Dynamic Management in a Global Economy

Dynamic Management in a Global Economy

Editor-in-Chief
Dr. K.N.S. Kang
Director
Punjab College of Technical Education (PCTE)
Ludhiana

Editors
Pawan Kumar Taneja
Sandhir Sharma
Gautam Bansal
P. P. Singh
Faculty, Department of Business Management
PCTE, Ludhiana

New Century Publications
New Delhi, India

New Century Publications
4800/24, Bharat Ram Road,
Ansari Road, Daryaganj,
New Delhi-110 002
Tel.: 23247798, 55396605
Telefax: 011-51017798
E-mail: indiatax@vsnl.com
www.newcenturypublications.com

Editorial office:
34, Gujranwala Town, Part-2,
Delhi - 110 009
Tel.: 27247805, 27464774

First Published 2006

ISBN: 81-7708-100-4

Published by New Century Publications and printed at Singhal Print Media, Delhi.

PRINTED IN INDIA

Punjab College of Technical Education (PCTE)

PCTE was established in August 1999 by Punjab Management Education Trust based in Ludhiana. Wg. Cdr. H.S. Gill, a retired pilot and industrialist, founded this institution with a vision to provide quality education to the young aspirants. PCTE, an ISO 9001:2000 certified institute, is located at Ferozepur Road, Ludhiana, an industrial hub of the country. It is an approved institution by AICTE, New Delhi and affiliated to Punjab Technical University, Jalandhar. It has 15 spacious lecture halls with audio-visual facilities, 3 computer labs, 3 play grounds, an auditorium, an indoor sports room, a conference hall and proper transportation and hostel facilities for the students. It offers MBA, MCA, BBA and BCA courses and runs Ph.D. programmes as well.

With a strong base of 34 regular faculty members, PCTE has the privilege of having visiting faculty from Bangladesh, Pakistan, Sri Lanka, Kenya and UK to interact with the students. It has grown from a student base of 100 at the start to more than 750 presently. PCTE faculty has already visited Pakistan, Bangladesh, Sri Lanka, UK, Malaysia, Thailand, Singapore under various programmes of students, faculty and curriculum enrichment.

Being close to the industry, all the courses at PCTE are run in academic-industry harmony. Since its establishment, PCTE has been maintaining the record of 100 per cent placements for its successful students. The major head hunters, *inter alia,* include: Air India, Vardhman, HERO, IAP Online, IBM, Reliance, ICICI Bank, Hughes, Infosys, Onida, LG Electronics, HDFC, JCT, Quark, Sapient, ACC Cements, Indian Express, Oberoi Cecil, Wipro, Dr. Reddy's Lab, India Bulls, Nestle, Standard Chartered, Kotak Mahindra Bank, HSBC, Eli Lilly, Citibank, IPCA Labs, Sun Pharma, Godrej, Cipla and TCS. PCTE believes in providing quality education in association with industry through lectures, management development programmes, workshops, seminars, research projects and consultancy assignments.

PCTE has 7 international collaborations with leading B-Schools and Universities of UK (City College, Birmingham), Pakistan (SZABIST, Islamabad, NCBA&E, Lahore, IQRA University, Islamabad, Quaid-i-Azam University, Lahore), Sri Lanka (Eastern University), Bangladesh (American International University of Bangladesh) and South Africa (Limpopo Province). PCTE has also attracted students from South Africa, Ghana, Tanzania and Zimbabwe who are pursuing different courses at its campus.

PCTE was ranked 44th among the top 50 B-Schools of India by Outlook Survey 2004 and rated best B-School of Punjab, HP and J&K by AIMA Surveys

2003 and 2004. Business India B-School Survey 2004 rated PCTE as A grade B-School. PCTE is the first B-School of the country to get its name included in the Limca Book of Records, 2005 for its unique mutual fund exercise under which students pool Rs. 1,000 each and invest the collected amount in the stocks. With this exercise, they are exposed to the stock market operations and provided first hand exposure to this branch of financial sector. At the end of their courses, the students get their deposited money back.

PCTE organises two extra-curricular events, viz. *Koshish* and *Ehsaas* every year for the students to show their talents in cultural and literary fields. Teams from Peshawar, Islamabad, Dhaka, and Lahore have participated in these events. Likewise, PCTE team of around 21 students and faculty members won overall trophy at *Dhoom-2004*, a cultural and literary festival organized by SZABIST, Islamabad in Pakistan.

PCTE faculty has contributed and presented more than 100 research papers and articles in various national and international conferences/journals/magazines. Furthermore, the faculty has published the following books in the field of management: *Business Families of Ludhiana, Business Groups in Punjab, Modern Business Environment, Environment and Pollution Education, Teachings of Environment, E-Publishing* and *Web Advertising and Online Marketing*. Besides, it publishes two international journals bi-annually on computers and management.

PCTE has organized two international and one national conference on issues pertaining to business management and information technology. Delegates from Bangladesh, Pakistan and Sri Lanka participated in these conferences to present their research papers. PCTE strives to produce high class professionals for industry and trade and to achieve this objective it is putting its best efforts to impart modern skills, knowledge and expertise to its students.

Editor's Profile

Dr. K.N.S. Kang is an Electrical Engineer with Post-graduation in Business Management and Doctorate in Marketing Management. A unique mix of an intellectual, a sportsman and artist, Dr. Kang has always achieved merit and distinction in education, sports and cultural activities throughout his student life. Fourth position holder in state higher secondary examination, national level athlete and a winner in inter-university culture events, Dr. Kang was conferred with the prestigious Shaheed Bhagat Singh State Youth Award for overall excellence by the then Governor of Punjab, honourable Shri S. S. Ray. Dr. Kang worked as an Assistant Professor in the Department of Business Management, Punjab Agricultural University, Ludhiana and has 14 years of professional experience to his credit. He was advisor to All India Management Association's Nodal Centre for imparting postgraduate management education in Ludhiana for 4 years. His fields of expertise include marketing management, international business and advertisement management. He has been guiding various research projects on management problems and current business environment.

To spread awareness about industry in Ludhiana, a book titled *Business Families of Ludhiana* has been published under his editorship. The book includes details regarding 15 reputed business families/groups of Ludhiana. Similarly, another book titled *Business Groups in Punjab* was published under his guidance which pertained to 10 leading business families/groups operating in Punjab. His latest contribution in the field of management is *Modern Business Environment.* He is a consultant to various industrial houses in the city of Ludhiana and a member of several committees and associations working in the field of education and business. These include: Executive Member, Ludhiana Management Association; Member, All India Management Association; Chairperson, Technical Sessions in the International Conference of International Digital Business Academy, Las Vegas; Chief Editor, M-World, quarterly journal of Ludhiana Management Association. Dr. Kang has visited leading B-Schools and Universities in England, Malaysia, Singapore, France and Pakistan to deliver lecture on management topics.

Editor's Note on the Book

The emergence of World Trade Organisation (WTO) has changed the world economic order. Economies of the world are opening up and integrating with each other. India too has shelved the earlier protectionist policy and opened up the economy to the world market.

Globalisation refers to widening and deepening of international flow of trade, capital, labour, technology, information and services. It involves liberalisation of national and global markets in the belief that it will result in higher growth rate and human welfare. Globalisation is not an end point, but a beginning for an enlarged process. It warrants liberalisation and privatisation of native economies. India too has adopted the path of liberalisation and consequently both positive and negative impacts of globalisation on the economy have been felt. It has been persistently a debatable issue over the losses and gains of globalisation on Indian economy.

The last decade of the 20th century witnessed the emergence of an all-pervasive global information infrastructure, commonly referred to as the Internet or the World Wide Web. This new medium of information and communication has revolutionized the work culture and living styles of human beings. Marketing of products and services has also been immensely influenced by the Internet. Various marketing activities can be performed more efficiently than ever before with the help of Internet.

Business environment in India is changing fast, bringing new opportunities as well as posing challenges. Economic liberalization and globalization have created keen interest in foreign investors resulting in comfortable foreign currency reserves, stability of Indian Rupee, vibrant stock market and expanding financial and services sector. However, the operations of multinational corporations (MNCs) and policies of (WTO) pose threats to some sectors of the Indian economy, especially to small and medium industries and agriculture. In some sectors of economy like automobiles, communications and entertainment the MNCs have registered their presence in a big way. Their marketing strategies are geared to create a new lifestyle, which is posing challenge to the traditional way of living and thinking.

The present volume contains findings of eminent scholars and young researchers on issues crucial to the contemporary business and economy in India. The book contains 42 articles which have been organised into four parts.

Part I is devoted to opportunities offered and challenges posed by the globalisation of the world economy. Part II deals with the management of human resources in the wake of new economic order. Part III relates to marketing of services in the context of revolution in information technology. Part IV focuses on the changing face of management functions following liberalization of world economies.

Each Part consists of papers contributed by scholars in their respective fields of specialisation. Thanks are due to all of them for their contributions and co-operation. Thanks are also due to the editors of New Century Publications, New Delhi for improving and standardising the texts of papers included in this volume.

October 15, 2005 K.N.S. Kang

Contributors

Adarsh Kumar Aggarwal
Lecturer, M.M. Institute of Management
Mullana, Ambala.

A. Lakshmi Kanth
Faculty, ITM
Warangal, Andhra Pradesh.

Aleena Sharma
Rai Business School
New Delhi.

Anwar Hossain
Dean
American International University
Dhaka, Bangladesh

Arunabh Mishra
Faculty, Aditya College of Engineering
Ahmedabad.

Bala Kiran
Research Associate
ICFAI University

Baldev Singh
Lecturer, Lyallpur Khalsa College
Jalandhar.

C. Muthuvelayutham
Lecturer, Raja College of Engineering and Technology
Madurai, Tamil Nadu.

Dhiraj Sharma
Senior Lecturer
Regional Institute of Management and Technology
Mandi Gobindgarh, Punjab.

Dindayal Swain
Assistant Professor
Institute of Management and Information Science
Bhubaneswar.

G.D. Sardana
Professor, Operations Management
Institute of Management Technology
Ghaziabad.

Geetika
Reader, School of Management Studies
Motilal Nehru National Institute of Technology
Allahabad.

Harpreet Kaur
Lecturer
BLS Institute of Management
Ghaziabad.

Hirak Das Gupta
Lecturer, M.M. Institute of Management
Mullana, Ambala.

H.M. Jha "Bidyarthi"
Professor, Department of Business Administration and Research
Shri Sant Gajanan Maharaj College of Engineering
Shegaon, Maharashtra.

Jasnoor Kaur
Lecturer, Department of Business Management
Khalsa College for Women
Civil Lines, Ludhiana.

Jaspal Singh
Deputy Registrar
Punjab Technical University
Jalandhar.

Julius Mogaka Gekonde
Researcher, Department of Business Studies
S.P. University, Gujarat.

Kashif-Ur-Rehman
Assistant Professor
Bahria University
Islamabad

Khushdeep Dharni
Faculty Member, School of Management and Social Sciences
Thapar Institute of Engineering and Technology
Patiala.

Kingshuk Das
Student, B.E. Electronics
Thapar Institute of Engineering and Technology
Patiala.

Komal Chopra
Lecturer, Marketing
Rai Business School
New Delhi.

Leena Shrivastav
Senior Lecturer, Human Resources
Rai Business School
New Delhi

Manisha Seth
Lecturer, Human Resource Management
Jaipuria Institute of Management
Lucknow.

Manohar Singh
Head, Department of Computer Science
Lyallpur Khalsa College
Jalandhar.

Mary Ipe
Professor, HRM and OB
ICFAI Business School
Kochi.

Meera Kulkarni
Assistant Professor
IMSCDR
Ahmed Nagar, Maharashtra.

MJF Fazeela Ahsan
Senior Lecturer in Marketing
Faculty of Management and Finance
University of Colombo
Sri Lanka.

M.K. Sehgal
Director and Professor
M.M. Institute of Management
Mullana, Ambala.

M. Mahmood Shah Khan
Lecturer, University of Management and Technology
Lahore.

Muhammad Iqbal Saif
Professor
Foundation University
Islamabad

Muhammad Shahbaz Shabbir
Lecturer
Foundation University
Islamabad

Nandita Sethi
Faculty Member
ICFAI Business School

Nasir Ahmed
Professor
Quaid-e-Azam University
Islamabad

Neelam Rani Suneja
Lecturer in Economics
Government College, Sector 46
Chandigarh.

Neeraj Pandey
Lecturer, School of Management and Social Sciences
Thapar Institute of Engineering and Technology
Patiala.

Neeti Agrawal
Lecturer, School of Management Studies
Indira Gandhi National Open University
New Delhi.

O.P. Sahni
Dean Academics
PCTE
Ludhiana.

Pawan Taneja
Faculty
PCTE, Ludhiana.

P. Kannadas
Lecturer, Madurai Kamaraj University College
Madurai, Tamil Nadu.

P.N. Jha
Director-cum-Professor
JD Institute of Management and Technology
Bathinda Road, Muktsar, Punjab

Prashant M More
PES College of Engineering
Nagsenvana, Aurangabad.

Part I: Globalisation: Opportunities and Challenges

HOLISTIC MANAGEMENT OF GLOBAL ECONOMY: THE FOURTH WAVE

H.M. Jha "Bidyarthi" and P.N. Jha

ABSTRACT

Management has been historically economy driven from the days of industrial revolution to those of quality revolution. It was British management followed by American management and then Japanese management. Now there is fourth wave management that seems to be making in-roads. Concepts like 'empowerment', 'brain stilling', 'servant leadership', 'transcendental management', 'trusteeship management' are fast replacing the practices of 'hire and fire policy', 'brain storming', 'autocratic leadership', 'ownership management' etc. The Indian management per se the Vedantic management per se the spiritual management per se the holistic management is taking the reign of global economic management. This is over 5000 years old management practice preached in Indian scriptures. The present paper surveys industrial cases of the recent past to study the trend of concurrent management style in the global context. It is observed that the conceptualization of global order has made a new beginning overturning "economy-driven management" to "management-driven economy" and holistic management has become the order of this 'knowledge workers era'. The authors submit that the genuineness of holistic management demands 'Indianization of globe' as against any possible attempt of 'globalization of India'.

INTRODUCTION

Society, economy, nations and regions have grown under a host of practices of governance and management since time immemorial. The nature and earth bestowed upon the human civilization unlimited resources for making a happy living. The desire for kingdom and its expansion coupled with political interests however reined the people and their prosperity in the early days. This led to the development of empires and emperors. Regions/nations rich in resources became the target of those poor in the same. The whole economic management thus relied on the practice of encroachment upon sovereignty of others. The entire human civilization was ravaged by a series of wars. Many dynasties rose and fell over the period of time. The last in the series was the British kingdom, which too started witnessing its end with the beginning of the last century. But this left almost all parts of the world economically bankrupt, and those with glorious past had lion's share of this bankruptcy. Hence with every nation getting independence from the so-called empires started its respective economic reconstruction for its people. They chose their own method of governance and management too.

ECONOMIC TRANSITIONS

On economic front several approaches were initiated which varied from region to region and even from nation to nation. Most of the European countries adopted capitalistic economic system, which continues even today. Countries like erstwhile USSR and Republic of China followed communistic socialistic economic system while Japan followed socialistic economic approach. Though USSR did grow into an economic giant but it could not sustain the same and it had to break causing an economic transition amongst the broken nations of the erstwhile USSR. China, on the other hand, too is initiating transition in its economy however under no backdrop of any failure of its earlier economic system like that of USSR but to integrate its national economy with the global economy. The application of the China to WTO for joining this world trade body is evidence to the ongoing economic transition in the Republic of China. Most of the Asian nations like India etc. adopted a mixed economic system giving way to both capitalistic and socialistic economic system what are popularly called as public-private sector economic regime. The neo-global economic order has forced an economic transition in India too initiated since 1991 and popularized as LPG economy.

MANAGERIAL TRANSITIONS

The approach to managing nations and its resources exhibits a different pattern than that of economic approach. The managerial transition can best be described as period specific than nation or region specific like economic transition. Since the British dynasty ruled the world during 17th – 20th centuries, the management during that period was broadly tool of governance. As time progressed there took place transition in management which may be categorized in to following distinctly defined management:

British Management: Compelled by governance requirements the British adopted a unique management approach, which is called British Management. They had to govern people of the nations outside their own and command their resources including human resources primarily for the benefit of their own community and nation. This resulted in to emergence of two classes – the managing class represented by British and the managed class represented by citizens of the British ruled nations. The characteristic features of British management were 'divide and rule policy', 'autocratic leadership', 'hire and fire system', 'fear-driven motivation' and so on and so forth. Many countries, even after freedom from British rule continued following this management as it had become an integral part of their system by then. It was the first wave management. However, as the dynasty ended, British management style started eroding.

American Management: The First World War created acute shortage of essential commodities. The gap between demand and supply became huge. Productivity therefore became the buzzword. Manufacturers, traders and businessmen rushed in to exploit this opportunity. Frederick Winslow Taylor's scientific management principles in United States ushered in a new management style – the second wave management - which we know today as American management style. This management commenced the industrial revolution in the world during the beginning of 20th century and continued even after Second World War. It was characterized by productivity and profitability orientation, hierarchical structure in organizations, monetary incentives based motivation schemes etc. and led to the unbridled consumption of material resources, including human resources, in order to fill the demand-supply gap. Many nations including India blindly copied this management style. In India, the Indian Institutes of Management were started on the blue print of Harvard Business School and MIT. However, application of the American management style brought about rapid expansion in industries, flooding of market with products and supply overtaking market demand.

Japanese Management: While the entire world was following the footprints of American management, Japanese invented their own methods. They did borrow American makes but did not copy them at all. They attempted to make improvements over American makes beginning the era of quality revolution. There began taking place a clear shift from production to product to process standardization. The Japanese management style was thus characterized by quality consciousness and concepts like Kaizen, ISO, TQM, quality circles, just-in-time etc. Companies started going for ISO certification as part of this management, the third wave management. Customer satisfaction became the final objective. This along with American management did bring about economic development and social prosperity to many nations but it missed to note down the true significance of people component in management. It continued to be treated as one of the resources in spite of the fact that it is the processor of all other resources.

CULMINATION POINTS OF TRANSITIONS

All economic systems of different nations and regions are now heading for market-free economic system. Economic transitions have thus culminated in to market forces driven economic system. It is the beneficiary of the economy – people at large – who will decide how economic development has to take place now. The national and regional trade boundaries are dissolving. People component is emerging as the single best factor of growth and development. Managerial transitions have also moved from visible – the product – to the invisible – the quality and customer satisfaction. Customer – who is people at its core – is the most pertinent deciding factor in all the management decision-making processes. And thus what has been thoroughly ignored in this transition process of both economy and management has become the point of culmination and convergence.

SIGNIFICANT OUTCOMES

The enduring British management saw the end of British dynasty. The American management style forced United States to look outward and create the globe as its market. Compulsions of both the management style are therefore obvious.

Several nations became developed nations due to the application of forgoing economic and management approaches. An economically prosperous man is however wandering after inner peace. Nations like America, Sweden and Japan, which are on the top of the list of the developed nations of the world, are on the top of the list of those nations where suicide rates are the highest. Books on 'How to commit suicide' are the best sellers, particularly in these nations. And there are cases reported where a man committed suicide with such book in hand with unfolded page on which the practiced suicide method was inscribed. Is this the purpose of adopting a particular management approach? A conspicuous omission of people component in these approaches seems to be the root cause.

Another significant observation of this transition is that management approaches have been mostly economy-driven. Thus materialism gained importance over spiritualism. A turnaround seems inevitable – management-driven economic approach.

A simultaneous technological development brought about information revolution and finally led to the emergence of knowledge era adding another dimension to the people component. The number of knowledge workers is fast increasing. There used to be 15 per cent managers and 85 per cent workers. Now there are 85 per cent managers (knowledge workers) and 15 per cent workers. Indeed, in companies like Matsushita employing thousands of people, there are found only two workers in a single factory in Japan – one to open and close the factory gate and other to switch on and switch off the servers and computer installations – rest all are managers sitting on their respective work stations and sending computer commands.

REGION-SPECIFIC MANAGEMENT AND ITS NEEDS

Management practices root in region-specific parameters. This is how the three management styles – British, American and Japanese management styles – grew and it did well to meet its ends. On the other hand, nations, which blindly copied them without looking in to their region-specific requirements, did not fetch the similar results. The lack of development of region=specific management approach or modification of the three above mentioned prominent management approaches in line with the regional requirements of different nations saw managerial transitions having headed it today to a naught. Now that the entire world has turned in to a global village the regional parameters have almost lost its significance. What remain omnipresent are man and his essential (fundamental) nature. And hence a further managerial transition is already on way.

FOURTH WAVE MANAGEMENT

This is Indian management per se holistic management per se spiritual management the core of which lies in man and his basic nature. Its principles and practices are rooted in more than five thousand years old cultures of Indian civilization. Indian ancient scriptures are its vast treasure source. The experiential learning of our ancestors who were saints and seers is the testimony of this management. The world is witnessing the offing of this fourth wave management today. The focus of this management is not on 'how' of management but on 'why' of management. It defines man (human resource) as *'atman'* based on the philosophy of *'tat-tvam-asi'* and *'aham brahmasmi'*.

The rising evils in the business and society and its resultant depression in mankind triggering restlessness in him are reasons that are showing signs of inclination towards this alternative management. It considers man as the most superior creatures of the nature. According to it the very purpose of this life is to achieve emancipation. It sees no difference between man and man immaterial of their cast and creed, rank and positions, age and sex, social and economic status. The business and profession has to be used for the manifestation of the divinity within each one of us. Swami Vivekananda says, "Each soul is potentially divine.

The goal is to manifest this divinity within by controlling nature, external and internal, or worship, or psychic control, or philosophy – by one or more or all of these – and be free ..."

This wave of management therefore talks about trusteeship management whereby we merely remain a custodian of all the resources at our command. This is what are we observing in the global phenomenon today where dissolution of global boundaries has made resource mobilization free within and without the national boundaries. Practices like servant leadership are being followed whereby leaders try to serve the interests of their groups by sacrificing their personal interests.

Corporate governance is today an integral part of managing business and organization. This speaks volumes about the accountability and responsibility being shown by the companies towards its major stakeholders – the public at large.

Prayers and uniform dress code have been accepted in the daily routine of top and leading Japanese firms and other firms too permeating the policy of oneness of human being in organizational practice. The side of the Board Rooms, at air terminals and railway stations abroad, has developed meditation halls. Indian scriptures identify meditation as an effective method of self-realization. Companies organize workshops on stress management on frequent basis using Indian scriptural methods. The tide of this fourth wave management can be seen everywhere now.

NATIONAL COMPANIES SHOWING THE WAY

Many Indian companies have designed programmes and initiated managerial practices conforming to the basic principles of holistic management. A list of a few such companies with their management practices has been given in Table 1.1 as an illustrative example. Offering employees stock option programme to its employees has turned many of the employees of WIPRO in to millionaires and at the same time has won their integrity and commitment of their company where they are now both the employees as well as employers.

MULTINATIONAL COMPANIES FOLLOWING SUIT

MNCs are also following suit. Ethics in business and service to society are finding place at the top of their agenda. Microsoft Corporations initiative to generously donate for fighting AIDS is one such illustration besides others as listed in Table 1.2.

Table 1.1: Holistic Management Practices of Select Companies

S. No.	Name of the Company	Holistic Management Practices
1.	Hindustan Lever Limited	Shakti Project for Rural Women Development
2.	WIPRO Limited	ESOP (Employees Stock Option Programme)
3.	Tata Steel Limited	Life Line Express – A Unique Effort of Health Services in Orissa
4.	Sahara India Limited	CEO designated as Chief Managing Worker
5.	Excel Industries Limited	Emphasis on individual and corporate Character

Table 1.2: Holistic Management Practices in Select MNCs.

S. No.	Name of the Company	Holistic Management Practices
1.	Hewlett Packard	Charity to health and education activities
2.	Matsushita	Prayers, meditation and uniform dress code
3.	Microsoft Corporation	Donations for fighting AIDS

INTERNATIONAL ACADEMICS STEP IN

Academic institutions world over have designed and introduced course curriculum for understanding the intricacies of this fourth wave management. Some call it 'Business Ethics', others call it 'Indian Ethos and Values', yet others have come out with credit courses on 'Human Values'. These include the likes of Harvard Business School, Kellogg Institute of Management, MIT's Sloan Management School and so on. The Indian Institute of Management, Calcutta long established a Management Center for Human Values.

DISTORTIONS AND DANGERS

There always appear resisting forces. The scope of distortion in the holistic management is not inescapable. Already there are agencies doing businesses in the field of business ethics. One of the most important distortions is the globalization of Indian management. This is causing uncalled for modifications in the basic Indian principles of management enshrined in Gita, Upnishada, Vedas, Patanjali Yoga Sutra, Epics and other scriptures. Yoga centers and meditation consultants have grown like mushrooms in the west noticing the current trend.

This is inviting dangers to the application of holistic management. It cannot be imbibed through courses but can only come through character. Ethics and ethos should not be used as a mask for doing all unethical practices underneath it. There is needed Indianization of the global management to make it truthful and meaningful

PRESCRIPTIONS

The days of military super power and economic power are fading. Welfare economics has come to stay. Service to humanity is the only mission all sections of society including industry, trade and business have to pursue for the well beings of the entire human civilization – "*Sarve Bhavantu Sukhinah*". The concept of global village that we are talking about is synonymous to brotherhood of the Indian tradition. We have to collectively work for the eternal economic regulation of the globe through this holistic management practices. This is the only wave to stay infinite, rest all had to naturally go through transitions. This would indeed be the management driven global economy.

REFERRENCES

Chakraborthy, S. K., Human Values for Managers, Wheeler Publishing, New Delhi.

Swami Vivekananda, The Complete Works of Swami Vivekananda, Advaita Ashrama, Calcutta.

Talk of Swami Nikhileshwarananda, Secretary, Ramakrishna Mission, Porebandar.

2

IMPACT OF GLOBALIZATION ON INDIAN AGRICULTURE PRODUCTION AND TRADE

Prashant Salwan

ABSTRACT

Policy regimes are required to help local autonomous operations. Out of the 1 billion Indians, about 300 millions may progress in today Global Business Environment due to their resources, capabilities to acquire technology & machineries. It is necessary to provide vision for the remaining 700 millions mainly for Agriculture Production and food security. Integration of skill and knowledge at village level and provision of urban facilities in rural areas may be the answer. Research must focus development of industrial, commercial technology, including biotechnology to help farmers to develop sustainable localized system of production and marketing. A nation whose economy focuses exclusively upon primary commodity production will be left behind in profit to nations involved in secondary & tertiary market. Relationship among regions and nation must be interdependent and not dependent. Nations has to maintain identity and integrity and act interdependently. Mantra of success is to built organization that has ability to learn faster than competition.

WTO regime will attract more efficiency seeking Foreign Direct Investment (FDI). Such FDI will require good infrastructure facilities, a science technology base and a skilled workforce, a good domestic consumption base. India has all this. The importance of expenditure on infrastructure, skill generation and R & D cannot be over emphasized. National policy must focus on smaller farmer and encourage the formation of small cooperatives that will help them to plan to convert primary commodity to tertiary market of value addition. The nations can be most productive through value addition. The nations can be most productive through specialization in the area where they have comparative advantage.

INTRODUCTION

Innovative activities, technology creation and transfer, Foreign Investments, Joint ventures, managerial practices and knowledge about markets is keys to success. It is no longer possible to protect Indian companies or sector of industry using outdated technology though business of high custom duties or a ban on imports. Indian companies have to compete against imports.

Over time force of the economy has moved from farm to capital and in the last fifty years to information. Information is more important than physical capital. The modern era is of knowledge and knowledge management. Peter Drucker calls it an era of knowledge economy. Knowledge worker and value added information. One must build an organization that has ability to learn faster than competition. It is all about finding ways to create, identify and distribute organizational knowledge to create, identify and distribute organizational knowledge value at least people who need it. Microsoft have made knowledge value at least ten times the value of its physical asset. This is what Globalization all about.

WTO regime is likely to attract more efficiency seeking Foreign Direct Investment (FDI). Such FDI are likely to be directed towards countries that have good infrastructure facilities, a science & technology base, a skilled workforce and a good domestic consumption base. India is a major candidate for this. The importance of expenditure on infrastructure, skill generation and R&D cannot be over emphasized.

WTO REGIME

To survive in WTO regime, there are no alternatives to continuous improvement. There may be many approaches to this. But ultimately result in the same thing, continuous and unending improvement. Companies must actively embrace continuous improvement principles. Passive acceptance is not enough. Maintenance of the status quo will result in an industrial base lacking the flexibility and efficiency to remain viable in world markets. We have to aim at improved product quality (Total Quality Management), improved productivity (reduce costs and cycle time) and increased customer satisfaction leading to higher sales and profitability.

In future there will be two kinds of companies those who perfect continuous improvement and those who have gone out of business. We in India have woken up but late to the pressure of Globalization. There are advantages of globalization in some area of the world economy. The manufacturing industry in the Third World has a lot to gain in globalization. Developing countries can produce goods cheaper to overseas countries and sell them at a competitive price in the developed world. This will reduce unemployment and poverty. The black side of globalization is dumping of overproduced goods in the Third World countries by developed countries. This will drive many companies into bankruptcy and loss of jobs. In order to win in this contrast situation emphasis has to be on knowledge sharing, innovation & technology creation.

IMPACT OF GLOBALIZATION ON AGRICULTURE TRADE

Economic motivation for globalization is creating comparative advantage. The nations can be most productive through specialization in areas where they have a comparative advantage.

The benefit of globalization are greater economic productivity achieved through efficient resource allocation and trade and political stability achieved through economic interdependent. It is fair to assume that if nations become economically interdependent, they will unlikely to wage war upon one another or tolerate political instability at home.

Primary markets are oriented towards the production of raw commodities (i.e. Food commodities, such as wheat, soybeans etc.) Secondary market focuses mainly on the further processing of raw commodities (i.e. corn syrup, bread, soy-based oil products etc.) Tertiary market specialize in facilitating production and trade by providing financing, access to market and assess to information about markets. Profit margin increases as goods move from primary to secondary to tertiary market. Thus a nation whose economy focuses exclusively upon primary commodity production will be left behind the profit to nations involved in secondary & territory market.

Environmental protection may be difficult by a nation if it is perceived as restricting free trade under WTO regime. In one of the WTO ruling, Japan was forced to lift its import ban on certain fruits that might bear dangerous insects, even through to get rid of those insects, Japan needed to use harmful pesticides.

INDIA'S AGRICULTURE SCENARIO AND GLOBALIZATION

We have a situation where farmers are being led by people who do not know where they want to go in first place. We still have many sectors where governments are still playing the role of referee and players, at the same time. The ultimate sufferer is the poor rural scale farmer who does not know what liberalization is all about – leave alone globalization. We must realize that before selling globalization that we have to take care of small scale businesses of farming. The only thing that they can do if they have to remain productive and useful to society & themselves is go cooperative. Good productive soils and favourable climate with low cost of production is the factors that may pave way for success of globalization in India. India cannot take WTO head on for the need of foreign aids, World Bank loans. Government need to address the following issues:

- Small farmers must be handled and addressed.
- Assessing the impacts of liberalization and globalization on the economies and system and decide the production lines that will help the farmer to sell the product in open market.
- Legal and policy framework which will support the district organization that can help the advocacy & lobbying for correct corps mix.
- Not withstanding the disadvantages of the liberalization and globalization, there is nothing else we can do. We must make best out of this.
- Food security issue must be handled seriously and negative side effects must be minimized.
- International community must be flexible enough to try and understand the fears of developing countries. They must be prepared to give preferential treatment to enable the developing countries access to world markets.

Large land holding farmers is the best position to take advantage of the Globalization. Rich countries with their political and economic advantage as well as advanced technologies are better placed for expanding in developing countries, export of cash corps, negotiate agreements at considerable cost for the new corps and deliver large quantities of mass produced food. They can move up the value chain and get into tertiary market.

Small farmers have neither technology nor the sophistication to easily and reliably sell to distant consumer. Only option to the small farmer is to pool their product and resources to form cooperatives. Lack of social safety network and powerful trade lobby may make life difficult for small farmers.

The question about social and environmental consequences of globalization that remains largely unanswered. Unless these issues are adequately addressed and legally examined into the trade regime sustainable of globalization for developing countries will be difficult.

The matter of society and culture we have the right and the responsibility to choose. We have right to preserve our unique national cultures. We have the responsibility to protect against the economics and political forces pushing us towards single global culture or social community.

WTO AND ECONOMY

Historically economic diversity among nations is a necessity to ensure choice and opportunity for health, growth, resilience and security of the global economy.

Is it wise for humanity to put all its eggs in one basket? If the answer is no, why WTO?. Is it motivated for short term gains of economy without long term consideration for human culture? The tremendous growth of the US economy over the past century is pushing all to competitive 'free market' economy. 'Culture of Economics' seems to be the only consideration.

Rich nations are taking advantage of poor nations. Coerced trade is not "Free Trade". Such economics is incapable of dealing with social consequences of trade. In economics it does not matter that the rich one made richer and the poor are made poorer only concern is greater total wealth and growth of overall economy. Can we forget issue of social equity or justice?

WTO is demanding ultimate removal of all social and ecological barriers to trade. All political constraints to trade removed, the multinational corporations would be free to treat the world as a single production area and single market and thus to maximize profits globally. Multinational corporations are best means of developing the "less developed economies" of the World. Will it result in transition out of agriculture and into some thing else like manufacturing? But it can only happen if we have technology to grow more food with fewer farmers. One must understand the implication of economic globalization i.e. destruction of ecological sustainability.

In India the Problem is that old economic & social structures continue to operate alongside the new setup of market driven dependency of production and consumption of capital inputs and technology transfers. Imbalances in productive asset, local constrains of inequality and oppression and regional imbalances keep the poorer section of the society left out. Land reforms, food far work programmes, mid-day meal programme and technology input reaching to the farmers is resulting in poverty reduction. Due to the present day policy of limiting the state and of economic modulation by global forces population growth in India has once again begun to outgrow agrarian growth with all its negative consequences. Public investment in agriculture, national research efforts, support prices, fertilizer subsidies and land reforms had in past contributed to the growth in India agriculture and in the reduction of rural poverty. Unstable prices in World market will have unsetting influences on the food security and agrarian production in India. Volatility will result in disaster under condition of poverty and low productivity. It is necessary to handle the Globalization and Agriculture with lot of caution and care.

TECHNOLOGY AND ECONOMY

Technology superiority and organizational capabilities are crucial to maintain a lead in competitive world. This is possible through right S&T policies. The

S&T policies have to be realistic about taking into account current realities of technological status, industry, capabilities of S&T institutions to respond to R&D required for industries facing international or global competitions. To fill the gap it may be necessary to have technology transfer from global companies and foreign technology sources by outsourcing, contract research and joint ventures. The emerging role for the developmental state in a gloabalized economy is the networking role or support of government to enterprises in order to penetrate linkages with globalized firms towards deep integration with them.

Generation of a whole range of human resource to suit the increasingly complex multinational operations can give India a special place in global contract research, albeit in parts of the systems at first and then in bigger system. The use of and participation by the vast NRIs should also become part of the policy.

The importance of infrastructure facilities, human resources, and skill content of population will decide how much share India will have in export market. Foreign firms invest in host countries not merely to exploit the host country market. They do so to take advantage of the technological capabilities and skill intensities of the host country and its population. As a result knowledge is not transferred but shared. India has advantage in these areas.

In order to survive in the atmosphere of Globalization in Agriculture, Technology inputs are essential that will add value to the product, built brand name and quality that is acceptable at the world level. It is an approach that is integration of skill, technology, high productivity and economy.

CONCLUSIONS

Following conclusions can be drawn from the study:

1. Small farmers must focus on their personal integrity, dependability, and commitment on developing personal relationship with their customers that big company cannot do
2. Relationship among regions and nation must be interdependent and not dependent. Maintain identity and integrity and act interdependently
3. Nation's first priority has to be food security for its people
4. One must build a organization that has ability to learn faster than competition.
5. The nations can be most productive through specialization area where they have comparative advantage.
6. Research must focus development of industrial, commercial technology, including biotechnology to help farmers develop sustainable localized systems of production and marketing.

7. A Nation whose economy focuses exclusively upon primary commodity production will be left behind in profit to nations involved in secondary and territory market.
8. The only way for small farmer to succeed is to pool their product and resources to form co-operatives.
9. Policy maker and human right activist have to answer that can we forget issue of social equity and justice.
10. Policy regimes are required to help local autonomous operations. Of the 1 billion Indians, about 300 millions may immediatcly aspire to product and services and may prosper in today global business environment but what will happen to remaining 700 millions? Kalam and Rajan, India 2020 – A vision of the new Millennium (1998) outlined how these 700 million can be part of this vision. Integration of skill and knowledge at village level and provision of urban facilities in rural areas is the answer.

REFERENCES

Gegre A F. Lunati, "Global Horticultural Impact: Fruits & Vegetables in Developing countries, International Society of Horticultural Science. World Conference on Horticultural Research, Rome, Italy, 17-20 June 1998

Grossman, Gene M and Elhanan Helpmen, "Innovation and Growth in the Global Economy, the MIT Press, Cambridge Massachusetts, 1991

John E. Ikerd, "The Globalization of Agriculture: Implication for Sustainability of Small Horticultural Farms" 3, 24, 2005.

Kalam, Abdul APJ and Y.S. Rajan, "A Vision for the New Millennium" India 2020, 1998 Penguin Viking India.

Kumar Venkat, "Globalization's Unanswered Questions" 'Common Dreams' Sep 2003 available at http://www.gloablpolicy.org.

Linford Martin, Mcc EL Salvador, "Globalization and Agriculture" Report of the Mennonite Central Committee.

Michael Boehlje, 'Globalization and Agricultures: New Realities", Strategic Business Planning for Commercial Product, Purdue University 15, 2003

Radossovic, S, "International Technology Transfer and catch up in Economic Development, Edword Elgar UK (1999)

Vandana Shiva, "The Threat of the Globalization of Agriculture" Research Foundation for Science, Technology and Natural Resource Policy New Delhi.

OPPORTUNITIES AND THREATS TO ENTER GLOBAL ECONOMY

G.D. Sardana and Sumeet Singh Jasial

ABSTRACT

Under the new regime of WTO, the balance of the trade restrictions is in the process of getting removed all over the world. The domestic produce is now no longer protected by the local legislation. The corporations can now import and export goods and services at fair competition. IT on the other hand has created an unprecedented awareness amongst consumers on what is available in any corner of the world and what performance corporations provide on products/ services delivered. These two aspects have resulted in shrinking of Global Market to the level of a Global village. Never before the parameters of cost, quality, delivery, flexibility, technical advantage and customer service become as relevant as now. Never before has the competition been so intense and the struggle for the survival been so acute as now. The companies have now to look for new mantras to survive.

Indian corporate world has so far enjoyed the luxury of safety, protection and resultant assured market. For last several decades, the Indian consumer has survived on poor quality of the products, unsatisfactory service and in many cases high prices charged by the manufacturers, in the absence of any alternatives. However, with the process of liberalisation ushered since last two decades, it is now recognised that survival in business will call for preparedness to meet the threats of globalized economy and not merely the domestic competition. There is no doubt that opportunities are unlimited. It requires only a will and a determination to exploit the same.

This paper examines some of the major threats and opportunities in the changed paradigm of the global economy. The study is carried out in context of Indian corporate world. This is illustrated by taking up the case of VIP, (Blow Plast India Pvt. Ltd.) This company has been facing stagnation in market growth in the last three years. As a result profits came down. The company is now on path to recovery as it has discovered the new mantra. With the new magic in its hand, the company is now poised to enter global market.

INTRODUCTION

Never before the business environment has been so turbulent as of late. It is complex, dynamic and increasingly changing in its various sub-systems. The pressures of globalisation and the rising expectations of the new economy triggered by Information Technology have brought new challenges and new threats for sustenance of business. But to conclude that this development has taken place all of a sudden and events have taken shape without any warnings, would be only naïve and illogical. Writings on the wall were very clear for a long time. Either these were ignored or wishful assumptions carried that Indian business would continue to be protected by the state at the cost of the domestic consumer and more importantly because of the socio-political beliefs nurtured over the years. However, entry into global economy has now become a necessity for sheer survival. This paper examines several issues in proper perspective. These include an analysis of the present day business environment, its genesis, the imperatives relevant today and the discovery of mantras to be successful in global economy. The paper has been organised in four sections:

- Business environment before liberalisation
- The aftermath of liberalisation
- The current scenario
- The *mantra* for success

In the closing sections, the paper takes up the case of VIP, which is now set to enter global market after it has imbibed the *mantra* of success

BUSINESS ENVIRONMENT BEFORE LIBERALISATION

The policy makers of a new independent India fully aware of its poverty, lack of infrastructure, absence of basic industry, chartered a unique path for the country to achieve development. This path which came to be known by several variants of socialistic society or the socialistic pattern of society etc. was not only the result of the socio-economic compulsions of our country at the time but was also the 'dream' perception of our political leadership as also the international alignments. The era which continued till early 1980's is characterised by several features which can be briefly examined as under:

State Protection: The state provided protection to the business and industry in several ways. This included protection against both the domestic and overseas competition. The imports were heavily burdened with excise duties and still higher penalties for any violations, that the domestic produce became heavily insulated against any competition arising from the marketing parameters of price, quality, delivery and service. Protection against the domestic competition sought to be delivered through licences to set up industry or increase output or controls on issues of important raw-material inputs such as iron and steel, coal. The state protected environment has come to be referred to as the period of *license-permit-quota* raj. The system allowed a flourishing business environment to the vested interests that could manipulate licences and permits and prevent the new entrants on pretext of likely creation of damage to the existing industry or socialistic fabric of the society. The system had serious fall outs:

- It killed the entrepreneurship of the Indian businessman. Not only he was provided protection against competition but was also assured of customers for all times to come. Capabilities to take risk necessary for any business venture came never to be developed. All business endeavours were safe, secure, insured and risk free.
- It gave birth to unprecedented corruption and a creation of a nexus between the businessman, politician and the beaurocrat. In his eagerness to get a licence or a permit or to prevent the entry of a new venture, a businessman will go all out to win the favours. Anything could be purchased, so the word went. Often the ethics and the values were sacrificed.
- Indian produce suffered in quality. Whatever quality was produced had an assured market. The customer had no choice except to accept it. Industrialist felt no need to improve upon quality. Indian products have come to be branded products of generally poor quality even as today.
- There was similarly no need to upgrade the technology or to carryout innovations both in the product or process. Indian businessman as a matter of fact rushed to world markets to purchase junks of old second hand plants and machinery discarded by the first owners in favour of new technology, higher productivity and better quality. The businessman as a matter of fact took pride to show to the visitors as to how he had been successful to recommission the old plant through his skilled technicians. Creativity, R&D and innovations became casualties.
- R&D was limited to carry out only the reverse engineering of the product models imported as samples or brought along as passenger baggage. It was a shoddy copy as the reverse engineering was carried out to manufacture a product on conventional machines as against the original process engineering on automatic machines. Quality could never be consistent and maintained.

- Indian consumer became 'phoren crazy'. Anything but Indian became a symbol of status. In many an instance an Indian traveller abroad purchased items carrying a foreign marketing label later to discover that the same had been manufactured in his own country. This legacy has not yet died and can be witnessed at airports and malls where the customer can be seen falling for the imported goods.

This is not to deny that the absence of liberalisation had no benefits. The permit–quota system laid foundations of fundamental /basic industries and the industrial culture over which the foundations of future industrial growth could be built. This was perhaps the only way that the then entrepreneurs could be persuaded to go for business ventures without any risks of failure. When advanced technologies were not available, a nation had to do with what was available as against relying on imports at the cost of sacrificing its political ideology. These were indeed the dilemmas before our founding fathers. This is a small price the nation had to pay for its endeavour to become self-reliant.

Missing Strategies: Businessman never felt the need to develop strategies or long range plans for expansions, product development or entry into uncharted territories. Thus Indian consumers continued to be served age-old fuel guzzling designs of the automobiles, when the automobile industry all over the world talked of new models introduced every year. In the domestic market it was a manufacturers market. Anything produced was easily consumed. Why should there be a necessity to think of future. If at all there existed a strategy, it could be termed as 'make hay while the sun shines'. There was hardly any need to enter global markets as the total produce had sufficient domestic market.

Even at the national level, the policy makers did not think in terms of strategic plans. There is otherwise no other explanation as to why long-term agreements had to be signed for export of raw materials, as iron ore, whereas national interests demanded value addition by setting up steel mills to generate employment. A large number of public sector undertakings employed old outdated technologies. These required to be updated from time to time. Companies rendered sick in the private sector were taken over by the state essentially to protect the employees, but no efforts were made as strategy to revive these through latest technologies or improve through value addition.

Long-term strategies called for emphasis on creation of infrastructure. The business needed power, roads, communication facilities, and construction. High rates of interest prevented competitive pricing of products besides inhibiting investments in new ventures.

Wrong fiscal policies only added to the woes. Heavy taxation and high rates of interest on advances and loans to the industry inhibited growth.

Aftermath of Liberalisation: The sad demise of the socialistic philosophy in the Soviet Union and the Eastern Bloc exposed the weak foundations of the Indian economy. The break up of the Soviet Union also led to the fall of the several citadels of Indian beliefs. India became signatory to WTO conventions and thus a process of liberalisation set in. Restrictions on imports had to go; FDI's had not only to be permitted but also rather welcomed, many a times at their conditions. Business sectors that only a couple of years before were closed had to be opened up to the foreign companies. Thus the Indian business was asked to move from an era of 'protection' to an environment of 'world class competition'. No one possibly bothered to check the preparedness of the industry. WTO regime had to be honoured. It is worth examining in brief as to what liberalisation has brought to the Indian business.

Entry of the Korean and Japanese: Conglomerates led by Samsung, Hyundai, LG, Honda, Sony etc. entered Indian market in a major way. Overnight a large number of TV's, refrigerators, washing machines manufacturers of Indian origin vanished. Indian domestic appliances are nowhere to be seen. Automobiles, both 4-wheelers and the two wheelers are dominated by Japanese and Koreans. At lower end, Diwali since last three years is now celebrated with decorative lamps and god-images manufactured in China. Foreign made fashion garments, shoes, cutlery, glassware, soft luggage, watches, imitation jewellery can be seen to dominate domestic markets. One does not have to employ a complex logic to arrive at the resulting unemployment. Many more products are in the line to throw out the Indian produce sooner than can be expected: electric fans of all types, medicines, packed foods, candies, furniture, fruits, vegetables etc. can be counted as some. At the other end of the spectrum, the electronic goods of the telecommunication sector, as mobile phones have no domestic competitor. These are but some of the threats of global economy.

Swadeshi Cry: A feeble attempt was made to invoke the slogans of the freedom days and the father of the nation to find protection for the Indian produce. But in face of globalisation this proved to be a feeble weapon. People have possibly a different view of nationalism after experiencing poor gains of freedom.

Exposure to World Class Practices: The Indian produce came to realise, so emphatically as to its weakness in dimensions of quality and cost. It also faced realities of its inability to innovate and go for creativity to produce a variety of models in a time bound programme. Product Development and R&D were never its strong points. An analysis of product cost and quality also convinced the manufacturers that these resulted from a host of practices followed in the operations management especially in areas of inventory controls, adoption of new technologies, manufacturing systems, performance evaluation and developing core competencies.

Customer is the King: For the first time the Indian manufacturer realised that the Indian customer could just ignore the decades old relationship with his Indian supplier when it came to availability of alternate choices. So it happened that the two Indian cars lost the ground no sooner than the alternatives came up. Never before the Indian consumer had such a wide choice of products and services. A customer had a choice of a variety of models of the same product, a number of shapes and sizes, prices, in many a cases far lower than he had been charged before, and quality which was perceived by him visible and transparent. The consumer had put on the clothes of a world citizen now and was no longer to be lured by the appeals of nationalism. CRM, service to customers and customer satisfaction came to be recognised as important performance parameters of an organisation.

Irrelevance of Cheap Labour: For generations, the Indian student has been fed the notion of India being the land of cheap labour. No doubt India possibly offers the cheapest labour thanks to massive unemployment and the failure of the political system to prevent exploitation of labour. However the element of labour in a product is only a fraction of the total sale price of the product. Bulk of the cost is built up through the expense on materials, processing and the overheads. The Indian businessman realised the same when it found the prices of the Chinese produce much lower. Those who have visited China swear that the standard of living enjoyed by an average Chinese worker is higher than that of an Indian worker, implying that the wages in China were at higher levels. And if China resorted to 'dumping' of its products, an always-vigilant Indian businessman would have been the first to cry loud on damage done.

Economies of Scale: The secret of low prices lay in the economy of scale. This became very clear when the Chinese goods appeared in the Indian market in quantity of millions. Apparently, the manufacture of large quantities necessitates installation of automatic lines of production. It also meant indirectly large investments, which could be afforded to by MNC's or large transnationals. It also signified that the organisations have to look for markets at new geographical locations to justify the capital expense. Economy of scale, globalisation and MNC's were observed to have interlinkages. The future business is increasingly getting reserved for the large organisations and the MNC'S.

Limited Role for the SME's: The lack of infrastructure to carry out innovation and R&D, The missing factors of economy of scale, limited access to markets (other than local neighbourhood) have put high restrictions on the viability of SME's. Financial constraints always posed problems as no financial institution considered these reliable enough for advancing of loans. And many a large customer treated them rough when it came to payments because of the leverage enjoyed. SME's which formed a backbone of the Indian business scenario have now been relegated to the background and confined to offer its services where it can best operate, that is low technology, labour intensive operations or to act as ancillary to supply parts to large organisations. Sardana (2004) details the limited role of SME's in the changed environment of globalisation.

Current Status: The process of liberalisation has now been largely completed. Besides new developments have taken place in the business environment. A brief review of the current status is carried out in the following sections.

WTO regime has come to stay: This means the market restrictions shall no longer exist. Capitalist economic theory holds that a completely liberalised global market is the most efficient way to foster growth, because each country specialises in producing the goods and services in which it has a comparative advantage. Yet, in practice, cutting trade barriers and opening markets do not necessarily generate development. Rich countries and large corporations dominate the global marketplace and create very unequal relations of power and information. As a result, trade is inherently unequal and poor countries often experience not rising well being but increasing unemployment, poverty, and income inequality.

An additional problem is that free trade is not entirely free. Agricultural subsidies and other trade barriers in the US and the EU prevent poor countries from gaining access to the most important markets, while they open up their own markets to US and EU exports. Critics of free trade point out that many of the world's richest countries sheltered their economies by protection when they were at the start of their own growth. Further, trade is so dominated by transnational corporations that new trade rules mainly benefit those companies.

Even though some of the provisions may not be conducive to our interests and may effect us highly adversely, India cannot retrace its steps. It has to live in the global community on the terms as decided by the world community even though the terms are dictated by nations as favourable to their interests. The recently passed Patents Bill is an example in this context. The bill was passed with the support of the leftists who always considered that WTO provisions favoured the developed nations. Cipla MD subsequent to passing of the bill has unequivocally stated in a press interview as reported by The Hindustan Times in its issue dated 25th March, 2005 that ' the prices of the medicines will rise sharply and by 2015, people will look back on the new bill and say that it was genocide'.

India's role in the world bodies: India with its large population, geographical status and demonstrated stability of political system has a role to play in the world bodies. This role has been wrongly denied to it so far. But the status cannot last any longer. However India shall require to continuously demonstrating its commitment to the various provisions of the world bodies to claim its central role to develop a global market. Globalization has increased the need for closer cooperation between the multilateral institutions with key roles in the formulation and implementation of different elements of the framework for global economic policy, in particular the International Monetary Fund (IMF), the World Bank and the World Trade Organization. Each of these organizations has a mandate for such cooperation in the agreements under which they have been established. They also have signed agreements among themselves, for mutual cooperation and regular consultation, which identify mechanisms designed to foster greater coherence in global economic policy-making.

Change is the only certainty. Change is an accepted consequence of modern life. Indeed, the phrase 'change is the only certainty' has become something of a business mantra. All organisations are subject to increasing levels of change. One can view change in terms of cyclical change and evolutionary change. Cyclical change involves variation that is repetitive and often-predictable (seasonal variation in demand or fluctuation in economic circumstances). Evolutionary changes involve a more fundamental shift. It may mean sudden innovation or a gradual 'creeping' process.

It amounts to the needs of continuous innovation and creativity. Organisations cannot sit back. It has to be on look out for new ideas and take lead over the competition. This is one of the mantras for survival.

Emergence of the Information Age: Almost simultaneously along with the process of globalisation and liberalisation, the global economy also ushered in the information age. Information technology and knowledge workers drive the information age. It is characterised by the dominance of knowledge workers, those who work with information rather than producing goods. Business in information age has different dimensions in various areas. Sahay et al (2000) explain, 'During industrial age, the success of a company was measured by how well it could capture the benefits from economies of scale and scope. Technology was important, but ultimately success accrued to companies that could embed the new technology into physical assets that ensured efficient mass production of standard products.' The information age environment requires new capabilities in organisations for competitive success, to mobilise and exploit its intangible assets. It calls for new organisational structures encouraging inter-organisational communication, global reach and rapid unpredictable innovations.

Customer awareness: IT has created an unprecedented awareness amongst consumers on what is available in any corner of the world and what performance corporations provide on products/ services delivered. Customers are more mature, wiser and knowledgeable and purchase the goods after a due consideration of all the factors. A customer expects value for the price he pays. Impulsive purchases are going down. Globalisation calls for properly assessing the needs of the customer who possibly is sitting thousands of miles away in a different culture and speaking a different language.

This awareness is not confined to selection of products or services alone. A customer is more conscious today of issues such as corporate governance and social obligations on the part of organisations. He expects corporations to follow fair trade practices, respect human and labour rights (avoidance of use of child labour, for example), and promote development of products, which sustain environment and lead to preservation of natural resources. Societal expectations include introduction of such products and services which help increase the standards of living, comfort levels and span of life and freedom from diseases.

Imperatives to Enter Global Economy: Sahay et al (2000) point out that globalisation of economy activity is qualitatively different. It is more advanced and complex form of internationalisation that implies a degree of functional integration between internationally dispersed economic activities. It is different from the operational management practices as carried out till now by the MNC's and the transnationals, who have largely restricted their operations to only boost their marketing operations in foreign lands. There have been few attempts to integrate their operations with local economic environment. Porter (1986) points out that global forces in several areas influence Globalisation. Globalisation can be characterised by the following attributes

- Tightly linked global financial markets
- Global sourcing of inputs
- Global marketing and distribution of production
- World Class Manufacturing of products and final products
- Global standards of product quality
- Globally accepted norms of product delivery schedules
- Globally accepted product price
- Global standards of customer service
- Evolution of business towards more comprehensive and continuous co-ordination and integration at global level, through IT and other means of communication.

In order to compete successfully in the global market and in the dynamically changing environment, a company requires to address several key strategic issues to prepare itself for the challenge. It has to discover a *mantra* to guide it on a religious zeal.

SITAR, The Mantra: A vast majority of Indian companies are essentially domestic market focused. These operate on small scales and have hardly taken any steps to differentiate the product models suiting the foreign markets. Another major handicap is projected in the inability or unpreparedness today of an Indian company to access the foreign market. The customer preferences, availability of various brands, their strengths, the opportunities available, expectations on service and service centres, the distribution channels, infrastructure to ensure safe storage and transportation and several other areas are yet unfathomed. Nor is information readily available. It will have to take up challenges of making entry in the global economy in steps taking advantage of the knowledge available with some that are in the field. The following sections examine basic imperatives in the form of mantra for success.

'S' for Strategic Partnership: As a first step, an Indian company may seek to enter strategic partnership with an MNC or a foreign based company which can provide it a head start. Strategic partnership will generate a global mindset to achieve economies of scale and hence cost excellence, quality expectations and knowledge on customer preferences. This will lead to strengthening of design capabilities, and innovation skills. Most importantly the company acquires a foothold or access to a foreign market. Another strategy could be to acquire some of the operating units. In strategic partnership one obvious advantage is the company gets exposed to the nitty-gritty of managing global operations and recognising the skills or talent needed. Strategic partnership can take many shapes.

- Acquisitions & Mergers should be viewed in this context of enriching each other core competencies and taking advantage of the size of operations
- Market segmentation so that transportation costs can be controlled
- Sharing of core competencies in areas of designs, know-how's, processing technologies
- Sharing patent rights, tools, dies and moulds
- Positioning of each other's products to mutual benefits
- Sharing functional responsibilities.

'I' for Information Technology: Sahay et al (2000) point out that Information technology enables today's organisations to integrate supply, production and delivery processes so that operations are triggered by customer orders and not by production plans alone. An integrated system right from a customer order upstream to supply of raw materials enables all business units of an organisation along the value chain to realise improvements in cost, quality and response time. It helps in providing links to both suppliers and the customers. Information Technology orientation combines the specialisation benefits from the functional expertise with the speed, efficiency and quality of integrated business processes functional. Speed and timely delivery is the essence of global operations. IT is possibly the most important tool to achieve these objectives.

'T' for Technology: Product life cycles are shrinking. New models are getting introduced more frequently. Many of these carry advantages of enhanced appealing looks, better operational performance, reduced costs, more safety and advantages to customers, and better compliance with environmental regulations. Competitive advantage enjoyed by a company on its model is no guarantee that it will have continuation of advantage for some time to come. A Company has to be vigilant and take the lead to introduce variety and innovations. Technology is not confined to only innovations. It also covers R&D, where Indian companies have traditionally lacked and have rather depended on borrowed designs or reverse engineering. In days of sever globalised competition when companies would like to capitalise on research, latest designs are not likely to be made available. Domestic players will need to develop their own long-term competencies. Another dimension of technology is in areas of processing. Appropriate process suited to the volume is going to determine both the cost and the quality of the end product. A Company has to keep itself fully posted about the latest developments in this field. Prem Vrat et al (1998) have highlighted the role of technology in achieving excellence in performance.

'A' is for Advantage-Competitive: India has several advantages, which it can gainfully exploit to its advantage in the global economy. It should endeavour to compete on its own turf, on its own core competencies, rather than taking up challenges where it is not on solid grounds. The opportunities and the advantages lie in several areas. Some of these include:

- Low wage rates*:* Apparently, the high boom in outsourcing of call centre jobs to India, Pakistan, China can be attributed to this factor.
- Labour intensive industries: This can include manufacture of toys, footwear, fashion garments. Civil construction jobs on a turnkey execution basis offer another opportunity.
- Aluminium products: India is the second largest producer of aluminium in the world. With its advantage of lightness, ductility and conductivity the metal can find several useful applications in the construction industry and electrical

products. Innovations are needed to discover such applications and offer the same to industry.

- Skill intensive industries: There are areas where India has already developed skills, which have also found an acceptance. Computer hardware, computer electronics, auto components and pharmaceutical intermediates (dyes and chemicals) are some examples.
- Textiles: This sector represents the oldest of the manufacturing sectors in India. So far exports have been confined to export of semi-finished cloth. It is time, value addition in the form of export of garments or fashion-apparel is considered.
- Knowledge work: India has one of the largest pools of doctors, technicians in the medical profession. It is time that businessmen recognise the opportunities it provides to promote medical treatment in India. Software development, civil engineering designs are other areas that can be exploited.

'R' is for Reengineering: Developed in 90's, Reengineering or more popularly known as Business Process Reengineering is an important tool to generate process orientation to comply and be aligned with the corporate objectives It focuses on examining the work-flow and processes within and between the organisations. Halevi (1999) points out that Reengineering can be viewed as a set of logically related tasks performed to achieve a definite business outcome. The approaches to carry out reengineering can differ in degree of change. These can be radical or incremental. The former may need heavy financial commitment with a long payback period. Whereas it is easier to go for incremental approach as the overall risk is small. In both the cases it is a structured exercise with emphasis on the outcome and not the tasks. Sardana (1997) has studied the positive impacts of BPR on productivity of an organisation and has recommended its adoption.

BLOW PLAST LTD.: A CASE OF RECOVERY

Jasial (2005) details that Blow Plast has been facing stagnation over the past 3-4 years. Principally this has occurred on account of entry of multinationals in the domestic market, thanks to the process of liberalisation. This resulted in Blow Plast facing stagnation in growth of volume and resultant down fall in profits. However with the new mantra in hand, the company is now poised to make an entry in the global economy. It is worth examining several initiatives it has taken which are responsible for its path to recovery. The following sections examine some of the steps initiated by the company.

Brief History: VIP is the market leader in the luggage industry in India and is the largest moulded luggage manufacturer in Asia. The company also has the honour of being world's second largest luggage manufacturer. It has a market share of more than 60 per cent in the luggage market in the country. The company is owned and managed by Dilip Piramal Group. Manufacturing of moulded and flexible luggage is done by VIP Industries, while the promoter company Blow Plast handles marketing. Blow Plast Ltd holds 50 per cent of VIP Industries equity.

Marketing of VIP and Alfa brands is done by Blow Plast Industries, the parent company. VIP has a strong positioning in the mid-priced and premium segment, while the low priced brands are marketed under the Alfa series. VIP has successfully maintained its leadership in the premium and medium priced luggage segment due to its well-established brand equity and an extensive distribution network.

Blow Plast Limited registered a turnover of Rs240.42 crore for FY 2004 as compared to Rs236.69 crore in the previous year. It maintained its market share in the branded segment, with the soft luggage and personal product division registering impressive growth.

The Threats: However, only three years earlier in 2001, the company was passing through a turbulent phase, which it never thought it would have to face. Samsonite, the world leaders in baggage industry had made an entry in India. It had done its homework well. It decided to take advantage of cheap labour in India and decided to set up its own manufacturing facilities. I t also took into account the inability of an average Indian customer to pay the fancy prices as charged by the company in international market. It therefore decided to introduce less costly versions. With its international brand image, proven and widely perceived good quality, this was a fit company to throw out the local VIP brand from the market in a repeat performance to what had happened to a number of domestic TV brands.

Besides there was also an increasing threat from the domestic players both from the organised and the unorganised sectors. Not all the market segments were brand conscious. Many customers were driven by cost considerations. The company had to find solutions. The following initiatives however saved Blow Plast.

Strategic Partnership: The company entered into a tie-up with Delsey-the world's third largest luggage manufacturer, to market the latter's premium luggage range in India. The move followed Samsonite's aggressive foray into the Indian market.

VIP was till now considered a standard luggage manufacturer, but not a company that produced premium lifestyle products. Therefore, the need to rope in Delsey arose. VIP introduced the Delsey range, which carried a worldwide warranty on the luggage items. This obviously made the international traveller more compliant to the idea of buying from a VIP showroom.

Marketing tie-up with Delsey was done to consolidate the premium luggage market in India, which was being poached upon by Samsonite. However the concern faced by VIP Industries had also been whether Delsey products would eat into the share of VIP Industries. To tackle the issues with brand dilution the company hiked its promotion budget from Rs. 16 crore by 20 per cent.

VIP has also been in fresh talks with Delsey on marketing strategy. Delsey has also agreed to pump about Rs. 5-6 crore into India as ad spend, to be spent on pushing the company's product.

Technology Initiatives: VIP Industries bought out the Europe based Carlton brand of luggage. With shrinking margins and a lopsided growth in the luggage industry, the company had to think of new ways to boost bottom-line growth. With the company toying with idea of boosting exports to South Asian countries and Europe in the first instance, buy out of Carlton was a step in that direction.

There are other advantages too for VIP Industries. Carlton's equipment and know-how could come in handy for the company. Also included in the deal are Carlton's moulds and intellectual property rights.

Entry into Global Markets: VIP (and Blow Plast) is actively working on a plan to create a presence in South East Asian markets like Singapore, Thailand, Hong Kong and others in the next nine months. From China, the group plans to outsource some of its manufacturing requirements catering to the mass segment of the luggage industry. Part of the SE Asian requirement of the group would be fulfilled from China. The long-term plan for its luggage business is to become an international player, by strengthening its presence in Europe and looking at bigger markets like the US. At present about 5 per cent of its turnover comes from global markets. VIP already exports to many countries, the Carlton brand would provide incremental volumes. VIP brand may not be so well established in European countries, but Carlton-the world's fourth largest luggage manufacturer could certainly be used as a piggyback.

The company wanted to make the VIP brand acceptable outside India. In this context it plans to launch 'Carlton' as a VIP product to the European market which has been slow to take off in the present circumstances. However, manufacturing costs needed to be stemmed if the company was to achieve a respectable sales volume.

Are exports the answer? Currently, exports account for a mere Rs. 15.75 crore out of V.I.P.'s Rs. 282 crore turnover. The company would like that to climb from the current 6-7 per cent of turnover to 15 per cent of turnover by 2006.

Cost as the Competitive Advantage: The company wound up Carlton plant in Europe and shifted the entire machinery to India. India, being competitive in terms of labour and resources to manufacture moulded luggage, is in position to provide the company a cost effective manufacturing base. The production of Carlton luggage is expected to start soon, and VIP is well placed to take on the show.

One conspicuous problem was that the company had more than 2,000 employees on its rolls. The Company went for VRS. Besides it took up restructuring of business operations. The company shut down two of its units in Maharashtra, and relocated some of the workforce to Nasik, while others were provided the option of a VRS.

Volume as the Competitive Advantage: VIP, which currently makes around 350,000 pieces of luggage, will boost its capacity by another 80,000 units. Carlton's plant moved from Europe shall provide the additional capacity. VIP was the world's second largest moulded luggage company even before the Carlton acquisition.

Reengineering: VIP Industries segregated its business into three specific business units, namely CBU-1 (catering to major towns and dealerships), CBU-2 (catering to smaller towns and rural segments), and CBU-3 (focusing specifically on Institutional/ Corporate Business).

By segregating retail and institutional business, the company's executives could focus on their key result areas.

In addition, the company developed its own premium range in line with international standards. VIP introduced the premium products such as Pepperworks and Oxford ranges, which were big hits with the consumers and offered a run for its money to Samsonite.

The Company continues to exercise rigid control on cost and other expenditure. Although a sum of Rs.13.85 Cr. was spent on the VRS exercise carried out during the year, this is expected to reduce the employee cost in the future years. Company's continued efforts in improving working capital management coupled with mobilisation of low cost debt have resulted in substantial savings in interest cost.

Higher profits and reduction in working capital has translated into steady cash flows which have been used to partly fund the acquisition of well known international luggage brand 'Carlton' and certain other assets.

Results Achieved: The company achieved a record growth in sales in the years 2002- 2004. Results exceeded expectations. Corporate business grew from Rs. 5 crore in 2001 to approx. Rs. 40 crore in 2004 (estimated figures as on January 2005). The turnover showed a marginal decline to a figure of Rs. 275.09 crore as against Rs. 279.60 crore achieved last year. However the profits rose to Rs. 9.13 crore as against Rs. 7.98 crore in the previous year. The retail segment has taken off equally well. The company is well poised to become the largest producer of soft luggage, globally in the next few years. It will be one more success story of Indian business that will demonstrate as to how global opportunities can be exploited and threats beaten with will, determination and magic mantra.

CONCLUSIONS

No doubt the Indian business has entered the age of globalisation with a clear disadvantage. It was simply not prepared. The WTO provisions are heavily loaded against the developing nations. It is known, for example that in the days of development, the present day developed nations had offered their domestic industry a strong protection against competition. Unprecedented economic aid was made available under Marshall Plan for restructuring to nations devastated in the Second World War. Yet the process of globalisation can neither be checked nor halted or retraced because it hurts the developing nations. A right combination of strategic initiatives by Indian corporations can still provide a challenge to many MNC's. There are several areas where the country possesses core competencies. These require being discovered and competitive advantages developed. Global economy has its opportunities. These are for exploitation by the ambitious entrepreneurs. Threats cannot debar them. VIP case demonstrates as how a company takes up the path of recovery through entering global economy.

REFERENCES

Jasial, Sumeet Singh (2005), Marketing Strategy Adopted by VIP in 'Management Case Studies' Ed. by Raj Singh, Sardana, G.D and Jhajharia, Parul, Amity University Press, New Delhi.

Porter, M.E(1986); Competition in Global Industries, Harvard Business School Press, Cambridge, Massachusetts

Prem Vrat; Sardana,G.D.; Sahay,B.S (1998), Productivity Management: A Systems Approach, Narosa Publishing House, New Delhi.

Sahay, BS; Saxena, KBC; Asish Kumar (2000), World Class Manufacturing: A Strategic Perspective, Macmillan, Delhi

Sardana, G.D, (1997), 'Integrating BPR with Productivity in Productivity', Vol. 39, No1, April-June 1998. New Delhi

Sardana, G.D, (2004), 'Determinants of SME Success: Formulating a Business Strategy', Productivity, Vol. 44, NO 4, Jan.-March 2004, New Delhi.

E-MARKETING AS A STRATEGIC TOOL FOR MARKETING IN THE 21ST CENTURY

Harpreet Kaur

ABSTRACT

E-Marketing includes any marketing activity that is conducted through the internet, from customer analysis to marketing – mix components, by virtue of rather low costs, wide geographic reach and many marketing roles, the internet should be a key part of any firm is marketing strategy – regardless of the firm's size or characteristics. The broadened scope of marketing in the decades ahead will require virtually every firm to have a web presence, much as they have a telephone, an answering machine and other technological tools, hundreds of millions of people around the globe are surfing the web, a number that will soon reach one billion individuals. As a major new-technology, the Internet will have a bright future, with some stumbles along the way and some challenges ahead. The impact of Internet and reason why the Internet is such a valuable marketing tool because of its multifaceted uses. In the future, Internet usage will grow exponentially with E-marketing being even more essential; high speed connections will lead to more multimedia rich websites, Business-to-Business E-commerce will greatly outstrip Business- to-consumer E-commerce.

E-marketing best supports the marketing activities. E-marketing has a growing impact on business-to-business and business-to-consumer markets. E-marketing includes any activity that is conducted through the internet from customer analysis to marketing mix components. The web enables a company to focus on a specific target market and offer a marketing mix specially devised for that target market. It leads to innovative high quality products that make life easier and more enjoyable.

E-MARKETING DEFINED

The first part of this definition illustrates the range of access platforms such as web, e-mail, mobile phones and interactive digital TV that comprise the online channels which e-marketers use to build and develop relationships with customers.

The second part of the definition shows that it should not be the technology that drives e- marketing, but the business returns from gaining new customers and maintaining relationships with existing customers. It also emphasizes how E-marketing does not occur in isolation, but is most effective when it is integrated with other communication channels such as phone, direct mail, or face-to-face. Online channels should also be used to support the whole buying process from pre-sale to post – sale and further development of customer relationships.

The final part of the definition summarizes approaches to customer centric E-marketing. It shows how it should be based on knowledge of customer needs developed by researching their characteristics, behavior, what they value, what keeps them loyal and delivering tailored web and e-mail communications.

TOP TEN STRATEGIC E-MARKETING ISSUES

Issue 1: E-marketing Planning Process

What is it?

The integration of E-marketing-specific objectives, strategies and activities into the traditional annual marketing planning process.

Key questions:

- Do we have a separate E-marketing plan?
- What should the E-marketing plan contain?
- Which objectives do we set to drive the contribution of E-marketing to the organization?
- How do we use align E-marketing activities with business strategies of market and product development?
- How do we integrate E-marketing communications with traditional communications?
- Which internet-specific strategies should we review?
- New channel structures- how do we partner / form alliances with online intermediaries, develop new intermediaries and manage channel conflicts?

Issue 2: Organising and Resourcing for E-marketing

What is it?

As the importance of online channels increase, the structure of the marketing organization and responsibilities may need to change to maximize the opportunities available through new media.

Key questions:

- Do we change the structure of the marketing organization?

- Which new responsibilities do we identify for E-marketing?
- How do we develop E-marketing specific skills within the marketing team?
- Does the organization have the database marketing and analytical skills to support E-CRM and E-mail marketing?
- Which E-marketing activities do we outsource?

Issue3: Defining the Internet Value Proposition (IVP)

What is it?

To achieve increased customer usage of online channels (web, E-mail, wireless), a distinct detailed proposition must be developed for these online channels and it must be clearly communicated online and offline.

Key questions:

- How can we vary the elements of the marketing mix online?
- How do we research the proposition?
- How is the combination of e-mail and web based personalization used to extend the proposition?
- How powerful is the IVP(research)?
- What are competitors offering as IVPs?
- Are there cannibalization issues?

Issue 4: E-brand Value

What is it?

How does the Internet contribute to and influence brands?

Key questions:

- How do we extend our brand online?
- Should we use brand variants?
- How effective is the emotional connection of an online brand?
- How is the online brand experience perceived by customers?
- How is online service delivery perceived by customers?
- Reputation management (or Personal relationship)- how do we manage how third-party sites present the brand through proactive promotion of the brand and reactive limitation of negative pr.
- Viral marketing- how do we use the efficiency of online networks to create involvement with a brand?

Issue 5: Setting the E-communications Mix

What is it?

Defining the proportion of online spend on different elements of the communications mix

Key issues:

- Percent of communications budget allocated to e-communications
- Online spend per cent on advertising, direct mail and pr
- Demonstrating return on investment for e-marketing tools
- Continuous Vs campaign spend
- Relative spend on different online tools, i.e. search, affiliates, online ads, rented e-mail lists, online sponsorship, etc
- How do we partner/form alliances with online intermediaries or should we develop new intermediaries?

Issue 6: E-mail Marketing Integration (Touch Strategy)

What is it?

Integrating different forms of marketing e-mail, i.e. rented list, house list e-blasts, service e-mails and e-newsletters with traditional communications, i.e. direct mail, advertising, etc to achieve maximum response.

Key issues:

- What is our touch or contact strategy defining minimum and maximum number of touches per customer in a period?
- What communications preferences do we offer customers for media type, format, frequency and content?
- How are e-mail newsletters used as strategic communications tools?
- How do we maintain responsiveness of e-mail marketing given the increasing volume of e-mail reaching recipients in-boxes including Spam (60 per cent of global e-mail) and blocking/filtering of legitimate permission –based opt-in e-mail marketing?

Issue 7: E-CRM

What is it?

Using online channels (web, e-mail, wireless messaging linked to customer databases) to build and deepen relationships with customers.

Key issues:

- How do we use online channels to create dialogue and build relationships with website visitors using a permission –based dialogue?
- How can we selectively target customer segments with different characteristics and value?
- What are the characteristics of customers who preferentially use the online channels?
- How do we manage customer data?
- How well does the web sites/e-mail support cross- selling/up-selling?
- How do we manage change associated with CRM?
- Which technologies do select to support CRM?

- What level of customer service do we provide online and how do we control the level of online versus offline enquiries?

Issue 8: Building and Exploiting Customer Knowledge

What is it?

Customer knowledge is profiling information and research characterizing customers including their characteristics, communications preferences, behaviors and perception of service.

Key questions:

- How do we acquire and update customer details as part of e-permission marketing? Who is responsible for customer knowledge?
- How do we assess and control the quality of customer knowledge?
- How do we motivate staff to improve knowledge quality?
- What are the legal liabilities and constraints of managing customer data such as in Europe, the data protection act, and the privacy and electronic communications act?

Issue 9: E-marketing Automation

What is it?

Developing personalized marketing messages delivered by web and e-mail in response to customer events and behaviors.

Key questions

- How do we build related products personalization into the website?
- How do we integrate personalization, technology into our existing infrastructure?

Issue 10: E-channel Optimization

What is it?

Develop in a continuous improvement process to monitor the effectiveness of web and e-mail marketing.

Key issues:

- Which web analytics tools do we use?
- What metrics / dashboards do we use to review E-marketing effectiveness?
- What testing programs do we use to improve E-marketing?
- What is the internal process of review and alter?

These issues give the value cluster, the market space offering, and the resource system and explain that E-marketing is hot. These issues suggest that strategic approach to E-marketing is a medium to accomplish the business aims. Therefore marketing in the electronic era requires creative and innovative strategies.

E-marketing is one of the most effective ways to keep in touch with customers. It is generally cost-effective, and if done properly, can help build brand awareness and loyalty. At a typical cost of only a few cents per message, it's a bargain compared to traditional direct mail at $1 or more per piece. In addition, response rates von e-mail marketing is strong, ranging from five-to35 per cent depending on the industry and format. Response rates for traditional mail averages in the 1-3 per cent range.

One of the benefits of E-marketing is the demographic information that customers provide when signing up for your email newsletter. Discovering whom your customer's really are- age, gender, income and special interests, for example – can help you target your products and services to their needs.

POINTS TO CONSIDER WHEN CREATING E-MAIL NEWSLETTER

- **HTML vs. Plain Text:** Response rates for HTML newsletters are generally far higher than plain text, and graphics and colors tend to make the publications look far more professional. The downside is that HTML email is slower to down load, and some email providers may screen out HTML email.
- **Provide Incentive to Subscribe:** Advertise the benefits of receiving of receiving of receiving our newsletter to get customers to sign up our newsletter, such as helpful tips, informative content or early notification of special offers or campaigns.
- **Don't Just Sell:** Many studies suggest that email newsletters are read far more carefully when they offer information that is useful to the customer's lives rather than merely selling products and services. Helpful tips, engaging content and humor are often expected to accompany email newsletters.
- **Limit Questions:** As each demographic question you ask may reduce the number of customers signing up, it's best to limit the amount of information you solicit or give customers the option of skipping the questionnaire.

It would seem that a framework is more useful than a definition in contributing to the analysis of a business model's structure and in determining the critical success factors in e-commerce. Osterwalder & Pigneur (2002) formulated and proposed an e-business model ontology (e.g. Rigorous framework) that highlights the relevant e-business issues and elements firms have to consider in operating successfully. This framework is founded on four main pillars, which are product innovation, customer relationship, infrastructure management and financial aspects as presented briefly in Table 4.1. According to these authors, a business model is nothing else than the value a company offers to one or several segments of customers and the firm's architecture and network of partners for creating, marketing and delivering this value and relationship capital, in order to generate sustainable revenue streams.

Table 4.1: Pillars of an E-Business Model

Pillars	Contents and Components
Product Innovation	The products and services a firm offers, representing a substantial value to the customer and for which he is willing to pay. The main elements are the value proposition a firm wants to offer to specific target customer segments and the capabilities that a firm has to obtain in order to deliver this value.
Infrastructure Management	This element describes the value system configuration that is necessary to deliver the value proposition. This comprises the activities to create and deliver value, the relationship between them, the in-house resources and the firm's partner network.
Customer Relationship	The relationship capital the firm creates and maintains with the customer, in order to satisfy him and generate sustainable revenue.
Financial Aspects	It is transversal because all other pillars influence it. This element is composed of the revenue model and its cost structure. The revenue model determines the firm's profit model and therefore its ability to survive in competition.

It is obvious that the four pillars are interrelated and mutually supported. As for the business strategy, it is worth stressing that e-commerce initiative is not an activity that might or should be developed an implemented independently and separately. it has been suggested (porter, 2001; Strauss Strauss & frost ,2002) that it is necessary to have a strategic approach to e-commerce as a medium to accomplish the business aims. Therefore marketing in the electronic era requires innovative strategies.

ESTABLISHING WEB PRESENCE

Even if one chooses not to sell ones goods or services online, a business web site can be a virtual marketing brochure that one can update on demand with little or no cost. Ones presence on the Internet can be a useful marketing tool by providing richer pre-sale information or post-sale support and service. This might temporarily differentiate ones product or service from competitors'. E-marketing has lessened the disadvantage that small businesses have faced for years when competing with larger businesses.

E-commerce has redefined the market place, altered business strategies, and allowed global competition between local businesses. The term "electronic commerce" has evolved from meaning simply electronic shopping to representing all aspects of business and market processes enabled by the Internet and other digital technologies.

Small business administration is preparing to help this new generation of Internet – enabled or e-small businesses.

Today's business emphasis is on e-commerce – rapid electronic interactions enabled by the Internet and other connected computer and telephone networks. Rapidly business transactions and unparalleled access to information is changing consumer behavior and expectations.

Inexpensive information processing and electronic media can help most small businesses provide better, faster customer service and communication.

IMPACT OF E-MARKETING ACTIVITIES ON MARKETING

Alvin Toffler explains the acceleration in development of technology by looking at the progress in transportation. In 6000 B.C. the fastest transportation available to man over long distances was the camel caravan averaging eight miles per hour. It was not until about 1600 B.C. when the chariot was invented that the maximum speed rose to roughly twenty miles per hour so impressive was this invention and so difficult was it to exceed this speed limit, that nearly 3500 years later, when the first mail coach began operating in England in 1784, it averaged mere ten miles per hour.

The first steam locomotive introduced in 1825, could muster speed of only thirteen mph. It was probably not until1880's that man, with the help of amore advanced steam locomotive managed to reach speed of one hundred miles per hour. It took human race million of years to attain that record. It took only 58 years, however, to quadruple the limit, so that by 1938 airborne man was cracking the 400mphline.it took mere twenty years flick of time to double the limit again. And by the 1960's rocket planes approached speeds of 4800 mph, and men in space capsules were circling the earth at 18,000mph. If technology has affected people so much, naturally it should have also had its impact on organizations.

EFFECT OF STRATEGIC E-MARKETING IN RETAILING

Currently the buzzwords amongst retailing circles are data warehousing and data mining. They create a warehouse of data about customers of various sources and then look for patterns that could be exploited is called data mining.

During a data mining exercise, the analysts in a retail chain found that beer and diapers were bought together. Upon further examination they found that most of the sale took place in the evening, mainly after office hours. Parents having young babies picked up diapers while going back home and also picked up the beer for the night. The retail chain profitably exploited this by having a special display of diapers and costly beers together near the entrance of the store. As people were anxious to get back home early, they did not go inside to pick up their favorite beer but instead selected for the costly beer kept near the diaper.

Technology has made it possible to transform the retail environment away from customer loyalty and towards customer intimacy away from mass marketing and towards micro marketing. With the of shopper I.D. cards it is possible to log in individual customers. The personalized shopper database is useful for moving towards one-to-one relationship marketing.

The Pola corporation example, illustrates how miniaturization of computer has been effectively tapped for selling of cosmetics.

Pola Corporation, one of Japan's leading cosmetics manufacturers developed a "make-up adviser", a hand held computer, which gave advice on make –up, and that, put up the same on the market in February 1987. As the newly developed computer was devised for 1,30,000 Pola door-to-door sales-woman throughout Japan, it was compact enough to fit inside a handbag. The computer used a question – answer routine to accurately analyze the client's skin type and gave advice on make-up.

India is not far behind, when we look at some of the new developments. The following attempt by Pond's is a case in point.

Pond's Institute, the division through which ponds has launched its interactive cell, advises on make-up through interactive touch-screen kiosks in addition to a telephone help line. Pond's consumers will also be able to access advice through a website 24-hours (www.pondsinstituteindia.com).

"We are using technology innovatively as a me3ans of marketing communication to contact the consumer directly at the retail level. This center will provide, inform, guide and advice customers on the various aspects of beauty and skincare", says a pond's spokesperson.

A customer can sit in front of computer terminal and design his own car or a fridge and it fabricated and delivered to his house on the same day; thanks to flexible automation.

Information Technology has greatly contributed to the retail revolution, which is sweeping the entire world. What used to be fragmented industry has got to be consolidated due to the sophisticated use of it systems. Large retail chains are gobbling up small-town retailers. Retailing has now become a global business, thanks to the sophisticated systems being used by them. Typically, owners all along operated the retail stores, but currently the shift is towards system-driven stores. The major shifts that are taking place in the retail industry are summarized in Table 4.2:

Table 4.2: Retail Revolution

From	To
Fragmented	Consolidated
Local	Global
Low technology use	High technology
Owner-operated	Systems-driven
Traders	Retail brand managers
Mass marketing	Individual relationship customization
Market place	Market space

Retail store chains are becoming more powerful than the manufacturing companies. They directly compete with manufacturers by introducing store brands. These private label brands typically offer more value for money, as they are priced low in relation to the company brands.

The days of mass marketing are over. The retailers are now moving away from the traditional segmented approach of marketing to customizing relationship with individual customers. With the introduction of tele-shopping, on-line shopping and virtual shopping malls, the retailing wars of the future are not likely to be fought in the market place but rather in the virtual market space (Table 4.3).

BENEFITS TO A COMPANY USING E-MARKETING

Communicability: The web makes it easy for a firm to communicate with every one of its constituencies: consumers, suppliers, resellers, employees, the media, government bodies, and others. As one observer noted," the internet allows you opportunities to talk to people on a continual, dialog basis in a way that we've never had before".

Focus/Tailored Approach: The web enables a company to focus on a specific target market and offer a marketing mix especially devised for that target market. For example," with the Internet, companies can keep track of purchase history- every single purchase a customer has ever made with organization. The reason that's so important is because purchase history is probably one of the most predictive things in understanding what somebody is most inclined to buy in the future. The other thing is good for is targeted e-mails.

Table 4.3: Internet Penetration of the Home Market by Top Ten Countries: As of January 2001

County	Active home users (million)	Average time spent per month	Average number of sessions per month	Active home users as a percentage of total population
United States	101.4	9 hours, 58 min.	18	36
Japan	15.4	7 hours, 57 min.	16	12
Germany	12.8	8 hours, 16 min	17	15
Great Britain	11.2	6 hours	12	19
Canada	9.0	10 hours, 48 min.	20	29
Italy	7.5	7 hours, 5 min.	13	13
Brazil	4.5	7 hours, 6 min.	12	3
France	5.6	6 hours, 32 min	15	9
Australia	4.5	7 hours, 8 min.	12	24

Source: Compiled by the author from Nielsen//Netratings, Www. Nielsen-Net Ratings. Com (March 8, 2001); and U.S. Bureau of The Census, International Data Base.

Information: A firm can amass information about almost any facet of its business from frce web sites, as well as from fee-based ones. Both primary and secondary data can be garnered via the Internet.

Timeliness: With the Internet, a company can operate in "real time", which means the ability to communicate, gather information, and so forth in a very contemporaneous manner. The time lags associated with other marketing tools are much shorter on web.

Cost Efficiencies: There can be reduced costs from Internet usage. Postal costs decrease inventory costs can be lowered because there is more efficient communication between the companies and their supplies. Sales personnel can follow-up with clients in a more efficient manner.

Dynamism/Flexibility: The Internet is very dynamic and flexible medium, which lets a company rapidly adjust its marketing mix. For instance, if a firm sees that a particular product is not selling well, it can instantly change the advertising on the web.

Global Possibilities: With the Internet, companies can effectively and inexpensively communicate with its various constituencies around the world, thereby increasing the reach of the firm's marketing strategy.

Multimedia Capabilities: The Internet has large multimedia possibilities for marketers, especially as additional users convert to cable or other fast connections.

E-BUSINESS STRATEGY OF IBM

IBM's declared strategy is to transform itself into an e-business in order to provide business value to the corporation and its shareholders. IBM views e-business as being much broader than electronic commerce because it serves a broader constituency and a variety of web- based processes and transactions. To assure successful implementation, IBM formed an independent division, called enterprise web management that has the following four goals:

- To lead IBM's strategy to transform itself into an e-business and to act as a catalyst to help facilitate that transformation.
- To help IBM's business units become more effective in their use of the Internet both internally and with their customers.
- To establish a strategy for the corporate Internet site. This would include a definition of how it should look, feel and be navigated- in short, create an online environment most conducive to customers doing business with IBM.
- To leverage the wealth of e-business transformational accumulated case studies to highlight the potential of e-business to customers.

Like many other companies, IBM started to use the Internet as a static digital brochure- or a publication model- basically posting information. Now however it is moving toward e-business, namely carrying out transactions of all kinds over the internet, intranets and extranets; transactions between IBM and its suppliers; among members of its business partner network; among its employees; and so on. IBM wants to become truly e-business oriented and to focus on how it can use this powerful networking technology to fulfill the diverse needs of its customers.

One of the major issues in moving to e-business was the reengineering of many of its core business processes on the internet- including commerce, procurement, customer care, and knowledge management. The company is developing consistent company wide business strategies that leverage the size and scale of IBM's web presence and investments. In addition, it is creating an Internet model that is both unified and user-centric. This involves the setting of site hosting and production standards related to design, functionality, and navigation.

The major goal that IBM has set is to become the premier e-business. That means being a leader in each of the business process areas. Leadership in these areas will improve customer satisfaction and will allow it to grow more profitably. As the recognized leader in e-business, IBM also adds tremendous credibility to its e-business marketing campaign.

CONCLUSION

E-marketing is a Relations Management Tool. E Marketing is a powerful tool for acquiring new customers. With the use of existing database of customers and prospects to build awareness, educate, sell and service. It is a global electronic superhighway of computer networks that is accessible to people worldwide. Strategic E-Marketing is a systematic process of forming a proper strategy related to Web-related activities to choose the scale of its Web presence. Procter & Gamble (www.pg.com), the consumer products giant, is a good illustration of how the Internet presents a variety of E-marketing opportunities beyond E-commerce. Today P&G operates about 70 user-friendly sites, often loaded with bells and whistles. The group lives on simply as FAST, a coalition to discuss and develop interactive marketing and advertising. The emphasis will be more on E-marketing as the web sites creating an exciting environment for browsing, entertainment, and shopping by users. The e-marketing is a reflection of those activities which transforms the consumer's unpleasant and painful experiences into pleasant and happy moments as it does not include the place or time-based boundaries-marketing strategy provides the sound framework for the marketer to vary the marketing mix to develop the relationships and increasing customer lifetime value.

REFERENCES

Electronic Commerce- A Managerial Perspective 'by EFRAIM TURBAN, JAE LEE, DAVID KING, H.MICHAEL CHUNG.

E-Marketing – Top 10 E-strategy issues is available at: http://www.marketing-insights.co.uk/wnimall.htm.

Kotler, P. and Armstrong, G. (1999) Principles of Marketing (8th edn.). New York, Prentice-Hall.

Marketing in the 21st century chapter 7 Marketing and the Internet.

Marketing in the new millennium by X Javier

Vlachopoulou, M. (2003) E-Marketing – Internet Marketing (2nd edn). Athens, Rosili Publications.

5

IMPACT OF GLOBALIZATION ON TECHNOLOGICAL ENVIRONMENT

Khushdeep Dharni

ABSTRACT

Interdependence among nations has been growing at a faster rate. The process of globalization has altered technology development, changing locations of manufacturing facilities, rising and greater role of Multinational Corporation as well as outsourcing of products, processes and even research and development. Increased R&D investment at the global level is clearly an impact of globalization and the emergence of global economy. The result has been increased pace of innovations and inventions. During the decade of 1960, consumer electronic industry was concentrated in the United States itself. However due to labour cost advantage most of the industry has been shifted to Pacific Rim countries like Taiwan. Role of technology also reflects in growth competitiveness. World Economy Forum calculates growth competitiveness index and it reflects competitiveness of nations. It can be seen from the example of United States that technology is an important determinant of growth competitiveness index. United States has been able to manage number two slot only because its lead in technology index. Average growth rate in the world trade during the decade of 1990's was about 7 per cent per annum with expected elimination of all forms of trade barriers under the institutional frameworks of WTO, the expansion of world.trade is further expected to accelerate. This calls for domestic companies to find out new ways to exploit the opportunities and to take on foreign competition in the emerging markets. With all these changes in store management practices will also undergo change. Managing the productivity of knowledge workers and technology will really be the key management areas of focus.

The waves of globalization are affecting every corner of the macro environment. There is no second opinion about its impact on social, economic and political environment. But if we look at a subset, which has been affected "the most" it is technological environment.

Technological environment is concerned with the level and direction of all technological progress or advancements taking place in a society, including new products, processes or material and the general level of scientific activity and advances in fundamental sciences.

Emergence of world economy is due to globalization and globalization can be referred to as the process by which the various nations in the world are increasingly being interconnected politically and economically through international trade. Interdependence among nations has been growing at a faster rate. The process of globalization has altered technology development, changing locations of manufacturing facilities, rising and greater role of multinational corporation as well as outsourcing of products, processes and even research and development. In the early seventies, only a few western countries were investing in research and development but off late many countries have joined the league. Increased R&D investment at the global level is clearly an impact of globalization and the emergence of global economy. The result has been increased pace of innovations and inventions.

Table 5.1 shows the spending on research and development as percentage of gross domestic product (GDP) for the leading countries in the category. Increased emphasis on technology has ensured that the scope of technological environment has broadened beyond the borders of the United States and Europe to Pacific region including countries like South Korea and China. Because of the cost focus many firms have shifted their manufacturing capacity from advanced industrialized countries to relatively underdevelopment economies of the world. During the decade of 1960, consumer electronic industry was concentrated in the United States itself. However due to labour cost advantage most of the industry has been shifted to Pacific Rim countries like Taiwan. Almost the same trend can be witnessed in case of Japanese automobile industry which was initially centered in Japan but now has spread allover the globe. Spread of R&D and manufacturing activities has ensured that role of multinational corporations will be more prominent and increasingly the number of non-US multinationals is on the rise. Technology based cost cutting has also led to expansion of outsourcing activities in the every sphere.

Role of technology also reflects in growth competitiveness. World Economy Forum calculates growth competitiveness index and it reflects competitiveness of nations. Growth competitive index is composed of their component indices: the technology index, the public institutions index and macroeconomic environment index. These indices represent a country's technological readiness because of increasing importance of technology in the development process, the state of the country's public institutions and the quality of macro environment.

Table 5.1 Expenditure on Research and Development

Country	Percentage of GDP
Sweden	3.78
Finland	3.37
Japan	2.98
USA	2.72
Korea	2.65
Switzerland	2.64
Germany	2.49
France	2.18
Denmark	2.09
Netherlands	1.97

According to the executive summary of global competitiveness report of World Economic Forum researches have emphasized that the role of technology in the growth process differs for countries, depending upon their particular stage of development. It is widely understood that technological innovation is relatively more important for growth in countries close to the technological frontier. Depending upon whether innovation is important for a country or technology transfer associated with foreign direct investment economies have been separated into two groups. These two groups are the core economies i.e. those for which technological innovation is critical foe growth and non-core economies i.e. those which can still grow by adopting technologies developed abroad. The weights differ for core economies. Lesser weight is given incase of non-core economies and more weight is given for core economies that are closer to the technological frontier.

Apart from competitiveness index two more indices are also good indicators of standing of nations on the global map. These indices are business competitiveness index and Networked Readiness index. Business competitiveness index is a complementary approach to macroeconomics approach of the growth competitiveness index in the medium term. It evaluates specifically two areas: the sophistication of the operating practices and the strategies of the companies along with the quality of the macro economic business environment in which a nation's companies compete. Because in absence of these microeconomic capabilities macroeconomic and institutional reforms are not going to yield full-scale results.

Table 5.2 shows the top 10 countries along with India and China on basis of growth competitiveness index. It also shows standing of these countries on basis of technology index, macroeconomic environment index, business competitiveness index, network readiness index and human development index. There seems to be a high degree of association between these indices. It can be seen from the example of United States that technology is an important determinant of growth competitiveness index. United States has been able to manage number two slot only because its lead in technology index. Almost the same seems to be valid incase of Taiwan.

Now let us try to find out how come India is going to be affected by globalization especially on the technology front. It is expected that over the coming 2-3 decades India's progress will be closely linked to events both with in the region as well as around the world. Opportunities and challenges will arise as the consequence of transformation of the regional and global trade scenario. Some major developments which are likely to affect India's progress in the coming time will be pressure on energy prices because of exponential economic growth, further diffusion of information revolution and more technological innovations.

Average growth rate in the world trade during the decade of 1990's was about 7 per cent per annum with expected elimination of all forms of trade barriers under the institutional frameworks of WTO, the expansion of world trade is further expected to accelerate. This calls for domestic companies to find out new ways to exploit the opportunities and to take on foreign competition in the emerging markets. Because of availability of global surpluses the competition is expected to be even more intense and scope of opportunities present in the business is going to be altered. It is expected that opportunities in business will slowly move from volume production to special value added categories of products and services. Another important area will be growth of service sector and associated labour shortages in the western world.

On the fronts of technology and Intellectual capital, it is expected that TRIPS will promote even faster technological innovation. Technology will get diffused a fast pace both in as well as across the national boundaries.

With all these changes in store management practices will also undergo change. No longer flexible management systems will be in the domain of private sector but public sector and government institutions will also have to show agility in line with the changing environments. Managing the productivity of knowledge workers and technology will really be the key management areas of focus. Management academicians will have to put in an extra effort to keep up with the emerging global scenario.

Table 5.2: Comparison of Select Countries on the Basis of Different Indices

Country	GCI		TI		PII		MEI		BCI	COSR	QNBE	NRI	HDI	
	Rank	Score	Rank	Score	Rank	Score	Rank	Score	Rank	Rank	Rank	Rank	Rank	Score
Finland	1	5.95	3	5.92	3	6.48	3	5.47	2	7	1	3	13	0.935
USA	2	5.82	1	6.24	21	5.74	15	5.04	1	2	2	5	8	0.939
Sweden	3	5.72	4	5.80	6	6.31	17	4.99	4	5	6	6	2	0.946
Taiwan	4	5.69	2	6.04	27	5.56	9	5.11	17	12	20	15	22*	0.895
Denmark	5	5.66	6	5.34	1	6.59	4	5.36	7	9	3	4	17	0.932
Norway	6	5.56	1	5.17	5	6.35	2	5.54	20	23	14	13	1	0.956
Singapore	7	5.56	11	5.11	10	6.21	1	5.79	10	13	8	1	25	0.902
Switzerland	8	5.49	7	5.25	8	6.22	5	5.24	5	4	7	9	11	0.936
Japan	9	5.48	5	5.68	16	5.88	29	4.67	8	3	11	8	9	0.938
Iceland	10	5.44	14	5.05	2	6.58	12	5.09	19	17	18	2	7	0.94
China	46	4.29	62	3.72	55	4.39	24	4.78	47	39	47	41	94	0.745
India	55	4.07	63	3.72	53	4.45	52	4.05	30	30	32	39	127	0.595

GCI: Growth Competitiveness Index, TI: Technology Index, PII: Public Institutions Index, MEI: Macroeconomic Environment Index, BCI: Business Competitiveness Index, COSR: Companies Operations and Strategies Ranking, QNBE: Quality of National Business Environment, NRI: Network Readiness Index, HDI: Human Development Index (All indices for 2004). Source: World Economic Forum and UNDP.

* Ranking for 2002

PARADIGM SHIFT IN MICRO FINANCE INSTITUTIONS: A FUTURISTIC MODEL

Geetika, Neeraj Pandey and Kingshuk Das

ABSTRACT

Today the micro finance is acquiring the status of a movement in the banking sector. Their role as an intermediary between banks and borrowers is becoming more relevant and it's model is undergoing 'reactionary' changes. The United Nations has designated Year 2005 as the International Year of Micro credit. Effective rural micro finance can very well be the elusive panacea to a host of social & emotive issues ranging from rural employment to empowerment. Thus given the increasingly centrality and relevance of the MFIs (Micro Finance Institutions), it requires proactive changes. The paper tries to unravel the existing model of MFIs, starting from the pioneering effort of Mohammad Yonus's Grameen Bank in Bangladesh to foreign banks like ABN Amro's innovative interventions in the field of micro finance in India. The present work proposes a totally new model of MFI, which shall be most suited to the targeted borrowers needs and demands. This model is based on exploiting the latent rural human-resource, bank-SHG (Self Help Group) linkages, bank-NGO (Non-Government Organization) linkages backed by innovative rural marketing strategies. This futuristic model is going to set new standards in approach, process & procedures of MFI functioning within India. The model is based on optimization techniques, given the constraints of diversity of borrowers, in which the ultimate goal is to make the MFI a dispenser not just of credit but also of a variety of social goods & services to the rural poor.

INTRODUCTION

The micro finance is changing the landscape of banking across the world. It has changed the lives of people and revitalized communities in the world's poorest and also the richest countries. The micro finance is a better targeted financial help to a clientele that is poorer and vulnerable than traditional bank clients. The broad classification of micro finance includes rural credit through specialized banks traditional informal micro finance like loans from friends and relatives moneylenders etc. BANK-NGO partnership based micro finance, non-NGO, non-collaterised micro finance, Grameen bank type micro finance etc. Anyone who has access to saving, credit, insurance and other financial services is more resilient and better able to deal with everyday demands. Micro finance helps poor and low income clients deal with such basic needs, like with access to micro insurance, which is a part of micro finance, poor people can cope with sudden expenses associated with serious illness or loss of assets. It also provides them access to formal saving accounts and thus an incentive to save. Clients who join and stay in micro finance programme have better economic conditions than non-clients.

MICROFINANCE INSTITUTION AND POVERTY ELIMINATION

A micro finance institution (MFI) is an organization that provides financial services targeted to the poor Its clients are generally poor and low income people .They may be female heads of households, pensioners ,artisans or small farmers .It obtains finance from banks and in turn provides small scale credit & other financial services to low income households & other informal business

The micro finance works around the concept of group lending where it allows a number of individuals to provide collateral or guarantee a loan through a group repayment pledge. The incentive to repay is based on peer pressure if one person in the group defaults, the other group members make up the payment amount .It is powerful tool for reducing poverty as it makes capital available to the unbanked poor at reasonable rates .A survey by ABN AMRO bank clients has shown that 58 per cent of those who have used micro finance for about 4 years, experienced a significant reduction in poverty and 41 per cent have come right out of it.

The micro finance institutions aim primarily to empower people to manage their resources on their own and build sustainable livelihoods. Development of local indigenous skills & vocational training to foster employment opportunities are integral part of the objective, with the ultimate goal to alleviate poverty.

EXISTING MODELS OF MFIs

Presently, the micro finance institutions are operating with diverse methods &means, with common end result to provide affordable financial services to the poor & low-income people. With access to range of financial tools such families can invest according to their own priorities viz school fees, healthcare, business nutrition, housing etc.

The micro finance was not popular before seventies. It was in late eighties & early 1990s that it started showing exemplary results in the field of poverty alleviation. The pioneering effort in this direction was done by Muhammad Yunus of Chittagong University .He established Grammen bank in 1976 in Bangladesh. Today Grammen bank has over 1000 branches- a branch covers around 25-30 villages around 240 groups & 1200 borrowers in every province of Bangladesh .It has borrowing groups in 28000 villages with 12 lakh borrows with over 90 per cent being women .The most important feature is the recovery rate of the loans, which is as high as 98 per cent yet another interesting feature of this bank is advancing credit without any collateral security.

GRAMMEN BANK MODEL

The bank lending system is simple but effective to obtain loans, potential borrower must form a group of five, gather once a week for loan repayment meeting and to start with learning the bond rules and "16 decisions" which they chant at the start of their weekly sessions. These decisions incorporate code of conduct that members are encouraged to follow in their daily life e.g. production of fruits and vegetables in kitchen gardens, investment for improvement of housing and education for children, safe drinking water for better health etc

Number of groups in the same village is combined into a centre. The organization of members in groups and centres serves a number of purposes .It gives individuals a measure of personal security and confidence to take risks and launch new initiatives. The formation of the groups, a key unit in the credit programme, is the first necessary step to receive credit. Loans are initially made to two individuals in the group, who are then under pressure from the rest of the members to repay in good time. If the borrowers default, the other members of the group may forfeit their chance of a loan. The loan repayment is in weekly installments spread over a year and simpler interest of 20 per cent is charged once at the year-end. Factors behind success of the Grameen Bank are participatory process in every aspect of lending mechanism, peer pressure of group members on each other, lending for activities which generate regular income, weekly collections of loans in small amount, intense interaction with borrowers through weekly meetings, strong central management, dedicated field staff, extensive staff training, willingness to innovate, committed pragmatic leadership and decentralized as well as participatory style of working.

PAG IBIG FUND (PHILIPPINES) MODEL

Pag IBIG fund, is one of the most financially stable government owned and controlled corporation in Philippines today. It has a total of 1.2 million members with a fund base of US 800 million dollars. The fund is a provident saving fund and a housing credit system for the wage earners. Its objectives are (a) to promote self - reliance and self – determination among workers through memberships in an integrated nation wide saving system, (b) to invest provident saving of its members taking into consideration the profitability and safety of the funds as a means of providing them provident benefits upon termination of their membership in the fund, (c) To promote home ownership through the establishment of an affordable and adequate housing credit system for its members and (d) to provide small and short loans and other benefits to its members.

Saving and housing are closely related and the first step was to take care of the member's basic need for housing. The fund instituted a systematic, regular and easy saving system and tapped new groups of savers who could not be reached by the commercial banks and became a major source of funds for developing the economy. Thus, pag IBIG helps every Filipino to have his own house by pooling the saving of its members and channeling them for the long term financing requirement of housing.

HDFC MODEL

HDFC has been making continuous and sustained efforts to reach the lower income groups of society especially the economically weaker sections, thus enabling then to realize their dreams of possessing a house of their own. Its response to the need for better housing and living environment for the poor, both in the urban and rural sectors materialize in its collaboration with Kreditanstalt fur Wiederaufbau (KFW), a German Development bank. KFW sanctioned DM 55 million to HDFC for low cost housing projects in India.

For the purpose of actual implementation of the low cost housing projects, HDFC collaborates with organisation, both government and non-government. Such organisations act as coordinating agencies for the projects involving a collective of individuals belonging to Economically Weaker Sections.

ABN AMRO PILOT STUDY

ABN AMRO did a pilot study with Cashpor Micro Credit in Uttar Pradesh and Bihar, on the use of " SIMPUTER"- a hand-held computer for real -time capture of data on -field for use by field workers in remote villages. Considering the success, the bank is now providing Cashpor with enough simputers to cover an entire district reaching out to thousands of its members for enhancing efficiency in the delivery of credit and other services to the rural poor.

Thus, ABN AMRO, along with other foreign banks like Citi Bank, HSBC etc., is working on Bank- NGO linkages to dispense micro credit to the targeted clients.

FUTURISTIC MODEL OF MFI

The micro financial institutions are today, no doubt, acquiring the status of movement in the banking sector. Its importance can be gauged from the fact that the United Nations has designated year 2005 as the international year of micro credit. Today effective micro-finance is seen as solution to many of the existing social and emotive problems ranging from rural employment to empowerment. The various micro finance institution models are quite effective in dispensing the much-needed credit to the targeted clients. However there exist certain weaknesses in existing micro finance institution models. There is enough space of more efficiency and better results in credit disbursement through micro finance institutions.

If we look back, it is found that Grameen Bank type micro finance institution model is one of most successful model in micro finance. The bank has successfully served the rural poor in Bangladesh with no physical collateral relying on group responsibility to replace the collateral requirements. This model, like other models, has also some weaknesses. It involves too much of external subsidy which is not replicable. Grameen Bank has not oriented itself towards mobilizing people's resources. The repayment system of 50 weekly equal installments is not practical because poor do not have a stable job and have to migrate to other places for jobs. If the communities are agrarian during lean seasons it becomes impossible for them to repay the loan. Pressure for high repayment drives members to moneylenders.

Most of the existing micro finance institutions are facing problems regarding skilled labour, which is not available for local level accounting. Drop out of the trained staff is very high. Also most of the models do not lend for agriculture.

The four pillars of micro finance credit system are

1. Supply of credit.
2. Demand for finance.
3. Intermediation by individuals or authorities.
4. Regulation by statutory bodies.

The end goal of any such basic model is accessibility of finance to poor.

The new model calls for exploiting the latent rural human resource by talent spotting and training them as per their potential, for example, the graduates can be trained in accounting or as Self Help Group leaders. The awareness campaign regarding various rights, subsidies and incentives given by various micro finance schemes may be disseminated by involving the local rural youth, which may very well connect to the local population based on similarity in dialect, living ways and culture.

It envisages the CENTRE as the hub of all activities. It is the place where all funding, responsibility and accountability is concentrated. This will ensure efficiency, better control and reduced cost of interfacing between dispenser and taker of the credit. The CENTRE will also do a grading system- A, B, C, D, E- under which grading would be based on number of years client has been attached with any of the micro finance institutions and its positive track record in repaying the loans, including the condition that at least one amount of the loan was greater than Rs. 5000. The criteria for grading are:

A ≥ 12 years attached with any MFI, subject to the conditions discussed above.

B ≥ 10 years attached with any MFI, subject to the conditions discussed above.

C ≥ 7 years attached with any MFI, subject to the conditions discussed above.

D ≥ 5 years attached with any MFI, subject to the conditions discussed above.

E ≥ 3 years attached with any MFI, subject to the conditions discussed above.

The client of A, B, and C can take loan directly from the CENTRE, other conditions for eligibility being the same. These are persons who have successfully came out of the vicious poverty cycle and are aspiring to grow big and still bigger, comparatively. For example they initially took loans of Rs. 1,000 then Rs. 3,000, then Rs. 5,000 and so on; and they have repaid the loan amount following all terms and conditions and within the time limits. Thus, their sincerity, a desire to excel and business acumen has been proved to a considerable level. Now a loan amount up to Rs. 50,000 for category C, up to Rs. 75,000 for category B and more then Rs. 75,000 for category A (upper limit Rs. 2 Lakh) can be disbursed directly from the CENTRE to such clients. This grading system would also help us in deciding whether the person has the capability of handling larger projects as compared to earlier and obviously, with larger financial stakes. A person with higher grades can be given additional loans for housing, vehicle, etc. This will help in reducing transaction cost and time, besides making the credit access easy and timely for the clients of this particular category.

The NGOs & CBOs have a vital role in this futuristic model e.g. CBOs (Community Based Organisation) have better access to the local information like type & timing of credit requirements. Since our rural areas have lot of diversity, qualitatively and demand wise, hence the active involvement of such organisation is a must for successful implementation of this model. The NGO linkage provides expertise, which they have gained over the years in executing such tasks. They are able to efficiently utilize local resources and involve voluntaries.

The model tries to optimize the end result and goals, given the constraints of diversity of borrowers, long recovery periods, scattered population, peculiar credit requirements of each SHG or a village centre. It also envisages that innovative rural marketing strategies like conducting informal workshops at village choupals, making the targeted people aware about the structure, benefits and excess points of MFI involving local people as "movement disseminators" and also giving "demonstration effect" where successful MFI-supported entrepreneurs are made to interact with the villagers and slum people so that they can get conviction about power of MFI.

The model takes into consideration a lesser-known fact that the poor repay their loans and are willing to pay for higher interest rates provided that the credit is provided to them. The peer group pressure and sequential lending provide strong repayment motivation and produce extremely low default rates. Therefore, banking on poor can be a profitable business.

Thus, this futuristic model of micro finance institution, taken in holism, is going to set new standards in approach, process & procedures in disbursement of micro-credit within India. The idea behind such an approach is to make micro finance institutions not just a dispenser of credit, but also of a variety of social goods & services to the unbanked rural poor.

REFERENCES

Barry, N.(1995), "The Missing Links: Financial System that Works for the Majority," Women's World Banking, New York.

Churchill, C.F. (1996)," An Introduction to Key Issues in Micro finance: Supervision and Regulation, Financing Sources, Expansion of Micro finance Institutions," Micro finance Network, Washington, D.C. February.

Ghate, P.(1992) Informal Finance: Some Findings from Asia, Oxford University Press, Hong Kong.

Grameen Trust (1995) Grameen Dialogue No.24, Dhaka, October.

Phelps, P.(1995) "Building Linkages Between the Micro enterprise and Shelter Sectors: An Issues Paper," GEMINI, Betuesda, Maryland.

7

IMPACT OF GLOBALISATION TOWARDS ETHICAL BUSINESS FOCUS

Surinder Pal Singh

INTRODUCTION

As from the mid-nineties, the discussion involving the question of ethics and social responsibility in business has been gaining prominence. In the face of worsening social and environmental problems (unemployment, social exclusion, deforestation, extinction of species, water, air, and soil pollution) in every part of the world, consumers, investors and society in general have begun to call on companies to assume their portion of social responsibility and to conduct their businesses in an The main impact of globalization on business ethics is found in cultural differences, which reflect on various social and business morals. What standards of conduct are to be adhered to when operating globally? Should companies adopt the standards of the country/company with which they are doing business, or remain faithful to their own standards? As the numbers of countries in which they operate grow, the probability of ethical conflicts may also increase.

The main objective of this paper is to analyze the implications of the globalization process on business management, in so far as it refers to business ethics.

This paper has been developed by means of a bibliographic research. Literature related to ethics, more specifically business ethics, and globalization was researched, together with more recent research of the theme directed at business ethics, from a globalization perspective. Data were qualitatively analyzed. Thereafter, a synthesis of the issue under study was prepared, in which the principal implications for companies having business interests in various parts of the world were underscored.

GLOBALIZATION

Globalization is, without doubt, the most used - and abused word – and one that has been least defined over the last and future years; it is also the most nebulous and misunderstood, and yet has the greatest political efficacy.

The globalization process has been widely discussed for a number of decades, although not always under this terminology. However, even nowadays, it appears rather difficult to arrive at any consensus regarding an acceptable definition. Some authors have defined the word as an absence of international commercial frontiers and barriers, while others see it as a process of changes in production standards, investment and commerce on an international scale. Another view defines globalization as the interlinking of society interests and business organizations (Parker, 1998).

Beck (1999) draws attention to the importance of the distinction between globalism and globalization. According to the author, globalism is seen as a banishment of political action. It relates to the ideology of neo-liberalism. It is restricted to an economic dimension, leaving all other aspects – relative to ecology, culture, politics and civil society – under the dominion of the world market. Globalization means the awareness of the fact that we are already living in a world society, whereby the notion of isolated spaces becomes fictitious. The author believes that globalization is an irreversible process, for the following reasons: geographic widening and growing international market interaction, the linking of financial markets throughout the globe and the increasing power of transnational companies; data and communication media revolution; universal demand for human rights; global cultural industry iconic trends; post-international and polycentric world policy (governments, companies, non – government organizations, national unions); worldwide poverty; the destruction of the environment throughout the world; and localized trans-cultural conflicts.

Bull (1977) has already discussed the decline of state systems, based on three of the elements mentioned above: the strengthening of transnational organizations, the flow of capital, and the development of technology. Ianni (1992; 1999) also calls attention to the crisis involving the principle of national sovereignty, which checkmates the idea of state-nation, in the proportion that trans-nationalization of the economy not only redirects but also reduces the capacity of national governments to make decisions.

According to Bull (1977), transnational organizations are those whose operations surpass frontiers. His view is that such companies have been in existence for a considerable time, giving as an example, the powerful Dutch East India Company. Czinkota and Ronkainen (1995) refer back to the Roman Empire comparing it to economic blocks, as a single currency system was used, commercial routes were protected, having its own legal system and forms of communication. Sposati (1999) cites the example of the Crusades, in the Middle Ages, as an attempt at unification. According to the author, "nowadays, capital is following the path that faith achieved 500 years ago".

Globalization can be seen as a consequence of the historic development of humanity, following successive integration processes, which have been impelled by technology (Ianni, 1992, Azevedo and Bertrand, 2000).

Some authors, however, single out the end of the cold war and the fall of the Berlin wall as fundamental milestones of the expansion of globalization (Czinkota and Ronkainen, 1995). Others, though, cite the maturity of the "triad" countries (U.S.A., Japan, and Europe), as also being strong impellers of the globalization process during the 80's (Abreu, 1999).

As far as Beck (1999) is concerned, globalization implies an interconnection of everything that happens in the world. No single phenomenon can be considered spatially bounded. All discoveries, disasters, good or bad facts, affect the entire planet, thereby creating the need for an adoption of new directions around the global-local axis.

However, this interconnected world is not monolithic (Ianni, 1999). Within it there is a coexistence of diversities and inequalities, nationalisms and fundamentalisms, regional and Imperialism blocks. Parallel to integration, there is also a fragmentation trend.

According to Sposati (1999), the globalization process is not uniform, and as such, affects each country in a different manner. Within the very same country, different people are also affected by this process in different ways.

Globalization is an essentially paradoxical process. If, on the one hand, it enables the economic development of a number of countries around the world, on the other, it also contributes to the ever-growing unequal distribution of wealth. There are many views regarding the opportunities and threats brought or imposed by globalization. Some see it as new clothing worn by and old process (Sposati, 1999), others regard it as colonialism revisited, in which the interests of powerful nations and corporations are reinforced.

Furtado (1998) and others, still see in globalization a hope of establishing a global community characterized by the union of different cultures in search of social justice, respect for human rights and nature, in fact, directed towards the common good (Boff, 2000).

However, the implications of this process in different arenas are undeniable: in economy, culture, technology and the natural environment. In the economic sphere, the increase of power enjoyed by independent negotiators in the financial market and an incredible volatility of capital can be clearly perceived, thereby making national economies more vulnerable to speculation (Parker, 1998).

In the political ambit, the destruction of frontiers at the same time in which business opportunities are created, also contribute toward the lessening of national autonomy. The movement towards privatizations, in turn, transfers responsibilities, that heretofore were seen as belonging to governments, into the hands of private companies. As a consequence, the weakening of national political leaders and the increase of influence wielded by business leaders who head veritable worldwide empires is clearly evident.

In the cultural field, companies appear as conductors of a "global culture", translated into consumer habits. National symbols and myths come face to face with the competition of world symbols and myths (Ianni, 1992; Ortiz, 1999, Parker, 1998).

In the technological sphere, the reduction of physical distances, due to the development of communication technologies and the possibility of the democratization of access to data and the distribution of knowledge, is also very evident. Parker (1998) draws attention to the fact that even with the use of the entire technological apparatus, this distribution of knowledge will only be possible if there is an equal investment in education.

In so far as natural resources are concerned, the increase in industrialization, while furnishing the potential for the creation of new employment, also contributes to a concentration of population in urban areas, which already have environmental problems resulting from garbage, drainage, atmospheric and noise pollution. The transfer of non-native animal and vegetable species increases the danger of an ecological imbalance, caused by the migration of pests and diseases where there are no natural enemies at destination. On the other hand, sustainable development requires greater economic equality among the regions. While the division of markets among rich and poor countries remains, we will find it difficult to reach sustainability of the planet and, life on Earth will continue to be threatened (Parker, 1998).

The surpassing of frontiers in all these dimensions violently transforms daily life. Everything surpasses frontiers – people, money, technology, data, drugs, and merchandise. Seen from this point of view, globalization means the end of distances, a process that subjects people to a transnational life, sometimes undesired and not understood (Beck, 1999).

In a general way, globalization impelled by development of technologies, especially telecommunications, by development of political institutions at a world level, by dissemination of cultural habits and the common consumption of various nations, has been bringing more and more accelerated changes to the business scenario and, as a result, a greater degree of uncertainty to business management.

At the same time that they are affected by globalization, the organizations are its own propellers, as they extend their economic objectives to cover the global sphere.

Azevedo and Bertrand (2000, p.28), based on a review of literature on globalization, propose the following definition for globalization, in so far as it refers to companies:

"Globalization is a set of transformations undergone by companies as a consequence of contemporaneous phenomena, typical of the post cold war era, characterized by:

- the strengthening of transnational organizations,
- massification of data technology,
- liberation of the flow of capital, products and data across national frontiers and
- a world trend towards the homogenization of markets".

The globalization process has contributed to markets, companies, and competition among them. Globalization, however, affects both the internal operation of companies as well as its external operations and market relations (Abreu, 1999; Azevedo and Bertrand, 2000).

Azevedo and Bertrand (2000) conceptually studied the transition of multinational companies to global companies. According to the authors, this transition implies a change from a low level to a high level of global integration of company operations; from decentralized strategic planning to centralized; from some key markets being served by the company to all key markets being served; from a predominant multidomestic marketing perspective to a global perspective and from a polycentric organizational view to a geocentric one.

The controversial case involving the non-ratification of the Kyoto protocol by the United States (the country responsible for approximately 25 per cent of gas emission causing the greenhouse effect), has brought to light the argument over the magnitude of global company power. The Kyoto protocol, originated in 1997, during a conference held in Japan, proposes that other industrialized countries reduce the emission of gases causing the greenhouse effect by 5 per cent by 2012, a percentage based on gas emissions as at 1990. The main element in these gases is carbon dioxide, produced as a result of burning oil, gasoline and coal (Bertolino, 2001).

The specific interests of each country relative to this issue are divergent. Tropical countries are extremely harmed by heating, while very cold countries may even be benefited by it. Countries having a coastline suffer damage caused by the rise in ocean levels, while countries that do not have direct access to the sea are not so much affected. Coal and petroleum producing countries would be affected if the world consumption of such products were to be reduced. On the other hand, countries that produce other types of energy would be benefited (Sachs, 2001).

In Brazil, a letter was sent by a group of non-governmental organizations (NGO's) to the 20 largest private American companies operating in the Country, requesting that they approach President George W. Bush for the purpose of convincing him to ratify the protocol. Thus, the companies were challenged to show their real undertaking with social and environmental responsibility, subject to the penalty of having their positioning in regard to the issue published in the press and other media. According to Rubens Born, general coordinator of Vitae Civilis, the NGO that leads this movement, international media reported the position adopted by the American president as a consequence of strong lobbying by principal American companies, seeking to maintain their private interests "ignoring the international agreement to protect the environment and all human beings on our planet". In this case, the United States, the country responsible for more than 30 per cent of the world's economy, in which the head offices of the largest multi-national companies are to be found, has adopted a position contrary to global interests, in favor of the private interests of American companies.

Parallel to the increase of global companies' power, their relationship with society also undergoes transformations. It is noted that there is a resurgence of the discussion related to corporate social responsibility and ethics in business.

SOCIAL RESPONSIBILITY AND BUSINESS ETHICS

Over recent years, there has been a growing debate on the social responsibility of companies. In the academic field, the theme has been studied for over half a century and the concept of corporate social responsibility has undergone various revisions, including the adoption of a variety of nomenclatures over this long trajectory: corporate social responsiveness (CSR2), with a more managerial focus, with emphasis on management relationships between company and society; corporate social rectitude (CSR3), incorporating normative ethics; and corporate social performance (CSP), more directed towards results (Frederick, 1986, *apud* Mitnick, 1995, Frederick, 1994; Preston, 1988, *apud* Clarkson, 1995).

In the 90's, a stronger idea arose advocating that a company should manage its relations with groups of stakeholders – people or groups having proprietary rights or past, present or future interests in an organization and its activities. Within the principal groups of stakeholders of a company, employees, consumers, suppliers, stockholders, business associates, community and the environment were highlighted (Clarkson, 1995).

Carroll (1998, 1999) proposes that corporate social responsibility involves the carrying on of business in a manner that is economically profitable, respects the laws, is ethical and supports the society in which it operates with contributions in a variety of forms (Clarkson, 1995). Thus, Carroll foresees four dimensions of corporate social responsibility: economic, legal, ethical and philanthropic. Of these four facets, ethics should be seen as the core dimension of social responsibility.

Ethics refers to the study and philosophy of human conduct, with emphasis on the determination of what is right and what is wrong (Srour, 2000).

There are two different concepts of ethics. The first is that which is considered a science of the *ends,* which guides the conduct of men and of the *means* necessary to reach that end. In this case, both *ends* and *means* are deduced from nature, essence or substance of man. The second concept is centered on the causes of human behavior, meeting the knowledge of facts, therefore, considering the science of *movable* of human behavior (Abbagnano, 2000).

In any event, ethics can be understood to be a manifestation of liberty, in so far as it involves the considerations of each one, relative to what is right or wrong (Chanlat, 2000). It is the human being exercising his conscience and consideration in order to decide on his own behavior or conduct.

Carried into business environment, *business* ethics embraces moral principles and standards that guide the conduct of firms. It is from the screen of different stakeholder groups that certain behaviors are classified as right or wrong, ethical or unethical. (Ferrell et.al., 2001)

Business ethics therefore serves as reference of company decision-making. Business decisions occur in the midst of conflicts of interests and roles. Many times, people see themselves obliged, due to the role they play in an organization, to take decisions that place personal interests or of those close to them (family, friends) or their cultural values, at risk. Apart from this, in the majority of cases, decisions in business affect, in some way or other, one or more groups of *stakeholders,* which may either positively or negatively influence the future of the organization.

Aiming at justifying their decisions relative to ethics, individuals resort to moral philosophies –principles or rules that each one uses when deciding what is right or wrong. Some of the types of moral philosophies can be cited as follows: consequentialism – study the moral value of conduct by examining its consequences; utilitarianism – analyzes the consequences seeking the greatest good for the largest number of people possible (greater social utility); deontology – concentrates on fundamental rights of individuals and on the intentions associated with behaviors (Ferrell et. al., 2001).

Max Weber (1959), *apud* Srour, 2000; 1919, *apud* Enriquez, 1997 proposed a division of ethics into conviction theories (deontology) and ethics of responsibility (teleology). The ethics of conviction is measured by values and norms established *a priori.* The ethics of responsibility state that people are responsible for their acts. The effects of their decisions should be appraised and an endeavor should be made to obtain positive results for society. While people who obey the ethics of conviction are guided by imperatives of conscience, projecting purist idealism, those that resort to ethics of responsibility are guided by an analysis of risks, following a pragmatic realism (Srour, 2000). A responsible man considers context when taking decisions acceptable to the majority, having to consider various responsibilities: organizational, technical, political, social, civic, ecological, and psychic.

The ethics of conviction is, therefore, used to a greater extent by those who accept an undertaking with beliefs and norms and are not willing to face ambiguities. In companies, however, it is very common to find decisions being taken according to the ethics of responsibility, in which costs and benefits are always weighed.

If there is a risk of fanaticism and the absence of questioning with the ethics of conviction, ethics of responsibility runs the risk of justifying the use of cruel means in order to attain the objectives aim at.

Ethical issues can be analyzed under a variety of perspectives. So, there is no single manner of taking ethical decisions. The different perspectives adopted by individuals are a potential source of conflict in organizations. Followers of the relativist perspective recognize that people in each society use different criteria to determine what is right or what is wrong. Each social group maintains its own system of moral norms. On the other hand, adherents to the ethics of virtue believe that what can be considered moral in a given situation is generally beyond the socially acceptable standards in another. Virtue would therefore have a universal character, surpassing cultural specificities (Ferrel *et.al.,* 2001).

IMPACT OF GLOBALIZATION ON BUSINESS ETHICS

With the intensification of international competition, arising mainly from the maturity of the triad nations and growing economic independence, companies were obliged to seek lower costs, more productive efficiency and new markets (Abreu, 1999). Thus, companies sought to obtain competitive advantages, drawing on resources and intakes from various parts of the world, wherever more advantageous.

Therefore, there is a distribution of roles between countries for each productive process. Some countries deal with research and intellectual production, others produce components and others concentrate on the execution of projects and assembly of products, furnishing low cost labor (Azevedo and Bertrand, 2000; Kon, 2000).

Herein lies an important ethical problem: the globalization process of business operations in itself, contributes towards accentuating the differences between developed and emerging countries, the former being responsible for the intellectual part of the process while the latter furnish their natural resources and low cost labor.

Kon (2000) reinforces this point when arguing that globalization implies exclusion and increases the relative backwardness of the nations that do not have the conditions for a satisfactory entry to the globalization process. Transnational companies would therefore have a fundamental role in determining which societies will be able to enjoy the usufruct of globalized world, raising its earnings and welfare and those who will tend to remain excluded from the process. The need for globalization process integration, therefore forces emerging countries to follow government policies that seek economic stability, frequently at the cost of negative social impacts. The decision relative to the internationalization of capital, therefore, would be a question of ethics in the face of a need for a greater international convergence at social development levels.

On the other hand, the globalization process contributes to a meeting of individuals from different nations, who bring their cultures, their values, their laws and different ethical and moral standards to business situations (Ferrell, *et.al.*, 2001). Professionals who are active in international negotiations have to be aware and sensitive to these differences, so that satisfactory business negotiations can be concluded. Different cultures can be present in communication, gestures, notions and the importance given to the time factor and in regard to what is morally acceptable or not, within a certain society (Ferrell *et.al.*,2001). Empathy and sensitivity in regard to other cultures must be sought as a way to deal with people coming from other countries or regions (Arruda, 2000).

One of the main impacts of globalization on business ethics lies, therefore, in cultural difference, which in turn, reflects on various social and business morals. What are the standards of conduct to follow when operating globally? Should companies adopt the standards of the country/company with which they are doing business, or should they remain faithful to their own standards? As the number of countries in which they operate increase, the probability of ethical conflicts also increases.

Klein (2000) furnishes some examples of the differences in morally acceptable standards. The first example relates to bribes. At the same time they are seen as morally problematic practices in the United States, they can be seen legitimate business practices in Egypt or Italy. Another example refers to the mere compliance with local laws: that which could be considered a legitimate product line in one country, may, on the other hand cause problems to the health of the population, as was the case of glue produced by H.B. Fuller, in Honduras, used as a narcotic by street children.

Sójka (2000) argues that the more a company becomes global, the more it needs to be aware of local values and habits. Based on the arguments put forward by Macintyre, the author does not believe in the possibility of a uniformity of ethical standards in business. Departing from the work of Georges Enderle (1996, *apud,* Sójka, 2000), which shows the differences between business ethics in North America and Continental Europe, Sójka also includes a comparison with standards relative to Central Europe and Eastern Europe.

In a research, based on a cultural individualism/collectivism dimensions proposed by Hofstede, Beekum at.al. (2001) tested positioning towards egoism and utilitarianism on Brazilian and American professionals. The results indicated a difference of appraisal in regard to ethics: on applying a utilitarian perspective, the Brazilian respondents are less inclined to see an action or decision as being non-ethical. This result can be explained by the collectivist characteristic of Brazilian culture. Thus, Brazilians tend to appraise an action or decision by using a parameter of consequences for the largest number of people in a group.

Ethical problems in an international sphere can take diverse forms. One of the most common is discrimination in the work place or in the hiring of staff, by sex, race, religion or physical handicap. In some cultures, for example, women do not have a place in the business world. Other points that create ethical conflicts are: the question of disrespect for human rights in work conditions, low salaries in developing countries, the differentiation of prices from country to country, bribes or gratuities, the sale of products harmful to health or the environment to countries having less rigid laws, violation of copyrights or patents (Ferrell *et.al.,*2000).

Global companies are constantly facing situations of difficult choice. While "when in Rome do as the Romans do" could bring serious moral implications, imposing the practice of their values onto another culture can be seen as imperialism. On the other hand, simply not doing business with other countries because of moral issues could represent a risky alternative (Werhane and Boyd, 2000)

DISCUSSION: FOR GLOBAL BUSINESS ETHICS

From all that has been presented up to now, it can be said that there are many challenges imposed by globalization on business ethics.

In so far as cultural differences are concerned, there are differing opinions. Some authors are more inclined to give a relative connotation to ethics, arguing that companies should endeavor, as much as possible, to operate within the standards of each society.

However, at the same time that companies become international, there is also an increase in ethical watchfulness on the part of consumers and investors, aided by the speed at which access to information is made possible, regarding the operation of companies at any place in the world. This vigilance is being extended throughout the entire productive chain. Therefore, it is not enough for a company to only operate in an acceptable form. Its suppliers, distributors and business associates should also perform in the same manner. The choice of associates who share the same standards of conduct now becomes the responsibility of the company.

Due to this type of surveillance, it is becoming more and more dangerous for a company to adhere to a relativistic perspective, that is, "dancing according to the music", in each of the places it operates.

On the other hand, the globalization process has brought enormous pressure to bear on companies, in the sense that they have to attract clients at any cost and obtain short- term results. As a result of this fight for survival in the market, we see some companies closing their eyes to the question of ethics, keeping themselves on a short term horizon, thereby going against their own values on many occasions. Hence, the greatest conflict faced by companies in the global era is: the difficult balance between ethics and competitiveness.

At this point, the position would seem to be that there is no way out for global companies, unless they develop standards of conduct to be followed in all the places in which they operate. Due to the existence of enormous cultural differences, this is a very arduous task. However, a good starting point would be to return to fundamental values of life and adopt respect for people and nature as a central point. In this respect, the guidelines established by SA8000 and AA1000 could serve as reference for such standards.

SA8000 is based on World Labor Organization conventions, in the declaration of Human Rights and in the United Nations Convention on The Rights of Children. AA1000, in turn, focuses on the undertaking of the organization in respect to stakeholders, linking social and ethical issues to strategic management and to the operations of the organization. Its objective, therefore, is to support organizational education and performance in general – social, ethical and economic – and, as a result, the contribution by the organization to sustainable development.

It is important to stress that the abovementioned norms can serve as a basis for company conduct, but they are not enough. The company needs to develop its own norms, applicable to its own particular case.

Finally, many companies have opted for the development of codes of ethics to be applied to all its operations. In order for this code of ethics to be really applied in practice, it must be more than just a declaration of intentions, thought out by top management. It is important that during the development phase, there is participation of employees from all the countries in which the company operates, since they are the ones who face ethical dilemmas on a daily basis.

As has been seen, ethics relates to the human being's capacity to deliberate over what conduct is right and what is wrong. When referring to business ethics, it must be borne in mind that decisions are not taken by the company, but by people, either individually or in group, performing their professional roles within the company.

It is necessary, therefore, that the people feel that there is space for deliberation. In order for people to make coherent decisions relative to company values, there must be an awareness of the importance of such values. The best way to do this is by means of examples. These examples must come from the top, thereby ensuring consistency between company mission and its practices. Employees at headquarters must feel they will be supported by top management in dilemmas related to ethics, even if this means the loss of some immediate "advantages" for the company.

If adhering to a code of ethics means, on some occasions, not doing business, this can be advantageous in the long run, because the company's image and that of its brand is, sometimes, worth much more than a few isolated business deals. In some cases the brand is the greatest asset of the organization. Once the reputation of the company has been stained, the recovery of its image is a much more difficult and costly process.

On many occasions, a global company acting ethically can contribute to a change involving more respect for people and their rights, in countries known for corruption and disrespect for human rights. Due to its power and influence, it can demand that local suppliers and business associates act in the same way. In this manner, the company can also be considered a moral agent.

Besides having strong values in so far as respect for people, diversity, obeying the law, refusing bribes and respecting the environment, are concerned, above everything else, if it requires that their employees behave ethically, the company must show respect for them. Ethical conduct begins "at home". So, human working conditions, fair salaries, openness to participation, and to the expression of opinions and respect of differences, are fundamental.

The distribution of roles among countries imposed by globalization also creates ethical problems for global organizations, increasing the difference between the extremely serious and complex problem, because its roots are fixed in the very logic of the business world, stamped into an eminently instrumental type of reasoning, which seeks efficiency at any cost.

The placing of investments needs to be rethought from a perspective of sustainable development. Poverty does not rhyme with sustainability. When talking about globalization, the question of sustainability must also be treated from a global viewpoint. With present social differences, this sustainability cannot be attained. This appears to be a utopian or ingenuous argument. However, it is a question of strategic intelligence and long-term vision. It deals "only" with the survival of the human species and the planet Earth as a whole.

The movement towards ethical business and ecologically sustainable operations is still in the embryonic stage, if the urgency of present social and environmental problems is considered. The theory considers medium and long terms, but actions continue, in its majority at short term, on the basis of "surviving" and "putting out fires".

CONCLUSION

Globalization in itself is a controversial phenomenon. There are many views surrounding it, including difficulty in being able to arrive at a definition. It is a process that has been affecting every sphere of world society: economy, politics, technology, culture and the natural environment, as well.

In the business world, globalization affects the productive process, relationships of companies with the market and with society, labor relations and the internal operation of organizations. The globalization process has also broadened discussion over the social responsibilities of organizations. It is based on the supposition that ethics must be the center of the social responsibility concept.

The role of drivers of globalization is to increase global company power, as was discussed previously, which in itself raises serious questions of ethics. Cultural diversity, in turn, imposes a challenge on organizations to deal with different ethical and moral standards around the world. On the other hand, the quest for competitiveness at any cost, opposes the pressure exerted by different stakeholders, in the sense that an ethical and responsible company performance increases the complexity of the debate on business ethics. How can an ethical attitude be adhered to, which, at the same time, sustains the values of the organization, respects the values of each society within which the company establishes business relations and furnishes a coherent global activity?

The discussion presented herein indicates that, in order to reach such coherence, global companies should seek a kind of ethics that is also global. The path of relative ethics, defined by some authors, is very dangerous, capable of affecting the reputation of the company in question in a matter of seconds. Thus, a return to respect for the human being and nature is defended, bearing in mind a perspective of sustainable development. There can be no sustainability without ethics. Therefore, at long term, there will be no human, animal, vegetable or business survival without ethics.

The reflection on ethics within the context of globalization as presented herein must not stop at business frontiers, because its consequences can be felt in national and international terms, affecting the quality of life of world populations as a whole. Such a discussion permeates the activities of people both personally and professionally, as well as company directors and national and international leaders.

It is worthwhile stressing that the main intention of the authors is not to categorically answer the issues raised, but to stimulate reflection on this paradoxical, controversial and above all, urgent theme.

REFERENCES

Abbagnano, Nicola. Dicionário de Filosofia. São Paulo: Martins Fontes, 2000.

Abreu, Rosamélia G. Processo de globalização e o gerenciamento de marcas globais: um estudo de caso. Dissertação de Mestrado. Departamento de Administração, PUC-Rio, 1999.

Arruda, Maria Cecília C. Ethics and Culture in Globalized Markets. Second ISBEE World Congress on Business Economics and Ethics. São Paulo, Brazil, July 2000. In: www.synethos.org.be/isbee.

Azevedo, Guilherme M, Bertrand, Hélène (orientadora). Transição de multinacional para global: as dimensões da mudança e os seus desafios.

Beck, Ulrich. O que é a globalização: equívocos do globalismo, repostas à globalização. São Paulo: Ed. Paz e Terra, 1999.

Beekun, Rafik I., Stedham, Yvonne, and Yamamura, Jeanne H. Business Ethics in Brazil and The U.S.: Egoism and Utilitarianism. Working Paper, Social Sciences Research Network. In: www.ssrn.com. 2001.

Boff, Leonardo. Ethos mundial: um consenso mínimo entre os humanos. Brasília: Letraviva, 2000.

Bull, Hedley. The Anarchical Society, A Study of Order in World Politics. New York: Columbia University Press, 1977.

Carroll, Archie B. The four faces of corporate citizenship. Business and Society Review. n. 100-101, p. 1-7, wntr. 1998.

Chanlat, Jean-François. Ciências Sociais e Management: Reconciliando o Econômico e o Social. São Paulo: Ed. Atlas, 2000.

Clarkson, Max B.E. A stakeholder framework for analyzing and evaluating corporate social performance. Academy of Management Review. v. 20, n. 1, p. 92-117, jan. 1995.

Cragg, A. W. Bribery, Globalization and the Problem of Dirty Hands. Second ISBEE World Congress on Business Economics and Ethics. São Paulo, Brazil, July 2000. In: www.synethos.org.be/isbee.

Czinkota, Michael R., Ronkainen, Ilkka, A. International Marketing. Orlando: Dryden Press, 4th edition, 1995.

Dissertação de Mestrado. Depto. de Administração, PUC-Rio, 2000.

Enriquez, Eugène. Os Desafios Éticos nas Organizações Modernas. Revista de Administração de Empresas. São Paulo, v.37, n.2, p. 6-17, 1997.

Ferrell, O. C., Fraederich, John, Ferrell, Linda. Ética empresarial: dilemas, tomadas de decisão e casos. Rio de Janeiro: Reichman & Affonso Ed., 2001.

Frederick, William C. From CSR1 to CSR2. Business and Society. v. 33, n. 2, p.150-164, Aug. 1994.

Furtado, Celso. O Capitalismo Global. São Paulo: Paz e Terra, 1998.

Ianni, Octavio. A sociedade global. Rio de Janeiro: Ed. Civilização Brasileira, 1992.

Klein. E. R. Ferengi 'Rules of Acquisition': A Case Study Toward a Global Ethic.

Kon, Anita. Os Países em Desenvolvimento no Cenário da Globalização: Repensando a Questão Ética. Second ISBEE World Congress on Business Economics and Ethics. São Paulo, Brazil, July 2000. In:www.synethos.org.be/isbee.

Mitnick, Barry M. Systematics and CSR: The theory and processes of normative referencing. Business and Society. v.34, n. 2, p. 5-33, Apr. 1995.

Ortiz, Renato. Mundialização, cultura e política. In: Dowbor, Ladislau, Ianni, Octavio e Resende Paulo-Edgar. Desafios da Globalização. 2. Ed. Petrópilis: Ed. Vozes, 1999.

Parker, Barbara B. Globalization and Business Practice: Managing Across Boundaries. London: Sage Publications, 1998.

Sachs, Jeffrey D. Protocolo de Kyoto. in: www. escolavesper.com.br/protocolo_de_kyoto.htm , 2001.

Second ISBEE World Congress on Business Economics and Ethics. São Paulo, Brazil, July 2000. In: www.synethos.org.be/isbee.

Second ISBEE World Congress on Business Economics and Ethics. São Paulo, Brazil, July 2000. In: www.synethos.org.be/isbee.

Sójka, Jacek. Globalisation of Business Ethics and the Role of Local Traditions. Second ISBEE World Congress on Business Economics and Ethics. São Paulo, Brazil, July 2000. In: www.synethos.org.be/isbee.

Sposati, Aldaíza. Globalização: um novo e velho processo. In: Dowbor, Ladislau, Ianni, Octavio e Resende Paulo-Edgar. Desafios da Globalização. 2. Ed. Petrópilis: Ed. Vozes, 1999.

Srour, Robert H.. Ética Empresarial: Posturas Responsáveis nos Negócios, na Política e nas Relações Pessoais. Rio de Janeiro: Campus, 2000.
Werhane, Patricia and Boyd, Douglas. Corruption, Globalization, and Moral Risk.

FOREIGN DIRECT INVESTMENT AND EXPORT GROWTH IN INDIA

Sadananda Prusty

ABSTRACT

Export growth in India has been higher than Gross Domestic Product (GDP) growth over the past few decades. Many factors appear to have contributed to this export growth including Foreign Direct Investment (FDI). It is true that there is an increase in FDI inflow in recent years. However, there has not much attempt to assess FDI inflow's influence on export growth in India. By using the quarterly data from April-June (Q1) 1990-91 to January-March (Q4) 2003-04, the present study explores the factors that influence export growth in India through Ordinary Least Square (OLS) and time series tools (i.e., unit root, causality and cointegration tests). Empirical results suggest that net FDI inflow is positively and significantly influencing export supply in India both in short-run as well as in long-run, thus contradicting the findings of Sharma (2000). Further it is evident from the result that higher domestic demand (proxied by the gross fiscal deficit of the Central Government as percentage of GDP) reduces export supply and higher lagged export (3 years lag) raises export supply in short- and long-run, which supports the empirical results of Sharma (2000). The empirical analysis, thus, clearly states that FDI inflow into India supplements higher export growth, which leads to higher economic growth. The above findings, thus, suggest that if India wants to achieve 8 per cent economic growth target as mentioned in the Tenth Five Year Plan, it should take some special measures and deepen the ongoing reform process through a consensus among all the political parties to ensure more and more FDI inflow.

1. INTRODUCTION

India's exports have grown much faster than Gross Domestic Product (GDP) over the past few decades. For example, its exports have grown by 4.75 per cent, 4.55 per cent, 17.71 per cent, 27.58 per cent and 22.06 per cent per annum while growths in GDP are 1.01 per cent, 7.17 per cent, 5.57 per cent, 4.37 per cent and

3.98 per cent in 1970-71, 1980-81, 1990-91, 2000-01 and 2002-03 respectively. Several factors appear to have contributed to this phenomenon including foreign direct investment (FDI) which has been rising consistently especially from the early 1990s. FDI inflow has increased to US$4660 million in 2002-03 from US$97 million in 1990-91. [1] However, despite increasing inflows of FDI there has not much attempt to assess FDI inflow's influence on export growth in India - one of the channels through which FDI affects growth. [2]

FDI inflow has proved to be a powerful tool of export growth in East and South-East Asian countries because multinational companies (MNCs), through which most FDI is undertaken, have the well-established contacts and up-to-date information about foreign markets. However, the experience of these countries cannot be generalized to India given the lower level of infrastructure, and the rigidity in both the factor as well as commodity markets (Srinivasan, 1998). Furthermore, the role of FDI in export promotion in developing countries remains controversial and depends crucially on the motive for such investment. If the motive behind FDI is to capture domestic market (tariff-jumping type investment), it may not contribute to export growth; if the motive is to tap export markets by taking advantage of the country's comparative advantage, then FDI may contribute to export growth (Sharma, 2000). Thus, whether FDI contributes to export growth or not depends on the nature of the policy regime. It is well known that an outward oriented regime encourages export-oriented FDI while an inward-oriented policy regime attracts FDI mainly to capture domestic rather than export markets (World Bank, 1993).

India has opened up its market since July 1991 by lowering tariff and non-tariff barriers, and liberalizing investment policy. However, the import-weighted tariff in India is much high as compared to many developing economies. [3] Furthermore, its factor market including infrastructure sector is less efficient compared with many East and South-East Asian countries with whom India competes in international market (Srinivasan, 1998). Hence, it is possible to argue that whether the liberalization policy in India has been successful in attracting a significant amount of export oriented FDI [4] or not. [5] In this situation, the export growth may have been brought about by factors other than FDI namely the domestic demand and lagged export.

In the light of the above debate, the aim of this paper is to examine the following propositions.

Proposition 1 (P1): Are there any causal link between the variables such as export supply, FDI inflow, domestic demand and lagged export in India?

Proposition 2 (P2): What is the correlation between variables such as export supply, FDI inflow, domestic demand and lagged export?

Proposition 3 (P3): What are the nature and degree of short-run relationship of FDI inflow, domestic demand and lagged export on export supply?

Proposition 4 (P4): Are there any long-run relationship among export supply, FDI inflow, domestic demand and lagged export?

The paper is organized as follows. Following an introduction in **Section 1**, the analytical framework is developed in **Section 2**. Data description and methodology are discussed in **Section 3**. The analyses of results are discussed in **Section 4**. The **last section** presents conclusion and policy suggestions.

2. ANALYTICAL FRAMEWORK

The role of FDI in export growth in developing countries is ambiguous and crucially depends on the motive behind such investment. If the motive behind such investment is to by pass trade barriers in the host country, then such investment would not result in better export performance. However, if FDI is motivated by the country's comparative advantage, then it may contribute to export growth. Thus, the nature of the link between FDI and export growth is not clear-cut.

On the basis of theoretical reasoning one would expect a fall in export growth when there is an increase in domestic demand for exportable items. This lead us to believe that there is a negative relationship between domestic demand and export supply (Joshi and Little, 1994).

The above discussions lead to the following specifications of export supply function, with expected signs given in parentheses.

XS = f (FDI, DD, LXS) **(Eq. 1)**

Where,

XS= Export Supply, measured as total export volume.

DD= Domestic Demand, proxied by the gross fiscal deficit of the Central Government as a percentage of GDP.

LXS= Lagged export supply.

3. DATA DESCRIPTION AND METHODOLOGY

The study uses quarterly data pertaining to a set of variables such as Export Supply (total export volume), FDI (net FDI inflow) and Domestic Demand (proxied by the gross fiscal deficit of the Central Government as a percentage of GDP). The study examines the linkage of such variables for a period of 56 quarters, i.e. from April-June (Q1) 1990-91 to January-March (Q4) 2003-04. [6]

In order to examine the linkage among Export, FDI, Domestic Demand and Lagged Export in India, the empirical analysis has been carried out in four stages. The study conducts Phillips-Perron unit root test to verify if the variables have unit roots in the first-stage of its analysis. [7] This is essential to ascertain that the concerned series are non-stationary in order to use cointegration analysis. In order to know the causal relationship between the above variables, the pair-wise Granger Causality Test is employed in the second-stage of analysis. The correlation matrix and the log-linear regression method are used in the third-stage of analysis in order to know the nature and degree of short-run relationship among the variables respectively. The Johansen and Johansen-Juselius's Cointegration Test is used in the final stage of analysis in order to know the nature and degree of long-run relationship [8] among the variables during the period of study.

Methodology

Granger Causality Test

The Granger (1969) causality test between X_t and Y_t which are stationary, i.e. I(0) can be expressed as:

$$Y_t = b_0 + \sum a_j X_{t-j} + \sum b_j Y_{t-j} + U_t \quad \textbf{(Eq. 2)}$$

$$X_t = c_0 + \sum c_j X_{t-j} + \sum d_j Y_{t-j} + V_t \quad \textbf{(Eq. 3)}$$

Where U_t and V_t are mutually un-correlated white-noise series. In order to test the pattern of causality, it is necessary to test the equations 2 and 3 and test the null-hypothesis that $a_j=d_j=0$ for all j (j=1,..., m) against the alternative hypothesis that a_j and d_j are not equal to zero for at least some j's. Acceptance of null-hypothesis implies lack of causal relationship between X and Y. Just as the acceptance of $a_j=0$ implies that X does not cause Y, acceptance of $d_j=0$ implies that Y does not cause X.

Cointegration Test

Sophisticated economic theories rely on the belief that certain pairs of economic variables should not diverge each other to a great extent, at least in the long-run. In the short-run, however, such variables may drift apart due to random and seasonal factors. But in the long-run, (if they continue to be too far apart) economic forces (market mechanism or government intervention) will bring them together again. Even if the economic theory involving equilibrium concepts might suggest close relations in the long-run, the correctness of the beliefs about long-term relatedness is an empirical question (Granger, 1986). Such empirical test underlies the idea of cointegration, initially introduced by Granger and subsequently developed and empirically examined by many other econometricians.

To define cointegration the concept of integrated series is necessary. A series X_t is said to be integrated of order d, denoted by I(d), if the series needs differentiating d times to be stationary. Consider a pair of series X_t and Y_t, each of which is I(d) and having no drift or trend in mean. There exists a constant A such that the linear combination of these series, say,

$$Z_t = X_t - AY_t \quad \textbf{(Eq. 4)}$$

is another I(d). The idea of cointegration is to search for a linear combination which itself is stationary, i.e., Z_t is I(0). The relationship

$$X_t = AY_t \quad \textbf{(Eq. 5)}$$

is considered as the long-run or equilibrium relationship with A as the cointegrating parameter. In the absence of a Z_t which is I(0), it may be inferred that X_t and Y_t have no tendency to move together over time. According to Granger (1986), "the term 'equilibrium' is not used to imply anything about the behaviour of the economic agents but rather describes the tendency of an economic system to move towards a particular region of the possible outcome space."

Unit Root Test

Time series theories starts by considering the generating mechanism, which should be able to generate all the statistical properties of the series, or at least the conditional mean, variance and temporal autocorrelations, i.e. "linear properties" of the series, conditional upon past data. A series is stationary, called I(0), denoting "integrated of zero", when the linear properties exist and are time-invariant. Some series needs to be differenced once to achieve these properties and these will be called integrated of order one, denoted I(1). More generally, if a series needs differencing d times to become I(0), it is called integrated of order d, denoted I(d).

There are many substantial differences between two series, I(0) and I(1). An I(0) series has a mean and there is a tendency for the series to return to the mean, so that it tends to fluctuate around the mean, crossing that value frequently and with rare extensive excursions (Granger, 1986). In an I(0) series autocorrelations decline rapidly as lag increases. On the other hand, an I(1) process without drift will be relatively smooth, will deviate widely and will only rarely return to an earlier value.

For testing cointegration, it is necessary to ascertain that the concerned series are not I(0) and the order of the concerned series should be the same. To verify this, the Phillips-Perron unit root test is employed.

Phillips-Perron (PP) Test

Phillips (1987), and Phillips & Perron (1988) suggested an alternative approach for checking the presence of unit roots in the data. They formulated a non-parametric test to the conventional t-test, which is robust to a wide variety of serial correlation and time dependent heteroscedasticity. The PP unit root test requires estimation of the following equation (without trend).

$$X_t = \mu_t + \sum_{i=1}^{T} X_{t-T} + u_t \qquad \textbf{(Eq. 6)}$$

The bias in the error term results when the variance of the true population

$$\sigma^2 = \lim_{T\to\infty} E(T^{-1}S_T^2) \qquad \textbf{(Eq. 7)}$$

differs from the variance of the residuals in the regression equation:

$$\sigma_u^2 = \lim_{T\to\infty} T^{-1}\sum_{t=1}^{T} E(u_t^2) \qquad \textbf{(Eq. 8)}$$

Consistent estimators of σ^2 and σ^2_u are:

$$S_u^2 = T^{-1}\sum_{t=1}^{T} (u_t^2) \text{ ; and}$$

$$S_{Tk}^2 = T^{-1}\sum_{t=1}^{T} (u_t^2) + 2T^{-1}\sum_{t=1}^{k} \sum_{t=j+1}^{T} u_t u_{t-j} \qquad \textbf{(Eq. 9)}$$

Where k is the lag truncation parameter used to ensure that the autocorrelation of the residuals is fully captured. It can be seen from equation 9 that when there is no autocorrelation the last term in the formula defining S^2_{Tk} is zero and $\sigma^2_u = \sigma^2$.

The PP test-statistic [$Z(t_\mu)$] under the null-hypothesis of I(0) is

$$Z(t_\mu) = \langle S_u | S_{tk} \rangle t_\mu - \tfrac{1}{2}\left(S_{tk}^2 - S_u^2\right)\left[S_{tk}\left\{T^2\sum_{t=2}^{T} \left(Y_t - Y_{t-1}\right)^2\right\}^{1/2}\right]^{-1} \qquad \textbf{(Eq. 10)}$$

Cointegration Test in a Multivariate System

Since the present study also deals with multivariate regression analysis, the cointegration testing procedure suggested by Engle and Granger (1987), Johansen (1988), Johansen and Juselius (1992), and Johansen (1995) will be the appropriate one. If we have a vector Z_t of n potentially endogenous variables, then it is possible to specify the following vector autoregression (VAR) mode involving up to k-lags of Z_t:

$$Z_t = A_1 Z_{t-1} + \ldots + A_k Z_{t-k} + u_t \qquad \textbf{(Eq. 11)}$$

$$u_t \approx IN(0, \Sigma)$$

Where Z_t is $(n\times 1)$ and each of A_i is an $(n\times n)$ matrix of parameters.

The Johansen estimation method is based on the error-correction representation of the VAR (k) model with Gaussian errors. Equation 11 can be reformulated into a vector error-correction method (VEC) form:

$$\Delta Z_t = T_1 \Delta Z_{t-1} + ... + T_{k-1} \Delta Z_{t-k+1} + \prod Z_{t-k} + BX_t + u_t \quad \textbf{(Eq. 12)}$$

Where, Z_t is an $n \times 1$ vector of I(1) variables, X_t is an $s \times 1$ vector of I(0) variables, $T_1, T_2, .., T_{k-1}$, Π are $n \times n$ matrices of unknown parameters, B is an $n \times s$ matrix. The T_i and Π contain information of the short- and long-run adjustment to changes in Z_t. The Johansen Maximum Likelihood (ML) procedure estimates equation 12 subject to the hypothesis that Π has a reduced rank, $r < n$.

The matrix Π can also be expressed as:

$$\Pi = \alpha\beta' \quad \textbf{(Eq. 13)}$$

Where, α represents the speed of adjustment to disequilibrium, while β is a matrix of long-run coefficients such that the term $\beta' Z_{t-k}$ embedded in equation 12 represents up to (n-1) cointegration relationships in the multivariate model which ensure that the Z_t converge to their long-run steady-state solutions. In this approach Z_t is assumed to be a vector of non-stationary I(1) variables, then all the terms in equation 12 which involve ΔZ_{t-i} are I(0) while ΠZ_{t-k} must also be stationary for $u_t \sim$ I(0) to be white-noise.

In the Johansen-Juselius (JJ) method the idea of cointegration is to search for linear combinations of the Z_t that are I(0). In other words, testing for cointegration amounts to a consideration of the rank of Π, i.e., finding the number of r linearly independent columns in Π. If Π has full rank, i.e., if there are $r = n$ linearly independent columns then the variables in Z_t are I(0). If the rank of Π is zero then there are no cointegration relationships. If Π has reduced rank, i.e., $r \leq (n-1)$, then cointegrating vectors are also present. In the testing procedure the hypotheses are:

H_0: $r = 0$ (no cointegrating vectors present), and the alternative,
H_1: $r \leq (n-1)$ [(n-1) cointegrating vectors are present].

4. ANALYSES OF RESULTS

Analyses of results have been discussed in four sub-sections: (4.1) unit root test analysis, (4.2) causal analysis, (4.3) correlation and regression analysis, and (4.4) cointegration analysis.

4.1. Unit Root Test [9] Analysis: We have used Phillips-Perron (PP) unit root test to verify whether the variables have unit roots, i.e. whether the data series are non-stationary. The PP unit root test statistic result shown in Table 8.1 reveals that all the variables (i.e., XS, FDI, DD and LXS) at level form are non-stationary and have unit root, i.e. the mean and autocovariances of all the variables depend on time. However, the PP test result with respect to all such variables at first differences confirm stationarity [10] of all the variables at 1 and 5 percent level of significance.

Table 8.1: Phillips-Perron Unit Root Test Statistic (with intercept)

Variable	Level Form	First Difference
Total Export Volume (XS)	2.7831 (-3.5523; -2.9146)	-10.6203 (-3.5547; -2.9157)
Net FDI Inflow (FDI)	-2.0955 (-3.5523; -2.9146)	-11.4187 (-3.5547; -2.9157)
GFD_c as per cent of GDP (DD)	-2.2260 (-3.5523; -2.9146)	-7.2304 (-3.5547; -2.9157)
Lagged Export (lag of 3 yrs) (LXS)	0.5323 (-3.5598; -2.9178)	-14.2877 (-3.5625; -2.9190)

Note: Figures in parentheses are critical value at 1 percent and 5 percent level of significance respectively.

4.2. Causal Analysis: The second stage of analysis has been carried out to explore the causal relationship between the stationary variables (i.e., the first difference of XS, FDI, DD and LXS). In general it is better to use more rather than fewer lags, since the Granger Causality Test [11] is couched in terms of the relevance of all past information. In Table 8.2, we have reported Pairwise Granger Causality Test results with lags 2 as two period lag is an appropriate lag order chosen in terms of Akaike Information Criterion (AIC).

The results of F-statistic stated in Table 8.2 reveal that export supply (XS) causes FDI [12], and lagged export supply (LXS) causes FDI as well as export supply (XS). The causality analysis, however, is silent about the nature and degree of relationship of such variables, which has been discussed in the following section (i.e., regression analysis).

Table 8.2: Pair-wise Granger Causality Test (with lags 2)

Null Hypothesis	F-Statistic	Significance Level	Inference
XS does not Granger Cause FDI	3.04	***	XS Granger Causes FDI [13]
FDI does not Granger Cause XS	0.36	N.S.	
DD does not Granger Cause FDI	0.95	N.S.	
FDI does not Granger Cause DD	0.64	N.S.	
LXS does not Granger Cause FDI	9.99	*	LXS Granger Causes FDI
FDI does not Granger Cause LXS	2.29	N.S.	
DD does not Granger Cause XS	0.34	N.S.	
XS does not Granger Cause DD	0.61	N.S.	
LXS does not Granger Cause XS	5.61	**	LXS Granger Causes XS
XS does not Granger Cause LXS	0.01	N.S.	
LXS does not Granger Cause DD	0.05	N.S.	
DD does not Granger Cause LXS	0.52	N.S.	

N.S. = Not Significant;
*, **, *** implies significant at 1 per cent, 5 per cent & 10 per cent level respectively.

4.3. Correlation and Regression Analysis: Before using the log-linear Ordinary Least Square (OLS) method to explore the nature and degree of short-run relationship among variables, it is pertinent to find out the correlation between such variables. The correlation matrix as shown in Table 8.3 clearly states that there is a high degree of positive relationship between export supply (XS) and FDI, and export supply (XS) and lagged export supply (LXS). However, there is less degree of negative relationship between export supply (XS) and domestic demand (DD).

Table 8.3: Correlation Matrix of FDI, Export Supply, Domestic Demand and Lagged Export

	FDI	Export (XS)	Domestic Demand (DD)	Lagged Export (LXS)
FDI	1.00	0.72	-0.08	0.73
Export (XS)	0.72	1.00	-0.40	0.97
Domestic Demand (DD)	-0.08	-0.40	1.00	-0.37
Lagged Export (LXS)	0.73	0.97	-0.37	1.00

In order to find out the combined influence and the extent of influence of FDI, domestic demand (DD) and lagged export supply (LXS) on export supply (XS), the log-linear OLS method has been used. The log-linear OLS method, which produces relationship, is reported below.

$$\text{Log (XS)} = \underset{(0.51)}{2.02^{*}} + \underset{(0.02)}{0.04^{***}}\ \text{Log (FDI)} - \underset{(0.13)}{0.30^{**}}\ \text{Log (DD)} + \underset{(0.05)}{0.84^{*}}\ \text{Log (LXS)}; \quad \textbf{(Eq. 14)}$$

No. of observation = 53

Adjusted R^2 = 0.97

DW = 2.11

[**Note**: Figures in parentheses are standard errors, Adjusted R^2 = coefficient of determination or "goodness of fit" adjusted for degrees of freedom, and DW = Durbin-Watson statistics (i.e., a measure of detecting auto-correlation). *, **, *** indicate 1 per cent, 5 per cent and 10 per cent level of significance respectively.]

From equation 14 it is clear that the coefficient of FDI variable is positive and significant at 10 per cent level. This implies that foreign investment helps in export growth in India, thus contradicting the findings of Sharma (2000). This could be due to an outward-oriented policy that India pursued in recent years, especially after liberalization and globalisation move since 1991, which might have encouraged export-oriented foreign investment. Another reason could be the motive of Multinational Companies (MNCs) to tap export markets by taking advantage of the country's comparative advantage. The negative elasticity of export supply with respect to domestic demand pressure indicates that export supply falls as domestic demand rises. The elasticity of domestic demand is 0.30 in the short-run. This result of export supply and domestic demand is same as the result obtained by Sharma (2000). The empirical result further states a positive elasticity of export supply in relation to 3 years lagged export, thus supports the findings of Sharma (2000). The elasticity of lagged export is highest at 0.84.

The log-linear OLS method is not an appropriate tool to explore the long-run relationship among the variables (especially when the variables are non-stationary in nature). In this situation, the cointegration technique is the appropriate tool to explore the long-run relationship among variables. [14]

4.4. Cointegration Analysis [15]: The Phillips-Perron (PP) unit root test statistic result shown in **Table 8.1** clearly states that all the variables are non-stationary and have unit root (i.e., I(1) series). It is necessary to examine the co-integrating relationship among various non-stationary variables through Johansen-Jessulius (1992) and Johansen's (1995) unrestricted cointegration Rank Test in order to draw the long-run relationship among variables. Here, we are only reporting [16] and discussing about the cointegrated equations [17]. The results of the normalized cointegrating equation based on the trace statistic and maximum-eigen statistic in a linear deterministic trend of more than two variables and 1 to 3 lags interval (in first differences), which produces relationship is reported below. However, the cointegration test results are given in **Appendix 1** and **Appendix 2.** Figures in parentheses in the following equation are standard errors.

$$XS = 0.03\ (FDI) - 7.06E\text{-}06\ (DD) + 0.11\ (LXS) \qquad \textbf{(Eq. 15)}$$
$$\quad (0.01) \qquad (7.1E\text{-}06) \qquad (0.04)$$

Equation 15 reveals that FDI and lagged export supply (LXS) are having positive long-run relationship and domestic demand (DD) is having a negative long-run relationship with export supply in India. This implies that foreign investment not only helps in export growth in short-run but also in long-run, thus contradicting the findings of Sharma (2000). Similarly, the negative relationship of export supply with respect to domestic demand pressure also holds true both in the short-run as well as in the long-run, thus supports the empirical result of Sharma (2000). The short-run positive relationship between export supply and lagged export supply also holds good in the long-run, thus supports the findings of Sharma (2000).

5. CONCLUSION AND POLICY SUGGESTIONS

Export growth in India has been higher than Gross Domestic Product (GDP) growth over the past few decades. Many factors appear to have contributed to this export growth including Foreign Direct Investment (FDI). It is true that there is an increase in FDI inflow in recent years. However, there has not much attempt to assess FDI inflow's influence on export growth in India by using quarterly data and cointegration test. By using the quarterly data from April-June (Q1) 1990-91 to January-March (Q4) 2003-04, the present study explores the factors that influence export growth in India through log-linear regression and time series tools (i.e., unit root, causality and cointegration test). Empirical results suggest that net FDI inflow is positively and significantly influencing export supply in India both in short-run as well as in long-run, thus contradicting the findings of Sharma (2000). Further it is evident from the result that higher domestic demand (proxied by the gross fiscal deficit of the Central Government as percentage of GDP) reduces export supply and higher lagged export (3 years lag) raises export supply in short- and long-run, which supports the empirical results of Sharma (2000). The empirical result of negative relationship between domestic demand and export supply suggest that tight monetary and fiscal policies are necessary especially at the time of higher domestic demand pressure. The empirical analysis, thus, clearly states that FDI inflow into India supplements higher export growth, which leads to higher economic growth.

Government has taken a number of measures to liberalize FDI policy, including allowing up to 100 per cent FDI in airports, courier services, real estate, banking and development of integrated townships including housing. The increasing rate of FDI is a positive reflection of global interest in India and the ease of entry into the country. Though, USA has traditionally been the largest foreign investor (accounting nearly 20 per cent of total FDI inflow), other leading investor countries have been Mauritius, UK, South Korea, Japan, Germany, Australia, Malaysia, France and Netherlands. The inflow from Mauritius has been substantial in recent years since investment is being routed through Mauritius. The small island managed to double its per capita income (with unemployment rate less than 2 per cent) in last two decades by giving special tax incentives along with creation of special export processing zones. This further proves the fact that FDI is an important prerequisite for increased economic growth.

In order to attain an annual foreign investment inflow of US$ 7.5 billion per year and 8 per cent economic growth in the Tenth Five-Year Plan, a high power committee under Planning Commission Member Shri N.K. Singh has favored enhancing FDI limits in telecom, insurance, civil aviation, non-retail trading, banking, plantations (other than tea, real estate) and others (DIPP Annual Report, 2002). The Committee has made some other major recommendations. These are (i) giving national treatment to foreign firms, (ii) making foreign investment in most sectors automatic by removing controls from FIPS and FIIA, (iii) allow up to 49 per cent investment in insurance and airlines (including FDI by foreign airlines) and (iv) permit up to 100 per cent FDI in petroleum refining, oil marketing, diamond mining, petroleum exploration, coal washery, airports, banking and investing companies, radio paging, advertising and trade, putting all proposals (except plantation and housing with only 49 per cent) on automatic route.

The export basket of India reveals that there is a scope to increase FDI in textiles, leather, gems and jewellery, machinery and metallic manufactures including steel. Furthermore, oil marketing, food processing, auto and auto components, airports, financial services and real estate are new FDI attractive sectors. India is a preferred destination for sectors requiring skilled labor and steps are being taken by the government to enhance FDI to US$ 10 billion in the next couple of years through FDI and disinvestment policy. As the FDI inflow depends on the Government's liberal policy, the ongoing reform process need to be accelerated through political consensus to supplement export growth and in turn enhance economic growth of the Indian economy.

Appendix 1: Normalised Multi-Variate Cointegrating Test Results

Equation Number	Eigen Value	Trace Statistic	5 per cent Critical Value	1 per cent Critical Value	r	k
15	0.41	42.31	29.68	35.65	1	3

Note: r and k indicate number of cointegrating relation and lag in the series of dependant variable respectively.

Appendix 2: Normalised Multi-Variate Cointegrating Test Results

Equation Number	Eigen Value	Max-Eigen Statistic	5 per cent Critical Value	1 per cent Critical Value	r	k
15	0.41	27.61	20.97	25.52	1	3

Note: r and k indicate number of cointegrating relation and lag in the series of dependant variable respectively.

NOTES

1. Handbook of Statistics on the Indian Economy, RBI, 2003-04, Table 153, p.238.

2. There are some studies (Sahoo, 2004; Helpman *et al.*, 2003; Mary *et al.*, 2002; Kundra and Sharan, 2000; Sharma, 2000; Lall, 1999; Atiken *et al.*, 1997; Bhalla, 1995; Young, 1995; Kumar, 1994; Fry, 1993; and Kumar, 1990) that examine the role of FDI in influencing India's export growth by using annual data until 1997 and Ordinary Least Square (OLS) technique. However, there has been a major reform since 1997. Moreover, these studies used OLS technique by using annual data only for a period of 10 or 15 years. Thus, their results must be interpreted with caution. Sahoo (2004) analysed the role of FDI in enhancing the technology intensive exports in India. Helpman *et al.* (2003)

and Sharma (2000) observed that FDI has statistically no significant impact on export performance in India. In the analysis of 43 Indian industries during 1975-76 to 1980-81 Kumar (1994) did not find any significant difference in the export-orientation of the affiliates of MNCs as compared with their local counterparts.

3. For example, by the mid 1990s import-weighted tariff in India was 33 per cent as compared with 9 per cent in Korea (1985-92), 10 per cent in Indonesia (1989-91), 10 per cent in Mexico (1990) and 14 per cent in Brazil (1993) (See Ahluwalia *et al.*, 1996).

4. Since there have been substantial liberalization in these countries their ability to attract efficiency-enhancing FDI depends on the availability of cheap unskilled labor (World Investment Report 2001 and 2002).

5. Efficient infrastructure facilities are vital in attracting efficiency-enhancing FDI in developing countries. Since there have been substantial liberalization in these countries their ability to attract efficiency-enhancing FDI depends not only on the availability of cheap unskilled labor but also on the quality of infrastructure facilities which are essential for MNCs in developing integrated production system (World Investment Report 2001 and 2002).

6. Data on Export Volume and Net FDI Inflow are Partially Revised (PR) from Q4 1996-97 to Q3 2003-04. Data on such variables are Preliminary (P) in Q4 2003-04. As monthly figures on Gross Fiscal Deficit of the Central Government (GFD_c) are available since April 1994 and quarterly figures on Gross Domestic Product at current market prices are not available, we have used same annual figures of the GFD_c as percentage of GDP for 4 different quarters in each year from 1990-91 to 2003-04.

7. Phillips-Perron Unit Root Test is used in the study as it is lag insensitive, which is advantageous as compared to lag sensitive Augmented Dickey-Fuller Unit Root Test.

8. The stationary linear combination is called the cointegrating equation and may be interpreted as a long-run equilibrium relationship among the variables.

9. A series is said to be (weakly or covariance) stationary if the mean and autocovariances of the series do not depend on time. Any series that is not stationary is said to be non-stationary. A common example of a non-stationary series is the random walk. For the random walk, if there is one unit root, then it is an I(1) series. Similarly, a stationary series is I(0). Standard inference procedures do not apply to regressions, which contain an integrated dependent variable or integrated regressors. Therefore, it is important to check whether a series is stationary or not before using it in a regression. The formal method to test the stationarity of a series is the unit root test.

10. The mean and autocovariances of all the variables do not depend on time.

11. Correlation does not necessarily imply causation in any meaningful sense of that word. The econometric graveyard is full of magnificent correlations, which are simply spurious or meaningless. Interesting examples include a positive correlation between teachers' salaries and the consumption of alcohol. Economists debate correlations, which are less obviously meaningless. The Granger (1969) approach to the question of whether x causes y is to see how much of the current y can be explained by past values of y and then to see whether adding lagged values of x can improve the explanation. y is said to be

Granger-caused by *x* if *x* helps in the prediction of *y*, or equivalently if the coefficients on the lagged *x*'s are statistically significant. Note that two-way causation is frequently the case; *x* Granger causes *y* and *y* Granger causes *x*. It is important to note that the statement "*x* Granger causes *y*" does not imply that *y* is the effect or the result of *x*. Granger causality measures precedence and information content but does not by itself indicate causality in the more common use of the term.

12. The statement "XS Granger causes FDI" does not imply that *FDI* is the effect or the result of *Export*.

13. *Ibid.*

14. See note 9.

15. The finding that many macro time series may contain a unit root has spurred the development of the theory of non-stationary time series analysis. Engle and Granger (1987) pointed out that a linear combination of two or more non-stationary series may be stationary. If such a stationary linear combination exists, the non-stationary time series are said to be I(0). The stationary linear combination is called the cointegrating equation and may be interpreted as a long-run equilibrium relationship among the variables. The purpose of the cointegration test is to determine whether a group of non-stationary series are cointegrated or not.

16. Here, we are only reporting the adjustment coefficients of FDI, domestic demand and lagged export of the multivariate normalized cointegrated equation.

17. See **Appendix 1** for the Eigen Value, **Trace Statistic**, Critical Values, and Rank & Order of the multivariate normalized cointegrated equation 15. See **Appendix 2** for the Eigen Value, **Max-Eigen Statistic**, Critical Values, and Rank & Order of all the multivariate normalized cointegrated equation 15.

REFERENCES

Ahluwalia, I.J., R. Mohan and C. Oman (1996), *Policy Reform in India*, Paris: Organization for Economic Co-operation and Development.

Atiken, B., H. Gordon and H. Ann (1997), "Spillovers, Foreign Direct Investment Export Behaviour", *Journal of International Economics*, Vol.43, No.1, pp. 103-32.

Bhalla, A. S. (1995), "Sino-Indian Liberalisation: The Role of Trade and Foreign Investment", *Economic of Planning*, Vol. 31, No.3.

Department of Industrial Policy and Promotion (2002), *Annual Report-2002*, Government of India.

Engle, R.F. and C.W.J. Granger (1987), "Co-integration and Error Correction: Representation, Estimation and Testing", *Econometrica*, Vol.55, pp. 251-76.

Fry, M. (1993), "Foreign direct Investment in South East Asia: Differential Impacts", *ISEAS Publications*.

Granger, C.W.J. (1969), "Investigating Causal Relations by Econometric Models and Cross-Spectral Models", *Econometrica*, Vol.37, pp.424-38.

Granger, C.W.J. (1986), "Developments in the Study of Cointegrated Variables", *Oxford Bulletin of Economics and Statistics*, Vol.48, pp.213-28.

Helpman, E., M. Melitz and S. Yeaple (2003), "Exports vs. FDI", *NBER Working Paper No. 9439*, NBER.

Johansen, S. (1988), "Statistical Analysis of Cointegration Vectors", *Journal of Economic Dynamics and Control*, Vol.12, pp. 231-54.

Johansen, S. (1995), *Likelihood Based Inference in Cointegrated Vector Autoregressive Models*, Oxford: Oxford University Press.

Johansen, S. and K. Juselius (1992), "Testing Structural Hypothesis in a Multivariate Cointegration Analysis of the PPP and the UIP for UK", *Journal of Econometrics*, Vol.55, pp. 211-44.

Joshi, V. and I.M.D. Little (1994), *India: Macroeconomics and Political Economy 1964-1991*, Washington D.C.: The World Bank.

Kumar, N. (1990), *Multinational Enterprises in India: Industrial Distribution, Characteristics and Performance*, New Delhi: Routledge Publication.

Kumar, N. (1994), *Multinational Enterprises and Industrial Organization: The Case of India,* New Delhi: Sage Publication.

Kundra, A. and V. Sharan (2000), "Performance Evaluation of Indian Export Processing Zones since Economic Liberalization", *International Economics*, Vol.53, No.3.

Lall, S. (1999), "India's Manufactured Exports: Comparative Structure and Prospects", *World Development*, 1999, Vol.27.

Mary, H., G. Larossi and K. Sokoloft (2002), "Exports of Manufacturing Products in East Asia: A Comparative Analysis with the Firm Level Data", *World Bank Working Paper*, 2002.

Phillips, P.C.P. (1987), "Time Series Regression With a Unit Root", *Econometrica*, Vol.55, pp.277-301.

Phillips, P.C.P. and P. Perron (1988), "Testing for a Unit Root in Time Series Regression", *Biometrica*, Vol.75, pp.335-46.

Reserve Bank of India (2004), *Handbook of Statistics on the Indian Economy 2003-04.*

Sahoo, P. (2004), "FDI and Technology Intensive Exports in India", *ICFAI Journal of Applied Economics*, Vol.3, No.3, pp. 25-36.

Sharma, K. (2000), "Export Growth in India: Has FDI Played a Role?", *Yale University Discussion Paper No. 816.*

Srinivasan, T.N. (1998), "India's Export Performance: A Comparative Analysis" in I.J. Ahluwalia and I.M.D. Little (eds.), *India's Economic Reforms and Development Essay for Manmohan Singh*, Delhi: Oxford University Press.

United Nations (2002), *World Investment Report 2001 and 2002*, New York.

World Bank (1993), *The East Asian Miracle*, London: Oxford University Press.

Young, A. (1995), "The Tyranny of Numbers Confronting the Statistical Realities of the East Asian Growth Experience", *Quarterly Journal of Economics*, Vol.110, No.2, pp. 641-80.

ROLE OF CORPORATE SOCIAL REPORTING IN GLOBAL ECONOMY

Suprava Sahu

ABSTRACT

Corporate Social Reporting refers to the measurement and reporting of information about the impact of a business enterprise and its activities on the society. In the wake of liberalization, Privatization and globalization, the importance of corporate social reporting cannot be denied. The concept of socialistic pattern of society, environmental protection and increasing awareness of the society towards corporate social responsibility, etc have all contributed towards the growing importance of corporate social reporting. The present study will be carried out with the following objectives: (a) to study the extent to which corporate enterprises are fulfilling their responsibilities towards the society and disclosing the same in their annual reports, (b) to assess the perceptions of stakeholders and other users like academicians, professionals and executives regarding the disclosure practices being followed in India and (c) to study the trend in corporate social disclosure across time.

A clearer idea can be formed about corporate social reporting by outlining the scope of corporate social reporting .It includes the following:

***Social Responsibility Accounting:** It deals with the internal and external Reporting of social costs and social benefits both in quantitative and qualitative terms by a business entity. Social costs refer to those expenses that a business entity has to incur to fulfill its obligations towards the society, such as protections of the health and safety of workers, community development etc. Social benefits refer to those returns that an enterprise is expected to realize from the society in return for fulfilling its social obligations.*

***Corporate Environmental Reporting:** It refers to the estimation and public reporting of environmental liabilities and financially material* *environmental costs. Companies with 'green' image fare very well in the consumer market and stock market.*

Social Audit: *It can be defined as an objective assessment of a business concern as to how it has been able to discharge its social obligation's while performing its day-to-day activities.*

The present study will address issues such as (a) whether the corporate sector is meeting the expectations of the society in the matter of fulfilling its social obligations and (b) whether the corporate sector is formulating the requisite strategies to shift their focus from profit maximization to enhancing the quality of life in the society.

The government of India appointed a committee under the chairmanship of Rajinder Sachaar, known as "sachaar committee". It recommended that a provision should be included in company law to make it mandatory for all companies to provide a social report along with director's report in the annual reports.

The government of India w.e.f. April 1989 requires a few companies to disclose information about conservation of energy, technology absorption and foreign exchange studies conducted in 1989 revealed that 96 per cent of public sector and 35 per cent of private sector units made some sort of social disclosures. The TATA'S have now started TCCI(Tata Council for Community Involvement) and as a group ,they are addressing community responsibility.

In the present scenario, corporate entities have to realize their obligations towards the society and do their bit to improve the quality of life in the society. They should show transparency while preparing the annual reports and make proper disclosure about social contributions like conservation of energy, pollution control, preservation of the environment and like.

INTRODUCTION

The corporate sector is expanding at a very rapid pace throughout the globe. The concept of scattered ownership gave birth to the concept of financial reporting whereas rapidly increased number of corporate sector particularly industrial corporate sector has given birth to corporate social reporting (Sharma and Gupta, 2001). The measurement and reporting of the social performance of business entities forms the core of corporate social reporting.

"Corporate Social Reporting" can be defined as the information communiqué with respect to discharge of social responsibilities of a corporate entity. In the last two decades, as companies expanded and globalization crept in, the issue of corporate social responsibility arose. Companies are accountable for their activities to a range of stakeholders like employees, shareholders, bankers, consumers, suppliers and finally to the society where the companies exist. Corporate social reporting safeguards future profit flows in some ways because profits are earned due to stakeholders. Today more emphasis is laid on how profits are made rather than on how profits are spent (Philanthropy). A company with good corporate social reporting practices gets environmental clearances faster, attracts better quality talent, wins more customers for its better practices and reduces transaction costs.

FEATURES OF CORPORATE SOCIAL REPORTING

Some main features of corporate social reporting are outlined below:

- It is related to the utilization of social resources.
- It is an application of accounting on social sciences.
- It is an expression of a company's social responsibilities.
- It emphasizes on both social costs and social benefits.
- It emphasizes on the relationship between the corporate entity and the society.

SCOPE OF CORPORATE SOCIAL REPORTING

Corporate Social Reporting includes the following:

Social Responsibility Accounting or Social Cost Benefit Analysis: It can be defined as "the reporting of the cost incurred in employing with anti-pollution safety and health and other social beneficial requirements and more generally the impact of a business entity on the efforts to protect society and the environment. Richard Dobbins and David Fanning have defined social responsibility accounting as "the measurement and reporting of information concerning the impact of an entity and its activities on society". It is also called as "Social cost benefit analysis" because it is concerned with the internal and external reporting of social costs and social benefits, both in quantitative and qualitative terms by a business enterprise social costs refer to those expenses that an enterprise has to incur to fulfill its obligations towards the society such as protection of the health and safety of industrial workers, proper disposal of garbage of industries, community development, protection of the environment, etc "Social benefits" refer to those returns that an enterprise is expected to realize from the society in return for fulfilling its social obligations. A company generally compares the social costs and social benefits before venturing into any socially viable project.

Corporate Environmental Reporting: It is an attempt to identify and highlight the resources used and costs imposed on the environment by a business entity. The concern for environmental issues has increased considerably attention to business social responsibility. (Glautier, Underdown; 1994) The environment therefore has become one of the key challenges facing the business sector during the 1990s. (Gupta; Chandra Shekhar, 1999). 'Corporate Environmental Reporting can also be defined as the estimation and public reporting of environmental liabilities and financially material environmental costs. (Chaklader, 2001)

Environmental Accounting is done either on a mandatory or on a voluntary basis. In industrialized nations, environmental information is being disclosed by firms voluntarily. Only a few nations like Sweden, Netherlands and the United States of America follow mandatory reporting of environmental information. Voluntary disclosure of environmental information is widely prevalent in environment intensive sectors like petroleum, energy, chemicals etc. In the United States, the Securities and Exchange Commission makes it mandatory to disclose much more than the conventional requirement about the current and potential environment liability on the part of corporate.

In India, the reporting of environmental information in the annual report is voluntary in nature But some reputed corporate houses like TISCO, Essar Power Limited, Paradeep Phosphates Limited, NALCO, etc are reporting about annual reports voluntarily. There is a need and a challenge for the companies to become greener. (Miller Szekely; 1995)

Specific Issues of Environmental Accounting: The specific issues of environmental accounting are:

- Identification of environmental costs.
- Capitalization of environmental costs.
- Identification of liabilities; and
- Measurement of liabilities.

Cost-benefit analysis is made by a company to find out the costs and benefits rendered to the environment and costs and benefits received from the environment by an enterprise during the accounting period. A comparison between costs and benefits obtained from the cost-benefit analysis must be made by a business concern.

COST IMPOSED BY A BUSINESS CONCERN ON THE ENVIRONMENT.

The costs imposed by a business concern on the environment can be listed as follows.

- Depletion of natural resources.
- Garbage and solid wastage.

- Spoiling waters of sacred rivers
- Loss of ozone layer
- Soil erosion and ground water loss.
- Acid rain
- High level of air pollution (Gupta; Thakar; Surayya; 1998)

BENEFITS RENDERED BY A BUSINESS CONCERN TO THE ENVIRONMENT

- River purification projects
- Greening barren land
- Green lawns and social forestry (Gupta; Thakur; Suaayya; 1998)

BENEFITS RECEIVED BY A BUSINESS ENTITY FROM THE ENVIRONMENT

- Rain, Snowfall, icebergs
- Oxygen and Carbon dioxide – live fuels
- Human resource supply
- Sand and Clay (Gupta; Thakar; Surayya; 1998)

COST IMPOSED BY THE ENVIRONMENT ON A BUSINESS ENTITY

- Destruction by wild animals
- Floods and droughts
- Cyclone, Storms, typhoons
- Extreme climatic conditions
- Famine and epidemics
- Fire accidents (natural)
- Earthquakes and volcanoes

STRATEGIES REQUIRED TO BE FORMULATED BY COMPANIES TO IMPROVE THEIR ENVIRONMENTAL PERFORMANCE

An attempt should be made by companies to formulate the following strategies to improve their environmental performance.

Green Business: Strategies should be formulated for green business. The company should be involved in new areas of research and formulate new strategies to inform customers about the environmental attributes of their products and to persuade consumers to buy these products rather than those of others.

Eco Mark: The Government of India has initiated a scheme of labelling the environment friendly products. (Gupta; Shekhar; 1999) This is done in order to provide accreditation and labelling for household and other consumer goods which satisfies the requirements of Indian environmental standard for that product. The Bureau of Indian Standards (BIS)/ Directorate of Marketing and Inspection (DMI) is the implementing agency for this scheme. Any product which is made, used or disposed of in a way that significantly reduces the harm it would otherwise cause to the environment is considered on environment friendly product. The label is called ECOMARK. (Gupta; Shekhar, 1999).

Quality and Environment: Quality and the environment share an important link. (Gupta, Shekhar, 1999). Total Quality Management (TQM) is a concept which is gaining importance in recent years. One of the main objectives of TQM is to eliminate defects. Under a quality based environmental programme, waste is reviled which reveals inefficiencies in a company's operations. Recently, a sub movement has emerged out of TQM, which is being called as "Total Quality Environment Management" or TQEM.

Social Audit: It refers to the evaluation or assessment of a company's performance against planned goals in the areas of social responsibility. The assessment may be carried out by internal or external bodies for internal or external use. Social audit includes everything that is concerned with the development and growth of the society at large.

The new annual report of companies contains the following financial and non financial information:

Mandatory Financial Information: Such information is required to be compulsorily shown by companies in their annual reports. It refers to the following information:

- Profit and Loss Account
- Balance sheet
- Cash flow statement
- Accounts of subsidiary companies
- Notes to Accounts
- Balance sheet Abstract
- Company's general business profile

Voluntary Financial Information: Such information may be shown by the companies on a voluntary basis. Such information includes the following :

- Economic Value Added (EVA)
- Social Audit
- Environmental Audit

- Brand Valuation
- Human resource valuation
- Financial Ratios
- Product information
- Market share

Mandatory non-financial information:

It includes:

- Director's report
- Auditor's Report
- Foreign Exchange earnings
- Particulars of employees
- Accounting policies
- Conservation of Energy and Technology Absorption

Voluntary non-financial information

Such information includes the following:

- Management Report
- Chairman's speech
- Director's profile
- CEO's Report
- Competitiveness and merger and acquisition plans
- Brand profile
- Corporate Governance
- Alliance and Joint Venture
- Industry Analysis.

CORPORATE SOCIAL REPORTING IN INDIA

The Government of India appointed a committee under the chairmanship of Rajinder Sachar which is popularly known as Sachar Committee. In 1978, the committee recommended that a provision should be included in company law to make it mandatory for all companies to provide a social report along with director's report in the annual reports. The Government of India w.e.f. April 1989 requires a few companies to disclose information about conservation of energy, technology absorption and foreign exchange.

Corporate Social Reporting has not yet gained so much momentum in India. In the Tata group, TISCO and TELCO are very socially conscious and have been sincerely practicing the principles that their founding fathers had set up. The

Tatas have now started TCCI (Tata Council for Community Involvement) and as a group, they are addressing community responsibility.

In India, majority of the business undertakings report about their social aspect through the Director's Report. Leading public sector undertakings like NTPC, ONGC, MMTC, Madras Refineries Limited and Cement Corporation of India, publish a social balance sheet. Mainly manufacturing companies like Reliance Industries Limited, MMTC, BHEL, TISCO, TELCO, NALCO, etc., fertilizer companies like PPL, Nagarjuna Fertilizers, etc and petrochemical companies like Lubrizol India Limited, Bharat Petroleum, Hindustan Petroleum, Indian Oil Limited, Hindustan Organic Chemicals Limited, etc. provide social information.

In the last decade or so, as companies expanded and globalization crept in, companies started laying more emphasis on fulfillment of their responsibilities towards the society. This is due to the fact that companies are accountable for their activities to a range of stakeholders like employees, bankers, suppliers, NBFCS, consumers, Government, shareholders and finally to the society.

In India, majority of the work done by companies is in the nature of philanthropy. Out of the six companies short listed for the Business World Federation of Indian chambers of commerce and industry (BW FICCI) award, five companies (Wipro, Gujarat Ambuja Cement Lupia, Indal and Canara Bank) are involved in community development work like running schools and hospitals, building roads, creating income- generating schemes and similar projects. (Business World, 29 December, 2003). The names of some companies which are Corporate Social Responsibility (CSR) practitioners are listed below:

- Kinetic Engineering
- Lupin
- Canara Bank
- Gujarat Ambuja Cement
- ITC
- Wipro
- Indal
- Apex Laboratories
- NALCO
- Jindal Steel & Power
- Forbes Marshall

CONCLUSION

Today the outlook of business towards social responsibility in India has changed from "Why should I do it?" to "How can I do it?" (Business World, 29

December 2003). This is corroborated by research. Earlier in the previous year, the UK-based International Center for Corporate Social Responsibility (ICCSR) carried out a survey of corporate social responsibility activity in seven Asian countries India, South Korea, Singapore, The Philippines, Malaysia, Thailand and Indonesia. India ranked at the top of the survey – 72 per cent of the sample reported extensively on the corporate social responsibility work done by them.

Since the society has become more conscious of its expectation from the corporate sector, the corporate sector is gradually realizing its obligations towards the society. Corporate houses are gradually accepting that they should report such information to the society which tells them how far they have fulfilled their social responsibilities. The Government has to play a pivotal role in this matter. Even though the Government has failed to provide even the most basic amenities to its citizens, it expects the corporate sector to actively participate in welfare programmes. For example, the State Government of Karnataka is very happy that an entity like Canara Bank has been actively involved in a number of welfare projects like granting educational loans to students at soft rates, giving vocational skills to the unemployed, etc.

A recent survey of 400 plants conducted by the Federation of Indian Chambers of Commerce and Industry (FICCI), shows that "96.7 per cent of the units had already initiated some steps for pollution prevention, and 86.1 per cent have taken measures for treating effluent wastes (Gupta, Shekhar, 1999).

In the present scenario, corporate entities have to realize their obligations towards the society and do their bit to improve the quality of life in the society. They should show transparency which preparing their annual reports. "True and Fair presentation" should be made about social contributions.

REFERENCES

Agarwal, Rajesh and Raghunathan, V, The Need for Transparency, The Chartered Accountant, January 1999.

Ball, A. Owen, D.L., & Gray, R.H., 2000. External Transparency or International Capture: The Role of third party statements in adding value to corporate environmental reports. Business strategy and the Environmental 9(1), pp. 1-23.

C. Awery, "Business and Human Rights in a Time of Charge, Amnesty, International Report, 2000, 11.b,

C.Hess and K.Key, "Good" Doesn't Always Mean Right, Across the Board, July – August 2001, p. 63. Department for Environmental, Food and Rural Affairs (Great Britain). (2001).

Gray, R.H., (2001, July 9). Social and Environmental Responsibility Sustainability and Accountability: Can the corporate sector deliver, paper presented at a seminar of the

CPA Australia and Accounting and Finance Research Unit of Victoria University, Melbourne, Australia.

Gray, R.H., & Bebbington, K.J. (2001). Accounting for the Environment (2nd ed), London : Sage.

I. Okonta and O. Douglas, Where Cultures Feast: Shell, Human Rights, and Oil in the Niger Delta (San Fransisco: Sierra Club Books, 2001) p.15.

Isenmann, R., & Leng, C., (2001) Customized Corporate Environmental Reporting by Internet – Based push and pull technologies. Eco – Management and Auditing 8,100, pp.100 – 1100.

Mishra, K. K., "A Case for Environmental Reporting", Indian Management, May 1998, p. 96.

P. Schwang and B. Libb, when Good Companies Do Bad Things: Responsibility and Risk in an Age of Globalization (New York: John Wiley, 1999), p.26.

Rees S., Wright S., (eds), Human Rights, and Corporate Responsibility: A Dialogue, Annandale, and Pluto Press, 2000.

Schaltegger, S. Burrit, R., & Petersen, H., (2003). An Introduction to Corporate Environment Management: Striving for sustainability.

Shepherd, K., Abkowity, M. & Cohen, M.A. (2001), Online Corporate Environmental Reporting: Improvements and innovation to enhance stakeholder value. Corporate environmental strategy, 8 (4), pp.307 – 315.

Stanton, P.A., & Stanton, J. (2002). Corporate Annual Reports: Research perspectives used. Accounting, Auditing, and Accountability Journal, 15(4), pp. 478 – 500.

Wheeler, D., & Elkington, J. (2001). The End of the Corporate Environment Report, On the Advent of Cybernetic Sustainability Reporting and Communication. Business Strategy and the Environment 10, pp.1 – 14.

Williams, S.M., & Pei, C.H.W. (2000). Corporate social disclosure by listed companies on their web sites: An international comparison. International Journal of Accounting, 34 (3), pp.389 – 419.

Wilson, Corporate Reporting in Indian Industry, The outlook weekly, August 25, 1998, p.25.

Part II: Management of Human Resources

10

IMPACT OF GLOBALIZATION ON HUMAN RESOURCES

Aleena Sharma

INTRODUCTION

'Planning is a forward looking function'- but do organizations plan its strategic moves in such a way that it does not have to resort to downsizing?

Downsizing has been a pervasive managerial practice for the past ten years. It has been the unquestioning norm that if a company finds itself in financial difficulties. The way out is to downsize by cutting personnel. Yet concern is growing about the human costs that accompany downsizing and questions are being asked about its impact on the people who are downsized out of job.

In general terms downsizing refers to an organization's voluntary actions to reduce expenses. This is usually, but not exclusively accomplished by shrinking the size f workforce. However downsizing is the term to encompass a while range of activities from personnel layoffs and hiring freezes to consolidations and mergers of organizational units

The paper will highlight the causes of downsizing and its viable alternatives. The long term effect of corporate downsizing has affected the way organizations are managed. This research looks at the economic problems facing the downsized organization and the psychological impact affecting the retained employees and the terminated workers.

WHY DO ORGANIZATIONS OPT FOR DOWNSIZING?

Organizations are still operating in the commodity era where in employees are treated as a commodity which can be discarded when not needed. Downsizing or rightsizing (putting it in a positive note) is reducing the number of head counts. 'Employees are our greatest asset' is what we hear very often from CEO's, the concept of Human Resource accounting where in employees are treated more of an asset than an expense. But if we look at what organizations do with their so called assets as opposed to what they say, we may derive a different conclusion.

Meeting Environmental Challenges: Organizations have to survive with the unrelenting market pressures and pace of change. The few strategies adopted by organizations to enhance their chance of success in an increasingly competitive global environment and to adapt to the changes in the environment are merger, reengineering, Total Quality Management and downsizing. To achieve sustained competitive advantage organizations will do anything and that 'anything' is primarily cost cutting, whether warranted or not. There are only two ways for firms to become more profitable: either increase revenue or cut costs. Cutting cost is the easiest way out. Human resource represents costs, so to become profitable it seems logical to reduce those costs by decreasing the number of employees.

Unreliable Human Resource Planning: The basic purpose of spending a chunk of the organization's resources on Human Resource planning is to get the right no. of people for the right jobs at the right time. But do firms ask themselves the following:

- What mix of skills do we need today?
- What skills are we likely to need in the future?
- Do we have the right number of people employed today?
- How will this number change in future?
- How does our staffing cost differ than those of our competitors?

If firms have the answers to these questions, thee wouldn't arise a need to cut cost resulting into downsizing.

ANALYZING DOWNSIZING

Corporate restructuring has become the fast track to business success. With staff the highest cost factor for most organizations, getting the balance right between over-resourced and under-resourced is critical. Downsizing got its bad name in the late 80s and 90s when it became synonymous with massive job cuts in recessionary times". So the bad downsizers got mixed up with the good downsizers, and this strategic corporate practice needed to find a new identity. Workforce re-alignments, company rightsizing, trimming positions, or job eliminations are some more positive names used.

Even the meaning of the word downsizing has got academics "troubled". The definition is so "loose" at present that is hard to research the phenomenon for fear of including or excluding too many workers. Good downsizers, are those organizations who shed staff, usually as a one-off event and as part of a broad growth strategy and are mainly private sector service organizations. "Good downsizers focus on a problem and a plan, and commit to future growth.

Corporate downsizing is bad for society as a whole. The costs to the fired employees outweigh the gains for firms. And what is more, downsizing increases unemployment and reduces economy-wide growth.

Like most other business phenomena, downsizing has both positive and negative attributes. When an organization gets "bloated", over-staffed, and non-competitive, or it the marketplace changes dramatically, a reduction in staff may be necessary for the health and often the very survival of that organization. Obviously, such downsizing is painful to those who are the casualties. There are many other pressures that can lead to downsizing. One of the most pervasive and fundamental pressures is new technology. Computerization and advances in automation cause the elimination or reduction of certain types of jobs. Another has been the switch to a global economy. Think back twenty or thirty years and remember the state of communications, transportation, computers, entertainment, home electronics, medicine, education, government regulation, foreign competition, and the fabric of our society. The changes are dramatic, and they exert part of the downsizing pressure.

Such downsizing pressures as these are virtually inevitable, and they are for the most part healthy. They are a natural result of change. Responding to such change is a real challenge for all of us.

IMPACT OF DOWNSIZING

The effect of downsizing on employees, and often on whole towns or cities, can be devastating. The effects of those "downsized" out the door are fairly obvious- loss of income and self-esteem, the need to seek new employment, and an uncertain future.

The effects on those left behind are often nearly as severe, for both themselves and their employer. This is a partially hidden and very negative consequence of downsizing, and it must not be ignored. The negative impact on the morale of those who remain after downsizing is deep and it lasts for years. Chief executives shouldn't assume that restructuring is good for a company. In fact, most are not good.

Corporations are paying severe penalties for laying off older, experienced workers. This takes the form of lost organizational memory and experience as well as the decline of morale. It is, after all, employees who have to provide customer service, make sales, build products, or provide services. In too many companies, downsizing has increased the workload on the remaining employees- the things that need doing don't get downsized. Sometimes new technologies have allowed fewer people to do these things, but often this is not the case. And the employees left behind are sometimes less qualified, have become demoralized, and feel that loyalty to the company will not provide loyalty by the company in return. The fear of downsizing even reaches employees of companies who are not downsizing and don't plan to. It has become a psychological epidemic of sorts. No one feels immune! And in too many cases, critical ties are broken between customers and suppliers when downsizing occurs, since the people who built these ties may no longer be present.

IS DOWNSIZING AVOIDABLE?

Organizations may adopt some of the following alternatives:

Voluntary Retirement Schemes: In this type of downsizing The firm offers opportunities to those near retirement to retire early with no financial cost. Others are offered financial incentives, usually based on age and length of service, to quit the organization. No one is forced to leave. This is often used as a first stage in the downsizing process. It is often followed by a less voluntary process. This concentrates the layoffs on those people most willing to experience them. Higher paid employees at each job level are likely to leave, so the positive cost impact is high -- though it may be offset by the cost of the retirement or severance package. On the other hand, People with most opportunity to be hired elsewhere (i.e., high performers) take the package and leave.

Changing the Organizational Structure: A horizontal slice of the organization is removed. Middle managers are reassigned or laid off and not replaced. This means that one of two things has to occur:

- more senior managers take over the decision making responsibilities of the managers who have left, or
- decision making is decentralized to lower level employees.

Which of these is the appropriate action requires careful diagnosis. Pain is shared across all departments, though it is concentrated at particular levels. Decision making, if decentralized, occurs at a more appropriate level -- closer to the customer, to where the variations in performance or demand happen. The disadvantage would be that transition costs may be high, top management may become overloaded and the costs of retraining may be excessive.

Cut Down on Outsourcing: Instead of contracting work out, the organizations can reduce the amount of work contracted out and bring the work "in house." For example components usually bought can be manufactured; services bought outside can be performed in-house. The feasibility of this approach will depend upon the skills and competencies of the current work force as well as the status of existing contracts with suppliers.

Have a Check on Human Capital: The demographic mixture of the organizational "survivors" is not skewed severely. Under most downsizing scenarios, older people leave the organization taking their experience with them. Counter-cyclic hiring can replenish the pool with persons with experience in other organizational settings and avoid dramatic "bulges" in certain age groups which play havoc with succession planning and hiring patterns.

Reassign and Retrain: Find out if anyone is interested in reduced hours. Many people would like to spend more time with their families or pursuing other interests, but aren't able to give up their whole income. If you need some jobs but not others, find out if people are willing to job share. Shorter hours may be taxed at a lower rate, which makes the cut hurt less.

CONCLUSION

What's the solution? Value people over profits? Recognize human capital as paramount? These answers are obvious. But given the high-handed, soulless treatment doled out today by many employers, it's a start. If appeals to integrity and character fail, there's always the bottom line: depressed and anxious personnel are unlikely to be productive, and absence from work costs employers and society money. The re-engineering of work ought to perpetuate fulfillment and productivity in employees, not illness and disability.

Employers often focus on the need to cut costs and underestimate how much work actually gets done by the people who are being laid off. The remaining employees get overworked and fall behind and/or burn out. The situation really doesn't become clear until a major problem develops. Organizations should take the time to sit down with employees and decide what work they are going to stop doing.

When a business is being reorganized, employers often talk about how terribly things were done in the past and how everything will be done much better in the future. This is a slap in the face to employees. Organizations should acknowledge thc accomplishments of the past and give credit to the great work that was done and talk about the changes as new opportunities.

Even if firms plan to cut back on staff just once, this is a promise they can't make. Business changes so quickly these days that they may have to cut one area of staffing even if firms are growing. Organizations may also find out that the cuts made the first time weren't deep enough

Employees need to be given the full picture. They need to hear it and see it several times. They need to have a chance to ask questions after the news has sunk in. They need to express their anger and concerns. It takes time for people to take in major changes in their lives.

11

LEADERSHIP DYNAMICS IN A GLOBAL ECONOMY

Dindayal Swain

ABSTRACT

Globalization, liberalization and privatization have posed lots of challenges for the Indian organizations and their leadership profiles. No doubt with every scientific and technological innovations, leaders are marching towards an era where they need global mindset, high level of adaptability, integrity of character, clear vision, high credibility, knowledge in cross functional areas , ability of self change ,managing and motivating knowledge work force, complex problem solving skills , bench breaking thirst , high risk takers, team workers , emotional intelligence , strong work ethics , honesty , high level of interpersonal skills , social commitment and cross cultural assessments. As the business is not confined to any national boundaries and is transacted in multidimensional way amidst highly speculative events the challenges for leaders thus demands high level of logical decision making with pin point accuracy. This paper will cover the above things in a systematic way with a strong belief that the real test of character for a leader will be not only to anticipate change but also successfully adopt change.

The real test of character for a leader is to nurture those people whose stars may shine as brightly as or even brighter than -the leader's own. Globalization, Liberalization and Privatization has thrown lots of challenges for the Indian organisations and their leadership styles.

In the new Millennium, which is characterized by technological change, the rapid pace of innovation and the communication revolution, organisations are learning new ways of communicating with each other. They are experimenting with new organizational forms to meet the demands of the global market. Management of a fast changing organisation is becoming the core leadership task.

In the Next millennium, India needs more leaders like Mr. Ambani, Mr. Premji, Mr. Narayan Murthy, but not mere mangers. Before going into an analytical discussion, I feel the importance of giving clear cut differential parameters between a Manager and a Leader.

Corporate in India can no longer operate in isolations and be immune to the changes in the business environment the world over. They should follow the trends and think globally but to act locally.

Now a day's change can be seen in every sphere economic, sociological, technological, socio cultural that has a direct bearing on the functioning of organisations and on the leadership profiles. In an organizational context, change encompasses not only change from the top level, but all levels where meeting organizational goal is a must. Leaders play a great role in managing change.

The resistance to change is an emotional /behavioral response to real or imagined threats to an established work routine. There are two types of reasons why people resist change:

- Situational variables.
- Socio-psychological and personality.

RESISTANCE DUE TO SITUATIONAL VARIABLES

- Threat of loss of position power.
- Fear of the unknown
- Habit & inertia
- Altered social relationships
- Disruption of organization culture reality
- Previous exposure to failed change efforts
- Summation of perceived personal loss and gains from the change.
- Previous exposure to failed change efforts
- Summation of perceived personal loss and gains from thc change
- Organizational climate
- Forced change and lack of participation in the change
- Poor communication
- Limited resources
- Vested interests
- Threat to self image
- Personal appeals
- Implied fault
- Sunken costs
- Loss of rewards and privileges

RESISTANCE DUE TO PSYCHOLOGICAL VARIABLES

- Cognitive dissonance
- Fear of the unknown
- Venturesome/need for change
- Faith in people/concern for others
- Dogmation
- Admiration for status

CHANGE MANAGEMENT

- Never institute change for changes sake
- Preparing the environment
- Showing concerns for projects and people
- Knowing the people and demanding best from them
- Sharing the knowledge
- Recognizing accomplishments

Finally change will always be present but it need not be traumatic. The question is one of Leadership. The Leaders need to recognize the different manifestations not only in others but also even in themselves, and they must also understand the common reasons employees resist change in the first place. Only then will the Leader be able to make a beginning to successfully handling the resistance.

Embracing the change as an opportunity can make all the difference.

LEADERSHIP PROFILES IN THE CHANGING SCENARIO

1. Leaders of the next century need to radically change their mindset because the leadership traits and qualities which were very important till now may not stand the test of time in the years to come. In keeping with changing times, it is important that leaders develop their adaptive capabilities.

In other words, to lead is to live dangerously. While leadership is often depicted as an exciting and glamorous endeavour, one in which you inspire others to follow you through good times and bad, such a portrayal ignores leaderships dark side; the inevitable attempts to take you out of the game. Those attempts are sometimes justified. People in top positions must often pay the price for a flawed strategy or a series of bad decisions. But frequently, something more is at work. We are not talking here about connectional office politics; mere talking about the high stake risks you face whenever you try to lead an organisation through difficult but necessary change. The risks during such times are especially high because change that truly transforms an organisation be it a multibillion-dollar company or a ten-person sales team demands that people give up things they hold dear: daily habits, loyalties, ways of thinking. In return for these sacrifices, they may be offered nothing more than the possibility of a better future.

We refer to this kind of wrenching organizational transformation as adaptive change, something very different from the 'technical change' that occupies people in positions of authority on a regular basis. Technical problems, while often challenging, can be solved applying existing know-how and the organization's current problem-solving processes. Adaptive problems resist these kinds of solutions because they require individuals throughout the organisation to alter their ways; as the people themselves are the problem, the solution lies with them. Responding to an adaptive challenge with a technical fix may have some short term appeal.

But to make real progress, sooner or later those who lead must ask themselves and the people in the organisation to face a set of deeper issues – and to accept a solution that may require turning part or the entire organisation upside down.

2. Leaders should have a clear "Vision" of how things should be. They should also be able to communicate the vision to others so that the vision becomes a shared vision and everybody willingly contributes towards fulfilling the vision.

3. To be able to deal effectively with the complexities of change in a more flexible manner, leaders of the future should possess cross-functional rather than narrow functional knowledge and expertise, but avoid thinking like an expert. Acquisition of knowledge should be viewed as a lifelong experience and not a collection of facts or skills. Not long ago what you learned in school and college was largely enough for the rest of your life. With knowledge expanding exponentially this is no longer true.

If we go back to our historical incidents Babur's success came because he had the courage to turn failure into success. He studied past failures to figure out which factors led to defeat and which ones could bring him success. Babur learned from his enemies. When defeated, he would acknowledge the superiority of their tactics, adopt them, experiment with them and even improve upon them.

By three methods we may learn:
By reflection, which is noblest?
By imitation, which is easiest?
By experience, which is the bitterest ......Confucius (BC 551-479)

4. Some of the important words a leader of the new millennium is required to put into action are: options not plans; they will not bother about perfection, only about possibilities; they will not seek obedience, only encourage participation and involvement (Handy, 1997).

5. As Benjamin Disrachi once mentioned that, "In a progressive country, change is constant. Change is simply unavoidable". The same is true for effective and successful organisations; Change will remain a core consideration for future leaders. The process of change starts with self change. You can't expect your people to change without you yourself willing to change.

Effective leaders will be those who had the ability to change gears with changing times and changing situations Just like a driver of a motor car changes gear in response to road conditions, effective leaders change gears in an organisation depending upon their skills, the competence and commitment of their people and organisation and the environment which impinges on their organisation and its performance.

6. Leaders need to realize what motivates the knowledge workforce. It requires a clear, unbiased understanding of the situation at hand, deep insight into the vagaries of human nature at individual and the group levels, the establishment of appropriate and reasonable expectations and goals, and the construction of a balanced set of tangible and intangible incentives. In other words, hard thinking and hard work.

Future leaders could possibly motivate people by following the PRIDE System (Smith, 1997) which stands for :

P – Provide for a positive working environment

R – Recognize everyone's efforts

I – Involve everyone

D – Develop skills and potential

E – Evaluate and measure continuously.

7. Leaders need to have a deep insight into the realities of the world and be receptive to the changes taking place and opportunities that these changes offer.

8. Leaders need to have high level of commitment to the organizational goal and the perseverance to achieve the goal in spite of all the obstacles.

9. As the tasks become too complex and information too widely distributed, leaders need to involve others and seek their participation in problem solving and decision making.

10. In large organisations, the leader should be willing to share power and control so that leadership is encouraged at various levels.

11. Leaders should test the assumptions and be prepared to change them but at the same time they should stick to their convictions.

12. Few obstacles on the way to excellence which leaders need to overcome are following the path of mediocrity and relying on connectional wisdom.

13. Successful leaders set their own standards and compare with themselves and not with others (Conger & Kanungo, 1998).

14. Leaders should learn to depend on themselves and not on other people, material rewards, prestigious position etc. for their self-worth as this is not long lasting. Self respect which comes from within cannot be taken away by anyone.

15. Innovation is the need of the hour. Only when a leader is innovative can he find opportunity in every crisis. Innovation is also to do with finding new application for old ideas which can't be discarded. Innovativeness will help the leaders to view the world not for what it is but for what it could be.

16. Leaders should be capable of taking risks as maintaining status quo leads to complacency and mediocrity. As the old proverb goes "you must learn from your past mistakes, but not lean on your past successes". It has been found that toward high achievers behave quite differently when taking risks (Mc Cleland, 1963), low achievers do one of the two things; either they minimize risk as much as possible or they take wild, irrational risks. High achievers, by contrast, typically take moderate risks, but the nub of it is that they calculate risks against circumstances and their own abilities.

17. To encourage teamwork within organisations mechanisms have to be created to broaden the concept of individual competence to include working with others and building trusting relationships by breaking barrier of communication across boundaries and encouraging collaborative rather than competitive behaviour.

18. The corporate environment has become increasingly unstable and unpredictable and vulnerable to outside forces and pressures. Managers must learn to cope with non-linear forces (Toffler, 1985). These observations have become even more relevant in the present day.

Ross and Nesbit (1991) puts it this way "tinkering, testing, piloting, experimenting – these are the strategic tools of the leaders of the 21st century. You can't really predict it; but you can experiment; you can flex the business; you can rearrange management teams worth noting, leaving things as they are can be just as predictable as changing every thing. You lose (or win) both ways."

19.Emotional Intelligence will be the key for successful leadership in the next century (Goleman, 1998).Like it or not, leaders need to manage the mood of their organizations. The most gifted leaders accomplish that by using a mysterious blend of psychological abilities known as emotional intelligence. They're self aware and empathetic. They can read and regulate their own emotions while intuitively grasping how others feel and gauging their organizations emotional state.

But the Questions like

Where does emotional intelligence come from?

How do leaders learn to use it ?

The Management literature (and common sense) suggests that both nature and nurture feed emotional intelligence. Part genetic predisposition, part life experience, and part old- fashioned training, emotional intelligence emerges in varying degrees from one leader to the next. Wisely and passionately deployed, emotional intelligence spurs leaders, their people, and their organizations to new heights.

Five Component Theory of Emotional Intelligence at Work

	Definition	Hall marks
Self-awareness	The ability to recognize and understand your moods, emotions, and drives, as well as their effect on others.	Self-confidence realistic self-assessment self-deprecating sense of humour
Motivation	A passion to work for reasons that go beyond money or status a propensity to pursue goals with energy and persistence	Strong drive to achieve optimism, even in the face of failure Organizational commitment.
Self-Regulation	The ability to control or redirect disruptive impulses and moods; the propensity to suspend judgment – to think before acting	Trust worthiness and integrity comfort with ambiguity. Openness to change.
Empathy	The ability to understand the emotional makeup of other people Skill in treating people according to their emotional reactions.	Expertise in building and retaining talent. Cross cultural sensitivity. Service to clients and customers.
Social skill	Proficiency in managing relation-ships and building networks. An ability to find common ground and build rapport	Effectiveness in leading change, persuasiveness Expertise in building and leading teams.

20. A successful leader should empower his/her followers but with a systematic way with the following considerations.

SIX WAYS TO COUNTER WAYWARD INFLUENCES

There is no guaranteed way of ensuring that you won't be misled by your followers. But adhering to these principles may help.

- Keep vision and values front and centre. It's much easier to get side tracked when you're unclear about what the main track is.
- Make sure People disagree. Remember that most of us form opinions too quickly and give them up too slowly.
- Cultivate truth tellers. Make sure there are people in your world you can trust to tell you what you need to hear, no matter how unpopular or unpalatable it is.
- Do as you would have done to you. Followers look to what you do rather than what you say. Set a good ethical climate for your team to be sure your followers have clear boundaries for their actions.
- Honour your Intuition. If you think you are being manipulated, you are probably right.
- Delegate, don't desert.

It's important to share Control and empower your staff, but remember who's ultimately responsible for the outcome. As they say in politics, "Trust, but verify".

21. Managing negative ego will be the key to success for the new millennium Leaders.

CONCLUSION

Let us now turn to the 21st Century organisation, the shape of organisations to come. In the last century the machine was the model of the organisation. However organisations in this century will not be machines; they will be characterized by alliances, networks, workgroups and temporary, ad hoc, fluid and amoeba-like-organisations. 21st Century organisations will not have plans, but only options, they will not bother about perception, only about possibilities, they will not seek obedience, only encourage participation and involvement. And the managerial role will be rechristened as coordinator, partner, facilitator, catalyst, or leadership roles (Handy, 1998).

The organization in this millennium will be a community of individuals, not a pool of human resources. Individuals will not be given authority; they will have to earn it. And, leaders will be those who will not receive power from position or election but through competence and commitment. Leaders will be those who will make things happen, prove themselves in time and space, and are skilled enough to handle virtual reality. They will be confident and trusted, exuding belief in themselves, showing respect for others, with a passion for excellence. These will be their key characteristics.

In the last 60 years, we have seen various new theories of leadership-charismatic leadership, wisdom leadership, transformational Leadership, integrative leadership (which integrates task, people and effectiveness), value – based leadership, strategic leadership, etc. All these theories search for one lever which will characterize effective leadership. In this fast changing world one lever won't work-one has to search for multiple levers.

Leadership is an improvisational art, you may be guided by an overarching vision, clear values, and a strategic plan, but what you actually do from moment to moment Can't be scripted. You must respond as events unfold. Leaders ignite imagination, inspire passion and surface the best in people. They are wedded to the principles of discovery, dream, design and deliver.

In the last century, great leaders were visionaries; Jamshedji Tata envisioned a steel plant to modernize India. Pandit Nehru envisioned India as a secular and democratic nation, where every Indian would have the quality of life which they are deprived of during the colonial era. John Kennedy had a vision to put man on the moon. Martin Luther king had a dream that people in America will not be judged by the colour of their skin but the quality of their character.

What all great leaders have in common?

- They are learners, thinkers and doers
- They are concerned with Outcomes and results.
- They hold themselves accountable and set an example for others.
- They want to make a difference in the organizations they lead.
- They are tolerant of diversity, unafraid of other people's strengths.

The most critical requirement of the leader in this new millennium will be to deliver results. It is unlikely that well-laid norms and standards alone will help people deliver results. Delivery will come through inspired action, the commitment and involvement of people, unleashing of energy, empowering people to innovate and achieve the strategic objectives. Hence the leader's role will be to review, communicate, appreciate and celebrate.

A leader in this Millennium must engage people in the process of discovery, dreaming, designing and delivering. His ability to collaborate with the people will ensure success and create opportunities to celebrate.

These will be the challenges for leadership in this millennium to discover, to dream, to design & to deliver.

REFERENCES

Conger, A Jay (1998), Charismatic Leadership in Organisations, Sage Publications, London (PP 189-200).

Covey, R Stephen (1989). The Seven Habits of Highly Effective People, Simon & Schuster, New York, P 71

Cox, T Jr (1991) "The Multicultural Organisation", Academy of Management Executive, 5(2), (PP 34-47).

Drucker, Peter (1977) "Introduction toward the New Organisation in the Organisation of the future" (Ed) Frances Hesselbein et al, Jossey-Bass, San Francisco.

Horn, Art (1998), Giffts of Leadership: Team Building through focus and empathy, Macmillan India Limited, New Delhi. Pp (56-58)

Howard. A (1995) A Framework for work change in a Howard (Ed) The changing Nature of work (pp. 3-44), Jossey-Bass, San Francisco.

Miliken, F.H & Martins, L L (1996) searching for common Thread: Understanding the Multiple effects of Diversity in Organisational Change, Academy of Management Review, 21 (pp 402-433).

Sims, Henry P & Lorenzi, Peter Jr (1992) The New Leadership Paradigm: Social Learning and Cognition in Organisations, Sage Publications, London.

Watson, W.E, Kumar, K & Michaelsen, L (1993)'Cultural Diversity's impact on Interaction Process and Performance comparing Homogenous and Diverse ask Groups", Academy of Management Journal, 36,590-602.

Work, John W (1996) "Leading a Diverse Work Force" quoted in F Hesselbein, M Goldsmith and R Beckhard (Eds), The Leader of the Future: New Visions, Strategies and Practices for the Next Era, Jossey-Bass Publishers, San Francisco (pp 71-79).

SECOND BASEL ACCORD (BASEL II): ISSUES AND CHALLENGES FOR INDIA

Dhiraj Sharma

ABSTRACT

Basel II compliance is becoming a global top priority within the financial industry. The initial Basel Capital Accord only took financial risks into account. Basel II will ensure that banks evaluate and measure other forms of risk, including operational risk. Introducing capital charge and measure for operational risk, Basel II encourages financial institutions to more actively address operational risk management. Today, managing risk is increasingly becoming the single most important issue for the regulators and financial institutions. These institutions have over the years recognized the cost of ignoring risk. Therefore, capital adequacy of a bank has become an important benchmark to assess its financial soundness and strength. Basel II offers a variety of options in addition to the standard approach to measuring risk. But these require strategising risk management for the entire enterprise, building huge data warehouses, crunching numbers and performing complex calculations. Compliance with Basel II poses great challenges for banks and financial institutions, which have been in the comfort zone of regulatory capital requirement. Like other countries, India also envisages many regulatory and supervisory challenges in implementing the Basel II recommendations. While there is no second opinion regarding the purpose, necessity and usefulness of the proposed new accord - the implementation poses considerable challenges for the banks especially in a developing country like India. The present paper gives an overview of the Basel II framework and discusses the issues and challenges in implementing Basel II in India.

The main objective of this paper is to explore the existing knowledge about the Second Basel Accord. Efforts have been made to judge how the Indian banking practices would have to be changed with the introduction of Basel II recommendations. Also, major issues, problems and challenges of implementing

Basel II in India have been examined. Thus, the scope of present study is confined to issues and challenges faced by Indian banking in complying with Basel Accord.

The paper draws information from a survey of research literature. Primarily, the data have been collected from Indian Bank Association's publications, RBI's reports, bulletins and Internet uploads, and by senior banking official's interviews to various papers and magazines.

INTRODUCTION TO BASLE COMMITTEE

It is a committee of banking supervisory authorities, which has established by the Central bank Governors of the group of Ten Countries in 1975. It consists of senior representatives of bank supervisory authorities and central banks from: Belgium, Canada, France, Italy, Japan, Luxembourg, Netherlands, Switzerland, Sweden, UK and USA. It usually meets at the Bank for International Settlements in Basle, where its permanent secretariat is located. The committee has stipulated in the five sections, the following eleven principles for banking supervisory authorities to apply in assessing bank's management of interest rate risk.

- Board of Directors, should approve strategies and policies with respect to interest rate, risk management and ensure that senior management takes the steps necessary to monitor and control these risks.
- Senior management must ensure that appropriate policies/procedures/ resources are available.
- Banks should clearly define the individuals/committees responsible for managing interest rate risks. Larger/complex Banks should have independent unit for administration/design of Banks interest rates/risk measurement, monitoring and control functions.
- Banks interest rate, risk policies and procedures be clearly defined and consistent with nature and complexity of their activities. Policies should be applied on the consolidated basis.
- New products/activities to be introduced subject to adequate procedures and controls.
- Assumptions underlying the system should be clearly understood by risk managers and Bank management.
- Banks must establish and enforce operating limits and other practices that maintain exposures within levels consistent with their internal policies.
- Banks should measure their vulnerability to loss under stressful market conditions including the breakdown of key assumptions and consider their results at the time of review of policies.

- Banks must have adequate information systems for measuring, monitoring, controlling and reporting interest rate exposures.
- Banks must have an adequate system of internal controls i.e. regular independent reviews and evaluations.
- Supervisory authorities should obtain from banks sufficient and timely information.

SECOND BASEL ACCORD (BASEL II)

The first Basle accord of 1988 is to be revised as it took into account only globally active banks in G10 nations and it focussed narrowly on minimum capital requirements. The New Accord commonly called the Second Basei Accord (Basel II) is to be implemented from 1st Jan, 2007. Therefore, systems and process changes needs to be made much sooner.

Basel accord II is currently engaging the attention of the banking community, not just in India but worldwide. Managing risk is increasingly becoming the single most important issue for the regulators and financial institutions. These institutions have over the years recognized the cost of ignoring risk. However, growing research and improvements in information technology have improved the measurement and management of risk. It's but natural therefore, capital adequacy of a bank has become an important benchmark to assess its financial soundness and strength. The idea is that banks should be free to engage in their asset-liability management as long as they are backed by a level of capital sufficient to cushion their potential losses. In other words, capital requirement should be determined by the risk profile of a bank.

The initial Basel Capital Accord only took financial risks into account. Basel II will ensure that banks evaluate and measure other forms of risk, including operational risk. Banks will have to make capital provision to effectively act as a contingency fund, to cover the direct and indirect losses that emergent operational risks could cause.

Bank for International Settlements (BIS) had asked RBI for vital inputs, including the Quantitative Impact Study (QIS) to help in calibrating proposals to arrive at a country-specific risk weightage in the revised Basle accord on capital adequacy for banks, scheduled to be in place by the year 2007.

QIS would help in crunching the numbers and provide an opportunity for dialogue between regulators and banks in the respective countries. The country-specific risk weightage model would depend on inputs from the respective countries including India, as risk perceptions varied among countries and region.

The treatment of credit risk determinants in standardised approach, in which "third parties" judge the risk, comprises probability of default, loss given default, maturity, exposure at default and concentration. On the financial collateral, standardised approaches cash on deposit with the lending banks, government securities rated BB- and above (includes public sector enterprises treated as sovereigns by national supervisor), bonds rated BB- and above, equities in a main index and certain mutual funds and gold. The Reserve Bank of India (RBI) is in process of finalizing the policy approach for the proposed new Basle capital accord.

The initial capital accord of 1988 was hugely successful with more than 100 countries accepting it as a benchmark. One of the major reasons for the success of this framework was its being simple. It brought in uniformity and attempted to make regulatory capital requirement consistent with the economic capital. Reserve Bank of India introduced risk assets ratio system as a capital adequacy measure in 1992, in line with the Basel accord of 1988, which takes into account the risk element in various types of funded balance sheet items as well as non-funded off balance sheet exposures. In fact, RBI norms on capital adequacy at 9% are more stringent than Basel Committee stipulation of 8%.

THREE PILLARS OF BASEL II ACCORD

The new Basel Accord has its foundation on three mutually reinforcing pillars that allow banks and bank supervisors to evaluate properly the various risks that banks face and realign regulatory capital more closely with underlying risks. The first pillar is compatible with the credit risk, market risk and operational risk. The regulatory capital will be focused on these three risks. The second pillar gives the bank responsibility to exercise the best ways to manage the risk specific to that bank. Concurrently, it also casts responsibility on the supervisors to review and validate banks' risk measurement models. The third pillar on market discipline is used to leverage the influence that other market players can bring. This is aimed at improving the transparency in banks.

INDIAN BANKING AND FINANCIAL SYSTEM

A feature, somewhat unique to the Indian financial system is the diversity of its composition. We have the dominance of Government ownership coupled with significant private shareholding in the public sector banks which in turn continue to have a dominant share in the total banking system. These public sector banks are listed on the stock exchange and their performance is reflected in their P/E ratios. The private sector banks especially the new ones are world class. We also have cooperative banks, whose numbers are large and pose a challenge because of the multiplicity of regulatory and supervisory authorities. There are also Regional Rural Banks with links to their parent commercial banks. Foreign bank branches operate profitably in India and by and large the regulatory standards for all these banks are uniform. The process of providing financial services is changing rapidly from traditional banking to a one stop shop of varied financial services and the old institutional demarcations are getting increasingly blurred.

The Reserve Bank's approach has been one of gradual convergence with international standards and best practices with suitable country specific adaptations. India's aim has been to reach global best standards in a deliberately phased manner through a consultative process evolved within the country. This has also been the guiding principle in the approach to the New Basel Accord e.g. as stated earlier, while the minimum capital adequacy requirement under the Basel standard is 8% in India, we have stipulated and achieved a minimum capital of 9%. On the other hand, banks in India are still in the process of implementing capital charge for market risk prescribed in the Basel document although since 1998 we have in place several surrogates such as an Investment Fluctuation Reserve of 5% of the investment portfolio plus a 2.5% risk weight on the entire investment portfolio – whereas Basel norms take into account only the trading portfolio.

RBI'S INVOLVEMENT IN BASEL II

RBI's association with the Basel Committee on Banking Supervision dates back to 1997 as India was among the 16 non-member countries that were consulted in the drafting of the Basel Core Principles. Reserve Bank of India became a member of the Core Principles Liaison Group in 1998 and subsequently became a member of the Core Principles Working Group on Capital. Within the CPWG, RBI has been actively participating in the deliberations on the Accord and had the privilege to lead a group of 6 major non G -10 supervisors which presented a proposal on a simplified approach for Basel II to the Committee.

The Basel Committee on Banking Supervision is in process of finalizing Basel II document. The Reserve Bank's comments on the 3rd consultative document on the New Capital Accord on the basis of the quantitative impact studies (QIS 3) undertaken in co-ordination with select banks has brought out the need for more simplicity and greater flexibility on account of the different levels of preparedness of the banking system in India.

In general, keeping in view the RBI's goal to have consistency and harmony with international standards and our approach to adopt the pace as may be appropriate in the context of our country specific needs, the RBI had in April 2003 itself accepted in principle to adopt the new capital accord Basel II. The

RBI has announced, in its Annual Policy statement in May 2004 that banks in India should examine in depth the options available under Basel II and draw a road-map by end December 2004 for migration to Basel II and review the progress made thereof at quarterly intervals. The Reserve Bank is closely monitoring the progress made by banks in this direction. Hence, at a minimum all banks in India, to begin with, will adopt Standardized Approach for credit risk and Basic Indicator Approach for operational risk. After adequate skills are developed, both in banks and at supervisory levels, some banks may be allowed to migrate to IRB Approach.

The regulatory initiatives taken by the Reserve Bank of India include:

- Ensuring that the banks have suitable risk management framework oriented towards their requirements dictated by the size and complexity of business, risk philosophy, market perceptions and the expected level of capital. The framework adopted by banks would need to be adaptable to changes in business size, market dynamics and introduction of innovative products by banks in future.
- Introduction of Risk Based Supervision (RBS) in 23 banks on a pilot basis.
- Encouraging banks to formalize their Capital Adequacy Assessment Programme (CAAP) in alignment with business plan and performance budgeting system. This, together with adoption of Risk Based Supervision would aid in factoring the Pillar II requirements under Basel II.
- Enhancing the area of disclosures (Pillar III), so as to have greater transparency of the financial position and risk profile of banks.
- Improving the level of corporate governance standards in banks.
- Building capacity for ensuring the regulator's ability for identifying and permitting eligible banks to adopt IRB / Advanced Measurement approaches.

ISSUES AND CHALLENGES

Like other countries, India also envisages many regulatory and supervisory challenges in implementing the Basel II recommendations. While there is no second opinion regarding the purpose, necessity and usefulness of the proposed new accord - the techniques and methods suggested in the consultative document would pose considerable implementation challenges for the banks especially in a developing country like India. Following are the major issues and challenges having profound implications for the banking industry:

Implementation of Basel II norms will prove a challenging task for the bank supervisors as well. Given the paucity of supervisory resources, there is a need to reorient the resource deployment strategy. Supervisory cadre has to be properly trained for understanding of critical issues for risk profiling of supervised entities and validating and guiding development of complex IRB models. Moreover, Basel II provides scope for the supervisor to prescribe higher than the minimum capital levels for banks for, among others, interest rate risk in the banking book and concentration of risks / risk exposures. In India, we have initiated supervisory capacity building to identify slackness and to assess / quantify the extent of additional capital which may be required to be maintained by such banks. The magnitude of this task to be completed by December 2006, when we in India have as many as 100 banks, is daunting.

The new norms will almost invariably increase capital requirement in all banks across the board. Although capital requirement for credit risk may go down due to adoption of more risk sensitive models - such advantage will be more than offset by additional capital charge for operational risk and increased capital requirement for market risk. This partly explains the current trend of consolidation in the banking industry. In addition, competition among banks for highly rated corporates needing lower amount of capital may exert pressure on already thinning interest spread. Further, huge implementation cost may also impact profitability for smaller banks.

The new standards are an amalgam of international best practices and call for introduction of advanced risk management system with wider application throughout the organization. It would be a daunting task to create the required level of technological architecture and human skill across the institution.

India has three established rating agencies in which leading international credit rating agencies are stakeholders and also extend technical support. However, the level of rating penetration is not very significant. So far, ratings are restricted to issues and not issuers. While Basel II gives some scope to extend the rating of issues to issuers, this would only be an approximation and it would be necessary for the system to move to ratings of issuers. Encouraging ratings of issuers would be a challenge.

The new framework provides for alternative approaches for computation of capital requirement of various risks. However, competitive advantage of IRB approach may lead to domination of this approach among big banks. Banks adopting IRB approach will be more sensitive than those adopting standardized approach. This may result in high-risk assets flowing to banks on standardized approach, as they would require lesser capital for these assets than banks on IRB approach. Hence, the system as a whole may maintain lower capital than warranted and become more vulnerable. It is to be considered whether in our quest for perfect standards, we have lost the only universally accepted standard.

Computation of probability of default, loss given default, migration mapping and supervisory validation require creation of historical database, which is a time consuming process and may require initial support from the supervisor. Though RBI recognises the inherent attractiveness of the IRB Approaches, which will result in better internal credit risk management but the minimum requirements stipulated even under the IRB foundation approach are difficult to be implemented, especially in the emerging markets. Most of the banks do not have robust rating systems and historical data on Probability of Default (PD), nor do the supervisory authorities maintain time series data for estimating Loss Given Default (LGD).

In case of unrated sovereigns, banks and corporates, the prescribed risk weight is 100%, whereas in case of those entities with lowest ratting, the risk weight is 150%. This may create incentive for the category of counterparties, which anticipate lower rating to remain unrated.

Basel II proposals underscore the interaction between sound risk management practices and corporate good governance. The bank's board of directors has the responsibility for setting the basic tolerance levels for various types of risk. It should also ensure that management establishes a framework for assessing the risks, develop a system to relate risk to the bank's capital levels and establish a method for monitoring compliance with internal policies.

Basel II norms set out a number of areas where national supervisor will need to determine the specific definitions, approaches or thresholds that they wish to adopt in implementing the proposals. The criteria used by supervisors in making these determinations should draw upon domestic market practice and experience and be consistent with the objectives of Basel II norms.

Pillar 3 purports to enforce market discipline through stricter disclosure requirement. While admitting that such disclosure may be useful for supervisory authorities and rating agencies, the expertise and ability of the general public to comprehend and interpret disclosed information is open to question. Moreover, too much disclosure may cause information overload and may even damage financial position of bank.

The new framework is very complex and difficult to understand. It calls for revamping the entire management information system and allocation of substantial resources. Therefore, it may be out of reach for many smaller banks. As Moody's Investors Services puts it, "It is unlikely that these banks will have the financial resources, intellectual capital, skills and large scale commitment that larger competitors have to build sophisticated systems to allocate regulatory capital optimally for both credit and operational risks."

Developing countries have high concentration of lower rated borrowers. The calibration of IRB has lesser incentives to lend to such borrowers. This, along with withdrawal of uniform risk weight of 0% on sovereign claims may result in overall reduction in lending by internationally active banks in developing countries and increase their cost of borrowing.

The working Group set up by the Basel Committee to look into implementational issues observed that supervisors may wish to involve third parties, such a external auditors, internal auditors and consultants to assist them in carrying out some of the duties under Basel II. The precondition is that there should be a suitably developed national accounting and auditing standards and framework, which are in line with the best international practices. A minimum qualifying criteria for firms should be those that have a dedicated financial services or banking division that is properly researched and have proven ability to respond to training and upgrades required of its own staff to complete the tasks adequately.

With the implementation of the new framework, internal auditors may become increasingly involved in various processes, including validation and of the accuracy of the data inputs, review of activities performed by credit functions and assessment of a bank's capital assessment process.

CONCLUSION

In conclusion, keeping in view the cost of compliance for both banks and supervisors, the regulatory challenge is how to migrate to Basel II in a non-disruptive manner. Undoubtedly, it would require commitment of substantial capital and human resources on the part of both banks and the supervisors. RBI has decided to follow a consultative process while implementing Basel II norms and move in a gradual, sequential and co-coordinated manner. For this purpose, dialogue has already been initiated with the stakeholders. A steering committee comprising representatives of banks and different supervisory and regulatory departments is taking care of all issues relating to its implementation. India should continue the process of interaction with other countries to learn from their experiences through various international fora. We should not forget that India is one of the early countries which subjected itself voluntarily to the FSAP of the IMF and our system was assessed to be in high compliance with the relevant principles. With the gradual and purposeful implementation of the banking sector reforms over the past decade, the Indian banking system has shown significant improvement on various parameters, has become robust and displayed ample resilience to shocks in the economy. Therefore, there is ample evidence of the capacity of the Indian banking system to migrate smoothly to Basel II.

REFERENCES

Banking Sector In Global Perspective, Inaugural Address by Dr. Y. Venugopal Reddy, Governor, RBI at Bankers' Conference, 2004.

Basel II: New Wine in an Old Bottle by Sabyasachi Bardoloi http://www.pinnacle-sys.com, June 12, 2003, Accessed Online.

Basel II: Position Paper on the Commission's Working Document, European Association Of Craft, Small And Medium-Sized Enterprises, July 2003.

Basel II: The Path To Promoting Financial Stability In The Asian And Pacific Region? by Lene Andersen, former staff member of the Development Research and Policy Analysis Division, ESCAP, Bulletin on Asia-Pacific Perspectives 2003/04.

Comments of the Reserve Bank of India on the Third Consultative Document of the New Basel Capital Accord, RBI, Jul 30, 2003.

Conference on "Indian Banking : Global Benchmarks" September 25-27, 2003, Mumbai. Presentation by Shri AK Purwar, Chairman, FICCI's Banking and FIs Committee and Chairman, SBI.

Implementation of Basel II: An Indian Perspective, Kishori J. Udeshi Deputy Governor, Reserve Bank of India.

Much ado about nothing? An alternative view of the Basel II rules for calculating regulatory capital by Tim Giles and Alistair Milne, Cass Business School, City University, London, 4th December 2003.

Risks Management and Indian Banking: The revelations of Basel Guidelines by R Prabahar, Confederation of Indian Industry (CII), June 2004.

The New Basel Accord - Implementation Perspectives by V Subbulakshmi, ICFAI Press, July 2004.

The New Basel Capital Accord and the Future of the European Financial System, by Andrea Resti, University of Bergamo, and Rym Ayadi, Researcher Fellow, CEPS (Centre For European Policy Studies), March, 2002.

Various Bulletins and Internet uploads by RBI and IBA.

13

MANAGING EMPLOYEES IN A GLOBAL MARKETPLACE

Mary Ipe

GROWTH OF INTERNATIONAL BUSINESS

Growth-minded companies are grooming employees to succeed in an increasingly global marketplace.

The business world isn't going global, it's already there. And as growth-minded companies are climbing aboard the international business bandwagon, they are grooming their future corporate leaders to successfully manage operations on a worldwide scale. In the global arena, business deals are heavily influenced by culture, and the contrasts are multifarious. Accomplishing the same task from one country to the next may be achieved with very distinctive approaches.

Companies operating in the business world today are faced with the challenges of hiring foreign employees for their American-based organizations or sending employees abroad to work in remote facilities, open new plants, or interface with an international clientele.

For example, Ford Motor company today is managed as a global business. Activities such as product development and vehicle design are conducted on a worldwide basis rather than in regional development centres. Manufacturing and purchasing are also handled globally. Ford approaches HR on the same global basis, "moving employees from anywhere to anywhere if they're the best ones to do the job."

This paper looks at some of the pressing challenges companies face due to the impact of 'going global' on the HRM systems. The major systems (such as recruiting, selecting, training, compensating employees) are complicated by cultural and political differences in the international arena.

DOMESTIC HRM VERSUS INTERNATIONAL HRM

International human resource management (IHRM) is the process of procuring, allocating, and effectively utilizing human resources in a multinational corporation. If the MNC is simply exporting its products, with only a few small offices in foreign locations, then the task of the international HR manager is relatively simple. However, in global firms human resource managers must achieve two somewhat conflicting strategic objectives. First, they must integrate human resource policies and practices across a number of subsidiaries in different countries so that overall corporate objectives can be achieved. At the same time, the approach to HRM must be sufficiently flexible to allow for significant differences in the type of HR policies and practices that are most effective in different business and cultural settings.

This problem of balancing integration (control and coordination from HQ) and differentiation (flexibility in policies and practices at the local subsidiary level) have long been acknowledged as common dilemmas facing HR and other functional managers in global corporations. Although some argue that IHRM is not unlike HRM in a domestic setting, others point out that there are significant differences, when specifically compared with domestic HRM.

INTERNATIONAL HRM

- encompasses more functions,
- has more heterogeneous functions,
- involves constantly changing perspectives,
- requires more involvement in employees' personal lives,
- is influenced by more external sources, and
- involves a greater level of risk than typical domestic HRM.

When compared with domestic human resource management, IHRM requires a much broader perspective on even the most common HR activities. This is particularly so for HR managers operating from a MNC's headquarters (HQ). The number and variety of IHRM activities are daunting. International HR managers must deal with issues as varied as international taxation; international relocation and orientation; various other administrative services for expatriates; selecting, training and appraising local and international employees; and managing relations with host governments in a number of countries around the world.

Even when dealing with one particular HR function area such as compensation, the international HR manager is faced with a great variety of national and international pay issues. For example, while dealing with pay issues, the HQ-based HR manager must coordinate pay systems in different countries with different currencies that may change in relative value to one another over time. An American expatriate in Tokyo who receives a salary of \$100,000 may suddenly find the buying power of that salary dramatically diminished if the Japanese yen strengthens in value relative to the US dollar. A US dollar purchased 248 yen in 1985, but less than 110 yen in 2000.

In the case of fringe benefits provided to host company employees, some interesting complications might arise. For instance, it is common in the United States to provide health insurance benefits to employees and the employee's family, which usually means spouse and children. In some countries however, the term "family" may include a more extended group of relatives—multiple spouses, aunts, uncles, grandparents, nephews, and nieces. How does the firm's benefit plan deal with these different definitions of family?

A final aspect of the broader scope of IHRM is that the HQ-based manager deals with employee groups that have different cultural backgrounds. The HQ manager must coordinate policies and procedures to manage expatriates from the firm's home country (parent country nationals, PNCs), host-country nationals (HCNs), as well as third country nationals (TCNs, e.g. a French manager working for an American MNC in the firm's Nigerian subsidiary) in subsidiaries around the world.

Although such issues are important for the HQ-based manager, they are also relevant to the HR manager located in a subsidiary. This manager must develop HR systems that are not only acceptable to the host country but also compatible with company-wide systems being developed by his or her HQ-based counterpart. These policies and practices must effectively balance the needs and desires of local employees, PCNs and TCNs.

It is at the subsidiary level that the increased involvement of IHRM in the personal lives of employees becomes particularly apparent. It is not unusual for subsidiary HR managers to be involved in arranging housing, healthcare, transportation, education, and recreation activities for expatriate and local staff.

THE BUSINESS CHALLENGE

With more employees abroad, HR departments have had to tackle new global challenges. For example, senior international HR managers in eight large companies were recently asked questions such as, "What are the key global pressures affecting human resource management practices in your firm currently and for the projected future?". The three broad global HR challenges that emerged were as follows:

- Deployment: Easily getting the right skills to where they are needed in the organization regardless of geographical location;
- Knowledge and innovation dissemination: Spreading state-of-the art knowledge and practices throughout the organization regardless of where they originate; and

- Identifying and developing talent on a global basis: Identifying who has the ability to function effectively in a global organization and developing these abilities.

Recruiting in a global employee market can be both time- and capital-intensive. Many thousands of dollars go into the process of recruiting foreign workers and integrating them.

Hiring the best employees worldwide is demonstrated well by ExxonMobil's Recruiting efforts.

"ExxonMobil's recruiting efforts span the globe. Our goal is to seek out and hire from among the best and brightest employee candidates worldwide. By hiring people from diverse cultures and with diverse backgrounds and experiences we gain essential local knowledge and the breadth of perspective necessary for achieving our business objectives. We rely primarily on college recruiting to hire management, professional and technical employees. Exxon Mobil has long-term relationships with more than 100 universities in the United States and hundreds more in other countries. We employ focused diversity recruiting strategies to compete effectively for qualified, highly sought-after women and minority graduates".

This process itself can be very complex: For example, consider some of the factors you would need to address just in deciding who to deploy to an overseas assignment and how to pay that person. From a practical point of view, the issues to be addressed are:

Candidate Identification, Assessment and Selection: In addition to the required technical and business skills, key traits to consider for global assignments include: cultural sensitivity, interpersonal skills and flexibility.

Cost Projections: The average cost of sending an employee and family on an overseas assignment is reportedly between three and five times the employee's pre-departure salary; as a result, quantifying total costs for a global assignment and deciding whether to use an expatriate or a local employee are essential in the budgeting process.

Assignment Letters: The assignee's specific job requirements and associated pay will have to be documented and formally communicated in an assignment letter.

Compensation, Benefits and Tax Programmes given the vast differences in living expenses around the world.

Relocation Assistance such as maintenance of the person's home and automobiles, shipment and storage of household goods.

Family Support, Cultural orientation, language training, education assistance and emergency provisions are to be addressed before the family is shipped abroad.

TRAINING FOR INTERNATIONAL ASSIGNMENTS

Multinationals have begun to realize that to be successful in the overseas projects, they need to prepare individuals to work in international assignments. For example, Honeywell surveyed 347 managers who lived abroad or travelled regularly and found that increased training was cited as critical for executives assigned overseas. Cross-Cultural training has been found to reduce the time necessary for managers to adjust to the culture, reach a level of cultural proficiency and become effective and productive in their assignments.3

A growing number of multinationals are investing in international training and orientation. Gillette has international assignments as a part of its junior trainee program. Colgate Palmolive trains recent graduates for multiple overseas assignments.

What are the specific training needs of overseas candidates?

HRM practitioners have prescribed a 4-step training process:

- **Level 1:** Impact of cultural differences on business outcomes.
- **Level 2:** How attitudes (both positive and negative) are formed and how they influence behaviour.
- **Level 3:** Factual knowledge about the country.
- **Level 4:** Skill building such as language and adjustment skills.

Apart from these special training programs, traditional methods sometime work in tandem with job rotational practices. At IBM, for instance, development involves a series of rotating assignments that permits overseas IBM managers to grow professionally. IBM and a number of firms as Siemens, CITIBANK have established management development centres around the world to hone their skills.

International management development, apart from honing functional skills, fosters global operations by building a unifying corporate culture. The firm brings together managers from far-flung subsidiaries, steeps them in the values, corporate strategy and policies. This facilitates homogenizing the corporate culture in conformity with the corporate mission.

PERFORMANCE APPRAISAL OF INTERNATIONAL MANAGERS

The major issue relating to appraising an expatriate's performance is who actually conducts the appraisal. Evaluation by the host-country bosses or by the home-office managers. Researchers have spelt out steps for improving the expatriate appraisal process.

- Weigh the evaluation more toward the on-site manager's appraisal than toward the home-site manager's distant perceptions of the employee's performance.
- In case the home-site manager does the actual written appraisal, use a former expatriate from the same overseas location to provide background advice during the appraisal process. This would help ensure that unique local issues are considered during the appraisal process.
- Modify the performance criteria for the position to fit the overseas position and its unique characteristics. For instance' maintaining positive labour relations' might be more relevant in Brazil, where labour stability might be more prevalent than in the US.
- Give the expatriate manager credit for his insights into the functioning of the operation and their interdependencies, along with the quantifiable criteria like profits or market share.

PARAMETERS OF SUCCESS

Thus we see that International business is important to almost every business today and firms must increasingly be managed globally. Companies have pressing international HR needs, for instance with respect to selecting, training, paying and appraising its global employees.

Research has identified traits that predict success in adapting to what may be dramatically new environments.

One study identified five factors perceived by international assignees to contribute to success in a foreign assignment. They were:

- job knowledge and motivation (managerial/ organizational ability, administrative skills, and creativity)
- relational skills (respect, courtesy and tact, display of respect and kindness)
- flexibility/ adaptability(resourcefulness, ability to deal with stress, flexibility, and emotional stability)
- extra cultural openness(variety of outside interests, interest in foreign countries and openness)
- family situation (adaptability of spouse and family, spouse's positive opinion, willingness of spouse to live abroad and stable marriage).

Thus multinationals need to gear their HR practices to gel with the international business scenario. They need to face key HRM challenges as outlined below:

Staffing: Host Country demands staffing policies contrary to maximizing Profits.

Decision Making: Conflicts-Diverse Constituent groups, Complexity in Decision processes.

Communication: Interpersonal Problems due to Geographical Dispersion & Cultural Differences.

Compensation: Perceived & Real Compensation Differences.

Career Planning: Perceptions regarding value of overseas assignments, difficulties in re-entry.

Performance Management: Difference in Standards, difficulties in measuring performances across countries.

Training: Special training for functioning in international joint ventures .

REFERENCES

Soloman, C. "Today's Global Mobility" *Global Workforce*, July 1998.

Roberts, K., Kosseck. E. and Ozeki, C. "Managing the Global Workforce: Challenges and Strategies," *Academy of Management Executive*,Vol.12, No.4, 1998.

Ronen, S. Training the International assignee in I.L. Goldstein & Associates (Eds.), *Training and development in organizations*,1989.San Francisco: Jossey-Bass.

Bernardin, H.J., *Human Resource Management:* An Experimental Approach, 2003. Delhi: Tata McGraw-Hill.

Human Resource Management – ICFAI (Text)

http://www.va-interactive.com/inbusiness/editorial/hr/articles/managing.html

http://www.ceoonline.com.au/content/expert_talk/human_resource_management/1359

http://www.hrmaster.com/hr-info/hr-practice/diversity.htm

http://www.strategios.co.uk/

http://ezinearticles.com/?Cross-Cultural-Solutions-for-International-Business&id=482

14

MANAGEMENT OF HUMAN RESOURCES IN THE GLOBAL ARENA: ISSUES AND CHALLENGES

Leena Shrivastav

ABSTRACT

One major trend with implications for HRD is globalisation. It is fostered not only by technological change and the continually falling costs of communication and transport but also by the decisions of countries around the world to embrace market oriented development strategies and to open their countries increasingly to the world economy. The world is thus fast becoming one interdependent global market place.

As world-wide competition has increased, the pace of economic change has accelerated and the process of development has become less predictable. In times to come, competitiveness will be decided on a country's or an enterprise's capacity to add value to global economic products, services and processes. A key contributor in this regard is the knowledge and skills of the workforce. In fact the education and skills of the workforce will be the key competitive weapon for the 21st century. Thus compared to the past, enterprises will need to update much more regularly the skills mix of their employees to respond to the opportunities or threats created by globalisation and rapid technological change.

As intense global competition is reconfiguring the market place, enterprises need to compete by differentiating themselves from their competitors by the quality of the human systems and processes behind their products and services. This quality of the human system and processes behind its products and services is determined by the attitudes, knowledge and skills of the workforce of the enterprise. This paper examines implications of globalisation on the human capital, key transformation as a result of globalisation, shifting HR paradigm, workplace diversity in global arena and speculations on the future of HR.

INTRODUCTION

One major trend with implications for HRD is globalisation. It is fostered not only by technological change and the continually falling costs of communication and transport but also by the decisions of countries around the world to embrace market oriented development strategies and to open their countries increasingly to the world economy. The world is thus fast becoming one interdependent global market place.

As world-wide competition has increased, the pace of economic change has accelerated and the process of development has become less predictable. In times to come, competitiveness will be decided on a country's or an enterprise's capacity to add value to global economic products, services and processes. A key contributor in this regard is the knowledge and skills of the workforce. In fact the education and skills of the workforce will be the key competitive weapon for the 21st century. Thus compared to the past, enterprises will need to update much more regularly the skills mix of their employees to respond to the opportunities or threats created by globalisation and rapid technological change.

As intense global competition is reconfiguring the market place, enterprises need to compete by differentiating themselves from their competitors by the quality of the human systems and processes behind their products and services. This quality of the human system and processes behind its products and services is determined by the attitudes, knowledge and skills of the workforce of the enterprise

The role of the Human Resource Manager is evolving with the change in competitive market environment and the realization that Human Resource Management must play a more strategic role in the success of an organization. Organizations that do not put their emphasis on attracting and retaining talents may find themselves in dire consequences, as their competitors may be outplaying them in the strategic employment of their human resources.

The purpose therefore of this paper is to focus on the particular challenges to human resources (HR) and other issues produced by the changes brought on by globalisation, and its implications.

This main objective of this paper will be on implications of globalisation on the human capital, key transformation as a result of globalisation, shifting HR paradigm, workplace diversity in global arena and speculations on the future of HR.

This paper has been developed by means of a bibliographic research. Literature related to issues and challenges to HRM, was researched, from a globalization perspective. Data were qualitatively analyzed. Thereafter, a synthesis of the issue under study was prepared, in which the facts and data were compiled under several headings as per the requirement of the paper.

The paper has reflected some glimpses into the implication of globalisation on human capital, key transformation as a result of globalizations, shifting HR paradigm, and speculations on the future of HR.

IMPLICATION OF GLOBALISATION

In this sense, HRM has emerged as a response to becoming part of the global economy. Globalisation itself has several implications for HRM, particularly in smaller countries. It has been suggested that one of the main competitive challenges for human resource management is globalisation, because it entails new markets, new products, new mindsets, new competencies, and new ways of doing business. Globalisation is shrinking the world through telecommunications, travel, and information. Competition on a global scale requires a complex of centres of excellence to draw on technologies created in one location, but that are shared on a worldwide basis. These centres of excellence are marked by a high degree of specialised knowledge, access to clients, and superior presentational and technical know-how skills. The resultant effect is the rapid movement of people, information, and products to meet local needs. One study, using in-depth interviews with leading global service firms concludes that competitive advantage is gained not through the sharing of activities, but through the transfer of intangible assets from country to country.

Hewitt (1997) suggests that in the new competitive landscape, industry is no longer a given, and that globalisation is radically altering the structure, boundaries, and definitions of many industries. Forces like global access and information have made most enterprises highly transparent, and value-laden resources (particularly intellectual ones) are becoming increasingly mobile, and so sources of the sustainability of competitive advantage need a rethink. Globalisation has resulted in flatter, less bureaucratic, less hierarchical, and faster and more responsive organisations. Much is now made of the notion of strategic flexibility, which is defined as the capability of the firm to respond or proact quickly to competitive conditions. Such notions require a different type of management thinking away from the rational, linear, and the predictable to more non-linear and innovative ways of handling issues. The global competition means that HR functions that are patterned on an external market model are beginning to take shape, as they operate more as "customer-centric" businesses. A number of contemporary HR commentators are stressing the need to identify and define clearly who HR's customers are .The new technology that is part of the globalisation process will allow universal access to HR-related information, and self-service options will increase greater customer convenience and freedom.

Some further implications on the impact of globalisation of business will be towards fostering a greater understanding of cultural differences and learning to adapt those HR practices to those differences. Ulrich suggests that in the politics of global markets, western rules do not apply worldwide. This means that to be successful in the global context, executives will need to develop a set of global capabilities that are able to deal with different forms of management thought and action. professionalism in HR that are common to all or many countries.

With the increase in competition, locally or globally, organizations must become more adaptable, resilient, agile, and customer-focused to succeed. And within this change in environment, the HR professional has to evolve to become a strategic partner, an employee sponsor or advocate, and a change mentor within the organization. In order to succeed, HR must be a business driven function with a thorough understanding of the organization's big picture and be able to influence key decisions and policies. In general, the focus of today's HR Manager is on strategic personnel retention and talents development. HR professionals will be coaches, counselors, mentors, and succession planners to help motivate organization's members and their loyalty. The HR manager will also promote and fight for values, ethics, beliefs, and spirituality within their organizations, especially in the management of workplace diversity.

KEY TRANSFORMATIONS AS A RESULT OF GLOBALISATION

The dual impacts of globalisation and the information revolution on HRM can be illustrated or represented as a journey of transition and transformation from HR being a specialist function, practiced only by HR specialists to a function that fosters people development through knowledge management. It is a journey that is a response to the inevitable changing world of business that is marked by a number of key transformations.

Transformation of Organisational Structures: The first is the transformation of the structure of organisations from rigid hierarchical pyramids to dynamic adaptive entities. The key conceptual shifts in structure are from rigidity to flexibility and from fixed to fuzzy boundaries. The flattening of organisations is only part of the journey, because the emerging organisational structures will look quite different. In these new integrated network organisations, the critical variable is knowledge, and the old traditional value chain is replaced by an emerging interactive service value net. So the idea of shared intellectual capital as part of the net is born. In this new scenario HR is, not just about people, but about the interaction of people, processes, and places. In the context of the practice of human resource management the end of its journey will be global networking.

The required mindset for managing in these types of organisational structures is quite different. The question is how many executives are prepared to move from the natural, linear world of the industrial society to the highly turbulent and chaotic environment of the global information environment. The command and control paradigms are no longer relevant, yet many of organisations still operate as though they are. The kinds of management skills required in the new environment are quite different and include collaborative, self-management, referral, partnership and relationship skills

Transformation of the Work Environment: The second point is that the changing environment has moved us from linear, standardised workplaces to an on-line network world, and in many respects nowadays, work no longer requires a workplace. This has a huge impact on management - it is not longer inward looking, it has become outward looking. According to Dunphy most organisations have handled this change by having "organisational lobotomies", which is a response to crisis and not a good learning approach. We are moving from a world of downsizing, cost cutting, and restructuring to a world that is competing on flexibility, sustainable performance and investing in technology and people. This sustainable performance leads to the question of ecological sustainability - we are facing the possibility of a global ecological crisis and now is the time to discuss it publicly. We need to create a world of regeneration not exploitation.

The new gatekeepers of our workplaces in this transformed world are the information technology (IT) people. Fat is out and lean is in - the dominant paradigm now emphasises knowledge. This has implications for people - there is more pressure to deliver, and more emphasis on personal responsibility for work. This has challenges for managers - facilitation and diversity are in, and knowledge workers are different to manage, the practices of traditional people management are no longer relevant.

Transformation of the Employment Contract: This is reflected between the generations, and the third point is that the values of the new generation of employees are quite different from those of their parents (the baby boomers). The essential feature of contemporary work is job insecurity. One of the deepest sources of anxiety is that both government and private employers are intent of employing as few people as possible. There are two contributing factors to this sense of job insecurity. First a sustained high level of unemployment, particularly youth (30-40%). The other is the burden of overwork. For example in Australia the amount of unpaid overtime amounts to about 500,000 full-time jobs (Mackay, 1998). The full-time employed are running faster than ever. A direct effect of this is the institutionalisation of poverty in a proportion of household, and a wealth and a poverty class has rapidly been created.

Job insecurity has become a major factor in our values - it is now assumed that disloyalty is part of the employers' value system - so why commit to an employer who may shed you tomorrow? Performance may not be a factor in the retention of jobs, and length of service can now actively operate against employees when change comes.

Therefore employees have worked out that the contract has changed. These values are evolving when HR people are bringing in enlightened thinking. Yet no amount of enlightenment can compensate for job insecurity. Ulrich sums this up by suggesting that the old psychological contract of corporate security has now been replaced by self-security. This change has huge implications for careers. Hall (1996) predicts that the 21st century will be about Protrean rather than organisational careers. A Protean career is driven by the person, not by the organisation. A person's career will be reinvented by that person from time to time, as both person and environment will change. To an extent this is already happening, as workplaces become progressively "de-jobbed", people will have to manage their own portfolios of "desires, abilities, temperaments, and assets" in a world where everything is a market.

Transformation of the Evaluation of Human Performance: The final point is that one of the difficulties with the emerging framework is that many of our measures of performance are no longer appropriate. The technology in terms of hardware and software that is developed is now out of sink with the organisation of our workplaces and our industrial relations. The knowledge economy is forcing us to redefine our whole concept of value and value creation. Value creation is a direct result of how well knowledge is generated and applied. The knowledge economy is different and it has laws that are moving us from finite to infinite resources (Allee, 1996).

The traditional value chain is being replaced by value networks, which give us fuzzy boundaries. The old measures like RO1, and share price are becoming irrelevant, and are being replaced with new measures like customer capital, structural capital, and human capital. The traditional assets in the accounting equation are visible, knowledge on the other hand is largely invisible, and the rules are quite different. In product transaction you exchange a product for money, and you lose that product. With knowledge you give it, but you also keep it (Sveiby, 1997). Knowledge management is the process by which the organisation creates wealth from its intellectual assets or intellectual capital. Like light that has both particle and waves properties - knowledge has both object and process guidelines. The key to the creation of intellectual capital is the flow of knowledge.

One definition of knowledge management is built around a core capabilities theme, in that the firm's knowledge is built to develop and exploit the core capabilities to achieve competitive success. The point is that there is not only one model of knowledge management, and the challenges are different depending on the model. As change occurs organisations may need to shift their models.

New Management: Knowledge Management: These transformations herald in the new ways of managing people. In some organisations, intellectual capital is equally important as the traditional stockholder capital (Edvinson, 1998). Intellectual capital is about relationships, not financial objects. There has been a fundamental shift in economics in the knowledge era; the law of diminishing marginal utility has given way to the law of increasing marginal utility. Traditional accounting systems do not capture intellectual capital, because their outputs (annual reports and accounting) are history. While many companies that have downsized may be profitable now, they are anorexic, characterised by a lack of future power. Knowledge management is about nourishing the future.

Intellectual capital (future accounting) is comprised of human capital, structural capital, and customer capital, and can be seen as the process of value creation. In companies, like Skandia, the starting point for an overall measure of this was market value less stock value. The largest in the equation should be the structural capital because human capital has two legs. The key challenge is to convert human skills into structural capital because human capital is the most critical.

Transformation into Diverse Workplace: According to Thomas (1992), dimensions of workplace diversity include, but are not limited to: age, ethnicity, ancestry, gender, physical abilities/qualities, race, sexual orientation, educational background, geographic location, income, marital status, military experience, religious beliefs, parental status, and work experience. The future success of any organizations relies on the ability to manage a diverse body of talent that can bring innovative ideas, perspectives and views to their work. The challenge and problems faced of workplace diversity can be turned into a strategic organizational asset if an organization is able to capitalize on this melting pot of diverse talents. With the mixture of talents of diverse cultural backgrounds, genders, ages and lifestyles, an organization can respond to business opportunities more rapidly and creatively, especially in the global arena (Cox, 1993), which must be one of the important organisational goals to be attained. More importantly, if the organizational environment does not support diversity broadly, one risks losing talent to competitors.

This is especially true for multinational companies (MNCs) who have operations on a global scale and employ people of different countries, ethical and cultural backgrounds. Thus, a HR manager needs to be mindful and may employ a 'Think Global, Act Local' approach in most circumstances.

In order to effectively manage workplace diversity, Cox (1993) suggests that a HR Manager needs to change from an ethnocentric view ("our way is the best way") to a culturally relative perspective ("let's take the best of a variety of ways"). This shift in philosophy has to be ingrained in the managerial framework of the HR Manager in his/her planning, organizing, leading and controlling of organizational resources.

It is also necessary for many local HR managers have to undergo cultural-based Human Resource Management training to further their abilities to motivate a group of professional that are highly qualified but culturally diverse. Furthermore, the HR professional must assure the local professionals that these foreign talents are not a threat to their career advancement. In many ways, the effectiveness of workplace diversity management is dependent on the skilful balancing act of the HR manager.

SHIFTING HR PARADIGM

The HR paradigm is shifting, some may argue that it has already shifted. Moreover some people support the wide recognition by HR professionals of the importance of strategic and effective HRM to organisational success, and that responding to changing challenges and priorities for HRM will require different skills and approaches. The survey also revealed a clear vision and role for HRM, one which continues to move away from the traditional personnel administration model. Specifically the respondents indicated that HR management will be transformed from a specialised, stand-alone function to a broad corporate competency in which HR and line managers build partnerships to gain competitive advantage and achieve overall business goals .

At a more global level, Cascio (1992) identified, in a survey of senior HR managers in multi-nationals across the world, the biggest challenges in globalisation as being associated with the new global environment. These specifically are summarised below.

- Translate their basic philosophies and norms (culture) to overseas operations
- Use global awareness training for all employees, and manage expatriots to reduce their failure in multi-cultural operations.
- Managing a multi-cultural work-force by exploiting rather than suppressing cultural differences
- communicate, cultivate, and capitalise on diversity.

- Developing management talent in a global business environment
- requires first-hand experience in multiple overseas assignments.
- HR aspects of international alliances
- Blending of cultures and management styles.

While HR people themselves may have a clear vision of the shifting paradigm away from the traditional personnel administration model, the contemporary environment of HR is one of ambiguity, paradox, and contradiction, which presents some real challenges for HR professionals, their professional associations, and the organisations they represent. For instance there is the paradox of economic growth. Handy (1995) describes this paradox, which goes something like this: "...if you want to make an economy grow, first of all you have to make organisations more efficient, that is produce more with less. This can be expressed very efficiently by the formula 0.5*2*3, which means that if a company wishes to be more productive within the next five years, it should halve the number of people who are employed full-time in its core. They will be paid on average twice as well, because the company will keep the best half, producing three times as much added value. If you look around successful businesses, that is exactly what they do. In a competitive global world you have to keep on doing that. So as a result, if you want to create more full-time jobs, your economy has to grow faster than the productivity gains of your companies."

But none of the advanced economies are actually doing that. The paradox is that economic growth does not mean more jobs it means less. If this is the case then, only half the workforce will be inside organisations, and the other half will be responsible for itself, that is self-employed, or temporary/part time employed or unemployed. These are not the people who will be trained, career developed, or even pensioned as well as those who are in full time employment. Nor are they necessarily the best qualified, because most of the people who are being pushed outside the organisation do not have MBAs and other such skills. In this sense the most vulnerable will be on the outside, and we then have a truly bifurcated workforce. The evidence today is that this is happening, and this I think represents a real challenge for HR, which traditionally has always been based on the management of full-time employees. This paradox of Handy's soon becomes a contradiction when we take away jobs on the one hand through restructuring, while promising on the other to prepare people for jobs and careers, which in all reality are probably not going to be there.

Another paradox relates to the building of trust and empowerment, Fukuyama (1996) suggests that the societies that will benefit and the economies, which will grow, will be those based on trust. The reason for this is because many organisations are now delayed, spread out, scattered, and virtual, managers, increasingly, have to manage people they may seldom see. Technology in the form of the PC, Internet, and other forms of electronic media, of course, have also made this possible in other words you have to trust people out of your sight. But here is the paradox, many of our organisations and management systems have been designed on distrust, they have been designed so that people will be punished if they make mistakes, they reward the winners and punish the losers.

The realisation that it is the people who are the real capital of an enterprise has not come too early, but it is not too late for HR people to take a leading role in the new millennium. Because, unlike all other assets, it is people who have the potential to appreciate not depreciate. It is the same with the knowledge that people have. For the first time some of the basic laws of economics are now being called into question. Under the industrial economies, we had the law of diminishing returns. Now in the knowledge era this law has been reversed and enlightened economists, that are not locked into the prevailing paradigm of economic rationalism, are realising that intellectual capital is about relationships not financial objects. Similarly the people are the real capital of the country, and consequently social issues are more important than purely market-based economic issues, if a nation is to realise the best out of its human resources.

The new paradigm focuses on people and relationships. Traditional accounting systems do not capture intellectual capital because their outputs are history. So there is challenge for HR people to work with accountants and other management professionals to deliver measurement and reporting systems that reflect the future, not the past.

SPECULATIONS ON THE FUTURE OF HR

Finally let me offer some speculations on the future of HR. First, the management of knowledge requires a different approach. The current economic policies do not seem to be congruent with this approach. To put it crudely "grabbiness" and relationship building do not go together. This brings me to the importance of measurement, and the use of new measures to measure intellectual capital. These measures are critical, and need to reflect the future, not the past as traditional accounting measures have. There is enough evidence now to suggest that the short term obsession with traditional accounting measures of shareholder wealth are increasingly leading to the making of poor long term decisions about the management and development of people in organisations. This may in turn force yet another reappraisal of the new employment contract.

The knowledge economy has the potential to completely overturn the existing managerial ethos. What then are some of the specific implications for HR and the HR profession? These are as follows:

- The knowledge economy has no truck with the exclusiveness of the traditional professions. The boundaries of the past are breaking down, and knowledge boundaries are "fuzzy". Expert knowledge is no longer necessarily the domain of particular people. HR is no longer the sole domain of HR people! This means that in developing associations of HR practitioners, the membership of such associations must be inclusive rather than the exclusive like the old traditional professions like lawyers and accountants.
- The knowledge economy has changed the role of the HR professional from that of reacting and responding to managerial prerogatives to leading the changes that our organisations must make. This has profound implications for the education and professional development activities of HR people. The new competitive landscape, as a result of globalisation, means that unless HR can actually add value to organisations it is likely to be reconstituted, given the shifting paradigm discussed in this paper.
- The global economy and environment will shift the emphasis from operating HR purely from a national to an international perspective. Employees in the global network will need to develop relational and cross-national skills. Executives will need to bring together organisations with different cultures, operating with diversified work teams in flexible structures, without the benefits of the traditional linear corporate structures. The most critical HR competencies in this respect will be communication and relationship building skills.
- Finally there is also a challenge for HR on a national basis. There is no point in restricting enlightened HR practices to only a minority of the work force. If organisational and governmental policies are neglecting the needs of a large proportion of the population, no amount of good HR practicc will prevent the onset of huge social problems in the future, if the current situation is not addressed. So I suggest that HR needs to think beyond organisational sustainability, and start arguing for ecological sustainability, which in the long term is going to be the real issue to be handled in our shrinking global environment.

CONCLUSION

The role of the HR manager must parallel the needs of the changing organization. Successful organizations are becoming more adaptable, resilient, quick to change directions, and customer-cantered. Within this environment, the HR professional must learn how to manage effectively through planning, organizing, leading and controlling the human resource and be knowledgeable of emerging trends in training and employee development.

The importance of HRD cannot be overemphasised. The Chinese philosopher, Guanzi (551- 479 BC) said that

"When planning for one year, there's nothing better than planting grain, when planning for ten years, there's nothing better than planting trees, when planning for a lifetime, there's nothing better than planting men".

In his own words he explained that grain is something that is planted once and produces only a single harvest. Trees are planted once but may produce ten harvests. Men are things that are planted once but may produce a hundred harvests.

HRD contributes to economic development. It does not by itself make such growth possible.

Employers' organisations of global arena face the challenge of defining their HRD role. Their decision will affect the standing, and relevance of their organisations to enterprises and their contribution to the economic and social development of their countries in the 21st century.

REFERENCES

Allee, V. (1997). *The knowledge evolution: Expanding organisational intelligence.* Boston: Butterworth-Heinemann.

Allred, B.B., Snow, C.C., & Miles, R.E. (1996). *Characteristics of managerial careers in the 21st century.* The Academy of Management Executive. 10(4), 17-27.

Alvares, K.M. (1997). *The business of human resources.* In D. Ulrich, M.R. Losey, & G. Lake (Eds.). Tomorrow's HR management (pp. 7-17). New York: John Wiley & Sons, Inc.

Armstrong, M. (1987). Human resource management: A case of the emperor's new clothes. *Personnel Management.* 19(8), 30-35.

Beer, M., Spector, B., Lawrence, P.R., Mills, D.Q., & Walton, R.E. (1984). *Managing human assets.* New York: Free Press.

Bridges, W. (1995). *Jobshift: How to prosper in a workplace without jobs.* St Leonards, NSW: Allen & Unwin.

Butler, J.E., Ferris, G.R.,& Napier, N.K. (1991). *Strategy and human resource management.* Cincinnati: South-Western Publishing Co.

Callick, A. (1991). Waiting for the kiwi godot. *Time Magazine.* 138(24), 52-57.

Cascio, W.F. (1992). International HRM issues for the 1990s. *Asia Pacific Journal of Human Resources.* 30(4), 1-18.

Cascio, W.F. (1998). *Valuing and costing human capital.* Paper presented to the 1998 Annual Convention of the Australian Human Resources Institute in May, Canberra, Australia.

Christensen, R.N. (1997). *Where is human resources?* In D. Ulrich, M.R. Losey, & G. Lake (Eds.). Tomorrow's HR management (pp. 18-24). New York: John Wiley & Sons, Inc

Crosbie, S. (1986). The future. In *Towards 2000: Proceedings of the 1986 Personnel Management Conference for the Asia-Pacific Region.* Auckland: Institute of Personnel Management New Zealand.

Dunphy, D. (1998). *The nature of work.* Paper presented to the 1998 Annual Convention of the Australian Human Resources Institute in May, Canberra, Australia.

Edvinson, L. (1998) *The Skandia corporate story.* Paper presented to the 1998 Annual Convention of the Australian Human Resources Institute in May, Canberra, Australia.

Fletcher, H. (1986). The future organisation. In *Towards 2000: Proceedings of the 1986 Personnel Management Conference for the Asia-Pacific Region.* Auckland: Institute of Personnel Management New Zealand.

Fombrun, C.J., Tichy, N.M., & Devanna, M.A. (1984). *Strategic human resource management.* New York: Wiley.

Ford, W. (1998). *Creating future organisations.* Paper presented to the 1998 Annual Convention of the Australian Human Resources Institute in May, Canberra, Australia.

Fukuyama, F. (1996). *Trust: The social virtues and the creation of prosperity.* The Free Press.

Gilbertson, D., and Fogelberg, G. (1991). Do New Zealand HRM staff have sufficient power and influence? *Asia Pacific Human Resource Management.* 29(1), 55 - 59.

Gowler, D. and Legge, K. (1986). Personnel and paradigms: Four perspectives on the future. *Industrial Relations Journal.* 17(3), 225-235.

Guest, D. (1987). Human resource management and industrial relations. *Journal of Management Studies 24(5),* 503-521.

Hackman, K. (1998).). *The nature of work.* Paper presented to the 1998 Annual Convention of the Australian Human Resources Institute in May, Canberra, Australia.

Hall, D.T. (1996). Protean careers of the 21st century. *Academy of Management Executive.* 10(4), 8-15.

Hall, D.T., & Mirvis, P.H. (1995). *New styles of management: career builders or career blockers.* Paper presented at the 1995 Work and Family Conference in April, New York, USA.

Handy, C. (1996). The white stone: Six choices. *London Business School Business Strategy Review.* 7(1), 1-8.

Hewitt, G. (1997). Corporate strategy and human resources: New mindsets for new games. In D. Ulrich, M.R. Losey, & G. Lake (Eds.). *Tomorrow's HR management* (pp. 39-47). New York: John Wiley & Sons, Inc.

Hitt, M.A., Keats, B.W., and DeMarie, S.M. (1998). Navigating in the new competitive landscape: Building strategic flexibility and competitive advantage in the 21st century. *The Academy of Management Executive. 12(4),* 22- 42.

Institute of Personnel Management New Zealand (1994). *Human resources priorities for competitive advantage.* Auckland: The IPM Survey Report

Kaplan, R.S., & Norton, D.P. (1996). *The balanced scorecard: Translating strategy into action.* Boston, Massachusetts: Harvard Business School Press.

Mackay, H (1997). *Generations: Baby boomers, their parents and their children.* Sydney: Macmillan.

Moore, K., and Birkinshaw, J. (1998). Managing knowledge in global service firms: Centres of excellence. *The Academy of Management Executive*. 12(4), 81-92.

Podder, N., & Chattergee, S. (1998). *Sharing the national cake in post reform New Zealand: Income inequality trends in terms of income sources*. Social Policy and Research Centre, Massey University, Palmerston North New Zealand.

Porter, M. (1997). *Strategy and human resource management.* Keynote Address to the IPD National Conference , October, Harrogate, United Kingdom.

Ransom, S.W.N., (1966). Background of personnel management. In G. Hanley (Ed.). *Personnel Management in New Zealand.* (pp 9-21). Wellington: Sweet and Maxwell (NZ) Ltd.

Rudman, R.S. (1998). *Beyond human resources management: What comes next?* Paper presented to the 1998 World Congress on Human Resources Management, July, Caracas, Venezuela.

Stablein, R., and Geare, A. (1993). Human resource management in New Zealand: Profession and practice. *Asia Pacific Journal of Human Resources, 31*(2), 26-38.

Storey, J. (1987). Developments in the management of human resources: an interim report. *Warwick Papers in Industrial Relations*, No 17, IRRU, School of Industrial and Business Studies, University of Warwick.

Sveiby, K.E. (1997). *The new organisational wealth: Managing and measuring knowledge-based assets.* San Francisco: Berrett-Koehler Publishers, Inc.

Tyson, S. (1985). Is this the very model of a modern personnel manager? *Personnel Management.* April, 22- 25.

Ulrich, D. (1997). *Human resource champions.* Michigan: Harvard Business School Press.

15

SUCCESSION PLANNING AND LEADERSHIP DEVELOPMENT IN A GLOBAL ECONOMY: THE INDIAN EXPERIENCE

V.V. Ramani, Nandita Sethi and Bala Kiran

ABSTRACT

In a competitive global economy, where geographic boundaries seem to be speedily disappearing and where competition for managers is growing rapidly, a major challenge faced is, how do you attract, develop and retain your key executives? The answer probably lies in an effective and visible commitment to succession planning and leadership development. While leadership development is recognized and well used as a tool, succession planning is still a latent weapon not fully exploited. Succession planning is - identifying and preparing the right people for the right jobs. Although it is applicable at all levels, the challenges however are the greatest at the key levels. Without proper, succession planning, organizations may find their key positions left open for long periods of time thus escalating recruitment costs, and delays in strategic decision making for the future.

This paper looks at the use of leadership development and succession planning as tools for fostering the developmental activities of organizations. It takes up the Indian experience associated with succession planning and leadership development. Many Indian companies are now beginning to appreciate the importance of succession planning especially after they have faced grave crisis.

The study takes up a few Indian cases and analyses the role and importance of succession planning & leadership development. The secondary information collected from the organizations and family business houses are analyzed and developed on a case-by-case basis. An important conclusion drawn is that most businesses are slowly moving towards being professionally managed. The bottom line however, is that there is a need for a mixture of professional approach, the basic acumen of the entrepreneur and the adaptability for change to meet the market demands

INTRODUCTION

In a changing global business scenario, to overcome the crises of finding the right person at the right place and at the right time, has become a major challenge for decision makers. Talent management therefore, has become an integral and important part of all strategic planning. Talent Management refers to identifying the employee talent, utilizing it effectively and retaining the same talent to compete with similar organizations. Talent is a competitive advantage and to manage it most Human Resource Plans use two important tools - succession planning and leadership development.

Succession planning is an on-going process, which addresses the future leadership needs. "Succession planning is not an issue of a position; you can plan for two or three years, but by that time the to-be-successor may have already left the organization; consequently it is not relevant. Instead of looking at a job to fill, organizations should profile it in terms of competencies, go to the data bank, and find whose competency profile matches the job." Succession planning is an essential part of corporate strategy. Organizations have to carry out a systematic succession planning at all levels. Choosing the right successor is not an easy job. It needs a lot of hard work and plan and at the same time processing it is the most important task. According to a report by US-based business research firm Cutting Edge, while many companies have succession plans, very few follow through with the rigorous implementation required. In fact, 70 percent of succession plans fail due to bad execution. The wise leader understands the difficulty and he will prepare himself that one-day he has to be replaced by his successor who can align the strategy for the future development of the organization.

Similarly, a strong need exists today for the development of leaders with integrity, character, and trustworthiness who are capable of leadership and management. The call for leadership development is not a new one and is felt across all sectors. The question therefore raised by most organizations is, "how do we develop the leaders, our organizations require for an uncertain future?" [1] Most experts and writers in this field express that the crises of leadership results from a lack of understanding of the nature of leadership itself. As Burns pointed out, "we know all to much about our leaders and far too little about leadership". [2] So, today the development of not just leaders, but leaders who possess strong ethical values is an important task for all societies.

This paper proposes to study succession planning and leadership development as important human resource practices for talent management in today's ever-expanding business world. The study takes up succession planning and leadership development in the context of the Indian experience through the analysis of a few corporate and family business cases. The paper is organized in six sections.

Section II studies succession planning, the practice as such and its problems. Section III analyses the Indian experience with succession planning, by a review of a few Indian cases. Section IV takes up the case of leadership development and its use as an HR practice. Section V studies a few cases of leadership development in the Indian business scenario. Section VI gives the conclusion and the main findings of the study.

SUCCESSION PLANNING

Succession planning has to ensure that the right people with the right skills are in the right place and at the right time. It can be done in three ways: role-based, individual-based and team-based. The first is about identifying key positions, the second focuses upon key people, and the last involves replacing a section of people or resources. This is possible only through the board and top management involvement. This will help to identify and nurture the talent. The transparency in this arena will make the employee to commit himself to fulfill the organizational and personal motives. The succession planning process can be a top down or bottom-up planning process.

The succession management approach should be aligned with the strategy, which is followed and also should be suitable for the future need. It should bring out a balance between the individuals and the organizations and should be helpful in developing the pool of talent within the organization. There is a key issue of retaining the talent in the organization, which is mainly related to the succession planning at the Mid-Management level. Mid managers play the most challenging roles in any organization. Middle managers are potentially seen as CEOs who can fit in those positions that the family businesses are looking forward. They are the vital link between the top management and the other employees. Even though they play an important role, most of the time they face the consequences related to leadership crisis.

Good leaders make a successful organization, but then it is the responsibility of the organizations to groom such leaders within its hierarchy. Liberalization, Privatization and Globalization have brought a tremendous change for the Indian family and other non-professional businesses, compelling them to become more professional and suitable to meet the international standards. Most of the family businesses across the world struggle to have succession planning in a formal way, and India is no exception. The family businesses are not realizing the contribution of the boards in the effective implementation of succession planning. The board's major contribution for succession planning is to ensure attraction of the right talent, evaluation of strategy and aiding the company in risk evaluation.

SUCCESSSION PLANNING: THE INDIAN EXPERIENCE

Today India is becoming an emerging world economy; most of the family businesses are following the global trends and taking the practice of succession planning as seriously as the rest of the world. For ex: Apollo Tyres, Apollo Hospitals, Ranbaxy, Dabur India, Murugappa Group, Birla Group, Wipro, and so on. Family run businesses earn some command and loyalty through concentrating on brand loyalty and building of culture. This brings pride, self-growth and knowledge of what is to be done in case of a mismatch. If they have to go out of the comfort zone and seek professional help, the companies have to be sure in building the social infrastructure. To build their social infrastructure the businesses have to track information, trap the roots and get in touch with the market. At the same time the organization should try to shape in the business positively, condense learning curves, and provide opportunities to enter new markets. During this process the family should have access to information, listen to key concerns, bring in a dialogue with the family members, and encourage interaction between family members. This will make the family members to become more professional. A learned professional can meet this competition with much vigor. For ex: Ajay Piramal worked for 33 yrs in 2 different multi-nationals and then stepped into his own business. This shows the strong focus on and the importance of professionalism.

According to Prof. John Ward, clinical professor and co-director, Center for Family Enterprises, Kelloggs School of Management, USA, there should be a clear cut succession plan even for family businesses, otherwise, there will be a rivalry between the kith and kin of the founder which can become a sensitive issue. Very often we can see this problem in the Indian Family Businesses, which may disturb the culture and work environment, for examples: Ambanis of Reliance Industries, Bajajs of Bajaj Auto, Nandas of Escorts, Modis of Modi Rubber and so on. Each of these families faced succession and ownership issues and found them tough to resolve.

The present sibling rivalry between Mukesh Ambani and Anil Ambani is causing lot of disturbance among the stakeholders. Similarly in the recent past a few more incidents typically like the Ambanis came into lime light. Rajan Nanda Chairman and Managing Director of Rs. 1,100-crore Escorts Ltd, and Anil Nanda were controlling stake in Goetze India Ltd. However, relations between the two brothers were under strain because of the controversy over the attempt to sell-off of a part of the stake of Escorts Ltd held in-group Company, Escorts Heart Institute and Research Centre (EHIRC). The same story repeated at Bajaj Company. Mr. Shishir Bajaj, wanted to acquire Bajaj Auto, but has not yet been able to reach a settlement with elder brother Rahul Bajaj on the valuation of his stake in the flagship Bajaj Auto.

Despite the succession problems in some of the Indian businesses, most of the professionals are coming forward to head the family owned organizations. In most of the Indian Family Businesses, the younger generations are well qualified and suitable to occupy the top positions in their organizations There are few Indian family businesses that have resolved the succession issues with better family values and brought about a professional touch. They are the Murugappa Group, Burmans of Dabur India and the new generation IT company like Wipro. A company which had problems in its succession planning, i.e., Reliance, is also discussed briefly here.

Case 1: Dabur: With the intention of manufacturing health care products, Dr. S.K. Burman set up a small business named Dabur in Calcutta in 1884, which became one of the well-known family businesses in India. It started its manufacturing plants in various places like Bihar, North East and Narendrapur. In 1936, Dabur became a full-fledged company and came to be known as "Dabur India Pvt. Ltd." After shifting the company's operations to Delhi in 1972, the company went ahead and established its Research Foundation in 1979 and became a public limited company in 1986. To compete with the international standards, with the advent of globalization, the company divided the entire flagship into three divisions- Health Care product Division, Family products division and Dabur Ayurvedic specialties Ltd. Later in 1997, it entered into the food division too. The company's established its offices and had a potential market for its products in the international markets like Europe, U.S, Africa, Middle East, Far East and Asian countries.

Today, Dabur family has entered into its 5th generation and handles all the businesses with the help of a family counsel consisting of 10 family members. This company that is worth 1,700 crore has also chosen professionals for operations. In 1998, it initiated the professionals to manage the company to compete in the international markets and to benchmark themselves with the best of companies. As a part of such an initiative Dabur promoted Mr. Sunil Duggal, who joined the company in 1995 as General Manager in Sales & Marketing (Family Product Division) as the CEO of the company in 2002. He was a professional with valuable experience who could steer the company ahead in its growth plans. While Pradip Burman (brother of G.C. Burman) is in charge of other group companies such as Ayurved and Sanat Products, London-based Sidharth Burman handles the overseas forays of the group.

It is essential for family businesses to acknowledge the distinction between ownership and management for which they require good corporate governance.

Based on the expert opinion, Dabur initiated good corporate governance and transparency in actions of the management. It provides a strong bond of trust to the Company's stakeholders and has constantly avoided an arbitrary decision-making process. It took initiatives to make the board fully professional by reducing of the members from 16 to 10, and also the number of promoters and independent directors on the board, and by encouraging more professionals. It meets all corporate governance code requirements and is finally governed through Board committees for Audit, Remuneration, Shareholder Grievances, Compensation and Nominations to groom the young talent within. Dabur also initiated the Young Managers Development Programme (YMDP). This is a clear example to indicate that Dabur has taken steps to develop the middle manager's skills and promote within for the hierarchal positions.

Case 2: Murugappa Group: The Murugappa Group's success is driven by its strong belief in the power of people. This is a team of ordinary people aspiring to do extraordinary things. It is one of the first Indian corporates to begin the process of transformation from being a family-owned business to a professionally managed organization.

Deewan Bahadur, who started the financial business or stock broking called Vellavan, started this Family Business way back in 1930's. The successors expanded and started new businesses and at present they have a total of 25 business units in 38 manufacturing locations spread over 11 Indian states and grown to a multiple thousand crore business. There are different products that consists bioproducts, confectionery, bicycles, steel tubes, chains, sanitary ware, etc. in the manufacturing sector and mutual funds, vehicle financing, stock brokerage, in the financial sector and sugar, fertilizers, pesticides, rubber, tea and coffee plantations in the agro sector. Family ownership of the companies ranges from 34% to 100%. There was a clear-cut strategy for leadership and control driven by values i.e. one leader for the family matters and other for the business. If there was a family crisis, the whole family would join and face the crisis together, irrespective of their prior commitments.

In 1999, for the first time the Murugappa Group consisting of seven companies officially formed the Murugappa Corporate Board (MCB) with a mix of both family members and independent directors. The various businesses were entrusted to competent professional CEOs from outside the family. The group planned to change its strategies involving succession, governance and leadership issues at a time when operational management had switched over for the first time from family members to professional non-family members in 1999. The professionals associated with Murugappa Group are Mr. P.S. Pai, Dr. Marti Subrahmanyam (Marti), Mr. Natalino Duo (Natalino) and so on.

The new initiative of promoting within their own organization led the HR to take up an innovative program on business leadership to encourage the employees to develop their talent and skills and to identify the potential leaders within the organization. The philosophy of the Business Leadership Program is to groom the business leaders, for which they adopted a new approach that involves conceptual learning, reflective learning, personal insight into one's own beliefs, values, attitudes and behavior, action-learning and internalization. Another initiative taken by the group is Competency Development Program, which will help employees to develop their careers at different stages. The Murugappa group has evolved a unique process, i.e., a team of 100 young managers will be under one director, out of them, at least for two or three highly talented managers will be identified to be mentored by their director . In this process, HR will get benefit and at the same time it will establish a channel for independent directors to seek out information. Competency Development Programs would help people to identify and work on areas that are critical to the group's competitive advantage - globalization, innovation, managing diversity, greater self-awareness and managing change. Processes of Succession Planning, Campus Relationship Program and Management Trainee Scheme cater to the employee's career at different stages in the Murugappa group. This process is possible only in those organizations that have an open culture of encouraging middle managers to interact with independent directors irrespective of hierarchy.

Case 3: Wipro: Apart from the manufacturing sector, the service sector is also striving for the leadership development within. One of the frequently debated topics in the recent years has been the lack of leadership skills among the middle managers in the IT industry. It forms an essential part in the corporate strategy in most of the IT organizations. Sanjay Mandik, HR expert with Emerson Network, has said, "Mid-level employees are often de-motivated and have high attrition rate, as a result of lack of good opportunities and challenges." This is the issue faced very commonly by most IT sector. This aspect has importance as most organizations have started adopting a succession planning policy to meet future leadership requirements.

Wipro Technologies is the global, technology services division of Wipro Ltd., with over two decades of IT experience. It is a $711 million company and delivers an integrated, one-stop solution for quality software to clients like Compaq, Nokia etc.

At Wipro, the succession-planning program is called Talent Review and Planning (TRP), and it is the most critical part of the organization's leadership building and talent management process that helps to identify the talent for emerging roles in the organization. Accountability and constant attention are the essential factors for the talent review process. According to Mr. Bijay Sahoo, Vice-President and Head of HR, Wipro Technologies, "The purpose of the talent review is to figure out the talent required to implement the business strategy and constantly strengthen the talent pool." The top management is also interested in reviewing the talent that makes the HR department to bring in initiatives related to talent issues. Specific programs that are designed for leadership development and succession planning at Wipro Technologies includes the New Leaders Programme, Wipro Leaders Programme, Business Leaders Programme and Strategic Leaders Programme for different leadership positions that an employee will assume in the organization.

In the Talent Review Process, everybody from the middle to the top level, including CEOs are critically analyzed and then the suitable employees who can take up certain positions between 1-3 years are identified. Talent Review and Planning will take place between the Strategic Business Unit (SBU) Heads and SBU HR Heads for the top three levels of their business, and then the strategy will be implemented and reviewed. When they conduct an internal talent review they can assess as to how many internal members are capable enough to occupy these positions. This provides an insight into the success of the talent review program and at the same time, the percentage of retention levels and its effectiveness. Apart from the above insights, this program helps in creating top class leaders.

Training plays an important role in nuturing the employees to become the future leaders. Here Wipro adopts the Leader Development strategy and designs a suitable training program and implements it. Sunder Rajan, general manager, HR & administration, ICS said, "The training could be through internal programs or on-the-job (local as well as global) to gain cross-functional or cross-geographical exposure for better maturity of the expertise that would enhance the confidence level of the person". Then there's just-in-time succession, which maps existing competencies of the staff to fill up important positions.

Case 4: Reliance: In 1958, Dhirubhai H. Ambani founded Reliance Industries Ltd (RIL). Initially, Reliance was into commodity trading and export. Later from 1977, the company expanded its operations. The activities of the group range from Exploration and Production (E&P) of oil and gas, refining and marketing, petrochemicals (polyester, polymers, and intermediates) to power, telecom and infocom initiatives. With its vast expansion the company soon became India's largest business house with total revenues of over Rs. 99,000 crore (US$ 22.6 billion), cash profit of Rs. 12,500 crore (US$ 2.8 billion), net profit of Rs. 6,200 crore (US$ 1.4 billion) and exports of Rs. 15,900 crore (US$

3.6 billion). Today, the products of RIL are exported to more than 100 countries all over the world.

With the efforts made by the company to promote its business it was awarded the 'Best Managed Company' in India in 2003. According to a global survey conducted by Price waterhouse Coopers in 2004, RIL was the only Indian company in the list of global companies that create value for their shareholders. Also it is listed in Forbes Global 400 best big companies and FT Global 500 world's largest companies. The company emerged 'India's biggest wealth creator' in the private sector over a 5-year period in a study by Business Today - Stern Stewart in 2004. With globally competitive capital and operating cost positions, Reliance Group was dominating the rapidly growing Indian market deriving over 80% of its revenues from the domestic market but the situation changed with the feud between the two brothers Anil Ambani (Anil) & Mukesh Ambani (Mukesh) over the ownership of RIL.

In many of the family-run businesses, lack of clear succession planning often leads to a situation where the personal relationships of the members are at stake, which also has a negative impact on the listed companies and also leads to the erosion in shareholder value. This was the situation of the Ambani brothers. The first hunch of a possible rift was the absence of Anil Ambani at the launch of Reliance Infocomm by his brother Mukesh in 2002. Mr. Mukesh had undermined evocation of a rift. Speaking to a business magazine in August 2003, he said: "We have perfect understanding. For us, it is really the goals that matter. Many times, I have not been there at board meetings or AGMs and I think people make too much of it. Our culture is, as papa (Dhirubhai Ambani) always used to say, kaam is more important than formalities. For us the end result is most important". However, this understanding was under strain when six of the 12 directors of Reliance Energy resigned from the board. The stock market reacted by hammering down the Reliance Energy (managed by Mr. Anil Ambani) stock by 13 per cent compared to the 8 per cent fall in the Reliance Industries (managed by Mr. Mukesh Ambani) stock since November 18.

This succession dispute between these brothers has given rise to several uncertainties regarding the Reliance Energy Project. Since institutional investors —domestic and international—hold nearly 40 per cent of the equity, their perception on the fallout of this succession battle will drive the valuation of the Reliance Energy stock in the near term. After several weeks of fight for the ownership of the major private business house, the board of RIL gathered to decide over this issue. However, the board failed to produce reconciliation. In spite of this, the older brother Mukesh announced that the company would spend $666 million on a share buyback to revive its stock.

The case explains that the Indian corporate sector is more or less promoter driven wherein the professionals have less control. Commenting on this Mr. U.K. Chaudhary, a senior Supreme Court advocate and a top corporate lawyer said, "A professional can never become a Chairman unless the ownership is divested from management". Further more investors are hoping that this ownership issue in this family business will drive regulators who have been silent to enforce reporting rules and corporate governance guidelines more vigorously. The split between the brothers would also pressure other family businesses to resolve their own issues. This case is a lesson for Indian business houses on how a lack of proper succession planning can shake big time corporates.

LEADERSHIP DEVELOPMENT

Business leaders need to have the important qualities of strategic thinking and planning. They need to adapt themselves to the changing global environment. They should be aware of their competitors, what challenges their organization faces and how to leapfrog those challenges. Leaders have to determine the management philosophy, goals and culture and also adopt a suitable management style. They should generate new ideas, encourage new experiments and at the same time should not control or command the employees but rather support them to work with passion to achieve the organization's goals and objectives. They should be able to keep the organization on the cutting edge. In short, they should play an important role to transform their companies from good to great. Therefore developing effective leadership becomes the most important and challenging task for an organization.

Good leaders make a successful organization, but then it is the responsibility of the organizations to groom such leaders within its hierarchy. A survey by McKinsey & Co. of 6000 executives at 50 large US corporations revealed that only 3% strongly agreed that their organizations develop talent quickly and effectively. Lean staffing, intense pressure from competition and the nitty-gritty's of day-to-day operations, make it difficult to focus on leadership development, although it is a well-known fact that for sustainable and profitable growth, strong leadership is a must. The CEO of GE, Jack Welch was known for his devotion to developing leaders and the results talk for themselves. GE's sales were up from US$ 28 bn in 1981 to US $132 bn in 2001, a compound annual growth rate of 14%.

Developing a good senior management team by fostering leadership skills is not only important for building current value, but also for increasing shareholder value when the business is sold (as most buyers want to see a strong management team that can execute without the CEO/owner). Moreover, most businesses and

CEOs get stuck with each other simply because there is no one else who has the skills to run it. This does not allow businesses to breathe fresh air.

As against the old philosophy accepted in most leadership development programs, which implicitly believes that leadership rests in individuals, a new concept of leadership is emerging which, is based on bottom-up transformation with emphasis on shared power and community building (Huey, 1994). Although the description of this new concept of leadership may differ, there are at least three common themes: shared leadership, leadership as relationship, and leadership in community. Shared leadership is collective, or group-cantered with the assumption that all of us have leadership qualities that can be pooled and drawn upon as needed, when working with others on vital issues. The second theme, leadership as relationship revolves around the idea of a network of fluid relationships and is built on the concepts of empowerment, participation, partnership, and service. The third theme, leadership in community, envisions community as the conceptual setting in which the leadership relationship takes place. A similar theme brought about in 'Communities of Commitment' (Kofman & Senge, 1993), represents a shift from competition and self-centeredness to a model for organizing a haven for the expression of new ways of relating, the promotion of important values such as trust, commitment, sharing, etc.

Thus a number of approaches to leadership development exist, from the classical' intellectual construct'- traditional classroom based instructions guided by academics to the action –oriented 'experimental learning' mechanism. Some of the Indian experiences with leadership development are discussed below with the help of a few cases.

LEADERSHIP DEVELOPMENT: THE INDIAN EXPERIENCE

While leadership development styles differ from organization to organization, they more or less involve the same steps. First of all, the organization should make leadership development a priority. This implies empowering the managers to assume real responsibility, take risks, and, also probably, do things differently than the CEO would. Secondly for the success of any Leadership Development Program it is necessary to identify the right managerial candidates who have the attributes to be effective leaders. Having the wrong person in the leadership positions implies opportunity costs, profitability may suffer, potential opportunities may be overlooked and most important, capable employees may not get the opportunity to develop in that leadership position. Then, it should be realized that daily routine experiences would not teach anything new to the upcoming leaders. It is the unusual, rare, 'hairpin curves or the stomach turning drops that forced them to look at themselves and their context through a different lens'. [3] Such opportunities should be provided for the potential leaders. Constructive and honest feedback should be given to the executives being groomed so that they get aware and alert of the blind spots. Finally, training can teach needed skills and competencies but it is the real world classroom that allows a manager to learn how to really use them. So the best way to encourage leadership is by involving them in the actual development and growth process of the organization. A few Indian experiences with leadership are taken up below. Most of these and the above cases show that succession planning and leadership development go hand in hand.

Case1: Infosys: Infosys, the most admired company in India, is a global leader in consulting and IT services, partners with global 2000 companies to provide system integration, application development, product engineering and consulting services. There are 25,000 employees spread over 30 offices worldwide. The company started its operations in 1981 in India and its first global operations begun in U.S in 1987. It is the first Indian company to get registered in the NASDAQ. It received its ISO 9001/TickIT quality certification and ISO 140001 certification for Environmental Management System. The present CEO is Nandan Nilekani.

The chief mentor of the company Mr. Narayana Murthy and also the founder of Infosys, paved the way for a professional succession planning and leadership development approach in the organization. For this they have established the Infosys Leadership Institute (ILI) in October 2001, in Mysore. The goal of the institute is to develop global leaders to compete efficiently with the future challenges of the organization. The leadership development program starts with defining leadership competencies, which exist in the context of the organization's vision and its core values. These competencies have been categorized along four broad dimensions i.e., Work, People, Technology & Business. Each of these is further amplified into smaller operational elements like, for eg under People category, the aspects gauged are (i) Developing leaders and (ii) Interpersonal effectiveness. These competencies are identified through a process of debate and discussion with an initial competency set developed through benchmarking studies of formal leadership development system across the world.

The operational elements of leadership development are called the nine pillars of the model. The nine pillars model is a unique leadership development model. Each pillar has its own uniqueness in the development of leadership competencies at the individual level. The individuals are free to choose one or more of these pillars for his/her own development. Participation in most of these is optional except for the 360-degree feedback, which is the starting point of the leadership journey.

The 360-degree feedback is used as a basis to prepare individual personnel development plans which will guide the individual to acquire new skills and helps to enhance the existing skills. The second pillar- development assignments- provides an opportunity for high potential employees to understand the different functions by providing job rotation and cross-functional assignments to gain skills outside his core area of experience. The third pillar is the culture workshops, which enable the participants to understand the culture of Infosys, by interacting within themselves, thereby empowering them to adhere and refine the Infosys culture. The fourth pillar helps to build one-on-one relationships, which may help to share and transfer their knowledge and experience thereby mentoring for leadership. The fifth pillar is a process where workshops are held and employees learn through interventions related to leadership. The next pillar provides a formal and informal feedback on behavioural aspects, from individuals with whom the employees interact. The next one is systemic process learning. Here the employees view the whole system comprising various interacting sub-systems and learn through plans for improvements in these systemic processes. The next pillar, Community Empathy, is the most important one, which talks about the social responsibility of each employee and creates opportunities for employees to take up social causes outside Infosys. In the final pillar, Action Learning, they will understand all the above-mentioned pillars by taking on a real time problem and trying to resolve it by formulating plan and strategies along with their teams. This model, thus assumes that learning processes differ from person to person and so caters to multiple learning modes. The process starts with the identification of high potential employees who then have one faculty member of ILI assigned to him who guide and mentor him to resolve real business issues

The leadership development model was further refined to improve its integration with succession planning across various levels of the company. For a good succession planning the organization has adopted a three-tier model in the company. Tier 1 consists of a business leader including heads of business units. To nurture the top-level leaders each tier-1 employee will be under 1 internal board of directors. Tier 2 and Tier 3 are hi-potential candidates and are trained through external development programs in India and abroad. This talent pool performance will be monitored and later they fill up the emerging vacancies in the company. This is a good management strategy to motivate and retain the best talent within.

Case 2: Tata Consultancy Services: Tata Consultancy Services (TCS) offers end-to-end strategy consulting and system integration services to Fortune 500 clients across 55 countries. With over 100 offices in 32 countries, TCS employs 24,000 consultants and has 100,000 man-years of experience. With its collaboration with industry and academia and its partnership with the global technology leaders, TCS could gain in-depth knowledge about the global economy. TCS follows a continuous quality-enhancement process, and 15 of its delivery centres in India have been assessed at SEI-CMM Level 5. All of TCS's major development centres are ISO 9001:2000 certified, and its quality management system is also ISO 9001:2000 compliant. TCS leverages its expertise in its service practices—e-Business, Application Development and Maintenance, Architecture and Technology Consulting, Engineering Services, e-Security, Large Projects, Quality Consulting, and Infrastructure Development and Management.

At TCS it is strongly felt that leaders need to possess multi-functional and multi-location experience and they should exhibit very high levels of physical, emotional and intellectual energy. As the two major activities of an organization are to develop good recruitment and retention processes for the employees, hence, the first step at TCS is to identify people with potential within or outside TCS. To retain the talent, there exists a common Training Centre for the TATA group- The Tata Management Training Centre in Pune. This centre helps to identify high performers through its leadership training programmes. The training center has also implemented the assessment centre model, which will closely look at the critical roles and functions of the employees. This way the organization tries to nurture the talent within the organization and also helps in employee career development. It analyzes and tracks the potential leaders in the group and harnesses their abilities for the group's progress. The centre also provides training and classroom facilities for non-Tata companies. Further as a process of developing the leadership qualities among the employees the Training Centre has to assist the employees in developing six major characteristics. They are: Functional competence; People management ability; Delivery capability; Conceptual skills; Competence with external agencies and Character/courage of conviction. At the organization level this has meant empowering people, building excellence and giving employees an ownership approach.

Case 3: ICICI: "The future will belong to those who can operate with extreme agility in the face of very high levels of ambiguity" K.V. Kamath MD and CEO, ICICI Bank."

ICICI Bank, the second largest bank in India offers a wide range of banking and financial services to corporate and retail customers through a variety of delivery channels and specialized subsidiaries and affiliates in the areas of investment banking, life and non-life insurance, venture capital and asset management. In October 2001, the Boards of Directors of ICICI and ICICI Bank approved the merger of ICICI bank with two of its wholly owned retail finance subsidiaries, ICICI Personal Financial Services Limited and ICICI Capital Services Limited. In 2002, ICICI Bank set up its international banking group to cater the cross-border needs of its clients and leverage on its domestic banking strengths to offer products internationally. ICICI Bank currently has subsidiaries in the UK and Canada, branches in Singapore and Bahrain and representative offices in the U S, China, UAE and Bangladesh. As on 2004, the bank's assets value was around Rs.146, 214 crore and profit after tax valuing at Rs. 1,391 crore. Substantial investments in technology right from the early years have resulted in systems that are today a competitive advantage for ICICI

The ICICI grooms its employees to become the future leaders. The management strongly believes in the principles of winning organizations, which have a surfeit of individuals who welcome the change and face it boldly. ICICI has created a lot of value in its e-platforms by empowering young (25-26-year olds) managers. It believes in the philosophy that if the employees are groomed with the leadership qualities and are empowered they would perform effectively and efficiently thus bringing success to the organization. ICICI has built a strong brand value in the banking and financial services sector due to its interpersonal skills.

The bank has overcome the barrier of glass ceiling and has moved on to nurture the women talent and has provided an opportunity to them to reach the top slot. With its efforts made to nurture the women employees it has grown to become the highest women recruiting company in the Indian Financial Services. The best examples in this regard are Lalita Gupte and Chanda Kochhar.

Women generally follow transformational style of leadership that is seen as a driver for organizational success. Lalita D. Gupte, Joint Managing Director, ICICI Bank brought the sea change in the private banking system. She made this possible through transforming her own employees and maintaining customer relationship and providing value to the stakeholders. For her successful endeavours in the corporate world she has received numerous awards Moreover, she was also listed as most powerful women in business by *Fortune* magazine. Ms. Chanda Kochhar is the Executive Director of ICICI Bank and Chairperson of ICICI Home Finance Company. Ms. Kochhar also heads the entire retail banking business of ICICI Bank. Apart from her distinguishing career in the retail banking industry, Ms. Kochhar, during her tenure of 20 years with the Bank, has held many key positions in Infrastructure, Project and Corporate finance divisions of the Bank. During her tenure as head of retail banking business, ICICI Bank has grown many folds and the Bank today has established itself as a clear "Leader" in the financing business. In the process of building this successful retail unit, Ms. Kochhar had to overcome many challenges. With her determination and perseverance, the whole Indian Banking industry has seen some breaking initiatives in the retail banking. Under her leadership the Bank has also won global recognition in the form of various awards including "Excellence in Retail Banking Award for Best Retail Bank in India" consecutively for the last three years and the "Best Multi Channel Strategy – 2003

CONCLUSION

When organizations moved from the founder dominated or family-owned to the professionally managed organizations there would be so many variants like culture conflicts, which one could overcome through understanding the emotional relationships between founders and employees. The basic skills required by the Indian family businesses to excel in the global arena are: Ensure maintaining right talent attracting professionals from outside and retain professional managers within, allow for transparency within the family, change vision of family business, and training them to provide value to shareholders.

The question is not whether companies have to hire professionals to succeed and stay afloat. The bottom line is a need for a mixture of professional approach, the basic acumen of entrepreneur and the adaptability for change to meet the market demands. The best example is Intel Inside board that delegates the rest of the work to other committees and concentrates on the above-mentioned issues and focuses on execution. There should not be anymore ceremonial boards that are always kept in dark. Today's business requires transparency and corporate governance. The family can own the stakes of the company but that does not automatically grant them right to manage the company. The stumbling blocks for the family businesses are their resistance to change, less consistency and ad hocism. Expert opines that only qualified family members should be engaged in the management of the business and there should be clear roles and rules of engagement for both owner-managers and professional managers. Above all, the perception of fairness should reign, which is true in the case of a few like Murugappa Group and Dabur India. Just as the family business tends to view the outsider professional with suspicion, the professionals on their part does not settle for a family managed company that easily. Brought up in a broader outlook, many of them dislike any hierarchical attitude or unprofessional approach of some of the family concerns. You need professional managers – from within the family or hired - who can take objective decisions to the overall benefit of the group.

NOTES

1. Dr Delia J Haak, (2002) "Leadership", Soderquirst Center for Business Leadership and Ethics.
2. Burns, J M (1978), "Leadership" Harper and Row, N.Y
3. The Daniel Group Ltd., 2002.

REFERENCES

A.V. Vedpurishwar, "Strategic issues in Succession Planning", "Talent Management: Concept and Cases", ICFAI Books.

Acharya, Ranjan," Wipro's way", Praxis Business line, June 2002

Barrett Jim, (1998) "Total Leadership", The Professional Paperback Series.

Byham, William, C, "Taking Your Succession Plan into the 21st century" http//www.ddiworld.com

CNBC live telecast on "Lessons on Family Business"

Huey, J (1994, Feb,21), The newpost-heroic leadership, Fortune, pp 42-50

Kamath, K.V," Leading in turbulent times", Praxis Business line, June 2002.

Kofman, F and Senge, P. M(1993), Communities of commitment: The heart of learning Organizations". Organizational Dynamics, 22 (2), 5-23

Piramal, Gita (2000), "Business Maharajas."

Ranjekar, Dilip, The Leading Within", Praxis Business line, June 2001, pg 15

Steeves, Rosie & Denroche, Barbara, Ross, "Using Succession Planning to Transform Organisations", The Centre for Exceptional Leadership, 2003.

V.V. Ramani & K. Guruswami (ed), (2003), "Talent Management: Concept and Cases", ICFAI Books.

V.V. Ramani (ed) (2004), "Effective Leadership: Concept and Cases" ICFAI Books.

V.V. Ramani (ed)(2004), "Leadership in today's World", ICFAI Books

V.V. Ramani, (ed) (2004), "Effective Talent Management", ICFAI Books.

www.businessweek.com

www.businessworldindia.com

www.dabur.com

www.directorship.com, "Leadership: Successful CEO succession planning"

www.icicibank.com

www.infosys.com

www.lessonsinexcellence.com

www.murugappa.com

www.sify.com

www.tata.com

www.tcs.com

www.wipro.com

MANAGING WORK FORCE DIVERSITY IN MNCs: A CASE STUDY OF MONSANTO INDIA LTD.

Neelam Rani Suneja and Shailja Verma

The most significant challenge in today's business world is the complex problem of diversity. As soon as a firm enters the exciting new world of international business, the sudden impact of diversity is almost challenging. Every foreign market is different- it's people are different, its whole environment is different. Firms entering a new market must develop new business techniques for dealing with that market's unique diversity or fail. When organizations become cross border entities, cross cultural factors start affecting every aspect of the business. Whether multicultural team or business interaction is the variants of diversity affects the business decisions. To achieve excellence in managing diversity, the global companies must strive to create a work place where the employees can contribute the best that they have.

The present study is an attempt to discuss the concept of work force diversity, elements of work force diversity, cultural diversity, elements & dimensions of cultural diversity.

The Present case study evaluates the practices of management of work force diversity and dimensions of cultural diversity at Monsanto India Ltd.

The research methodology designed to study the present problem comprises the data collection of both types' i.e. primary & secondary data. Primary data is collected from a sample size of fifty employees including one country manager, two regional managers with position of Regional Coordinator & forty seven employees at branch level with position of executive/managerial/supervisory category from all disciplines by using the technique of structured questionnaire from employees at branch level & schedules from Regional Coordinators & Country manager. The results are presented in pie charts & graphs. The data regarding the elements of work force diversity is obtained from the questionnaire designed on the basis of Hofstede's & Trompenaar's diversity dimensions.

Diversity is defined as a variety of similar & different characteristics among people including age, gender, race, religion, national origin, physical ability, sexual orientation, thinking style, background & all other attributes that make each person unique.

Work force diversity is an approach to understand the new work force in terms of its size, gender, race/ minorities, physically challenged, age, education, work experience, productivity, rural-urban background, location, culture etc.

The term culture refers to the result of human interaction. It is acquired knowledge that people use to interpret, experience & generate social behaviour. This knowledge forms values, creates attitudes & influences behaviour. Culture can affect technology transfer, managerial ideologies, business-government relations, managerial attitudes, & trying to do international business without prior cross-cultural training is a recipe for disaster.

Each culture is composed of cultural universals. The major cultural universals are language, religion, material elements, customs, temporal factors, societal organizations, status, education, age, gender & common interest. Culture refers to the sum total of values, beliefs, morals, laws & customs acquired by humans as members of a particular society. A global organization needs to adapt its business practices to the cultures of different regions where it operates. The management of diversity is a composite function involving:

- Managing cultural diversity
- Managing individual diversity & work force diversity.

Different cultures value different aspects of credibility more than others. Dutch researcher Geert Hofstede (Hofstede, 1980) developed four dimensions of culture to explain how & why people from various cultures behave differently. Hofstede's well known four dimensions of culture are;

Power Distance: Power distance is the extent to which workers accept the idea that people in an organization accept that power is distributed rightfully. The affect to this dimension can be measured in a no. of ways. Organisation in high power distance tends to be more centralized whereas low power distance is more decentralized. In high power distance cultures, workers follow orders as a matter of course.

Uncertainty Avoidance: The extent to which people feel threatened by ambiguous situations and have created beliefs & institutions that try to avoid these.

Individualism: The tendency of people to look after themselves and their immediate family only. Individualism is the philosophy by which workers think of themselves fist as individuals and give priority to their own interests.

Masculinity: Masculinity refers to the extent to which the dominant values in a culture are success, money and things. Work culture with low masculinity index (high femininity) reflects great importance on cooperation, a friendly atmosphere, and employment security.

Trompenaar developed five relationship orientations that address the ways people behave with each other.

Universalism and Particularism: Universalism is the tendency to apply same ideas and practices everywhere without modification where as particularism is the situation in which ideas and practices are applied with modification as dictated by circumstances.

Individualism and Communitarianism: Individualism refers to people regarding themselves as individual & giving priorities to their own interests whereas communitarianism refers to people regarding themselves as a part of the group.

Neutral and Emotional: Neutral culture is tendency to keep the emotions in check where as in emotional culture emotions are expressed openly and naturally.

Specific and Diffuse: In specific culture individuals have a large public space they readily share with others and a small space private space they protect closely and share only with there close friends but in diffuse culture both private and public space are similar in size and people protect their public space carefully.

Achievement and Ascription: In achievement culture people are accorded status on the basis of their performance whereas in ascription culture status is given on the basis of relationships.

PROFILE OF MONSANTO INDIA LTD.

Monsanto India Ltd. is a subsidiary of a U.S. based multinational (headquarter at St.Louis), which is a leading provider of agricultural products and solutions in 52 countries the world over with 13,900 employees around the world. Monsanto's work in India began over 50 years ago, soon after independence. The principle businesses of Monsanto comprise of

- Herbicides
- Seeds
- Biotechnology

Monsanto India's Head Office is in Mumbai India.

In India, there are 11 regions in which the company's work is distributed & 12-14 branch offices

SIZE AND COMPOSITION OF WORK FORCE

The organization has a total of around 350 employees of which about 200 are in the managerial or supervisory category.

Background: Rural/Urban/Agricultural

Age groups:	20-30 yrs	20% employees
	31-40 yrs	60% employees
	40-50 yrs	20% employees

Men & Women: 10% of females working for the company in India.

DIVERSITY MANAGEMENT INITIATIVES

Monsanto initiated diversity management efforts as a formal program in 2003, however, Monsanto's parent organization commenced its diversity management programs about eight years back.

The top management recognized the need to formally manage the diversity in the organization to effectively manage the International business. The diversity of perspectives & experiences would lead to innovative ideas & solutions, better problem solving & affective decision making, so Monsanto's formal diversity management programme originates from its parent organization's global initiatives who's practices to manage diversity is reflected in two major components:-

- Monsanto listens carefully to diverse points of view and engage in thoughtful dialogue to broaden our understanding of issues in order to better address the needs and concerns of society and each other.
- Monsanto respects the religious, cultural and ethical concerns of people throughout the world.

PRESENT SCENARIO

The company recognizes that the customer profile in India is changing with changed modern agricultural practices so as to manage the business with the diverse marketing conditions. The company needs a diverse base of employees who in turn develops new ways of maintaining the satisfactory customer & consumer relations.

OBJECTIVES OF DIVERSITY MANAGEMENT PRACTICES

Company is committed to bring diversity into the organization at all levels and the organization has launched formal practices to ensure that diverse work force are managed properly and the work force in the organization learns the skills & behaviour required for a conducive work environment so that company can leverage the diversity among its employees to achieve overall business success, growth & acceptance of biotechnology.

Monsanto has designed the practice of recruiting diverse work force to improve the diversity in the organization. The company is recruiting the employees having education in agriculture, biotechnology & these biotechnology workers are given formal training in agriculture. Company selects the candidates for positions in sales having experience in FMCG (Fast Moving Consumer Goods) sector.

- Company promotes the work force on the basis of internal job applications as well as through advertisements. Company encourages cross-functional transfers.
- Company lets the employees determine their work timings as per their specific needs.
- Company has a formal diversity team headed by CFO having expertise in diversity management programme.
- Monsanto culture has been to encourage people to express their opinion as well as their apprehensions. The company has participative culture to manage the diversity.

ANALYSIS OF CULTURAL DIVERSITY ON THE BASIS OF HOFSTEDE'S DIMENSIONS OF CULTURE

- It was found by the interaction with the employees that Monsanto India Ltd. has High Power Distance.
- Company is low in uncertainty avoidance & collectively face the uncertain situations. The merger of Pharmacia (earlier a part of Monsanto) with Pfizer in the year 2002 led to the crisis period for the company but the company has been successful in overcoming the crisis tenure.)
- It was found that the culture promotes a work environment to motivate employees to take greater responsibilities of their careers and contribute to the success of company throughout their careers. It was revealed that the company's culture is neither high on the Individualism nor high on Collectivism.
- A transition is observed in the Masculinity Index of the company due to change in the work force composition. The company's culture is now on High Femininity Index. However, there was a resistance from the market place for women in front line sales but gradually this is disappearing.

ANALYSIS OF CULTURAL DIVERSITY ON THE BASIS OF TROMPENAAR'S DIMENSIONS OF CULTURE

- Monsanto's culture is High Universalism & the focus is more on formal rules in all the conditions for every branch of the company.

- On Trompenaar's dimensions of communitarianism, the employee's culture is highly communitarianism.
- The company has Individualistic culture along with a team work environment.
- Interaction with employees reveal that 80% of them believe that the company has neutral & specific culture
- The company recognizes the employee's good performance & give performance based rewards & status. Company is high on achievement culture.
- The company has trained its employees that they seek the qualities which encourage the team oriented culture & they expressed their fascination for these qualities & most of them prioritized these qualities in the following order:

✓ Value for Learning
✓ Sense of Responsibility
✓ Ability to Communicate
✓ Good Manners/Politeness
✓ Independence
✓ Tolerance & Respect for Others
✓ Loyalty
✓ Conscientiousness at Work

- 70% of the employees express that Monsanto's basic approach to International business is Geocentric.

SUGGESTIONS

Building a more diverse & effective work force for the future success of a company needs that the management have a well-development programme to manage diversity with support from top management.

- Continuous efforts to access the diversity management programmes.
- Flexibility in recruitment, training, retention, promotion/upward mobility of diverse work force.
- Alternate work schedules & flex time.
- Use of high level managers to guide high potential women & other diverse employees.

CONCLUSION

Diversity is essential for outstanding business success. Monsanto reflects diversity among its employees & in the ways it does its business.

Monsanto is committed to a diverse & inclusive work environment. The culture at Monsanto is team oriented & entrepreneurial, encouraging people to take great responsibilities for their careers to grow personally & professionally & to contribute to the success of the company though out their careers.

Company provides various incentives for recognition of employee's good work. The team oriented culture encourages creativity, decision making & entrepreneurial spirit & achieve its pledge to create a *Great Place to Work.*

REFERENCES

Dev, Sudipta (2005), "Cross- Cultural Training: The Melting Pot" Express Computer, Jan 1.pp 29-30.

Hodgetts M Richard & Fred Luthans, "International Management: Culture, Strategy & Behaviour" TMH, V Edition.

Hofstede, Greet, "Culture's Consequences: International Differences in Work-Related Values, Sage Publications, 1980.

Hofstede, Greet & Michall Bond(1984), "The Need for Synergy among Cross-Cultural Studies" Journal of Cross- Cultural Psychology, Dec, pp 419.

Thakur, Manab & Gene F. Burton, "International Management Concept & Cases, IV Edition.

17

TALENT MANAGEMENT

Renu Luthra and Manisha Seth

ABSTRACT

High performing employees are great people to have around. They achieve targets, add value, contribute to the organization and above all inspire others. For these same reasons they are most likely to be pursued or at least actively welcomed by other organizations. Top performers also tend to have an inconveniently realistic idea of their own worth and an uncarry knack of knowing what other career options are available to them at any time. All this taken together makes the managers job of retaining the best employees a delicate amalgam of motivation, support, diplomatic chastising and inspiration. Between providing resources and setting challenges, agreeing to compensation and coaching for higher performance, rewarding achievements and encouraging teamwork, the top performers' manager is increasingly expected to be some sort of corporate superman or wonder woman. Organisations perceptions of the meaning of talent management can vary from the mechanical (reduce this employee turnover figure to an acceptable level) Some companies view it as a distinct, controllable element of labour management (it's a matter of compensation and benefits) and others consider it a cross-functional, pervasive, and seemingly all encompassing set of values or methodologies about our culture and how we treat people.

Talent management is each of the definitions cited above. It can also be a specific combination of two or more definitions. Talent management is best seen not as a set of topics, but as a perspective or a mindset. A talent management perspective presumes talented individuals play a central role in the success of the firm. All corporate issues are seen from the perspective of "How will this affect our critical talent?" and "What role does talent play in this issue?" Just as the finance and the customer perspective should be (but often is not) pervasive, so too talent management is a set of tools and technologies that help organizations make good decisions about talent.

The objective of this paper is to examine whether there are any positive linkages between talent management methodologies specifically training and development adopted by organizations and performance outcomes be it sales or productivity in Indian conditions. Most managers are concerned with the day-to-day talent management decisions such as, "is it worthwhile interviewing more candidates or should we just pick from the ones were seen?" However, the CEO, the board, and the financial markets are interested in the big picture and are looking for some overall measures of the "talent asset." Academic papers such as Eric Flamholz's book "Human Resource Accounting Advances in Concepts, Methods and Applications" (1985) have dealt with the field of study called Human Resources Accounting. Dr. Eric Flamholz's gave the "Stochastic Rewards Valuation Model," which develops concepts such as expected realizable value of an employee and an organization service state matrix. The essence of the Stochastic Rewards Valuation model is that it looks at the return an employee generates through his career (for eg. from retail shop assistant to assistant manager to store manager) taking into account the probability of promotion and the probability of turnover. In this way the value an average employee will return over, say, a ten year period can be estimated.

It is difficult to imagine a firm using this concept except in unusual situations. It requires too much data and that is not readily available. Human Resource Accounting has not made the transition from academia to practice because it has not produced methods of everyday usefulness to firms.

The failure of human resource accounting to devise practical tools is a concern working organization should heed. Trying to compute "what is our human capital worth?" as if it were just another asset to be entered on the balance sheet, has not been productive. This paper is an attempt to find out if there is any direct link between an important talent management, technique i.e. training and development and financial performance. It also deals with a number of measures firms can use right away to indicate whether their human capital is healthy. These measures have a straight forward relationship with performance. There are a number of well known simple measures that should be of interest to senior managers with a talent mindset.

These include absenteeism, turnover and retention. These useful indicators tell us, "are things getting better or getting worse?" and "how do we compare to other firms?" That absenteeism, turnover and retention have meaningful direct and indirect costs is not in doubt. A more powerful simple measure is employee engagement, which has been popularized by Gallup in their best seller "First, Break All the Rules" Engagement is a type of employee attitude survey which assesses the satisfaction level of employees across a number of factors including culture and purpose of company, work environment, fairness, relationships with people in the company, rewards and recognition, work life balance, etc. It is particularly useful because it is demonstrably and even quantitatively related to performance.

Another approach is to create a strategy map and then track the elements of human capital that are most important in driving success.

In this case, a key human capital measure would be an indicator of how successful training was at increasing product knowledge. This approach abandons the notion that we should be asking "What is the value of our human capital?" or even "is one human capital getting better or worse?" Rather it suggests concentrating on the elements of talent management that most impact strategy execution. The consultancy firm Watson Wyatt has created a Human Capital Index that allows firms to judge their practices against what Watson Wyatt's research has shown to be important. Watson Wyatt found critical practices involve things such as effective use of rewards, creating a collegial, flexible workplace and excellence in recruiting. While firms could build there own measures of best practices based on the research from academics it is clearly easier just to engage a consulting firm that has already put together a methodology.

Today, firms should be capturing and reporting some simple measures of human capital such as turnover, some measure of engagement, any strategy map measures and some assessment of human-capital practices. These measures give a pretty good idea of how well a firm is doing in managing its human capital and if things are getting better or worse.

There are no proven methods for putting a number on "the value of human capital" and perhaps there never will be. However, the measures discussed above will influence the market value of the firm and give the CEO and the board evidence as to whether they are fulfilling their fiduciary responsibility in nurturing the human capital asset.

There is a place for big-picture thinking that asks, "How is our talent asset doing?" However, organizations also need to focus attention on improving the day-to-day management of talent decisions, the question being, Is this investment in talent worth making?

"Where would an investment in talent have the biggest impact on the execution of our strategy?" "Will this investment provide a good return?" Their question focuses our attention on the execution of strategy rather than making a number of disconnected investment decisions."

FOCUSSING ATTENTION WHERE INVESTMENTS WILL HAVE THE GREATEST IMPACT

Rather than asking about HR services they suggest that the first question must be, "Which talent pool should we focus our HR services on?" The key is where the investment in talent can have the biggest effect. In the launch of a new product the sales representatives may be the most important talent pool. However, in all likelihood management has already invested a lot in the selection, motivation and training of sales reps. An additional investment in this talent pool may not have much impact. On the other hand, it is quite possible that an investment in the sales support talent pool would have the biggest impact. Dr. David Ulrich and Norm Smallwood have a somewhat different approach to Boudreau and Ramstad. They argue that firms should identify a few strategic capabilities, such as innovation, closely managing costs and teamwork, and then invest to make these capabilities world class. The essential point their approach shares with Boudreau and Ramstad is that it begins with strategy. In both cases these thought leaders are saying, "Decide what the strategy is, then invest in the human resources initiatives that will support the execution of that strategy."

The emphasis on strategy execution as a starting point in tackling the ROI of talent management has a couple of very important benefits. One is that it captures the full attention of line management. In a case where it is clear that an investment in talent will drive the success of the strategy, there will be little difficulty getting senior management to put in the kind of time needed for good decision making.

LIMITATIONS OF ALL ROI METHODOLOGIES

The text book answer to determining if an investment is worthwhile is to calculate the expected Net Present Value (NPV) and from that determine an ROI. The fundamental idea of NPV is simple enough: Determine the cash that will flow from a given investment – whether that be a new machine tool or a new assessment method – pick a discount rate and with some suitably clever math, you can calculate the NPV and ROI.

However, ROI is full of assumptions that derail its usefulness as a business method, particularly for more complex problems. The input of a talent management initiative is going to have many outcomes. For example, enhanced training of call centre operators may improve short-term performance, increase retention of some employees provide a forum where unrelated but critical business issues are unveiled, or provide a catalyst for employees to meet together, leading them to form a union.

Furthermore, the value chain from an outcome (e.g. better phone manners) to revenue can be a long one. Predicting the series of cash flows is near impossible. Even after the fact it can be hard to tell if something worked because any output has many causes. Better assessment tests may have contributed to improved performance from programmers, but performance is also determined by teamwork, leadership, programming tools, culture and a host of other things.

The good news for talent management professionals is that ROI doesn't work well in most areas of business. Talking ROI is important; actually using the equation is not. A near universal practice in using ROI is to do the calculation then go back and change the estimated cash flows until a suitable answer is derived. Managers do this not because they are incompetent or dishonest, but because they don't believe the textbook approach is giving them the right answer. This reality check can keep us from chasing holy grails. Thousands of managers have struggled with calculating ROI for training and other talent initiatives for decades. This is good evidence that it won't work. What is needed is to talk ROI but use semi-quantitative or even qualitative method.

Serious business decisions are made using semi-quantitative methods. The idea is not to capture all the costs and benefits, much less calculate a present value. Rather, it is simply to try and get a handle on some key impacts in a quantitative way to support qualitative evidence.

This may mean following focusing on intermediate variables in the value chain rather than cash flows. For example, a product-training program can be assessed by measuring how much knowledge the participants retained. This does not give an ROI, but it provides some quantitative data that can lead to an informed judgement as to whether the training makes sense-particularly so where there is a strategy map so that managers have a qualitative sense of how important product knowledge is.

ASSESSMENT VERSUS MEASUREMENT

There is a pro-measurement school that argues, "If you can't measure it, you can't manage it." This is nonsense - unless it is merely a rebuke to those who refuse to look at any numbers at all. We manage all the time based on limited, ambiguous, qualitative information. Qualitative assessment is powerful and can play an important role in supporting good decisions on investments in talent. There are two main qualitative methods, observations and conversation.

Consider a case where you are concerned about the service in a restaurant. A metrics-based approach would insist on getting diners to fill out little cards rating service on a scale of 1 to 5. A more powerful way of assessing service is for an experienced restaurateur to sit quietly in the corner and observe what is going on.

It's common to hear seasoned managers say, "I can walk into a plant and tell you in five minutes if its well run or not. The other powerful approach is conversation. Talking to the staff and patrons will reveal a great deal about what is right, what is wrong and how to improve matters. Measuring the return on investment in soft-skills training is notoriously difficult because the benefits are qualitative, multi-faceted and spread out over time. However, a set of structured conversations can provide the evidence needed to make an informed decision.

Measuring the return on investment in soft-skills training is notoriously difficult because the benefits are qualitative, multi-faced and spread out over time. However, a set of structured conversations can provide the evidence needed to make an informed decision.

Database and Methodology: Extensive review of the literature on talent management revealed a tendency by companies to use quantitative measures to measure the impact of training and development on employee performance. However, our hypothesis is that it is actually more efficient to determine which qualitative measures of training and development lead to improved performance/productivity. The electronic database Prowess was used to obtain information on such quantifiable measures like Return on Capital Employed and Return on Net Worth, etc. Data on ten companies namely Dr. Reddy's Laboratories Ltd., HCL Technologies Ltd., Hughes Software Systems Ltd., Infosys Technologics Ltd., NTPC Ltd., Patni Computer Systems Ltd., Sasken Communication Technologies Ltd., Satyam Computer Services Ltd., Thermax Ltd., HDFC Ltd. was taken from the Business Today Nov.21, 2004 issue on such parameters like percentage of attrition, average career tenure training budget and training man hours.

Statistical analysis was done using multiple regression analysis techniques (Table 17.1).

In this section we analyse the impact of training and development on the different performance measures of the firm. The intensity of training and development has been measured using number man hours of training and training budget. The different performance measures which have been taken in this study are attrition rate, career tenure, sales per employee, sales per rupee of salary and wages, return on capital employed (ROCE) and returns on net worth (RONW). For this a cross sectional analysis is conducted using the data or the above variables at the firm level for the year 2003-04. The analysis has also been conducted to find the impact of the size variable on the training and development intensity. Sales have been considered as the measure of size as far as this study is concerned.

Table 17.1: Independent Variable: Training Hours

Dependent Variable	A (t value)	β (t value)	R^2
Sales	210.39 (0.14)	0.01 (3.56)	0.61
Attrition Rate	19.77 (2.56)	-1.26 (-0.86)	0.085
Career Tenure	7.00 (3.11)	2.76 (0.65)	0.05
Sales/Employee	0.61 (2.14)	-1.79 (-0.33)	0.01

The results showing the regression model explaining the relationship between training hours and different performance measures have been shown in Table 17.2. The results indicate that number of man hours of training has come out to be insignificant to explain the variation in the different performance measures.

Table 17.2: Independent Variable: Training Budget

Dependent Variable	α (t value)	β (t value)	R^2
Sales/Employee	0.28 (2.31)	6.78 (1.16)	0.16
Attrition Rate	22.51 (2.78)	-0.01 (-1.19)	0.17
ROCE	23.38 (4.32)	0.00 (0.04)	0.00
RONW	19.90 (4.56)	-0.00 (-0.15)	0.00
Sales/Salaries & Wages	3.14 (1.50)	0.00 (2.27)	0.42

The results showing the relationship between training budget and different performance measures have been shown in Table 17.2. The results indicate that the explanatory power has increased when training and development budget (i.e. training budget) is used intensity. The t-coefficient was found to be significant in case when the impact of training budget on sales/salaries and wages is computed. In the case of other performance measures such as attrition rate, sales per employee and career tenure the training budget coefficient was not found to be highly significant but the t-value of the coefficient was greater than 1 in all the cases.

Thus the training budget plays some role in explaining the variation in the different performance measures. Thus we can say training budget can be used as a tool to improve the performance of the firm. From the results of the Table 17.1 and Table 17.2 we can conclude that it is the quality of the training (training budget) and not the quantity (training hours) which positively influence the performance of the firm.

The results indicating the impact of the size variable on training and development intensity has been shown in Table 17.3. The results indicate that the size has come out to be a significant determinant of both training hours as well as training budget. The results show that the larger the size of the firm, the more emphasis they give to the trainings and development.

Table 17.3: Independent Variable: Sales

Dependent Variable	α (t value)	B (t value)	R^2
Training Hours	139538.44 (1.20)	60.74 (3.50)	0.64
Training Budget	259.71 (1.17)	0.27 (8.23)	0.91

The results indicating the impact of training and development intensity on the profitability measures. (ROCE, RONW) show that both training hours and training budget are insignificant determinants of the profitability. Thus the results show although training and development intensity (training budget) may increase the productivity of the employees but the same is not translated in terms of increase in the profitability of the firm.

Since expertise in "ROI methods" is not as important as a deep understanding of the business, we recommend some qualitative measures for retaining talent such as balancing work life, coaching competency mapping, performance management systems and team building.

BALANCING WORK LIFE

According to a survey conducted by Coopers & Lybrand talented people are not as impressed with money as with a balanced lifestyle.

Flex Schedules, part time options, job sharing, telecommuting and phased retirement all offer choices that are becoming increasingly popular. Organizations need to depend on contingent workers to fill gaps caused by employees pursuing family duties.

Recruiting a contingent work force from retirees who are interested in continuing their employment in non traditional terms can result in a highly qualified part time workforce. More flexibility with options such as telecommuting job sharing and more flexible hours is mandated if super keeper men and women needing these arrangements are to stay in corporate positions.

COACHING

Coaching key employees is becoming increasingly popular trend to retain talent. Successful implementation of coaching brings significant benefits such as retention increases in productivity, development of high potential performers, greater job satisfaction for the participant and achievement of organization objectives. Super keeper coaching that targets 'must keep' individuals should be adopted to retain top performers. This coaching is based on a collaborative relationship among the employee his/her boss, the human resource manager and an executive coach – coaching for super keepers must be positioned in the company as an essential 'perk'.

COMPETENCY MAPPING

Competencies are the observable and measurable skills, knowledge and behaviours that contribute to enhanced performance and organizational success.

Competency mapping means making transparent the skills an organization needs to be successful. There are a variety of ways of developing and using competency models in organizations – but first it's useful to understand some of the history of how competency models became popular in HR departments.

Until the early 1970s, most organizations viewed the characteristics required for success as either very solidly based on the technical skills needed for roles or a belief that intelligence mattered most. Some organizations, particularly the military, that depended so much on deep leadership skills, had tried to classify some of the personality traits that their leaders needed. They tested for these but rarely made them transparent and certainly could not translate what they meant in terms of the roles that people had to perform.

David Mc Clelland, an eminent Harvard Psychology professor, had already widely published work on the personality characteristics that describe entrepreneurs. He showed that a measure of motivation he termed "need for achievement" predicted success among entrepreneurs. Later on Mc clelland and his fellow researchers at a consulting firm, Mc Ber and Company, discovered that skills such as the ability to network widely or to sense others' feelings were more important for determining an individuals' success.

Thus Mc Cleland's research studies provided a momentum and many HR people in large organizations and consultants started reviewing their work in the light of Mc clleland's findings.

COMMON COMPETENCY MODELS

There is now a whole industry in describing the characteristics of great leaders. One of the best of these is Daniel Goleman's emotional intelligence. In his book "Working with Emotional Intelligence" Goleman proposes that emotional intelligence is shown in four areas; self awareness, social awareness, self management, and relationship management (Table 17.4)

Table 17.4: Aspects of Emotional Intelligence

Self Awareness ✓ Emotional Self-Awareness ✓ Accurate Self-Assessment ✓ Self Confidence	**Social Awareness** ✓ Empathy ✓ Organisational Awareness ✓ Service Orientation
Self Management ✓ Transparency ✓ Adaptability ✓ Achievement ✓ Initiative ✓ Optimism	**Relationship Management** ✓ Developing others ✓ Inspirational leadership ✓ Influence ✓ Change catalyst ✓ Conflict management ✓ Teamwork and collaboration

Each of these is a set of competencies or characteristics that can be behaviourally observed. Each of these competencies has a set of behavioural descriptions.

A firm hiring a new employee would have been well served by choosing some of these aspects of EQ as a base for its selection decision.

BUILDING A MODEL FOR A CRITICAL ROLE

This model emphasizes on defining a key role or set of characteristics associated with a job. A company can do this in two ways (i) by looking at job holders it already has and identifying the critical things that differentiate people who are really good in the role from those who are average performers (ii) by identifying the defining characteristics of job incumbents through a panel of managers who manage these people.

What is really important is to look at all aspects of a person. Think of all the attributes the job incumbent can possess. What do the outstanding managers show or know that average performers do not show with the same degree of consistency? Next look below the surface from how we observe a person. First, at their self image. How do outstanding project managers look at themselves in comparison with average performer? May be we have a clear view because of the way he or she talks about problems or situations. The next level digs further below the surface and looks for the traits that the person brings to the role that will make a difference. The next level should look at the fundamental motivational issues that make a difference.

BUILDING MODELS FOR JOB FAMILIES

This approach involves finding the right set of technical attributes that people need to know in order to perform a specific function. In this case, the leadership group needs to come together and agree on fundamental understanding of where the business is going and what the individuals in this functional area must contribute. At the end of the day, the management group must have a clear view of what they must do, then at the skills and competencies in this light start from the entry level and answer the question. What do people need in order to perform well at this level? Then imagine a second level and answer the question "What would a person have to demonstrate in order to move to this level. This method should produce or chart with the skills that a function needs in order to complete its mission. Managers should be able to compare their people and decide which skills they possess and whether they possess enough know how at each level of the function.

BUILDING MODELS OF LEADERSHIP

This approach aims to review the characteristics a company wants to see in key leaders who will drive a strategy or organizational change.

There are three connected methods management groups can use to build a model of competencies that they agree should drive leadership or key roles in their company.

- Managers can use a list containing important leadership characteristics and agree which of these are most important in their company. If they had to choose only five, which of these would really differentiate the best performers from average performers. Which two or three would have the most devastating impact if they were missing? This requires a hard discussion about what really matters for this company. Is there is an agreement on 8 to 12 that make the most difference, that would be necessary for top-notch, superior performance or a killer if missing?
- Management team can decide on the key requirements for the role. How are leaders for expanding business supposed to add value. The managers might have a debate that ends up with a list of the seven (plus or minus two) accountabilities that define what that role is about. Then managers make a matrix and map out the critical competencies.
- The group of managers should think concretely about whom they see as the top performers in these key roles and then keep a picture of them in mind. They find out what the top performers are doing that are really different from the average performers? What makes them outstanding? What motivates them? How do they think? Thus the managers not only focus on results but also on what the top performers are actually doing.

Competency models used in any of these approaches can be adopted by organizations' HR departments to describe their recruitment standards, training requirements or promotion criteria. Thus it would lead to successful management of talent.

SELECTING THE RIGHT PERFORMANCE MANAGEMENT SYSTEM

Selection of a suitable and effective Performance Management System is also very crucial for retention and development of talent in an organization.

Dr. Mason Haire, an industrial organizational psychologist while discussing the importance of right performance management system once commented "What gets measured gets done. If you want to change how an organization behaves, change the measurement system." Bill Gates also said the same thing, "People behave as they are measured."

Therefore, it is important to develop a right performance Management System having two primary parts: performance appraisal (the process of measuring performance) and performance review (the process of communicating the results of the performance appraisal to the person whose performance was measured).

CHOICE OF APPRAISAL SYSTEM

Appraisal Systems can be categorized by what they assume and on what they focus. These include:

Trait-based

Assumptions that certain traits drive performance; measures personal characteristics of the position incumbent.

Behaviour-based

Assumptions that certain behaviours drive performance, measures what the position incumbent does.

Knowledge/skill-based

Assumptions that certain knowledge drives performance; measures what the position incumbent knows/applies. When traits, behaviours, skills and knowledge are linked to organization success expectations, they are sometimes called competencies.

Result-based

Assumptions that achievement of objectives equals performance; measures what the position achieves.

Determining which type of appraisal system best fits in an organization depends primarily on its objectives i.e. what the organization is trying to achieve i.e. increased job understanding on the part of the incumbent, individual growth and development, or performance planning and control.

Other important factors to be considered are:

- Business environment
- Strategy and objectives of the business
- Organization size and management levels
- Corporate climate
- Values and style of the senior management group
- Available resources

Further, not all appraisal systems can be utilized effectively with all types of employees. Appraisal systems are best suited to employee types as follows:

- Trait based – all employees;
- Behaviour based – supervisors and below;
- Knowledge/skill based – production workers, and some professionals
- Result based – administrators/managers, most professionals, and executives

Table 17.5 presents a comparison of the general characteristics, advantages and disadvantages of the four systems.

Table 17.5: Comparative Advantages and Disadvantages of Different Systems

System Type	Characteristics	Strengths	Weaknesses
Trait-Based	Assumption that certain traits drive performance • Emphasis is on personality, style, values • Traits are generic and may apply to all employees/groups • Evaluation based on perception • Rating tied to degree/ frequency trait is exhibited	• Simple to conduct evaluation • Can apply to different employee groups • Communicates important traits	• Simple to conduct • Can apply to different employee groups • Communicates important traits
Behaviour-Based	Assumption that certain behaviours drive performance • Behaviours are specific to the work environment • Tailored to different jobs/groups • Evaluation based on demonstrated actions • Rating tied to degree/ frequency behaviour is exhibited	• Can be tailored to specific jobs • Helps employees understand specifically how job is to be done • Behaviours help reinforce culture/ values	• Time-consuming to develop and evaluate • Must be able to observe and measure discrete behaviours • Behaviours may not produce desired results

Knowledge-or Skill-based	Assumption that certain knowledge/ skills drive performance • Emphasis on employee capabilities • Tailored to each knowledge/ skill area • Evaluation based on acquisition of knowledge/ skills • Rating tied to degree/ diversity of knowledge/ skill achieved. • * Knowledge/skill tied to organizational objectives	• Competency required on each job • Reinforces cross training and flexibility • Direct link to pay system • Strategic view: pay for competencies required in the future	• Assumes link between knowledge/skill s and results • Employee may not use certain knowledge/skill • Difficult to measure diverse skills.
Results – Based	• Assumption that achievement of objectives drives performance • Objectives tied to job or organization goals • Develop objectives specific to individual/ group by which performance is measured • Evaluation based on results achieved • Rating tied to degree of achievement	• Tailored to specific jobs/ organization • Emphasizes results • Encourages dialogue and employee buy-in if goals are jointly established.	• Time-consuming to develop and evaluate • Limited to work where specific objectives can be established and measured • Debate between short term and long term emphases.

Table 17.6 presents a different kind of comparison of the four types of performance appraisal system, focusing on the utility of each for different program objectives.

Table 17.6: A Different Kind of Comparison

	Type of Measurement			
Programme Objective	Trait – Based	Behaviour – Based	Knowledg e/ Skill-Based	Results – Based
Increased Job Understanding	*	X	X	XX
Remedial Performance Improvement	X	XX	XX	XX
Career Development	XX	X	XX	X
Focussing Employee's Efforts on Specific Tasks	X	XX	X	X
Increasing Output	X	X	X	XX
Human Resources Planning	XX	X	X	X
Linking Pay and Performance	*	X	X	XX
Improving Teamwork	X	X	X	X

X = has utility for that objective
XX = has a high degree of utility for that objective
* = lack of utility for that objective

DETERMINING EVERY EMPLOYEE'S POTENTIAL FOR GROWTH:

Finding talented business leaders is a growing challenge for today's organizations. In the past, where structures, strategies, and even markets were relatively static, leadership was less complex. One model for leadership was all most organizations needed. Those who fit the model were groomed overtime – in those days when employees stayed with one organization for their entire career, they weren't going anywhere else and eventually were moved into leadership roles.

Today developing star leaders is even more difficult than developing star athletes and artists. For starters, the days of a single leadership model are gone. Even within a company a variety of leadership models are needed. And those models are constantly evolving.

To identify potential leaders, organizations can rely on three proven processes – a trio of crystal balls, that will help them "gaze" into possible leaders and ascertain whether they have the right leadership attributes. These crystal falls can help organizations identify three critical attributes:

1. How a person thinks?
2. How a person works with other people?

3. How resilient a person is?

CONCLUSION

Organizations need not be so concerned with exact ROI calculations of talent managements. In fact its actually more efficient to determine which qualitative measures of training and development lead to improved performance. These simple qualitative measures of human capital like competency mapping, some measures of engagement and performance appraisals give a pretty good idea of how well a firm is doing in managing its human capital. This paper recommends that investment in the above mentioned techniques would provide answers to the moot-question, "Is this investment in talent worth making?" Over the last few years HR expenditures have been fairly consistent, the top five priority areas for Human Resource allocation being employee benefits, employee recruitment, training and development, compensation and employee relations. This paper focused on training and development man hours and training budget and attempted to establish relationship between these two independent variables and factors like attrition rate, career tenure, sales, sales per employee. In significant relationship between training man-hours and these variables has emerged while there is a low significant relationship between the training budget and the dependent variables. Hence we conclude that in the absence of any highly significant relationship between these two independent variables and the identified dependent variables, companies would be more effective in retaining talent if they rely more the above discussed qualitative measures like competency mapping, work life balance, employee engagement and performance appraisal.

REFERENCES

Argyris, Chris (1991, May-June) 'Teaching Smart People How to Learn', Harvard Business Review, Vol. 69, No.3, p. 99.

Burke, Michael J., and R.R. Day, 'A Cumulative Study of the Effectiveness of Managerial Training' Journal of Applied Psychology, Vol. 71, No.2, April – May 1986, 232 – 245.

Chandramouli, V.V & Sankaranth V. 'Grow Talent to Keep', HRD Newsletter, July 2004, Vol. 20, Issue:4, p.33.

McClleland, David C, 'Toward a Theory of Motive Acquisition,' American Psychologists, Vol. 20, No.5, May 1965, pp. 321 – 333.

Wolf, Martin G., 'Selecting the Right Performance Management System', The Talent Management Hand Book, Tat McGraw Hill, Edition 2004, 85 – 97.

Young Rob, 'Finders Keepers', Accountancy Magazine.com, Nov.2004.

CHANGING FACE OF HUMAN RESOURCE MANAGEMENT IN THE NEW MILLENNIUM

Varsha Dixit

ABSTRACT

Emergence of the service society after the last world war brought increased realization of the role of employee knowledge and creativity in adding value to the company. The subject generated interest after 1990's with rapid emergence of information and communication. The progress in the field of IT is changing the way organizations do business. A new style of organizational structure based on communication and information is being seen in the organizations. Organization structure has totally changed from tall structure to flat. The information age permits communication with widely spread organizations that are not closely controlled by the automakers. The environment in the organizations is changing day by day. In the past, we had uniform products manufactured with low and simple technology and sold in known markets in stable environment. However, in this emerging competitive scenario we have high and complex technology so the uncertainty prevailing in the market has made the environment dynamic. Diverse products are available in new markets. Globalization confronts managers with some Herculean challenges. The author in this paper wants to stress upon globalizations impact on HR management system. In order to cope up with the changing world HRIS, TQM, Kaizen, Quality circles, job re-engineering, strategic workforce management, 360-degree appraisal, mentoring, emotional intelligence etc are being practiced in the companies. The integration of technology & these tools has enriched the human resource and increased his productivity. Hence, it is believed that changing face of HR plays a significant role and this shall help the Indian organizations to compete with the MNC entering Indian markets.

INTRODUCTION

Human resource is the asset to the organization. Human resource is the only resource in an organization, which appreciates; else, all depreciate with the passage of time. So, to develop human resource becomes important and ultimately lead to the development of resources and the organization as a whole. HRM emerged in 1970s. Many people continue to refer to the discipline by its old traditional title such as personnel management or personnel administration. The trend is changing. Nowadays industry circles use the latest nomenclature Human Resource Management. Human resource management is not only paying salaries and keeping up personnel registers and other personnel administration related matters, but it is also a strategic issue. Personnel structure, skills and competences, recruitment, education... strategic issues! The kind of employees you have in your organization today and tomorrow are the cornerstone of future success. You will need better tools to help you to manage and develop your personnel, their competences and skills. You need tools and processes to recruit the best possible employees - and keep them

Chankaya's Arthshastra states that there existed a sound base for systematic management of resources in 4th B.C. the government took active interest in the operation of public and private sector enterprises and provided systematic procedures for regulating employer employee relationships. In 1990s, the emphasis shifted to human values and productivity through people. This decade have brought a revolutionary change in our business. Post liberalization is marked by a shift from command economy to market driven economy, from sheltered market to competitive market, from monopoly to competition & from domestic trade to global trade. Such, shifts calls for a new approach to HR activities.

During the pre-economic liberalization, the HR manager had adopted reactive strategies to people's problems. The need of the hour is proactive approach, a strategy that helps HR managers foresee events and take appropriate actions before the events occur. The proactive strategies call for awareness about the likely challenges the HR managers will face in future and the solutions to overcome the problems.

The major challenges are-

- Globalization
- Corporate re-organization
- New organization structure
- Changing demographics of workforce
- Changed employee expectations
- Renewed focus on people
- Managing managers
- Interests of the weaker sections of society.

GLOBALIZATION

The demise of capitalism, the breaking up of trade barriers and the rise of networked information have unleashed a revolution in business. Growing internationalization of business has its impact on HRM functions. The HR department is required to cope with the problems of unfamiliar laws, languages, practices, competition, attitude, management styles, work ethics, and more. The HR manager should know that international operations have many additional functions such as taxation & co-ordination of departments, coordination of multiple salary currencies, and more involvement in the employee's personal life, such as housing, health, education and recreation. As the HR, functions will change and the role of HR manager will be modified.

CORPORATE RE-ORGANIZATIONS

The corporate mergers, take-overs and massive re-organizations are in news. These pose a greater challenge for HRM as it has impact on organizational levels .The employees experience anxiety and uncertainty about their places in a new organization. There is little indication that the pace of mergers and acquisitions will slacken in the near future.

Organizations have been compelled for internal re-structuring due to competition from MNCs and domestic industries. Many Indian companies are busy reducing the number of management grades, eliminating layers and redrawing reporting lines within their organization. ITC, HLL, Godrej & Boyce, Raymond woollen mills, Shaw Wallace, Crompton Greaves are some of the companies that have embarked on a flattening exercise. The re-organizations increase growth opportunity for performers, fast decision-making, better communication etc.

Although flat structures reduce the chances for promotion and increase the workload on individuals. The role of HR manager becomes important. He should arrange to train and develop his people to cope up with the change with high morale.

In the emerging forms of organizational structure multidisciplinary teams organized around core processes and not around functions do work. The entire organization is flat or horizontal with few layers and is led by a president and a skeleton group of senior executives who support functions such as finance and HR.

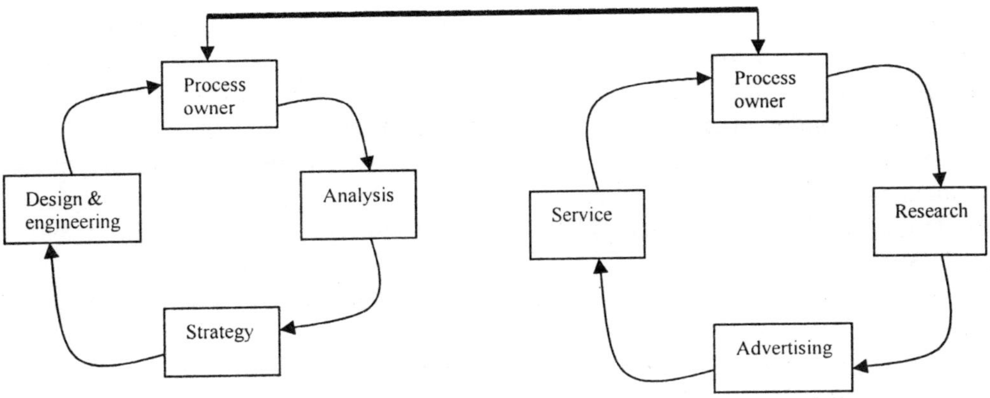

THE HORIZONTAL CORPORATION

Eg: **Eastman Kodak** which eliminated several Vice Presidents positions and built 1000 self directed teams.

Xerox which now develops new products through multi disciplinary teams that work in a single process.

General Electric moved from vertical structure to a horizontal one with more than 100 processes and programs.

CHANGING DEMOGRAPHICS OF WORKFORCE

Another change in the workforce demographics relate to the growing number of youngsters. People working in companies established in 1990s and 1950s are now superannuating. Those who join are fresher and young in new organizations. As they are highly energetic and creative, the HR manager should take special care to protect the interests of the diversified workforce. As it is believed that human, efficiency doubles if he gets congenial, homely environment at the workplace. Some companies like Infosys have made a leap forward for the same.

In Infosys, the employees are taken to office about 45 minutes away from the city by bus; the day starts with breakfast in consideration for single employees. The company is doing everything that it can, to make it more than a desk and a telephone. Dormitories are provided for those who want to rest and sleep. Gymnasium is built for breaks during the day.

CHANGED EMPLOYEE EXPECTATIONS

The change in workforce leads to changes in employee expectations and attitudes. Traditional allurements such as job security, attractive remuneration, housing etc do not attract and motivate today's workforce. Employees demand empowerment and expect equality with the management.

The job of empowerment again is of concern to HR manager. Empowerment also means that a worker can bring his children to the workplace so that they can look around and gain knowledge about work methods. Owners of enterprises usually enjoy this privilege.

Expectation of equality break ups the traditional relationship between employer and employee.

Another expectation is that the electronic and tele-communication revolution will improve the quality of work life. Today's average worker demands better treatment, challenging jobs and career advancement. The HR manager must therefore redraw the profile of the worker and discover new methods of hiring, training, remunerating and motivating employees.

RENEWED FOCUS ON PEOPLE

For too long, managers believed in structures, strategies and systems. For decades, this philosophy served companies well. It supported successive waves of growth as companies integrated horizontally in 1950s, diversified in 60s and expanded into global market in 70s & 80s. But over the last decade, technological competitive and market changes have eroded its effectiveness. The structure strategy, systems approach, which worked during the post-war era, is no more relevant in today's economic environment, which is characterized by over capacities and intense competition. Now, the HR managers have to adopt people-oriented philosophy. The manager should re-define them so that they support and not subvert the top management's ability to focus on the organizational people.

MANAGING MANAGERS

The biggest challenge to an HR manager is to make all employees contribute to the success of the organization in an ethical and socially responsible way. The business organization provides several things to society and the failure will adversely affect the society. It must be the endeavour of everybody to ensure success and stability of organization. Responsibility is more on the HR manager as he/she who co-ordinates the activities of people and it is people who make or mar organization.

PROTECT THE INTERESTS OF THE WEAKER SECTIONS

A HR manager has to protect the interests of weaker sections of the society. Dramatic increase in the no. of women, minorities and other has resulted in the need to re-examine their policies, practices and values.

In order to survive in this changing environment the HR managers have to be specific in their choice of selecting right man at the right time and place him at the right place. To make the work easy and faster we can adopt the new technologies and train the human resource to make best use of it. To make the working environment congenial it becomes essential on the part of the manager that he should be aware of the new emerging trends of HRM like

- HR & IT
- HRIS (Human Resource Information System)
- CAREER PLANNING
- HUMAN CAPITAL
- EMOTIONAL INTELLIGENCE
- MENTORING
- TQM (Total Quality Management)
- QUALITY CIRCLE
- KAIZEN

HR and IT

The merger of computer technology with the communication technology has given birth to IT. The strides made in the area of IT have virtually transformed the face of the world into a global village. IT is being profitably used in various areas of HRM like:

- Recruiting on the internet(using video-conferencing facilities to connect the university campuses and the employees)
- Record-keeping
- Holding computer –aided interview
- Holding computer-interactive performance tests
- Career counselling
- Computerized job evaluations
- Monitoring safety

For a HR manager the knowledge of IT has become a must .He has to be conversant with the use of IT in managing human resource effectively. In order to use the technology to get the jobs done the employees are to be trained on-the-job. The importance of IT has to be highlighted in order to lessen the resistance.

To be successful in the new millennium the HR manager has to go for the upcoming HR strategies like HRIS, Emotional Quotient, Mentoring, 360 degree appraisal, TQM, Quality circle, Kaizen etc. which shall help him to survive.

HRIS

It is the sum total of all systems that store data, classify data and to be made easily available to the decision –maker. HRIS provide the storage, retrieval and analysis of that information and data. Having good HRIS enhances the accuracy and effectiveness of managerial decision-making and hence its presence is always an important asset for a company. Indeed, it is the lifeline of IR, HRP, HRD, and HRA function within HRM.

HRIS is an absolute necessity for the smooth and effective functioning of strategic HR interventions.

CAREER PLANNING

To prepare the executives to function effectively career progression of executives is to be linked to their career path. HR manager should make sure that individual's goals of employees are satisfied. This is possible by planning of career by means of education, training, development and job search. The main focus is of HR process is development

Eg: - BPCL believes in performance management, which links business goals with individual's performance. ITC aims to provide accelerated career growth opportunities for its people, same as IOC.

MULTI SKILLING

Such program aims at importing job skills and knowledge to employees. It helps to further organization and personal goals. BPCL introduced multi skilling to encourage employees to take up new initiatives.

HUMAN CAPITAL

According to Sumatra Ghosal of London Business School, it has three elements

Intellectual Capital: It consists of stock of knowledge , skills and expertise that all members of the organization collectively possess and the knowledge skills and expertise embedded.

Social Capital: It relates to the structure, quality and flexibility of the human relations. Like HLL, SBI had built strong network of formal and informal relationships through job rotation, joint training etc. trusting relationships.

Emotional Capital: Apart from other capital companies also need emotional capital like self confidence, courage, risk-taking ability, resilience etc.

EMOTIONAL INTELLIGENCE

EI has become the buzzword now a day. It is the ability of manager to manage his emotions at the workplace and calmly deal with stressful corporate situations than on his I.Q. or technical skills. Control of emotions like anger, hatred, frustration, confusion, sadness etc can substantially increase performance and effectiveness. Byron Stock and associates have proved that Motorola could reduce-

36% stress problems
56% insomnia
33% indigestion
27% headache
33% heartburn
By improvement in emotional control

MENTORING

A process whereby a senior manager acts as a friend philosopher and guide to anew recruit. It is a kind of emotional support given by experienced person to younger people through teaching coaching, counselling, guiding etc. A mentor performs all types of elucidation to his or her proteege from job content. It is a kind of personal counselling from drawing up a dress code to, teaching table manners. Organization training takes care of knowledge and skills while mentoring complements it with personal instruction in the intricacies of operating in that corporation.

It develops self-confidence and empowers managers to operation stress while retaining the quality standards and values. At SmithKline Beecham consumer healthcare mentoring consists of following steps:-

1. Initiation
2. Progression
3. Assimilation
4. Integration

360 DEGREE APPRAISAL

360 degree appraisal systems involve evaluation of a manager by everyone. This method is much in practice now a days.

- Self appraisal

- Superiors
- Subordinates
- Peer

ESOP – These are becoming popular in IT firms. The employees are offered company's share at a concessional price. Stock options are considered performance-based incentives. This is a method to retain efficient employees with companies it inculcates a sense of ownership and responsibility. This scheme establishes significance of team effort among employees. However, it is used by only profit making companies.

TQM

The HR managers can facilitate introduction, maintenance, renew and reinforcement of TQM in organization by implementing following ways.

- Develop collaborations between management and trade union for implementing TQM.
- Train the people in the principles and techniques of TQM.
- Identify the need of TQM.
- Guide work team in quantity improvement.
- Develop communication system for the launch of TQM.
- Create awareness within the orientation courses. If required then redesign the appraisal system.
- Assess the effectiveness of TQM infrastructure and systems.
- Benchmark effectiveness of TQM with competitors and global best practices.
- Facilitate the operation of internal reviews
- Conduct quality and ethics audit.

QUALITY CIRCLE

These circles play an important role in quality improvement of the product. The employees are clubbed into groups of 4-5ormore. Then these groups search for the problems in their area .The reasons are sorted and solutions are searched. The groups are rewarded for the fruitful answers, which add to product quality.

KAIZEN

It means continuous improvement with the involvement of everybody .it is different from innovation. Innovation involves a drastic improvement in the status quo because of a large investment in new technology. Kaizen programs like-

1. Management Oriented Kaizen

2. Group Oriented Kaizen
3. Individual Oriented Kaizen

Steps in Kaizen programs:

1. **SEIRI**: Straighten up i.e. distinguish between necessary and unnecessary.
2. **SEITON**: Arrange the things in order
3. **SEISO**: Clean the work area
4. **SEKETSU**: Personal cleanliness
5. **SHITSUKE**: Discipline

In the new paradigm, the job of HR manager has become quite challenging. The companies have started paying special attention to career planning and on-going training of their staff as they realize the importance of retention. According to a survey sponsored by Kelly Services India has emerged as a star performer in the call center industry and expects a dramatic growth rate in near future. The study covers four countries- India, China, Korea and Philippines. The growth trend is led by India by 64%, Philippines with 53% and china at 50% (Tables 18.1 and 18.2).

Table 18.1: Number of Call Centres and Number of Seats in Select Countries, 2004

Country	Number of organisations operating call centre	Number of seats
China	525	49,000
Korea	955	1,09,000
India	324	1,72,000
Philippines	162	51,000

Table 18.2: Growth of Number of Seats in Select Countries

Country	Number of seats (2003)	Number of seats (2004)	Number of seats (2005)	Growth %
China	38,000	49,000	76,000	56
Korea	N/a	1,09,000	1,26,000	16
India	96,000	1,72,000	2,83,000	64
Philippines	20,000	51,000	78,000	53

Source: Exclusive Call Centre Markets in Asia, *HT Power Jobs*, 22/02/2005.

The study revealed that during the last 12 months all markets except of Philippines spent considerable time and effort developing and upgrading their human resource and technology. It is evident that this industry is still in the growth stage in Asia. When demand exceeds supply due to the fast growth, the scale is tipped towards the workers. As e result, companies have started paying special attention to career planning and on-going training as they realize the importance of retention. Most of the Indians & Chinese prefer to work from their homes. Although India experiences a high level of agent turnover but only 11% of the call centres are experiencing recruitment problems as compared to Philippines and Korea where it is 50% and 45%. The study revealed that agents in India received the highest no. of days of training i.e., 24 days in comparison with others. Respondents reported that there has been 50% growth in seat no. the Indian economy is doing well but organizations have to be very careful about the salaries they offer. Compensations tend to creak when there is rush for talent. Therefore, it is important to weigh productivity against remuneration in order to retain the best professionals.

CONCLUSION

The professionals, the HR managers must be ready to face the various challenges through appropriate and suitable HR practices. To have better HR practices into the organization, it is important to have a conducive atmosphere. By understanding the human beings and providing the appropriate environment it is possible to harness that latent power within the human being, which will make all difference between success and failure, in time to come, "the power of the human spirit." We conclude that being a function HR has evolved to be a strategic partner in value addition. The HR manager is responsible for seeking talent, nurturing talent and retaining talent. The HR manager should use the available human resource to face the challenges of globalization, corporate reorganizations, changing demographics of work force etc. Employees expects more than the financial benefits for motivation i.e., flexi time, paid vacations, career development, recognition of personal achievements, outings of project team at the end of the successful completion of the project etc. Many companies mentioned in the paper have proved the worth of new practices of HR like mentoring, 360-degree appraisal, and kaizen, TQM etc. It is the time to reinvent employee's roles and careers and integrate technology into business. In, essence the HR functions now must have the ability to make a company spin a new direction quicker. Thus, it is time to rethink about the changed role of HRM in the new millennium.

REFERENCES

Biswajeet Pattanayak, HRM, Prentice Hall of India.
C.B. Gupta, Human Resource Management
David A. De CENZO &Stephen P. Robbins, HRM, Prentice Hall of India
Ian Beardwell & Len Holden, HRM, Mac Millan India Ltd
Internet Data-various websites
Journals and magazines- Effulgence, Business world
News paper – Hindustan Times
Tarek Khalil, Management of Technology, Mc Graw Hill International Editions

19

MANAGEMENT OF GLOBAL HUMAN RESOURCES

Vivek Kumar

INTRODUCTION

Globalisation means managing human resources around the world. The globalisation of management is a fact of life. Today's business leaders are challenged to build dynamic, entrepreneurial and truly global organizations in pursuit of excellence. Globalisation of systems and processes facilitates the management of global operations. As new technology continues to change the face of the business, the last vestige of opportunity for a company in a competitive environment is its Human Resource. Globalisation of HR affects the global business. Gone are the days when the scope of human resources entailed little more than employee training and benefits programs. Although traditional back office functions are still important, today's global HR professionals are expected to deliver far more.

It is said, "people are our biggest assets". Human Resource Management and distribution defining the new age supply-demand chain. As new economies emerge from the shadows to jostle for space on the world business map, there is a distinct shift from the old "everything in-house" model to the "outsource everything except core competence'' model.

First of all before managing the human resource in globalised world we have to understand the global environment, which starts with the following points:

- Importance of Understanding the Global Environment
- The Evolving Global Economy
- The Political Landscape
- Regional Trade Zones
- Evolving Technologies
- The Global Workforce
- Cultural Diversity in the Global Environment

Formal processes include:

- Scanning and detecting changes in the environment
- Monitoring environment to determine changes
- Using forecasting to predict what will happen

- Selecting strategy to follow

Now after scanning and detecting the environment, the role of HR department starts with Line managers, HR professionals and employees.

ROLE OF THE HR TRIAD

Growing internationalisation of business has its impact on HRM functions. The HR department is required to cope with the problems of unfamiliar laws, languages, practices, competitions, attitudes, management styles, work ethics and more. As little as 10 years ago, the market value of a company was largely determined by its financial track record. But that's no longer the case, now about 85 percent of the market value of a company is determined by intangible factors. The HR function deals directly with all those intangibles, making it much more important in today's global organisation.

Managing international HR activities is an elaborate and complex task, it includes following activities:

- HRP
- Recruitment and Selection
- Training and Development
- Performance Management
- Remuneration
- Repatriation
- Employee Relation

The global HR manager proceeds with the job of hiring the number of people of the right type. The global HR manager not only selects people with skills, but also employees who can mix with the organisation culture.

International businesses are said to adopt three approaches to staffing-ethnocentric, polycentric, geocentric.

Ethnocentric Approach: In this approach, all key management positions are held by parent-country nationals. It is appropriate during the early stage of business, because at this stage firms are concerned with transplanting a part of business that has worked well in their home country. Firms such as P&G, Philips originally followed this approach.

Polycentric Approach: The polycentric staffing requires host-country nationals to be hired manage subsidiaries, while parent-country nationals occupy key positions at corporate headquarters. For example Hindustan Lever Limited (HLL), the Indian subsidiary of Uniliver, has locals as its chiefs.

Geocentric Approach: This staffing philosophy seeks the best people for key jobs throughout the organisation, regardless of nationality.

For example, Coca-Cola is one of the most successful multinational enterprises. Coca-Cola manages its global operations through 25 operating divisions that are organised under six regional groups- North America, the European Union, the Pacific Region, the East Europe/Middle East Group, Africa. It achieves the corporate HRM functions into two main ways: 1. By propagating a common HR philosophy within the company. 2. By developing a group internationally minded mid level executives for future senior manager responsibilities. Coca-Cola believes that since it is a global company, senior manager should have had international exposure.

The seven workplace practices which are strongly related with the superior performance in the new economy are:

- Change leadership
- Pay and incentives
- Stakeholder Commitment
- Strategy
- Talent creation
- Business discipline
- Structures

In globalisation, many companies are going for merger, acquisitions and take over to enter into foreign market or to be big. For example there were two major acquisitions between P&G and Gillette and Dabur and Balsarsa recently. The whole HR activities of a company change due to these business processes:

HR ACTIVITIES DURING INTERNATIONAL JOINT VENTURE PROCESS

Formation

- Initial Planning
- Select business dev. Mgr.
- Facilitate Communications
- Select skilled negotiators

Development

- Surface Concerns of Senior Heads
- Evaluate proposed structure for impact on learning/knowledge
- Recruit and select Sr. staff

Implementation

- Select participants for mission, vision, values, strategy
- Design HR policies and practices
- Assist mgrs. to implement HR policies and practices

Advancement & Beyond

Evaluate and revise HR systems to support knowledge flow to the parent and learning by the parent

KEY HR ACTIVITIES IN THE STAGES OF THE MERGER, ACQUISITION PROCESS

Stage 1: Recombination

- Participate in assessment of target firm
- Assist in thorough due diligence assessment
- Participate in planning
- Assist in developing HR practices for rapid learning and knowledge transfer

Stage 2: Combination

- Recruit and select integration managers
- Transition team design and staffing
- Assist in deciding who goes
- **Facilitate establishment of new culture**

Stage 3: Solidification and Assessment

- Establish criteria and procedures for assessing staff
- Monitor and strengthen new culture
- **Develop and implement plans for adjustment and learning**

CHALLENGES OF INTERNATIONAL HRM

The 1990s have brought a revolutionary change in our business. Post liberalization is marked by a shift from command economy to market driven economy; from sheltered market to competitive market; from monopoly to competition and from domestic trade to global trade. Such a shift calls for a different approach to HR activities. The need of the present is a proactive approach, a strategy that helps HR managers to foresee events and take appropriate actions before they occur. The major challenges are;

- Global culture
- Corporate reorganisations
- New organisational forms
- Changing demographic of workforce
- Different laws

The cultural differences make the HR function complex. The working style, language difference, cultural values should be first studied by a parent company before entering into a new country.

The early 1990s brought us news about corporate mergers, takeover, and massive reorganizations to fend off hostile take over bids. It is difficult to imagine circumstances that pose a greater challenge for HRM than reorganizations resulting from acquisitions, mergers, divestitures or take-over threats. The reorganisations will have impact on organisational levels and employees.

The organisational forms in which people are employed shape the practice of HRM. Elsewhere, economies have been undergoing fundamental change and the structures of organizations and the relationships between them have been transnational. The basic challenges to HRM and enterprise management come from the character of competition. The issue is not large firms or small firms but large firms, medium firms, and small firms. Competition in many sectors is no longer between individual firms, large or small, but between constellations firms. The HR managers will have to cope with the implications of networked relations more and more. For eg. to manage its global expansion Ranbaxy ids trying to build a "Human Bridge" across its operations in various countries. The objective is to ensure that its Indian Workforce is turned into global market needs.

The major challenge that has resulted from changing workforce demographics concern dual career couples, couples where both partners are actively pursuing professional careers. Organizations have been accustomed to using job moves and physical relocation as an important means of development talent. The increasing number of dual-career professionals limited individual flexibility in accepting such assignments and may hinder organizational flexibility in acquiring and developing talent.

India's private bankers are encountering problems of attrition and inadequate manpower. Over the last few months, banking have been finding the going tough at a time when some of the foreign banks have been expanding their private banking business. Given the shortage of trained manpower for these operations, salaries have grown by close to 25-30% annually. In the private banking segment, a stiffer who joins normally makes the progression from a relationship manager to a financial advisor, and then to private banker. Bankers are adopting different methods to surmount the problem of attrition and the paucity of manpower Some, like ABN Amro, they are picking up people from other segments like debt and equity capital market, mutual funds and insurance companies.

As the law changes the organisational functioning get affected. *For example,* the Japanese govt. has unveiled a new migration plan. The Japan's justice ministry asked its cabinet to firmly consider bringing unskilled foreign workers. While the focus is on unskilled labour, the policy will also try attracting more professional & technical skills by allowing them a larger stay & making them easier to take up permanent residence, as against the current proactive of issuing three-year visas.

The reason for it is the country's impending demographic crisis. According to the UN, Japan's population will decline from 127 million in 2004 to 109 million in 2050. In fact a small working population will have to support a larger group of pensioners.

So due to this new policy more foreigners will move to Japan and the T&D activities of Japanese companies will increase.

GLOBAL WORKFORCE

The World Bank report on global workforce growth predicts a jump of 19% during the period 1998 to 2010, from 2.85 billion to 3.38 billion workers. And this growth will predominantly be fueled by what the World Bank categorises as the "low income" countries of the world. It adds that another quarter of global workforce growth will come in the middle income countries while just 3% of the world's increased workforce will come in the high-income countries. In fact, among developed countries, only the US will show any worthwhile growth during this decade. The European Union will actually lose about a million workers during the period while Japan will lose about 2 million workers.

With market opening up, the dynamics are changing fast. For the developing world, the most encouraging aspect of the report is that among the low-income countries, between themselves, India (21.5%) and China (14.8%) will contribute 36% of the total growth of the world's workforce.

FUTURE OF HR

As the new dimensions of workplace are increasing the Human Resource Management is becoming much more compatible for MNCs as well as domestic companies. Best in class companies believe globalization of resources is the true measure of globalisation. Global resources help harness diverse perspectives within an organization. India's top tier IT companies are truly global entities. Companies like Infosys and Wipro have built a global workforce that has been successfully integrated into the respective companies' culture and ethos. Even the companies like L&T are going global. Through outsourcing the HR function is changing from administrative to a strategic one. The information technology is helping the personnel to be more tech savvy. Through technology the workforce has become virtual as employees can work any time anywhere. Management and workers are learning to coexist. The provisional figures for last year show that the number of mandays lost cumulated to about 14.5 million against the yearly average of 26.8 million in the 2001-03 period. So we can say, according to the changes and challenge HR is changing it and is playing a dynamic key role in raising the world economy.

REFERENCES

Business Today magazine, 27 march, 2005
Economics Times, April05, 2005.
Globalisation-An Overview, Dr. Hiru Bijlani
HRM Review, ICFAI University Press. March, 2005
Human Resource & personnel Management, K. Aswathappa, 2004.
The Times of India, March19, 2005.
www.altavista.com.

Part III: Information Technology and Marketing of Services

20

INDIA: A GLOBAL TOURISM HUB

M.K. Sehgal, Adarsh Kumar Aggarwal and Hirak Das Gupta

ABSTRACT

Tourism provides the second highest net foreign exchange earnings to our economy. Tourism industry is the largest employment generator of the world. It is estimated that, by 2010, this industry will create 7 million new jobs, may contribute Rs. 1,30,000 crore in capital investment and may have 7% share in GDP. Foreign tourist arrivals are at 2.64 millions during 2000. This is the only industry, which requires less or no investment, yet generates billions of foreign exchange to the country's exchequer. Many small nations viz. Singapore, Srilanka, Malaysia, Thailand etc. woo millions of foreign tourists and bag billions of foreign exchange. India, albeit, the country houses rich tourism locations, yet, figured in the bottom of the rank table in wooing foreign. Apart from foreign tourist, domestic tourist has emerged as a powerful source for the development of tourism. Around 1.50 million domestic tourists have made a trip outside their places. This paper examines the importance of this area, the challenges and opportunities that awaits to make the customer satisfied and to lift the economy of the country. This paper touches strategies to enhance tourism through Corporate Market Responsibility and role of tourism in economic growth. To conclude, India possesses every thing. The rich cultural heritage, sculptures, sprawling deserts, highest mountains, palaces, temples, delicious cuisine, rare mixture of life style etc, which makes it a 'Cross Cultural Paradise' stays on 'Unity in Diversity'. The Government and private sector need to work earnestly and with a commitment to develop India, a most attractive tourism destination in the world. The paper touches all the facts and figures, option of marketing, strategies and techniques to woo international visitors and also to encourage domestic tourism.

INTRODUCTION

"A complete digital experience will be created on-line to meet the requirements of travelers. Banners will also be displayed on all leading travel portals. And we soon plan to have a one stop travel shop on our website. Focus will be on all facets of travel like leisure, pilgrim, adventure and business." Ministry of Tourism, Government of India, November 2002.

"We have been promoting health tourism as one of our niche tourism products. Although traditionally Ayurveda was there, but healthcare has also gained lot of ground with India offering better facilities at a reasonable cost." Rathi Vinay Jha, Secretary, Ministry of Tourism, Government of India, December 2003.

"States are busy extending Brand India to a niche, exclusive, hi-end trajectory - from Goa developing itself into a business destination to Chhattisgarh aiming to become an eco-tourist's delight; from Gujarat, Karnataka and Maharashtra targeting the upper-end tourist for their luxury trains to Andhra Pradesh using IT to market its destinations." A Financial Express Article, February 2004.

As an economic activity (traditionally tourism is included in the tertiary sector) tourism on the one hand is defined by the demand and consumption of visitors. On the other hand, tourism refers to the goods and services produced to meet that demand. That means it comprises a whole range of different activities, for example transport to and at the destination, accommodation, catering, entertainment, shopping and services of travel agencies and outgoing and incoming tour operators.

A look at a travel brochure these days, shows a tendency by travel writers to speak in superlatives. "Grand colonial architecture", "sparkling beaches", "amazing monuments" and so on; and yet, for a country like India, all these adjectives and more, are totally appropriate. India's tourist industry is booming due to a rush of foreign tourists and increased travel by Indians to domestic and overseas destinations.

Nearly three million foreign tourists visited India in 2004, a 15 percent increase over the previous year. Prospects look even better this year, with tourist arrivals already up nearly 20 percent. The visitors are pouring in from all over the world: Europe, Africa, Southeast Asia and Australia. At the same time, the number of Indians traveling abroad last year increased by 30 percent, to 4.5 million. The boom has come even as global tourism has dropped, due to the September 11 terrorist attacks in the United States, the outbreak of Severe Acute Respiratory Syndrome in East Asia, and the Iraq war.

Tourism professionals cite several reasons for the buoyancy in the Indian industry. The recent surge in the Indian economy has raised middle class incomes, prompting people to spend money on vacations abroad or at home.

At the same time, India's emergence as a global information technology hub and an aggressive advertising campaign by the government are credited with changing India's image from that of a land of snake-charmers, and sparking new interest among overseas travelers.

Domestic tourists are also fueling the industry's revival. Many of them escape from the summer heat on the plains to resorts in the Himalayan Mountains. One of the major beneficiaries this year is Kashmir, where a cease-fire between India and Pakistan has reduced violence, if not completely, at least enough to help revive the state's sagging tourism industry.

However, for a country bursting with tourism opportunities, we have been slightly slow on the uptake, as far as promoting these destinations goes. A point highlighted by the First Planning Commission way back in 1955, which ranked tourism 269th on their priority list of industries – lower than even the development of light-houses! At that time, the average number of tourists who came knocking at our door, was around 15,000.

Growing wealth will continue to produce new tourists as vast numbers of people in developing countries join the middle class. More over the programmes initiated by WTO and other agencies resulted in moulding a new perception on tourism. Some qualitative development trends in tourism include the development of the concept of sustainable tourism, increased market segmentation, development of new forms of tourism, especially those related to nature, wildlife, rural areas, culture, sustainable tourism, eliminating poverty etc. India having considerable touring potential, today occupies a very tiny place in the international market of tourism.

Evaluating the touring potential of India, the rich historical- cultural heritage, the variety of nature, the main forms of tourism can be singled out , that can develop the most successfully. They are mainly forms of specialized and non-traditional tourism.

- **Cultural, Historical, Cognitive Tourism:** Generally they are of amateur or professional interest (this form of tourism is very perspective in India and always had a predominant place due to the rich historical-cultural heritage of India).
- **Echotourism:** The potential of India is great due to landscape variety and virgin nature, besides the flora and fauna contain very special elements. According to the definition of WTO "Tourism Statistical Consultation" -

"Tourist" –a person in another country, with various purposes not forbidden by the given country, from 24 hours to one year period, not performing any paid activity in the country or place of arrival, who in the lodging of collective or single distribution has slept at least once and who travels. At the same time historical monuments are in harmony with the nature and with the area, which gives the opportunity to combine successfully these forms of tourism.

- **Religious Tourism:** India was the first to adopt Buddhism and having rich traditions, pilgrim journeys in religious areas is a great potential for religious tourism to be formed and develop.
- **Ethnic Tourism:** The existence of great diaspora can play a decisive role in the sphere of inbound tourism. In future, Indians visits to their ancestors' birth-place can be a share in the segment of inbound tourism of India
- **Rural and Agrotourism:** These forms of tourism develop more and more in the whole world. Indian fruits, vegetable are very attractive by their taste and ecological purity, and Indian gardening, wine-making, making dry fruits, canning are very special, so it is a very great potential in the sphere of existing rural tourism development. As Indian historical monuments are generally situated near villages, and Indian ethnographic traditions are well preserved in these very places, so it allows combining successfully rural and cultural forms of tourism.
- **Winter Sports Tourism:** The variety of locality creates favourable conditions for the development of such kind of tourism.
- **Health Tourism:** This type of tourism has its traditions in India
- **Business Tourism:** Business visits can include an element of tourism such as sightseeing and special activities that can lead to repeat visits and the tendency of growth of this type of tourism was very noticeable during the recent years.

GLOBAL MARKET TRENDS

Consumer trends in tourism are gradually changing and require an appropriate response in terms of both policy formulation and investment.

Current market trends indicate that:

- Long haul travel should grow faster than intra-regional travel. A growth of 24 per cent is expected by 2020.
- People with less time for leisure are likely to take more frequent but shorter trips nearer home, opening up opportunities for 'neighbouring country' tourism.

- The experienced traveller wants authentic, off-the-beaten-track vacations in remote and less well-known places as against luxurious five-star vacations, leading to an interest in rural and ethnic tourism.
- The increase in the number of people with lots of money but little leisure time has resulted in a growing emphasis on rest and relaxation, and 'wellness' and 'health' holidays.
- The elderly population in key tourism generating markets has shown a preference for cultural tourism against sun-and-sand vacations.
- There is notable and increasing interest in spiritualism.
- The demand for eco-tourism and nature based holidays is expected to double and even triple in the next 20 years.
- Sports and adventure holidays continue to be popular with the young.

The interest in cultural tourism, spiritualism, 'wellness' holidays, eco-tourism and rural tourism would tend to favour India, provided the country can avail of the opportunities offered to maximise its natural advantages in these areas. The development of new tourism products and destinations during the, must be based on market research and demand, keeping the source markets and the age groups of the tourists in mind. At the same time, the Government must develop new source markets nearer home and make India a safer destination for women tourists and family holidays.

Tourism the sector that integrates a wide range of economic activities is now regarded as the world's largest industry. The dramatic growth of tourism over the last 50 years is one of the most remarkable economic and social phenomena of the period. International Tourist arrivals grew, in real terms, from a mere 25 million in 1950 to 698 million in 2000, which represents an average annual growth rate of 7 pc over the period. But for the industry 2003 and 2004 are exceptional years. According to FHRAI, foreign tourist arrivals are expected to reach at 2.6mn in FY04, an increase of 10% yoy. There has been a consistent growth in international arrivals and travellers from new markets such as SE Asia, China and Russia are increasing their presence. The resilience and opening up of the Indian economy is likely to attract foreign investors. According to the World Tourism Organization (WTO), international tourist inflow in India is expected to grow at 6.5% CAGR, which means increase in the tourist arrivals from the present 2.5mn to 6.0mn in 2010 and 10mn by 2020.

Placing the growth of tourism in the analytical framework, we can say that this is due to three factors

- Social factors that enhance demand
- The technology, which makes traveling easier and

- Information technology, which transforms selling strategy of tourism.

The innovations of new products (selling holidays by new methods, time-share resorts etc) played its own role in the development of the industry. The development of tourism is characterized by continuous expansion of area and diversification of destinations. All these increased the demand for tourism, which is determined mainly by wealth.

ECONOMIC IMPACT OF TRAVEL AND TOURISM IN INDIA

The main positive economic impacts of tourism relate to foreign exchange earnings, contributions to government revenues, and generation of employment and business opportunities. These are discussed briefly here.

Total Demand: India Travel & Tourism is expected to generate INR1,846.3 bn (US$38.8 bn) of economic activity (Total Demand) in 2004, growing (nominal terms) to INR7,027.7 bn (US$90.4 bn) by 2014. Travel & Tourism Demand is expected to grow by 8.8% per annum, in real terms, between 2004 and 2014.

Capital Investment: India Travel & Tourism capital investment is estimated at INR485.3 bn, US$10.2 bn or 7.2 per cent of total investment in year 2004. By 2014, this should reach INR1,663.9 bn, US$21.4 bn or 7.8 per cent of total.

Personal and Business Travel and Tourism: India Personal Travel & Tourism is estimated at INR927.3 bn, US$19.5 bn or 5.0 per cent of total personal consumption in year 2004. By 2014, this should reach INR3, 612.9 bn, US$46.5 bn or 6.1 per cent of total consumption. India Business Travel is estimated at INR114.5 bn, US$2.4 bn in year 2004. By 2014, this should reach INR387.4 bn or US$5.0 bn.

Exports: Visitor Exports play an important development role for the resident Travel & Tourism Economy. India Travel & Tourism is expected to generate 6.7 per cent of total exports (INR283.2 bn or US$6.0 bn) in 2004, growing (nominal terms) to INR1, 267.3 bn or US$16.3 bn (5.4 per cent of total) in 2014.

Foreign Exchange Earnings: Tourism expenditures and the export and import of related goods and services generate income to the host economy and can stimulate the investment necessary to finance growth in other economic sectors.

On a broader scale though, finding accurate figures and statistics is something of a problem even today, and in the absence of a centrally appointed and vigilant monitoring body, one can only make estimates. Immigration figures based on disembarkation cards are unreliable as they make little distinction between visitors coming only to India or backtracking from Nepal or other neighbouring countries. Also, a large number of arrivals stay with family or friends and do not contribute much to the forex kitty.

Forex earnings are the best criterion of the quality and number of tourists a country is attracting.. In 1989, our earnings in forex were Rs. 2,103 crore, which rose to Rs. 5,000 crore in 2001 (Table 20.1).

Table 20.1: Foreign Exchange Earnings from Tourism

Year	Tourism Earnings (Rs. crore)	% Annual change
1980-81	11,66.3	43.8
1981-82	10,63.9	-8.8
1982-83	11,30.6	6.3
1983-84	1,225.0	8.3
1984-85	1,300.0	6.1
1985-86	1,460.0	12.3
1986-87	1,780.0	21.9
1987-88	1,890.0	6.2
1988-89	2,103.0	11.3
1989-90	2,456.0	15.0
1990-91	2,444.0	10.0
1995-96	4,000.0	9.0
2000-01	5,000.0	5.5

Source: Department of Tourism.

Contribution to Government Revenues: Government revenues from the tourism sector can be categorized as direct and indirect contributions. Direct contributions are generated by taxes on incomes from tourism employment and tourism businesses, and by direct levies on tourists such as departure taxes. Indirect contributions are those originated from taxes and duties levied on goods and services supplied to tourists.

The World Travel and Tourism Council estimates that travel and tourism's direct, indirect, and personal tax contribution worldwide was over US$ 800 billion in 1998 - a figure it expects to double by 2010. (Source: WTTC/Michigan State University Tax Policy Center)

Contribution to GDP and Employment: India's T&T Industry is expected to contribute 2.0 per cent to Gross Domestic Product (GDP) in 2004 (INR 618.4 bn or US$ 13.0 bn), rising in nominal terms to INR 2,002.3 bn or US$ 25.8 bn (2.1 per cent of total) by 2014. The T&T Economy contribution (percent of total) should rise from 4.9 per cent (INR 1,477.4 bn or US$ 31.1 bn) to 5.2 per cent (INR 4,972.5 bn or US$ 64.0 bn) in this same period.

Employment: India T&T Economy employment is estimated at 24,456,600 jobs in 2004, 5.6% of total employment, or 1 in every 17.8 jobs. By 2014, this should total 27,790,000 jobs, 5.7% of total employment or 1 in every 17.5 jobs. The 11,404,000 T&T Industry jobs account for 2.6% of total employment in 2004 and are forecast at 12,441,200 jobs or 2.6% of the total by 2014.

Accounting for 3.6% of world's GDP and 2.8% of world's employment, the travel and tourism sector has emerged as one of world's largest service sectors. In terms of the larger travel and tourism economy concept, travel and tourism accounts for 10% of world's GDP and 7.8% of the world's employment. An investment of Rs 10 lakh in tourism, creates 89 jobs, as against 45 in agriculture, and 13 in manufacturing for the same investment. In the Indian context, although travel and tourism sector accounts for 2.1% of India's GDP and 2.6% of India's employment, its relative share in relation to both Southeast Asia and the world is considerably lower. Although travel and tourism sector accounts for 2.1% of India's GDP and 2.6% of employment, its relative share in relation to both Southeast Asia and the world is considerably lower (Tables 20.2 and 20.3).

Table 20.2: Travel and Tourism Sector (2002 – 2012)

	2002			2012		
	Value	Share	Y-o-Y Growth	Value	Share	CAGR Growth
T&T Economy GDP (in US$Bn)	3283.00	10.0%	-1.1%	6352.00	10.6%	4.0%
T&T Economy Employment (in millions)	198.10	7.8%	-1.6%	249.49	8.6%	2.3%
India						
T&T Economy GDP (in US$Bn)	24.40	4.8%	3.3%	72.00	5.5%	8.9%
T&T Economy Employment (in millions)	23.66	5.6%	0.1%	30.64	6.4%	2.6%

Source: World Travel & Tourism Council.

Stimulation of Infrastructure Investment: Tourism can induce the local government to make infrastructure improvements such as better water and sewage systems, roads, electricity, telephone and public transport networks, all of which can improve the quality of life for residents as well as facilitate tourism.

The Govt. has finally granted the tourism industry "infrastructure" status, and an increase in plan outlay. The international airports in the four metros are to be upgraded to world-class standards and six comprehensive tourism circuits will be developed to help promote tourism.

Table 20.3: Benchmarking India with the World

	India	World
T&T Economy contribution to GDP (in % terms) 2002	4.8%	10%
T&T Economy contribution to Employment (Nos) 2002	23.7 million	198.1 millions
Domestic Tourists (Nos) 2001	234 million	NA
Foreign Tourists (Nos) 2001	2.53 million	<699 million
Dom Tourists (Average spend in rupees) Ballpark estimate	Rs. 630 per day	NA
Foreign Tourists (Average spend in USD) Ballpark estimate	$ 1250 per person	NA

Contribution to Local Economies: Tourism can be a significant, even essential, part of the local economy. There are other local revenues that are not easily quantified, as not all tourist expenditures are formally registered in the macro-economic statistics. Money is earned from tourism through informal employment such as street vendors, informal guides, rickshaw drivers, etc. The positive side of informal or unreported employment is that the money is returned to the local economy, and has a great multiplier effect as it is spent over and over again. The World Travel and Tourism Council estimates that tourism generates an indirect contribution equal to 100% of direct tourism expenditures.

Future-wise: Forecasts provided by World Tourism Organisation on a longer time frame are presented in Table 20.4.

As can be seen from the exhibits presented above, the tourism growth rates projected in the sub-continental region are higher as compared to other regions and the world average as a whole.

Going forward for India, the travel and tourism sector holds immense potential for employment generation and income growth. According to World Travel and Tourism Council's (WTTC) forecast most of the growth in tourist arrivals is expected in South Asian countries over the coming years. WTTC projects India's travel and tourism industry to grow at CAGR of 9.3% up to 2012 with corresponding employment growth expected at 3%, much above the expected growth in South East Asia and the world aggregate level. The WTO projects an annual average growth rate of 6.2% in South Asia over a larger timeframe till 2020.

Table 20.4: International Tourist Arrival Forecasts by Region (millions)

	Base Year	Forecasts		Average Annual Growth Rate (%)	Market Share (%)	
	1995	2010	2020	1995-2020	1995	2020
Total	565.4	1006.4	1561.1	4.1%	100%	100%
Europe	338.4	527.3	717.0	3.0%	59.8%	45.9%
East Asia/Pacific	81.4	195.2	397.2	6.5%	14.4%	25.4%
South Asia	4.2	10.6	18.8	6.2%	0.7%	1.2%

Source: World Travel & Tourism Council.

It can thus be argued that the next decade is a window of opportunity for India. This statement finds its basis in a couple of interesting facts and trends. There is a visible shift in regional preferences of the global tourist from the US and Europe to Asia. India, with its multifarious tourism strengths embedded in natural resources, culture, ethnic diversity and heritage can attract a lion's share of this potential shift.

Domestic tourism in India is another oft ignored opportunity. With a robust domestic tourist base in excess of 200 million tourists coupled with rising middle class incomes and tourism wants, the domestic traveller is bound to grow in numbers in the next decade. This further buttresses our point for making tourism a focus sector for India and logically for Indian states.

The more significant findings of the many reports done for the international travel and tourism industry show that the focus of the industry is gradually shifting from Europe and N America to east/South Asia and the Pacific. A research forecast by the

World Travel and Tourism Council pegs tourism industry growth at 4.5% over the next ten years. Turkey is expected to be the fastest growing travel and tourism economy over the next 10 years at a rate of 10.2%, while India will have a growth of 9.7%. This buoyant outlook also reflects a possibility of the creation of nearly 7 million jobs over the next 10 years

BARRIERS TO GROWTH

There are several factors that are responsible for the inadequate growth of the tourism sector in India. These are: barriers related to approach, barriers that discourage private investment, factors that affect competitiveness and factors that affect the long-term sustainability of tourism.

Approach-Related Barriers

- Absence of consensus on role of tourism
- Lack of priority to tourism on account of unappreciated potential
- Relatively low levels of investment.
- Lack of interest on the part of the state governments – the primary players.
- An unprofessional ad hoc approach.

Barriers that discourage private investment

- Absence of legislative support
- Lack of policy integration and co-ordination
- Lack of long-term investor-friendly policies.
- Heavy and multiple taxes, restrictive aviation and
- Land policies.

Factors that affect competitiveness

- Lack of concern for competitiveness
- Complex visa procedures
- Inadequate facilitation services
- Lack of quality infrastructure
- Lack of emphasis on product quality
- Lack of training at the 'cutting edge'
- Lack of hygiene
- Low utilisation of modern marketing and publicity tools.

MAIN PRECONDITIONS FOR INDIAN TOURISM DEVELOPMENT STRATEGY

1. To create legislative and normative-legal field, which in the conditions of market economy will promote the formation of equal competition in the sphere.

2. To define the low boundaries of service quality by classifying the sphere standards and hotels creating a base to protect the interests of consumers in the sphere.
3. To form a favourable field for inbound and local tourism.
4. To promote investments in the sphere of tourism and to stimulate the reconstruction of materio-technical base.
5. To promote the progress of domestic touring result in local and foreign markets with the help of informational-advertising provision, creating conditions for increasing the in-flow of tourists.
6. To form a permanent education system in the field of tourism industry and create conditions for providing the sphere with high-qualified specialists, promote the local population to get involved in the sphere of touring services.
7. To create favourable conditions for the development of various types of tourism.
8. To create favourable tax field for the exportation of Indian touring services.
9. To create among the society and especially state employees special attitude towards the sphere.
10. To create a security system for tourists particularly for non-traditional services.
11. To create preconditions for India to participate in international and regional touring programs and to cooperate with international organizations effectively.
12. To develop a national consensus on the role of tourism in the development agenda of the nation through the National Development Council.
13. To enhance the effectiveness of public sector investment through the inter-sectoral convergence and prioritisation of tourism-related infrastructure programmes in other sectors like special tourist trains, rail and aviation links, rural roads etc..
14. To remove the barriers to growth to leverage private sector investment.
15. To mobilise the support of the primary players, viz. the State Governments, in tourism development.
16. To mobilise public support by creating awareness of the socio-economic benefits of tourism for the host community.
17. To provide legislative and regulatory support to protect the tourism industry, the consumer and the environment.
18. To involve the rural sector in tourism and start mobile training units for service providers in rural areas identified for the development of tourism.
19. To augment training facilities in hotel management and food craft and build the capacity of service providers at the cutting edge.

20. To create world class circuits and destinations, eschew haphazard development

STRTEGIES FOR DEVELOPMENT

- Improving and Expanding Product Development: Product development strategy related to the special interests of tourist target markets.
- Cultural and heritage tourism should be expanded. India has a vast array of protected
- For the development of beach and coastal tourism, identify sites on the west coast of India for the development as beach resorts by the private sector. The sites should be offered on long-term lease at preferential terms. These sites should primarily be on the beaches of Goa, Kerala, and North Karnataka because of easier access by air. Kochi in Kerala and the Andaman and Nicobar Islands should be developed as international cruise destinations because of their proximity to international cruise routes and their exotic appeal.
- India's unmatched variety of cuisine is becoming increasingly popular in the world and should be developed as a special attraction. It is proposed to create a highly skilled workforce of culinary professionals through an innovative incentive scheme not only for India but also to promote Indian cuisine internationally.
- Village tourism should be promoted as the primary tourism product of India to spread tourism and its socio-economic benefits to rural areas.
- India's great wildlife variety has not been developed as a tourist attraction. Wildlife sanctuaries and national parks should become an integral part of the Indian tourism product. Priority should be given to the preparation of site and visitor management plans for key parks. The quality of tourist facilities available at the parks should be enhanced after a prioritisation of parks. Tentatively these should be: Corbett National Park, Kanha National Park, Bandhav Garh National Park, Kaziranga, Madhumali, Bharatpur, Periyar, Ranthambore, Little Rann of Kutch, Chilka, and the Sunderbans.
- India has the greatest adventure tourism assets in the world in the Himalayas and its rivers. Mountain-based adventure activities should be developed and promoted. Regulations and certification for adventure tourism operators should be introduced so that the minimum standards of safety and conservation are met.
- India receives only a minuscule proportion of the global meetings, conventions and exhibition market. It is important that India develops a

world-class international convention city not just for the sake of tourism development but also for international and domestic trade and commerce.

- India's most unique tourism product should be holistic healing and rejuvenation packages. In focussing on this, it should capture the essence of Indian culture for international and Indian visitors alike.
- India's fairs and festivals, some of which are already well established such as the Pushkar mela, the Desert Festival at Jaisalmer, the Kumbh Mela etc. should be promoted as unique products of India. The Festivals of India programme should be re-introduced in the top 12 future markets for India - initially with an annual event in the United Kingdom and the United States, to be followed by triennial events in the other markets.
- Shopping should be recognised as an integral part of tourism. The development of dedicated shopping centres for traditional crafts designed along the lines of village haats such as Dilli Haat and Shilpgram should be encouraged and information on where to procure specific crafts made available through shopping guides.
- Delhi should be positioned as the cultural capital of India supported by an ongoing and vibrant calendar of cultural events. The development of such a niche-based special interest product mix should position India as a unique and
- competitive destination.

CREATION OF WORLD CLASS INFRASTRUCTURE

- The need for physical infrastructure for tourism ranges from ports of entry to modes of transport to destinations (airways, roadways, railways or waterways), to urban infrastructure such as access roads, power, water supply, sewerage and telecommunication. This underscores the need for inter-sectoral convergence of infrastructural schemes and programmes that could support tourist destinations.
- The road network is vital for tourism as almost 70 per cent of passengers in India travel by road. Many tourist circuits are entirely dependent on roads. The current government plan for the road system in the country covering both inter-state highways and improvements to rural roads directly supports tourism development. There is urgent need to construct and improve highways linking the 22 world heritage sites and places of tourist significance. The Ministry of Road Transport and National Highways should collaborate with the Ministry of Tourism in this effort.
- The Indian railway system can also become an enormous asset to the development of the tourism and hospitality industry in the country. The

railways hold a special fascination for foreign tourists who wish to travel the country. For the vast majority of domestic tourists also, the railways is the most affordable means of travel linking the length and breadth of the country. Introduction of special tourist trains with pre-set itineraries and private sector participation should be encouraged.

- The Indian Railways plan to establish 100 hotels at railway stations to serve specific tourist centres. The private sector should be given incentives to operate these hotels on long-term leases. These hotels should provide clean and inexpensive accommodation for budget tourists. The Indian Railways also owns a number of heritage structures, which, if effectively maintained and marketed, could serve, both as railway stations and places of tourist interest.
- India has five hill railways, which compare with the best hill railway systems in the world. The enormous tourist potential of these products should be tapped -. As steam-hauled trains like the Royal Orient, Buddha Parikrama, Palace-On-Wheels and Fairy Queen are extremely popular with tourists, steam traction for special tourist segments should be continued. Trains like the Shatabdi and the Rajdhani with a special tourism and hospitality focus should be planned both for foreign and domestic tourists.
- India's 7,000-km coastline and her mighty rivers should be tapped for the promotion of cruises. Care should be taken to develop world class tourism products. As the Ministry of Tourism's financial assistance to the states has not been able to have the desired impact in terms of creating of world class tourism infrastructure, the emphasis must shift to the development of specific travel circuits as internationally competitive destinations and the convergence of resources and expertise for these circuits.
- The availability of trained manpower is essential to achieve excellence in the tourism sector. At present, there are 21 Institutes of Hotel Management and Catering Technology (IHM&TC) and 13 Food Craft Institutes in the country. In addition, a good number of accredited institutes also cater to the growing demand in the service sector. It is estimated that only 50 per cent of the requirement of the market is met by these institutes. In addition, 15 more Food
- Craft Institutes should be set up ,and efforts should be made to take culinary crafts and training to the rural areas through mobile training units. A new scheme on capacity building to train service providers in the unorganised sector such,as small hotels, dhabas, restaurants and other eating joints is also suggested.

STRATEGY FOR EFFECTIVE MARKETING

- As there is fierce competition for tourists from India's source markets, India needs to change its traditional marketing approach to one that is more competitive and modern. It needs to develop a unique market position, image and brand, which cannot be held by any other competitor. India's positioning statement should capture the essence of its tourism product to convey an 'image' of the product to a potential customer. This image should be related not only to its ancient Vedic civilisation with a cultural heritage that continues to thrive especially in its rural areas but also to its essentially secular nature.
- An extensive market research programme should be launched in the target source markets and tourism products developed to cater to the interests of each source market. An effective and ongoing market representation presence should be established with the travel trade in each source market and an Internet portal should be set up in various languages to provide information, a description of the product and the product requirements of the target market segments. The Internet has a great impact on the marketing of travel and tourism. It has already established itself as a channel through which tourism organizations can promote their destinations and products. Indian tourism should utilise both the Internet and other emerging interactive technologies to avail of the benefits to be gained.

THE PATH AHEAD

- The tourism sector needs a national consensus on the role and place of tourism in national development and the early removal of impediments that have hitherto handicapped its growth. For the creation of 18 million jobs through tourism requires a substantial investment of Rs. 38,800 crore at the rate of 47 jobs per one million rupees of investment, both from the public and the private sector..
- Public sector investment, though limited, can be made more efficient through the intersectoral convergence of policies and programmes supportive of tourism. An integrated inter-sectoral investment plan that provides effective infrastructural support to tourism through the Ministries of Railways, Surface Transport, Shipping, Civil Aviation, Urban Development, Rural Development and Environment and Forests etc. can be achieved through the preparation of a tourism component plan. Private sector investment can be enhanced by removing the barriers to growth and expediting critical policies that are being

evolved. Public and legislative support should be essential for the sustainable development of the sector.

CONCLUSION

Tourism is the third gross foreign exchange earner after gems, jewellery and textiles. India's share in the global tourist arrivals is less than 0.4 percent while its share in the country's GDP is 1.2 percent. Tourism industry is the largest employment generator of the world. This is the only industry, which requires less or no investment, yet generates billions of foreign exchange to the country's exchequer. Even with this tiny global market share, the economic impact of tourism on the country has been significant.

South Asia received only0.8 percent of world's total tourist arrivals and only one percent of the total foreign currency generated by tourism globally. According to WTO India was the most favoured destination among countries of the south Asian region receiving more than 50 percent of the total foreign tourist traffic in the area. India had always beckoned visitors from all over the world to experience its 5000 years old civilization. The country's diversity of culture, faiths, languages, fairs and festivals, majestic monuments and captivating wildlife made for a variety which could take in almost the whole world. All these provide a unique set of opportunities for tourists to enjoy.

Still, tourist arrivals are still just a fraction of those in such popular Asian destinations as Bangkok. Even with the recent boom, industry experts say that in order to attract more visitors, India needs to upgrade its airports, roads and other infrastructure to global standards. The Government and private sector need to work earnestly and with a commitment to develop India, a most attractive tourism destination in the world. The success of tourism industry will be largely determined by the success achieved on all strategic fronts

REFERENCES

Arun Kumar Sarkar, action plan and priorities in tourism development, Kanishka publishers, New Delhi.

Bhatia, A.K. 1983: Tourism development principles and practices, sterling publishers (P) ltd.

Krishan K. Karma, Tourism Theory, planning and practice, Indus publishing company, New Delhi.

Pran Nath Dhar, 2000: International Tourism, Emerging Challenges and future prospects, Kanishka publishers, Delhi.

Pran Nath Seth, 1997: successful tourism management volume I, fundamentals of tourism, sterling publishers (P) ltd, New Delhi.

Praveen Sethi, 1999: handbook of effective travel and tourism, Rajat publication New Delhi.

Rakesh Kapoor, tourism policy organization and management, Kanishka publisher, New Delhi.

Ratandeep Singh, 2000: tourism marketing: principles, policies and strategies, Kanishka publishers, Delhi.

Sharma J.K. 2000 tourism planning and development: a new perspective, Kanishka publishers, New Delhi.

21

IMPACT OF RELATIONSHIP MARKETING ON BEHAVIOURAL CUSTOMER LOYALTY

MJF Fazeela Ahsan

ABSTRACT

Customer loyalty is increasingly seen to be crucial for the success of business organizations, with the growing realization that attracting new customers is far more expensive than retaining existing ones. It has been suggested that a way of increasing behavioural customer loyalty is through secure relationships between buyers and sellers. Despite the growing body of literature on relationship marketing issues, little empirical research has been conducted on the link between relationship marketing and customer loyalty in a Sri Lankan context. This paper attempts to address this gap by analyzing whether the practice of relationship marketing can enhance behavioural loyalty among business customers of courier companies. Following a literature review four hypotheses were developed and required data was collected. Then the correlation been the two variables in the courier has been analyzed. Findings reveal that trust and commitment between parties involved is crucial to enhance loyalty among customers.

INTRODUCTION

Relationship building and management, which has been labeled as relationship marketing, is one of the leading approaches to marketing which eventually has entered the marketing literature. Relationship marketing practices are becoming more and more important today as they can be used as a competitive tool to fight the increasing competition.

The evolution of relationship marketing has been one of the most notable topics in marketing over the last two decades in general and in business marketing in particular. Even though the term is recently used in consumer marketing, relationship marketing originated from and has thus far been discussed mainly in business marketing. And researchers indicate that a paradigm shift towards relationship marketing is taking place and has taken place in service marketing in particular. Thus this research paper will analyze the correlation between, relationship marketing and behavioural customer loyalty in the service sector taking courier companies as a representative sample.

For the past few decades Sri Lanka has been slowly moving towards industrialization, in this process the service sector of the country has also been growing steadily. As a result of this the service sector became more and more competitive and focused on customer satisfaction, delight etc. All in all they all wanted to earn a loyal set of customers for them to survive in the long run. The situation was similar in the courier industry as well. And today the industry is crowded with both national and multinational companies. Some of the companies which operate in Sri Lankan courier market are ACX International, Air action, Aramex Airbone Lanka (Pvt) Ltd, Dee Pee Ex International (Pvt) Ltd, Sprint Pronto Lanka (Pvt) Ltd EMS speed post – Sri Lanka, Express transportation solutions, TNT International express, United parcel service, DHL and Federal Express. Out of two kinds of customers existing in the courier company business buyers account for a larger proportion of company revenues almost 80% of revenue is generated by them.

Around the globe courier industry has become very popular due to inconveniences faced with postal and other related services. Therefore the industry is becoming very competitive and industry players have been using various marketing strategies from time to time. Advertising in particular has been heavily used by major multinational players. It seems that the paradigm shift from marketing mix to relationship marketing is being experienced in the courier industry as well, where companies feel the practice of relationship marketing will give a competitive edge over their competitors. The ultimate objective of relationship marketing is to create loyal customers. Loyalty has two main components – attitudinal loyalty and behavioural loyalty and this research paper analyses whether the practice of relationship marketing creates behavioural loyalty among its customers, because the aim of every marketing strategy is to add value to the bottom-line.

RESEARCH ISSUE

Customer loyalty is increasingly seen to be crucial to the success of business organizations, with the growing realization that attracting new customers is far more expensive than retaining existing ones. It has been suggested that a way of increasing customer retention is through secure relationships between buyers and sellers. Surprisingly, however, and despite the growing body of literature on relationship marketing issues, little empirical research has been conducted on the link between relationship marketing and behavioural customer loyalty in Sri Lankan context. It is said that effectiveness of relationship marketing tactics should be evaluated in terms of the behavioural changes they create. Behavioural loyalty is a composite measure based on consumers' purchasing frequency and amount spent at a retailer compared with the amount spent at other retailers from which the consumers buy. Because it is assumed that customers who committed to relationships might have a greater propensity to act because of their commitment. Also length of contact is another measure of behavioural loyalty.

Relationship Marketing is a relatively new concept emerged within the marketing literature over the past decade. Essentially developed from theories of services marketing and the network approach to industrial marketing, relationship marketing has been argued to cause a fundamental directional change in mainstream marketing. The term "relationship marketing" is becoming widely used, although consensus on a definition of the construct has yet to be reached. Gronroos (1996:5-14) defines relationship marketing in the following way: "marketing is to establish, maintain, and enhance relationships with customers and other parties, at a profit, so that the objectives of the parties involve are met". This is achieved by mutual exchange and fulfillment of promise. This definition sets out the ultimate goal of relationship marketing, rather than what relationship marketing actually entails. The ultimate objective of relationship marketing is to create loyal customers. Loyalty has two main components – attitudinal loyalty and behavioural loyalty.

Also this definition is supplemented by a statement that such a marketing approach should lead to trusting relationship between the parties involved. The underlying aspects of such an approach to marketing are that not only getting customers and creating transactions (identifying and establishing) are important, but also maintaining and enhancing ongoing relationships ; that not only giving promises is the responsibility of marketing, but also the task of fulfilling promises; and that profitable business relationships rely on the capability of a firm to develop trust in itself and its performance among its customers and other stakeholders.

Pessy and Mathews (1998) suggested that a high level of trust and commitment between both parties, a long time horizon (or length of relationship), open communication channels between both parties with information exchanged between both parties, having the customers best interest at heart, a commitment to quality for both parties and attempt to favourably lock-in or retain the customer should be considered as some of the indicators of relationship marketing.

Loyalty is a concept which has enjoyed wide currency and usage within the field of consumer behaviour for many years. In the words of Disney (1999:491), "the organizations become increasingly customer focused and driven by customer demands, due to a need to meet the customers' expectations and retain their loyalty becomes more critical". To a business organization, loyal customers are a competitive asset (Dekimpe et al., 1997). Indeed, customer loyalty represents a basis for charging price premiums, and a barrier to competitive entry (Aaker, 1991). Customer loyalty is also a key determinant in predicting market share (Baldinger and Rubinson, 1996: Jacoby and chestnut, 1978) and profit levels (Reichheld, 1996). Furthermore, the dynamics of evolving business trends have dictated an increase in the importance of customer retention. Neal (1999:21) defines customer loyalty as "the portion of times a purchaser chooses the same product or service in a category compared with his or her total number of purchases in the category, assuming that acceptable competitive products or services are conveniently available".

Customer loyalty describes the tendency of a customer to choose one business or product over another for a particular need. Customer loyalty becomes evident when choices are made and actions taken by customers. Customers may express high satisfaction levels with a company in a survey, but satisfaction does not equal loyalty. Loyalty is demonstrated by the actions of the customer; customers can be very satisfied and still not be loyal.

Customer loyalty has become a catch-all term for the end result of many marketing approaches where customer data is used. In relationship marketing or database marketing or permission marketing or CRM, the ultimate target is to increase customer loyalty – getting customers to choose to buy or visit more. Increased customer loyalty is the end result, the desired benefit of these programmes. All of the above approaches have two elements in common – they increase both customer retention and the lifetime value of customers. Hence to a business organization, loyal customers are a competitive asset.

Where the construct of loyalty is concerned existing research has generally focused upon segmentation and measurement issue rather than integrating the loyalty concept into a wider body of marketing theory, thus the process by which customers develop a sense of loyalty to a particular firm still remains largely misunderstood.

"Brand loyalty is a highly sought after goal in the market place and building loyalty is seen as the central task of the marketing manager" (Bhatia and Bawa, 2002:39-45). The conceptual definition of brand loyalty coined by the authors was, "Brand loyalty is the tendency of a decision making unit to repeatedly purchase the same brands because it is propelled by positive attitude, perception, motives, and intentions for the brands. Also the authors declare that marketing managers should therefore know which of the strategic alternatives at their disposal give the best results vis-à-vis brand loyalty. Why brand loyalty is considered as such a phenomenon today is because brand loyal customers are difficult to for competitors to take away and brand loyal customers of competitors are hard to attract.

Theoretical literature on customer loyalty conceptualizes loyalty as an interaction of attitude and behaviour. In other words, loyalty (or the absence of it) is exhibited both through customer behaviour and also through attitude. Loyal behaviour might be manifested as repeat and relatively frequent purchase. Such behaviour may or may not be associated with a loyal attitude, which leads a customer to value the service of a company. Such attitudes may, not necessarily lead to repeat purchase, but might provoke loyalty behaviours such as participation in a petition to resist closure of a branch. Dick and Basu (1994:99-113) argue that loyalty is determined by the strength of the relationship between relative attitude and repeat patronage, and that it has both attitudinal and behavioural elements. One of the basis of attitude behaviour relationship, they propose four conditions related to loyalty: loyalty, latent loyalty, spurious loyalty and no loyalty.

There is a debate about the relationship between attitude and behaviour, and there is some support for the belief that attitude causes behaviour. On the other hand, East (1997) comments that attempts at establishing causal primacy may be unrealistic. He states that thoughts and feelings are interwoven and that changes in one component of the construct may affect others in the system. Other variables such as the social and physical environment as well as personal abilities have been found to pre-empt action. Incompatibility between attitude and behaviour may also occur because attitudes which embrace a set of circumstances make it difficult to predict a single behaviour. In certain circumstances, attitude may even be a consequence of behaviour (Uncles and Laurent, 1997) and both attitudes and behaviour may change over a period of time.

It is said that effectiveness of relationship marketing tactics should be evaluated in terms of the behavioural changes they create. Behavioural loyalty has been defined as a composite measure based on a consumers' purchasing frequency and amount spent at a retailer compared with the amount spent at other retailers from which the consumers buy. Furthermore some empirical evidence have been found for relationships between dimensions of relationship quality and behavioural loyalty. Bolton (1998), Macintosh and Lockshin (1997) report a positive paths from relationship satisfaction to both relationship duration and purchase intentions, which can consider behavioural indicators of loyalty.

In this respect this study focuses on measuring whether the practice of relationship marketing creates behavioural customer loyalty. The reason for choosing behavioural loyalty is because, whatever strategy is used, the marketer ultimately wants it to impact the bottom line. Consequently this study helps measure whether the practice of relationship marketing is profitable for the company. With reference literature, and the researcher's subjective judgement and convenience, purchasing frequency, amount spent at retailer and duration of contact have been chosen as indicators of behavioural loyalty.

CONCEPTUALIZATION MODEL

Central to the success of relationship marketing is trust of t buyer in the supplier (Mohr and Nevin, 1990). Trust can be defined as "the belief that a party's word or promise is reliable and that a party will fulfill his/her obligation in exchange relationship"(Schurr and Ozanne, 1987). The also identified that trust as the critical factor for the move from discrete market transactions towards continuous exchange relationships. Trust was viewed as one of the most relevant antecedents of stable and collaborative relationships. "It has been understood that commitment and trust are the key drivers of cooperative relationships within and outside the organizations", (Hunt and Morgan, 1994:24). The Centrality of trust in marketing relationships are made evident by the many research and some wide literature review that are already available. Trust is defined by the perception of reliability that, in buyers' view, is based on experience, or rather on the sequence of transactions/interactions characterized by the confirmation of expectations regarding performance and satisfaction. Hence trust increases the tendency of the customer to engage in repeat purchases.

It is thus expected that

H1 = A higher level of trust between parties involved leads to higher customer behavioural loyalty

Commitment is defined as the 'durable desire to maintain an important relationship', and is considered and antecedent of loyalty. Morgan and Hunt (1994) have identified its determinants as: trust, the degree to which customers and firms share the same values (value congruence), the level of shared aims in the relationship (goal congruence), and the value of the benefits deriving from the relationships, as well as the costs which interrupting the relationship would cause. Conceptual distinction between customers' commitment and loyalty are still unclear. As a result of this, the link between the commitment and the loyalty has received little empirical attention (Pritchard et al., 1999). However, a main difference can safely be said to reside in the context in which both constructs have been studied to date. More specifically, while commitment traditionally refers to the commitment a customer may feel to a marketing relationships with a given organization, customer loyalty traditionally refers to loyalty attitudes and behaviour towards the organization in general, or the organization's brands.

The relationship becomes the key component of delivering the utility, whereas loyalty is a reflection of the utility derived from the purchase itself. The greater the mutual commitment to the relationship, all other things being equal, the more loyal the customers. Furthermore, and as reported by Gruen (1995), commitment can be viewed as the motivator to act, rather than the act itself. It is therefore posited that the commitment to the relationship between the company and the customer affects the level of customer loyalty.

Scanzoni (1979) identified a number of stages two organizations might well experience going through a relationship. The most highly evolved stage was referred to commitment, a point in the relationship when both organizations attempt to strengthen the relationship and continue it just as long as it remains profitable. There is a high degree of trust and sensitive material may well be swapped between both organizations. Researchers have observed that information swapping (two-way information flow) between organizations is frequent, and important. Whatever the industry might be it is important to build commitment between parties involved. Hence:

H 2 = A higher level of commitment between parties involved leads to higher customer behavioural loyalty

Theodore Levitt (1983:111) noted "the sale merely consummates the courtship, how good the marriage is depends on how well the relationship is managed by the seller". If the relationship is to remain successful the customer should be at the hub of it and so it is important to have the customers' best interest at heart. Related to this issue is co-developing products and service augmentation. These will, in many instances, be employed by organizations adding extra service to differentiate from its competitors' offerings. In this context the "extras" must be valued by the consumer and not readily available elsewhere. Also a high emphasis on enhanced service and service quality is further cited as an essential element within relationship marketing (Christopher et al., 1991), because if customers are to be satisfied, their needs should be understood and if so the chances of that customer becoming loyal increases. Hence:

H3 = having the customers best interest at heart leads to higher customer behavioural loyalty

The above factors constitute an attempt to favourably lock-in or retain the customer and many academics espouse the importance of customer retention regarding relationship marketing theory (Wright et al., 1998; Ward et al., 1998). Barnes (1994) observes that tactics such as frequent buyer schemes, where the customer has to return to the same company to accumulate "points", develops a barrier to exit.

According to Philip Kotler (2000:48) the key to customer retention is "customer satisfaction". A highly satisfied customer stay longer, buys more as the company introduces new products and upgrade existing products, talks favourably about the company and its products, pays less attention to competing brands and advertising and less sensitive to price, offers product and service ideas to the company and costs less to serve than new customers because transactions are reutilized. Schneider (1980) observed: "What is surprising is that researchers and businessmen have concentrated far more on how to attract customers to products and services than on how to retain them". Selling products to existing customers is essentially more cost effective than the costs incurred while searching fro new ones.

Customer loyalty is the result of well-managed customer retention programmes; customers who are targeted by a retention program demonstrate higher loyalty to a business. All customer retention programmes rely on communicating with customers, giving them encouragement to remain active and choosing to do business with a company. The reason why organizations increasingly concentrate on customer retention is because "new customers cost 10 times to acquire" line is one of the most frequently made claims in marketing. Sometimes claim is that new customers cost five times, or six times or every ten times. Thus:

H4 = A higher level of keenness by the service provider to retain customer leads to higher customer behavioural loyalty.

Behavioural loyalty was being measured using the variables such as purchasing frequency, amount spent at retailer and the duration of contact.

Based On the research theme, literature review and conceptualization, the conceptual model depicted in figure was developed. In this model four hypotheses/causal relationships are assumed. Trust between parties involved, commitment, having the customers' best interest at heart, attempts made to retain the customer are assumed to be the independent variables. These four variables are considered to be indicators of relationship marketing; hence the degree to which the variables are present will indicate the degree to which a company practices relationship marketing.

Behavioural loyalty intern is the dependent variable, which will be measured with the aid of purchase frequency, amount spent at retailer, duration of contact and tendency to buy new products.

RESEARCH METHODOLOGY

Due to time and cost limitations and lack of expertise in the field of research it was decided that a survey among selected samples may be conducted instead of a census. Also a census may not be suitable when comparing cost and the benefit. The sample is to include business customers of courier companies. This segment was selected because the senior managers interviewed identified it as the main income generator (approximately 80%) of courier companies. Also relationship marketing strategies are commonly used with business customers whereas its use is very rare with personal customers. Subsequently in order to find the correlation between relationship marketing and behavioural loyalty the segment containing business customers was considered more appropriate. Geographically the sample will be limited to Colombo and suburbs due practical constrains.

Data collection is conducted using convenience method. Business customers' will be selected based on industries which generate the highest proportion of business to courier companies, consequently based on the importance questionnaires will be distributed. While consulting industry experts it was found that banks, garment factories, and tea exporters are the major clients of a courier company. Questionnaires were also distributed to friends and acquaintances who work for the chosen companies.

The sample size was determined as 35 respondents and it was decided to distribute 50 questionnaires to allow room for non-response. The reason for deciding upon the above sample size was because it was thought difficult to reach a bigger sample because courier is not a service which is regularly used across all businesses. As express deliveries are not required by all industries, a smaller sample of 35 was considered representative enough. At the end 37 questionnaires were collected from respondents.

The researcher had to engage in primary data collection as data on the research theme was not readily available. Especially data in Sri Lankan context was not available; also the courier industry is not which has been adequately researched. Primary data collection was conducted mainly using self administered questionnaire and personal interviews with industry experts. Also certain amount of observation was also used. The researcher had to settle with the above mentioned data collection methods due to practical difficulties associated with other data collection methods. Focus groups in particular were not used because considerable amount of expertise is required to play the role of a moderator.

A structured questionnaire was used, where it contained 19 questions, of which 16 were multiple choice questions and three were open ended questions. Out of the three open ended questions one was used to identify the courier company and two were used to obtain demographic data of the respondent. And out of the multiple choice questions one was used to identify whether the respondent has obtained the service of a courier company, one to identify the level of satisfaction with the service, three questions were pertaining to behavioral loyalty and eleven were related to relationship marketing.

Most questions were operationalized as a five-point likert type scale with high ratings indicating agreement, low ratings disagreement and the mid point was neutral indicating neither agreement nor disagreement. Although a high level of discrimination in responses leads to better understanding on the problem, too many responses might confuse respondents therefore a five point scale was considered more appropriate. Information was sought on the length of the respondents' patronage to the service provider (i.e. factual information was sought rather than intentions). And all questionnaires were printed in English.

It was decided that personal interviews should be conducted with Industry experts in order to get more detailed qualitative information and to understand relationship marketing practices of their respective companies. In this respect Marketing managers and Executives of DHL, Federal Express and TNT International express were interviewed. They were interviewed on the relationship marketing practices currently undertaken by their respective courier companies. Also their views on the different variables used in the research were also obtained.

The researcher spent around four and half hours at TNT Fort branch observing the company operations. This helped the researcher understand how a courier company operates. However the observation did not help obtain any information regarding behavioural loyalty because the researcher's presence at the company was very limited in time. And it was not practical for the researcher to observe individual respondents – as business customers generally contacted the courier company by telephone and gave details on the package to couriered. Therefore the use of observation was very much limited in scope.

DATA ANALYSIS

The collected data is part of a correlation research. Correlation is a measure which indicates both the strength and the direction of the relationship between pair of variables. There are two types of correlation measures, measure of linear correlation using interval variables and measure of rank correlation using ordinal variables. This study involves a linear correlation study as the data collected by the questionnaire is interval. Cohen and Holliday (1982) suggest that a value below 0.19 indicates very low correlation, 0.20 to 0.39 is low, 0.40 to 0.69 is modest, 0.70 to 0.89 is high and 0.90 to 1 is very high. These are rules of thumb and not considered as definite indicators however for analysis purposes a definition is needed hence the one above is used.

Data was mainly analyzed with the aid of SPSS 10.1 for windows. Analysis has been conducted under six major headings behavioural loyalty, service quality, trust, commitment, serving customers best interest and efforts made to retain customers respectively.

Service quality is an important determinant of customer loyalty. In times even though there might be good relationship between parties involved if the service quality is poor customers will be forced to switch. This study measures behavioural loyalty with the aid of duration of contact, frequency of use and relative expenditure.

Table 21.1 shows the Correlation between the independent variables (Service quality, Trust, Commitment, Customers' best interest, retaining customers and relationship marketing) and the dependent variable (behavioural loyalty):

Table 21.1: Correlation between Independent and Dependent Variables

Independent variables		Behavioural Loyalty
Service quality	Pearson correlation	0.522**
	Sig (2-tailed)	0.001
Trust	Pearson correlation	0.625**
	Sig (2-tailed)	0.000
Commitment	Pearson correlation	0.533**
	Sig (2-tailed)	0.003
Customers best interest	Pearson correlation	0.476**
	Sig (2-tailed)	0.003
Retaining customers	Pearson correlation	0.560**
	Sig (2-tailed)	0.000
Relationship marketing	Pearson correlation	0.740**
	Sig (2-tailed)	0.000

The Correlation between service quality and behavioural loyalty was found to be 0.522, and a correlation value of 0.40 to 0.69 is considered modest (Chen and Holliday, 1982). The coefficient of determination (r2) is 0.272. This means 27.2% change in behavioural loyalty is due to changes in service quality. Hence courier companies and service organizations in general should give serious consideration to service quality as it is also a determinant of behavioural loyalty.

The correlation between trust and behavioural loyalty was measured as 0.625, which means relationship is modest. Significance was found to be 0.000 which means the sample represents the population and the probability of the population not having a correlation is 0.000. This indicates that there is very correlation between the variables. Having the coefficient of determination (r2) as 0.390 means 39% change in behavioural loyalty is due to changes in trust between the customer and the service provider. Hence courier companies and service organizations in general should give serious considerations in building trust.

The correlation between commitment and behavioural loyalty was measured as 0.533, which means relationship is modest and the significance was found to be 0.001 which means the sample represents the population and the probability of the population not having a correlation is 0.001. By having the coefficient of determination (r2) as 0.284 it can be said that 28.4% change in behavioural loyalty is due to changes in commitment of both the customer and the service provider. Hence courier companies and service organizations in general should improve commitment between parties involved.

The correlation between serving customers best interest and behavioural loyalty was measured as 0.476, which means relationship is modest and the significance was found to be 0.002 which means the sample represents the population and the probability of the population not having a correlation is 0.002. And the coefficient of determination (r2) is 0.226. This means 22.6% change in behavioural loyalty is due to changes in the level of serving customers best interest. Out of all the chosen variables this recorded the lowest correlation.

The correlation between effort made to retain customers and behavioural loyalty was measured as 0.560, which indicates a modest relationship. And the significance was found to be 0.000 which means the sample represents the population and the probability of the population not having a correlation is 0.000. And the coefficient of determination (r2) is 0.313. This means 31.3% change in behavioural loyalty is due to changes in efforts made to retain customers. Hence courier companies and service organizations in general must put more effort in retaining their customers.

It is clear that this study measures relationship marketing with the aid of chosen indicators of relationship marketing such as trust, commitment, serving customers best interest and effort made to retain customers. When calculating an integrated mean fro relationship marketing a sum of 2.473 was found. This means respondents agree that courier companies practice relationship marketing to a satisfactory level. Also the correlation between the variables was measured as 0.74. Hence the relationship is considered strong. And the significance was found to be 0.000 which means the sample represents the population and the probability of the population not having a correlation is 0.000. This reveals strong significance. And the coefficient of determination (r2) is .5476 which means

54.76% of change in behavioural loyalty is due to changes in relationship marketing practices.

FINDINGS AND CONCLUSION

As a whole it can be concluded that relationship marketing palys a vital role in determining behavioural loyalty thus any expenditure incurred in developing relationship marketing is an investment. Therefore the courier industry and service industries in general should give more emphasis to relationship marketing practices in order to increase behavioural loyalty among their customers.

Service quality is an important determinant of customer loyalty. In times even though there might be good relationship between parties involved if the service quality is poor customers will be forced to switch.

Due to ever increasing competition in service industries, organizations are striving to differentiate them from competitors. In this endeavor relationship marketing has caught the attention of many marketers today. On the other hand customer loyalty is increasingly seen to be crucial to the success of business organizations, with the growing realization that attracting new customers is far more expensive than retaining existing ones. It has been suggested that a way of increasing behavioral customer loyalty is through secure relationships between buyers and sellers. This study has taken a dyadic, empirical, approach to the study of customer loyalty and relationship marketing.

Following a literature review on relationship marketing and loyalty hypotheses were developed. It was then transformed into a conceptual model. Subsequently the methodology of conducting the research was defined and then it was decided that personal interviews with industrial experts, self administered questionnaires and certain amount of observation and will used for data collection. In this respect three senior managers of DHL, FedEx and TNT were interviewed and the consumer survey conducted recorded a response rate of 74%.

From a more substantive point of view, the results provide evidence of, and insights into, how relationship marketing can enhance customer loyalty. All four indicators of relationship marketing which were chosen for this study trust, commitment, serving customers best and effort made to retain customers' revealed strong correlation with behavioural loyalty. Interestingly neither of them had a correlation value above 0.7 where as a strong correlation of 0.74 was found between relationship marketing and behavioural loyalty, also the significance between the variables was very strong. Hence relationship marketing is an important determinant of behavioural loyalty.

Another finding was that service quality and behavioural loyalty recorded a correlation of 0.52, which means the customer being satisfied with the product is also important to retain customers.

With regard to suitability of relationship marketing practices it was found that, since a large proportion of the offer is intangible, perceptions of customers play a major role in their success. And in order to persuade the customer their product offerings are superior strategies like relationship marketing is considered essential.

Also another factor which was commonly found was that, almost all companies made their best effort to find the most profitable customer and build relationships with them. And relationship marketing was mainly practiced among business customers than personal users. Because industrial buyers generated majority of the revenue and they were few in number, so focusing on them is easier. These findings on the courier industry can be generalized on service industries as it was chosen as a representative sample. Therefore service industries should give more emphasis to relationship marketing practices if they were to create behaviourally loyal customers. Hence it can be concluded that any cost associated with relationship marketing is an investment but not a cost.

MANAGERIAL IMPLICATIONS

Since a significant correlation between relationships marketing and behavioural loyalty was found it is necessary that top managers of courier companies be more conscious about their relationship marketing practices. Major changes in the business philosophy may be required if relationship marketing is truly to be adopted. To do this, employees should be trained especially on interpersonal skills and motivated continuously. And importantly they should be empowered, so that they can respond quickly to customer requirements. Another strategy would be, making regular contacts with customers and getting feedback on service quality. And rewarding loyal customers is necessary to make them feel important.

Also employees should be facilitated with necessary resources; a comprehensive data base in particular should be developed because to build a relationship one needs to know the person. The data base should include all relevant data pertaining to the client and clients' purchase behaviour. Thereby when a customer reduces or stops usage they can be contacted and reasons can be found. Also the data base will help predict consumer behaviour thereby the company can act proactively and satisfy consumer needs.

Since business customers generate majority of the revenue satisfying them to the fullest possible level is necessary. Because they are few in numbers, often there is contact with competing firms so any dissatisfaction will quickly spread through out the industry. Such problem can be avoided if organizations maintain good relationships with their customers.

RECOMMENDATIONS FOR FURTHER RESEARCH

Given the small sample size generated for this study, some statistical analysis was necessarily restrained in its sophistication. In itself, the size of the sample is not, however, a major weakness. Indeed, hypotheses were supported, despite the fact that the major drawback of small samples is the risk of not detecting true relationships (Speed, 1994), indicating that low statistical power was not an issue. And also the questionnaires were distributed among companies operating in greater Colombo area; hence the findings cannot claim to be representative of the entire country. And of the many indicators of relationship marketing only four were selected. Also the relationship between relationship marketing and behavioural customer loyalty has been tested, not other aspects of loyalty.

The study focuses on a single industry, namely that of courier industries. While useful in controlling for potential extraneous influences unrelated to the study, the limitation involved in studying a single industry constrains the generalization of the findings. Future research should seek to replicate the study onto different business sectors in order to assess whether the linkages uncovered here hold across different industrial and consumer populations. Also other attitudinal components of loyalty require search in Sri Lankan context.

Finally, as Iacobucci and Hopkins (1992, p.5) point out, " the focus in the analysis of 'dyadic interactions' is on a single relationship between two parties". Relationship marketing, however, should include efforts directed at "establishing, developing, and maintaining successful relational exchanges" with many other partners including, for example, suppliers, competitors, the government, and employees (Morgan and Hunt, 1994, p. 22). The future researchers involved in the study of links between firms' relationship marketing strategies and their partners' loyalty should consider examining the responses of more then two partners in the chain of business.

REFERENCES

Andrew D Pressey, Brian P Mathews (2000:272-28), "Barriers to relationship marketing in consumer retailing", Journal of Services Marketing, Volume 14, Number 3

B.S Bhati and Anupam Bawa (2002:39-45), "The arduous path to brand loyalty", IIMB Management Review, September

Christian Gronroos (1994:4-20), "From marketing mix to relationship marketing; towards a paradigm shift in marketing", Management Decision, Volume 32, No. 2.

Christian Gronroos (1996:5-14), "Relationship Marketing: strategic and tactical implications", Management Decision, Volume 34, Number 3

Jai Boem Kim (1999:118-129), "Relationship Marketing in Japan: The buyer – supplier relationship of four automakers", Industrial Marketing, Volumes 14, Number 2

Kristof De wulf, Gaby Odekerkeh, Schrode and Dawn Lacobucci (1999), "Investment in consumer relationships: A cross country and cross industry exploration",

Leanne H. Y. Too, Anne L. Souchon & Peter C Thirkell, "Relationship marketing and customer loyalty in a retail setting": A dyadic exploration by Martin Christopher and Adrian Payne (2000), "Relationship Marketing",

Mosad Zineldin (2000:9-23), "Beyond relationship Marketing: technological ship marketing", Marketing Intelligence and Planning, Volume 18, Number 1.

Pressey and Mathews, B.P (1998:39-53), "Relationship marketing and retailing: comfortable bedfellows?" International Journal of Customer Relationship Management, Volume 1, Number 1

Rajesh Singh (2003:34-43), "Developing relationship marketing with customers: a Scandinavian perspective", Library Management, Volume 24, Number ½

Stephen S. Tax, Stephen W. Brown, & Murali Chandrashekaran (1998:60-75), "Customer Evaluations of service complaint experiences: Implications for Relationship Marketing", Journal of Marketing, Volume 62, April

Susan M Keaveney (1998:71-82), "Customer switching behaviour in service industries: An exploratory study", Journal of Marketing, Volume 63, April

Prashanth U. Nayer (2000:9-19), "An investigation into whether complaining can cause increased consumer satisfaction", Journal of Consumer Marketing", Volume 17, Number 1.

Christine T. Ennew and Martin R Binks (1996: 219-230), "The Impact of service quality and service characteristics on customer retention: Small Businesses and their banks in the UK", British Journal of Management, Volume 17.

LINKAGE MODEL FOR BUSINESS EDUCATION INSTITUTIONS

Rukhsana Kalim and Rahmat-Ullah

ABSTRACT

Collaboration among academic institutions is highly admired to enhance the quality of education. A range of integration and collaboration models among academic institutions are available. Many key factors identified in these models e.g., curriculum development, distance education, institutional management, internalization of education, partnership of institutions in some programs, faculty exchanges, joint research, access to research equipments, committee membership, collaborative projects, library and documentation exchange, contracts, exchange of pedagogical material, joint participation in seminars and conferences, formal agreements like Memoranda of Understanding (MOU), etc. indicate the common forms of collaboration. None of these models take into account all of these factors together. One way or the other, some of the important factors are missed out.

This paper is an attempt to fill the gap in collaboration models already mentioned in the literature. A proposed collaboration model is developed covering all possible key variables determining collaboration among business institutions. To fit the model to the current situation of the business institutions, a survey of 12 leading public/private business institutions located in Lahore is conduced.

Results show a low degree of integration among the existing institutions, thus necessitating the need to plan and work on enhancing collaboration.

I. INTRODUCTION

Academic institutions are centers of learning involved in acquiring, creating, and disseminating knowledge. Academic institutions, especially universities, are becoming learning organizations as they are applying new ideas and changing into new ways of operating, mainly because of changing environmental pressures and conditions (Patterson, 1999).

The strategies of collaboration and alliances are considered important to strengthen learning organizations and to enhance the learning process. By learning, the organizations strengthen and extend their core competencies–a motive for alliance formation. Stata (1989) and Garvin (1993) emphasize the powerful lever given by the opening up of organizational boundaries and disciplines in stimulating the exchange of ideas and experience. Collaboration however, does not entail only one factor. It is a combination of different joint activities undertaken by academic institutions.

This paper attempts to develop a linkage model for business institutions. To explore the degree of linkage among institutions, primary data is collected from 12 leading business institutions located in Lahore.

The paper is organized into different sections. Section II discusses the importance and rationale of collaboration in the new era of information technology. Section III develops a model of collaboration. Section 1V discusses methodology and data collection. Section V analyzes results. Finally section V1 concludes the main findings of the paper.

II. COLLABOARTION AND INFORMATION CULTURE

In the era of mass information, every society desires to achieve not only the satisfactory levels of traditional (basic) literacy but also to face successfully new challenges posed by Internet Age and the Information Society. New types of illiteracy have sprung up, purely as a result of the new information and communication technological developments that have increased the ability of people to access, use, and distribute information (Ponjuan, 2002). New information products and services are generated virtually every second in this virtual cornucopia of online information resources with which we are now conformed.

The new concept of information literacy has emerged which entails several kinds of literacy such as conceptual, intellectual, cultural, and technological skills (Kokkonen, 1997). The information literacy is considered as a prerequisite for successfully pursuing academic studies and research in today's fast moving and highly competitive society. An information literate person is capable of (a) locating the information required (b) determining the relevance and reliability of the information, and (c) using the information in problem solution and decision making (Skovira, 1997). Hagerman (1995) and Pinnacle (2002) regard this new kind of literacy technical and instrumental which facilitates cross-cultural and intra-cultural comprehension and communication.

The information literacy process in the teaching and learning sector takes place through cooperation which is established among the various component members, including the academic authorities of various departments, laboratory managers, faculty members, university and school staff, and so forth. Such cooperation is viewed as a partnership between stakeholders with pedagogical expertise, subject expertise, and expertise in information organization and technology (Breivik, 1994).

Universities/colleges are the institutions which can be the effective source of information literacy. For building and developing learning organizations, five vital dimensions or disciplines have been introduced by Senge (1990, 1994)– personal mastery, mental models, building shared vision, team learning, and the crucial fifth discipline 'systems thinking'. Systems thinking, according to Senge (1990), is the cornerstone of how learning organizations think about their world. The strategies of collaboration and alliance are system solutions arising from systems thinking (Patterson, 1999). Grafting refers to the process whereby organizations internalize knowledge not previously available to them and add this to their store of knowledge (for example through mergers, and joint ventures). Ponjuan (2002) has identified various closely knitted dimensions and components of information culture such as human, information, infrastructure, cooperation, leadership, and social conditions. These dimensions and their components help in promoting information culture and building organization culture in the society.

Recently, various foreign universities and institutions are making efforts to collaborate with each other. The objective behind this closer interaction is to promote academic and research activities. In the United States, twenty collaborations between historically black colleges and universities (HBCUs) and Doctoral/Research universities were reported in the literature in 2003 (Adessa and Diane, 2003). These collaborations tend to focus on medicine and science, and were initiated basically to promote research and training activities. In Australia, for instance, greater synergies and collaborations among Publicly Funded Research Agencies (PERAs) and universities are to be proceeded (Clark, 2003). The University of the Sunshine Coast and the Agency for Food and Fibre Sciences (Department of Primary Industries) have signed and begun to implement, a Memorandum of Understanding that involves a commitment to create synergies, integrate infrastructure, jointly develop R&D programs and projects, undertake staff exchanges and joint appointments, collaborate in research training, and align institutional development (Clark, 2003). Perimeter Institute of Canada has adopted specific methods of interaction between Perimeter and Canadian universities e.g. cross appointment is facilitated for any of its senior researchers with any relevant local university. The University Linkage Program (U-Links) has been introduced in the United States that builds mutually beneficial relationships between Thai and American colleges and universities. It facilitates the transfer of knowledge, expertise, and technical assistance from the United States to Thailand (KIAsia, 2003). Network research group in Malaysia is also making an effort to create linkage among research and education institutions.

Knowledge effects refer to the benefits of the outcomes of university activities, notably the production of highly educated graduates, and the production and dissemination of knowledge to local businesses. Collaboration facilitates the transfer of knowledge, expertise, and technical assistance between academic institutions. Alliance and integration may result in an increased range of qualifications and fields of study, and consolidation and dominance in particular areas of teaching and research.

Collaboration can bring cost efficiencies for the institution for sharing capital, intellectual, and servicing resources. Institutions having insufficient resources or lack of necessary infrastructure to support faculty and student research or doctoral education can benefit from collaboration with those institutions which are rich in all these resources. Faculty research may contribute to local and national development. Students' research participation via integrated system may also enhance learning experience as well as motivate to acquire more knowledge.

Collaboration leads to provide more learning opportunities through pooling of partner's resources, skills, capabilities, and knowledge. The students benefit from alliance and integration arrangements. They can have access to a fuller range of disciplines, stages and awards, and can have more choice and flexibility. They can be equipped with the experience, skills, and knowledge that will allow them to work across cultures and nations in an increasingly interconnected world.

I11. COLLABORATION MODEL

A range of models of integration and collaboration among educational institutions have been discussed at length by Patterson (1999). These models represent distinct features of collaboration among universities. For instance, contract model postulates formal arrangements to be made for availability of particular subjects or units of a course by one institution to the students of another. Under these arrangements, each institution has specific contract obligations.

In collaborative model memorandum of understanding can be signed for the broader cooperative relationship.

Validation model facilitates students to gain a university qualification or part-qualification of the validating university, through another institution. These models highlight the widespread and growing trend for post-secondary education to move away from the traditional segmented system of elite (usually university) and 'other' (usually vocational) institutions towards fusing of complementary institutional strengths, and system permeability.

Many key factors from these models can be identified to discern the degree of collaboration among different institutions. These factors may be listed as:

1. Curriculum development
2. Exchange visits of faculty and students
3. The existence of exchange programs to provide a two-way flows of students.
4. Joint programs with other institutions
5. Joint curriculum development
6. Contracts and franchise arrangements with different institutions
7. Participation in national conferences
8. Joint research and publications
9. PhD co-supervision
10. Shared laboratories
11. Sharing library facilities

All the aforementioned models take and discuss one or the other factor of collaboration. The model presented here is a unique model covering different areas of collaboration. Linkage or collaboration can be initiated via signing formal agreements like MOUs or by arranging some types of joint academic and research activities. Four key factors, curriculum, exchange, research, and resource sharing synthesize the linkage. Sub factors further synchronize these key factors. Equal weight age may be given to all the key factors of linkage. The model can be tested by collecting data on the factors.

IV. METHODOLOGY AND DATA COLLECTION

Primary data was collected to find out the degree of collaboration of different academic institutions. For this purpose, a questionnaire was developed that contained different factors contributing towards linkage among academic institutions. A survey was conducted to get the data from twenty leading business education schools located in Lahore (Educational Guide of Pakistan, 2003). The response rate was 60 percent and the data was obtained only for 12 institutions. The respondents were deans and faculty members of the respective institutions. Data is analyzed simply by making frequency table distribution.

V. ANALYSIS

Basic profile of these institutions (Table 22.1) show that on average four programs i.e BBA, MBA, M.Sc Economics, B.Com are offered. Data depict a reasonable number of faculty members. Number of students on average enrolled in these institutions does not seem very high.

Table 22.1: Profile of Institutions (Average)

Institutions	12
Programs Offered	4
Faculty Ph.Ds Associate professors Assistant Professors Lecturer Research Fellows	 2 3 5 5 1
Students enrollment	440
Books provided	5811
Computers	91

When asked about the liaison with other institutions, 58% replied in affirmative (Table 22.2). However, liaison with local institution was lower (16.7%) than foreign institutions (33.3%). This may be the marketing strategy especially of private business schools to collaborate with foreign institutions. The results are further supported by other two variables "student exchange" and "faculty exchange" where respondents showed their partnership more strong with foreign institutes than with local institutes (Table 22.3)

Table 22.2: Liaison Response (%)

	Yes (%)	No (%)
Liaison with other Business Schools	58.3	41.7
Local	16.7	83.3
Foreign	33.3	68.7

Identifying factors determining collaboration it is found that the degree of link among business institutions is extremely low (Table 22.3). Only one factor i.e. the sharing of library has gained the highest score (41.7%) among all other factors determining collaboration. Some degree of foreign student exchange (25%) and foreign faculty exchange (27%) do exist. Joint seminars carry the weight age of 18.5%. Joint Publication is nil.

Table 22.3: Factors Determining Collaboration

Factors	Yes (%)	No (%)
Curriculum		
Distance Learning	16.7	83.3
Joint Program	9.0	91.0
Exchange		
Student Exchange		
Local	16.7	83.3
Foreign	25.0	75.0
Both	8.3	91.7
Faculty Exchange		
Local	8.5	91.5
Foreign	33.0	67.0
Research		
Joint Research	8.0	92.0
Joint Publication	0	100
Joint Seminars	16.6	83.4
Resource Sharing		
Library	41.7	58.3

Many limitations of the data warn to interpret the results with caution. Sample size is not large enough to test the model rigorously. Many institutions were not ready to share the basic information as a matter of their institutional policy. Nevertheless, a crude idea may be obtained about the degree of linkage among business institutions. The results show that the degree of linkage among business institution located in Lahore is extremely low. If these institutions want to enhance collaboration and to increase the sharing of knowledge jointly, they will have to think seriously on different aspects of collaboration.

VI. CONCLUSION

Linkage and collaboration among academic institutions is essential for the enhancement of the knowledge and for the receipt of the benefits associated with it. An effort has been made, in this paper, to build a linkage model and to explore the degree of linkage among business institutions in Lahore. For this purpose a questionnaire was developed to gather primary data from twelve leading institutions. The results have shown that on average liaison with other institutions is high. It is quite possible that liaison may be confined to only one particular activity. By considering all factors of linkage together, an extreme low degree of collaboration seems to exist. Only library sharing sources has shown a comparatively high degree of response. Foreign student exchange and faculty exchange do also exist. Results indicate that business institutions have not yet started thinking on the lines of strong and effective collaboration.

REFERENCES

Adessa C. and Diane H. (2003), "Exploring Collaboration Among Historically Black Universities & Doctoral/Research Universities in the USA."

Breivik, P. (1994), Literacy in an Information Society, Information Reports and Bibliographies, 1991, 20 (3): 10-14. cited by: Bruce, C. S. Information Literacy Services–Computing Training, Information Literacy Blueprint. Clark P. (2003), "Review of Closer Collaboration between Universities and Major Publicly Funded Research Agencies",

Garvin, D. A. (1993), "Building a Learning Organization", HARVARD Business Review, Vol. 71, No 4, pp. 78-91.

Glenys Patterson (1999), "The Learning University", The Learning Organization, Vol. 6, No. 1, pp. 9-17.

Hagerman, J. (1995), "quoted by Ponjuan G." (2002) The Role of Collaboration Among Leaders from Various in Creating an Information Culture", White paper prepared for UNESCO, the US National Commission on Libraries and Information Science, and the National Forum on Information Literacy.

Kokkonen, O. (1997), New Trends in Information Literacy. Linkoling Electronic Articles in Computer and Information Sciences, Vol. 2, no. 10.

Pinnacle L. quoted by Ponjuan G." (2002) The Role of Collaboration Among Leaders from Various in Creating an Information Culture", White paper prepared for UNESCO, the US National Commission on Libraries and Information Science, and the National Forum on Information Literacy.

Ponjuan, Gloria (2002), "The Role of Collaboration Among Leaders from Various in Creating an Information Culture", White paper prepared for UNESCO, the US National Commission on Libraries and Information Science, and the National Forum on Information Literacy.

Senge, P., (1990), "The Fifth Discipline, The Art and Practice of the Learning Organization, Currency Doubleday, New York, NY; Random House, Sydney; Century Business, London.

Senge, P., (1994), "Building Learning Organizations", in Costin, H.I. (ed), Readings in Total Quality Management, Dryden Press, Fort Worth, TX.

Skovira, R.J. (1997), "On Being Information Literate. En: Systems, Peole, Understanding. Proceedings of the 45th Annual Meeting of the American Society for Information Science. Vol. 28, Medford, N.J.L. Learned Information, Inc. P. 341.

Stata, R., (1989), "Organizational Learning – the Key to Management Innovation", Sloan Management Review, Vol. 30, No. 3, pp. 63-74.

23

MANAGEMENT EDUCATION AND NGOs: ROLE AND ISSUES

Ranjana Agarwal

INTRODUCTION

The stream of management education deals basically the art and science of accomplishing tasks or achieving goals with the available resources. Management focuses on managing best the resources available with a complete set of techniques and skills. Hence, mgmt education can help all sectors of the economy to achieve its goals in best possible way by efficient management systems. Recent trends in management education show that management education has now expanded to a range of subjects. The scope of management schools is not restricted to the corporate sector. It now covers issues of non profit sector as environment, health, education and micro enterprises.

Changing attitudes in the global scenario show that various issues of social sector are being dealt in great detail by non government organizations (NGO's). A slow pace of poverty alleviation and the enormity of social deprivation make the presence of NGOs more relevant today than ever before. Any institution created for a purpose needs to be managed in order to survive and prosper. These NGO's perform many roles. Some of the functions of NGO are Development and Operation of Infrastructure, Advocacy for and with the Poor, Technical Assistance and Training, Facilitating Communication, Supporting Innovation, Demonstration and Pilot Projects and Research, Monitoring and Evaluation.

NGOs are key players in the development field, they need to be process-oriented, quality-oriented and result-oriented. There is a need today to reorganise NGOs to inject professionalism, to market their causes and to create a distinct brand image for donors and beneficiaries. The need is for a strategic refocussing to develop a holistic approach/allied diversification, position itself, evolve to ensure continued relevance to move along the learning curve and grapple with change.

How does management education help in functioning of NGO's in the changing global scenario? The present paper examines these aspects. It examines firstly, some of the functional areas where NGO's are making use of management education. Secondly, the paper discusses some aspects of business school interface with social sector.

SECTION 1: NGOs AND MANAGEMENT EDUCATION

Management education can help NGO sector in many different ways. Some of the key areas where management education can directly contribute are capacity building of NGO's, issues of microfinance and small scale enterprises.

Capacity Building: In the changing context of development in global environment, voluntary organisations are working towards improving the conditions of socio-economically disadvantaged and marginalised sections of society. For effective functioning, these organisations need to acquire skills to manage their organisations and develop appropriate and sustainable interventions. Thus Capacity building of personnel working in non-government organisations (NGOs) becomes crucial for enhancing their managerial skills and leadership potential. It is this context that management education becomes crucial for NGOs.

Capacity Building is required in areas as are namely Leadership development, Operating Systems management-Administration, Financial and Reporting Systems, Developing performance standards as well as Monitoring and evaluation. There is need for Fund Raising and resource mobilisation as well as Communication, Presentation and Documentation Skills. Institute of Rural Management, Anand offers a Management Appreciation Programme for Voluntary Organisations (VOLAG-MAP). The main aim of the programme is to meet the demand for professionalising the NGO sector. VOLAG-MAP is designed for senior personnel from voluntary organisations in developing countries who have spent considerable period of time in these organisations, and whose job content is managerial rather than involving direct implementation. Today these managers coordinate the activities of many people, guide younger entrants into the working of the organisation, maintain critical interface with external agencies and perhaps manage an entire project or programme for the organisation. These senior NGO personnel would benefit from a formal exposure to the principles and applications of development management, which form the core of this programme.

Microfinance: Microfinance (MF) has emerged as a popular and a credible instrument of livelihood promotion and empowerment. MF intervention refers to provision of access to small loans without physical collateral to the poor, especially the women, while encouraging them to save regularly in order to combine thrift and self-help for their own development. At the core of microfinance is the idea of addressing the problem of poverty and deprivation by enabling the poor to access financial capital hitherto denied to them. The goal is sought to be achieved through creating innovative mechanisms or channels whereby poor could access easily savings, credit, insurance and other services for overcoming their vulnerability. Efforts are being made in India to scale up MF interventions which call for a major thrust in terms of both creating an enabling policy environment as well as promoting strong network of institutions for delivering MF.

The MF intervention in India which started with a few local NGO initiatives in the mid 1980s has now spread widely and includes agencies which are active both in the formal and informal sectors. The effort to mainstream the sector started with the initiative of National Bank for Agricultural and Rural Development (NABARD) to link-up Self-help Groups (SHGs) promoted by NGOs and MF Institutions (MFIs) with the formal banking sector. By March 2004 more than one million SHGs have been linked with the banking system in the country. Besides the linkage programme, there have been many other initiatives in the microfinance sector. The Government of India has set up Rästriya Mahila Kosh (RMK) to support and finance micro-finance programmes. Similarly Small Industries Development Bank (SIDBI) has established SIDBI Foundation for Microcredit (SFMC) for supporting the sector. Many NGOs have promoted MFIs which have emerged as role models. In the coming years, MF sector is expected to grow in a big way with a major emphasis being placed on it by Government of India. An estimate by the Task Force on Micro Finance of NABARD puts the demand for MF to be in the order of Rs. 15,000 to Rs. 50,000 crore involving about 7.5 million families, supported by about 1000 MFIs, 2000 NGOs and 10,000 branches of the commercial banks by 2004.

The growth visualized requires careful direction and active support from various quarters. Given the fact that the sector consists of a large number of informal institutions like NGOs dealing with the poor and very small clients, the support may have to go beyond financing. This may include capacity building, institutional development, policy advocacy etc. Capacity building of MFIs has come to be regarded as one of the major prerequisites for mainstreaming the MF sector. Except for few, most MFIs in the country are still in their nascent stage of development. Moreover, much of the MF intervention by the NGO sector is in the form of a project lacking the much needed organisational form and capacity. Upscaling the operations of MFIs and NGOs would require strengthening their organisational capacity. Professionalising the management of these institutions is one of the possible ways of building their capacity. Relevant and quality training, research and other activities become important in the effort towards capacity building of MFIs. The existing arrangements for training and research in the country need to be geared-up to suit the specific and emerging needs of the MF sector.

Management Education and Microfinance: Institute of Rural Management Anand (IRMA) is a premier rural management institute set up 25 years ago with the purpose of professionalising development organizations. IRMA has set up a Chair in Microfinance in 2004 with the support from Microfinance Management Institute, Washington for contributing towards capacity building of the sector. The Chair seeks to achieve its goal mainly through training, research and other activities focusing on microfinance

The MF Chair integrates MF issues into the existing structure of progammes and activities of IRMA. The activities of the Chair may be classified under two broad categories: Knowledge Dissemination and Knowledge Development in MF. Under knowledge dissemination, there are Courses in PRM Programme, Doctoral/ Fellow Programme, short-Term Training/ Management Development Programmes(MDPs). For Knowledge Development, there is Cases and Training Material Development, Research and Consulting Activities, Distance Education Programme and various Workshops and Seminars.

Small Scale Enterprises: With the Indian economy getting integrated with the global economy, it has become important for small scale enterprises to gear up their operations to explore, penetrate and develop new markets. With its distinct advantage of adaptability and flexibility, SSEs have great potential to generate employment opportunities and spur the growth of the economy. In the rural context, SSE development has emerged as a major strategy to combat the problems of poverty and unemployment. Small enterprise development, a proven developmental initiative towards employment and income generation is being widely accepted and implemented by the voluntary sector. Their role has also been recognized in the latest plan documents of government as well.

Entrepreneurship Development Institute of India (EDI), is an international resource organisation for training, teaching and research in entrepreneurship development. EDI organizes a 8 week programme for preparing a cadre of development consultants titled "Certificate Course for Rural Business Development Service Providers / Consultants".

Through this programme, EDI would create a cadre of independent development consultants and equip them with skills that are critical to the functioning of NGOs and execution of income generation and economic development programmes. These consultants would in-turn provide necessary professional advice and support to various players in different ways i.e.

- NGOs: in exploring sources of funds, pursuing income generation activities and rural industries development programmes more vigorously;
- Funding agencies: in project monitoring, evaluation and impact assessment;

- Budding entrepreneurs: in providing escort services and counselling for speedy implementation of their proposed business activities.

After completing this 8 week programme, the participants would become versatile counselors for executing diverse tasks. As majority of NGOs are generally not in a position to hire full time experts for managerial counselling and functions, these trained counsellors can also provide their services to NGOs on the management front.

SECTION 2: MANAGEMENT SCHOOLS INTERFACE WITH NGOs

Post Graduate Diploma in Management of NGOs (PGDMN): EDI, Gujarat gives a postgraduate diploma in management of NGO's of 1 year duration. The emphasis throughout the course is on action learning and use of the class room inputs to real life situations in NGOs. The classroom inputs focus on applied aspects and are based on participatory learning through discussion, case based teachings, experience sharing, group work and field visits. Case studies and simulation exercises are extensively used to provide theoretical and conceptual understanding on various topics. The Class room inputs of 780 hours are spread across the following broad modules: foundation module, perspective module, management module and application module.

IBAT, a B School offers an MBA Programme to develop professional managers who would be responsible for running organizations in various capacities and sectors in the world economy. It offers specialization in field of Human Resource Management, Marketing Management, Financial Management, Information Technology Management, Managing Non-Government Organizations (NGOs) and Entrepreneurship.

For NGO Management, students are trained in areas of Environment Management, Integrated Marketing for NGOs .and Financial Management in NGOs. The other courses are HRM in NGOs, Building Organisational Capacity-Strategic Planning and Management in NGOs and Religious Non-Profits and Community Building. Students are also trained in issues regarding Ethics and Professionalism in NGO, Social Movements and Advocacy-The Role of NGOs

Theory and Practice of NGOs and The Law Regarding NGOs. NEHU, North Eastern Hill University, also runs PG level courses in NGO management.

Management education can contribute immensely to the functioning of ngos. To increase the efficiency of NGOs, it is necessary to for ngo's to be trained in management education.

REFERENCES

Business Environment www.iiml.ac.in/faculty/be.html

CALumni Volume 5 www.iimcal.ac.in/calumni/archives/vol.5/In%20Focus.html - 22k
Dean Speak www.indiainfoline.com/bisc/ximds.html
http://www.ediindia.org/courses_pgdmn.asp
http://www.ediindia.org/fellowship_pgdmn.asp
http://www.irma.ac.in/mfmi/wsnote.html
http://www.nehu.ac.in/admision_foreign.html
XIMB Postgraduate Programme in Rural Management www.ximb.ac.in/academics

24

RETAILING IN A GLOBAL ECONOMY WITH SPECIAL REFERENCE TO INDIAN INDUSTRY

Jasnoor Kaur and O.P. Sahni

INTRODUCTION

Globalization is something of a buzzword today. With trade and investment barriers between countries rapidly breaking down, companies are spreading their operations across the globe and consumers are able to access an ever-growing basket of goods and services. More and more companies are increasingly beginning to take into account what is happening across the world, rather than in only the country in which they are based. In short, globalization is affecting the process of industrialization in all the developing countries. The effect of globalisation is thus on the development of all types of industries both in private and public sector in these countries.

Although business has been conducted on an international scale for a long time, international business has gained greater visibility and importance in recent years because of WTO which resulted in the growth and movement of large multinational corporations. International businesses engage in transactions across national boundaries and a global manager tries to integrate the various cutting edge ideas and concepts that are shaping the global business environment. In today's highly competitive scenario, where barriers between countries are rapidly collapsing, globalization is less a choice and more a compulsion. Firms conduct business differently today than they did a few years ago. The organizations that are stagnant and are bound by traditions are increasingly fading from limelight because one of the biggest problems in managing an organization today is failing to adapt to the changing world. Economies throughout the world are going through turbulent change. The following table demonstrates 1960s stars and early 21st century stars in the US that can be seen as future development in the countries like India.

In rapidly changing world, the demand on countries to produce, expand develop and advance has become overwhelming. This would lead to an alarming change in competition for goods and services not only within the country but would go beyond national boundaries. The emergence of a global economy and a global trade has transformed the world into one massive business community. If corporations do not prepare for the global market they would lag behind those that prepare themselves to face international competition.

The purpose of this paper was to understand the nature and the dynamics of the Indian retailing. It also studied the importance of supply chain management its effect on emerging retailing system. It discussed the changes in branding scene in the country. The paper also details the dimensions of retail industry with respect to rural markets and throws light on various strategies to be followed by managers in the changing global economy.

The paper was based on secondary information. This was procured from journals, magazines, case studies, internet, etc. Various articles related to dynamics of the Indian retailing, supply chain management, the changes in branding scene in the country, and the dimensions of retail industry with respect to rural markets were reviewed. In the end the information so collected was synthesized to draw conclusions.

CHANGING SCENARIO OF INDIAN RETAILING

After the much hyped IT and BPO booms, retail is one of the crucial sectors of the economy that requires urgent attention. Unlike the other two sectors, the scene in the retailing industry is largely unorganized. The country has witnessed a retail revolution in recent years. Significant developments have taken place in urban area in the form of a number of outlets in organized retailing sector such as mega stores and malls . All of the metros or mini-metros have superb shopping malls to rule shoppers heat, e.g. in recent years Gurgaon has seen the mushrooming of so many swanky stores that shoppers' dream has come true. The city is all set to become the retail capital of the country. Actually, both the corporate as well as government sector have shown keen interest in the retail sector. Thus, the retail sector has become the impetus of the Indian industry.

Retailing has witnessed drastic changes in the last few years- from a poorly stacked dirty karyana stores in the by-lane of a residential area to an aesthetically decorated store with properly arranged goods, offering ambience and convenience. Instead of lanes and by-lanes growing into a bazaar, planned shopping centers well connected with all main roads, freeways are emerging today in all towns and cities. These shopping centers are complete in themselves, capable of meeting all the essential requirements of the population starting from perishable to durable goods or shopping to specialty goods.

The concept of organized retailing has gained momentum in the last few years. The large corporate houses have displayed more than a fleeting interest in this sector. Big houses like Tatas, Piramals, Rahejas, S Kumar's, RPG etc. have already made their presence felt in organized retailing by investing in either of the format like- malls, big departmental stores, chain stores, discount stores.

Weekend after weekend Indian shopaholics, movie freaks and gluttons are creating a virtual chaos at shopping malls, restaurant chains and movies theatres. While the end of hectic working week has always spelled moolah for business, the sudden burst of voracious consumerism with new age options has created its own "weekend economy"

Most of us are aware that retailing was started with big departmental stores in the metros like Mumbai, Delhi etc. and then there was appearance of big showrooms in small cities and towns. In the recent past, the large format retailing has picked up like wild fire. Centrally air conditioned malls like Ansal Plaza in Delhi, Crossroads in Mumbai and Spencer Plaza in Chennai seems to be perpetually crowded everyday. The well off population, middle level executives college goers of cities looks forward to make shopping an experience in an unhurried and relaxed air-conditioned atmosphere, convenient ambience or space to hang around.

The concept of malls started with Ansal Plaza's Shopper's Stop in Delhi. Within a short span of time a few more names appeared on the competitive scenario like –Pantaloon, Lifestyle, Westside, Ebony, etc.

Dynamics of retailing is evident from the fact that thirty years after landing up in Bahrain with $5000 in his pocket to open a shop, the Dubai based CEO of Landmark group has built up one of the largest and most profitable retail chains in the Middle East, with more than 280 stores, 6000 employees and an estimated $ 650 million in revenues. Retail operations of the group now span the UAE, Saudi Arabia, Kuwait, Bahrain, Qatar, Oman, and India. It includes a wide variety of formats-department stores ranging from baby products to footwear.

Kishore Biyani's Pantaloon Retail is already India's biggest retail chain of outlets. It was started a little over seven years ago. Now, it is targeting a revenue of Rs. 8,800 crore in 2010. It expects to close this year with a turnover of Rs. 1,100 crore; the last year revenues were Rs.650 crore. It has grown from a three-store retailer with just Rs. 60 crore of revenue.

In north India Ebony and Shopper's Stop have become big brands themselves. These outlets cater to the requirement of entire family. Sort of Wal-Mart of India, these provide complete shopping experience with huge number of options to choose from. The development of retailing in India is evident from Table 24.1.

It is worth mentioning here that Gurgaon is all set to add twenty-five malls with a total retail space of forty-four lakh square feet in the period of next three years. Already, this booming suburb of Delhi is home to three big malls i.e. MGF Metropolitan, DLF City Centre, and Sahara Mall.

Table 24.1: Present Scene of Retailing in India

Name of the Store	Location	No. of outlets	Projected outlets
Shopper's Stop	Mumbai, Delhi, Bangalore, Hyderabad, Jaipur, Chennai	13	40 (by 2004)
Pantaloon	Hyderabad, Mumbai, Bangalore, Kolkata, Kanpur, Jaipur, Nagpur, Pune, Chennai, Ahmedabad	31	74 (by 2005)
Ebony	Delhi, Noida, Jalandhar, Ludhiana, Chandigarh, Chennai, Faridabad	8	14 (by 2005
Westside	Mumbai, Hyderabad, Bangalore, Kolkata, Chennai, Pune	13	21-23 (by 2005)
Lifestyle	Hyderabad, Bangalore, Chennai,	7	15 (by 2005)
RPG	Hyderabad	1	12 (by 2006)
Bombay Store	Mumbai, Pune	5	10 (by 20050
Globus	Indore, Mumbai, Chennai	7	17 (by 2005)
Fun Hours	Ahmedabad	1	

Source: Business World, 16th Feb., 2004.

More than a dozen years after the first of India's retail chains (Shoppers' Stop) launched itself from out of a defunct movie theatre, organized retail has come a long way. The industry had to negotiate a long list of hurdles, like poor quality of real estate, messy supply chains, etc. Some of the issues still exist, but with an estimated revenue of Rs. 22,500 crore, organized retail has reached an inflexion point.

It is to be pointed out that even in the developed countries, it took Mc Donald's around eight to ten years to break even. It can be said that profits don't come immediately, but only after one puts everything together and reaches customers, and continue to look at the requirements of customers and continue to match them when one thinks to expand. This requires creation of a system.

To bring forth a fact in India, every location and every region is different. It takes time to understand a particular location or a particular market. Thus one of the biggest mistakes a retailer could make is in forecasting the demand for a new store without considering the uniqueness of a location.

The fundamental issue in India from grocery point of view is that the organized retailing is still very nascent. It is seven to eight years old. So one needs time to see the required results. The size of the market is huge, extremely complex and there is very little synergy as far as supply chain is concerned. The real challenge and opportunity for the existing pioneers is how to scale up rapidly, otherwise the retailers could lose the advantage they have created.

It can be said that Indian retailers already have a head start and many of them would perform very well along with a few the international retailers who are thinking to invade India.. Some of these foreign retailers may also be successful in India. At the end of the day, it will be all the retailers working together. India is a big market, but it is fragmented into one billion customers. But for many retailers, the market may not be as big as they would like it to be. Tesco, Wal-Mart, Carrefour are multibillion corporations, if one looks at India from their perspective, the market should offer them an opportunity of at least $4-5 billion.

RETAILING PERSPECTIVE IN RURAL MARKET

Rural consumers have unique customs and behavior and marketers may find it difficult to serve them, as they are mostly equipped with urban-based marketing skills. The Indian rural community amount to over two- thirds of the total population and it offers a vast and growing market opportunity. Indian rural areas are emerging as important and huge market, as it is much larger as compared to urban market in terms of population, number of households across specific income groups, and above all consumption levels for many product categories like tea, soaps and shaving blades.

The relative importance of rural markets requires a review and assessment of distribution infrastructure available to the marketers. Village shops are run on a low scale. They deal in a limited number of products and brands. The number and size of retail outlets depend upon the population of that village. Studies have shown that the influence of the local retailer is perceived to be high in the rural market. Rao, (1997) observed that rural retailers are the main link between the producers and the consumers in India. Normally they buy products from the nearby towns, deal in limited variety of products, mostly on the basis of customer requirements and tastes and earning a low level of income. Their understanding and vision is limited to the area they belong and to the rural consumers they serve. Rural marketers are required to understand that the Indian rural market can be segmented as given below:

1. Rural rich consumers

2. Rural consumers around urban areas
3. Rural consumers above poverty line
4. Rural consumers below poverty line

The consumption pattern of rural people is changing in recent years. The rural consumer wants to acquire urban life in their buying behavior. Sales executives prefer to serve rural markets. A strong retail setup is emerging in the villages of Punjab, Haryana and parts of Rajasthan and Uttar Pradesh parallel to periodic markets. There is going to be a boom in Indian rural market and small retail outlets. The factors responsible for rural market boom are:

- Increase in population leading to increase in demand. The rural population in 1981 was Rs. 2.50 crore which increased to Rs. 68.50 crore in 1991 and Rs. 72 crore in 2001
- A market increase in the rural income due to agrarian prosperity.
- Large flow of investment for rural development programs from government and other sources.
- Increased contact of rural people with their urban counterparts due to development of transport and wide communication network.
- Increase in literacy and educational level and inclination of sophisticated lives by the rural folks.
- Inflow of foreign remittances and foreign made goods into rural areas.
- Change in land tenure system causing a structural change in the ownership patterns and consequent changes in the buying behavior.

All these developments have resulted in the changing retail scenario in the rural markets. Large retail showrooms were a feature of major cities. But now these retail outlets are being opened in small cities to cater to different customer segments.

Thus, the scope and concept of rural marketing has changed over years. In earlier days, rural marketing was used to designate marketing of agricultural produce and village artisan products. In modern society, villages have acquired a new profile by receptively adopting themselves to the technological change taking place in an unimaginable trade in major cities. There is a direct impact of modern means and methods of marketing and requires strategic changes in attitudes and policies pertaining to rural markets.

SUPPLY CHAIN MANAGEMENT

Supply Chain Management is a process of moving goods from the customer order through the raw material stage, supply, production and distribution of products to the customer. Supply chain in an organization vary depending upon the size of organization and the type of product manufactured. These networks obtain supplies and components, change these materials into finished products and then distribute them to the customer. Managing the chain of events in this process is known as supply chain management. Effective management must take into account coordinating all the different pieces of this chain as quickly as possible without losing any of the quality or customer satisfaction, while trying to keep costs down. The role of supply chain has changed considerably and good retail management is required to give special emphasis to this activity to improve the services to be provided to customers and to create customer satisfaction which would lead to higher level of performance in retailing.

Middle and executive level corporate leaders are usually able to comprehend potentials of supply chain management. However, they often lack clarity about how to develop a supply chain strategy for their companies. The main objectives of supply chain management are:

1. The need to maximize the value added for each activity or member organization in the supply chain for both customers and suppliers.
2. The need to achieve synergies that improve the performance of the supply chain in reducing the cycle times, reducing system inventory and reducing costs.

Supply chain strategies should be oriented toward:

- Ensuring the best process.
- Enhancing relationship between customers and suppliers.
- Creating electronic communication possible.

CONCLUSION

To conclude it can be said that within 7-10 years India will become one of the largest retail markets for major brands. Some of the factors that are driving the retail industry in India are favorable demographic and psycho graphic changes relating to India's consumer class, international exposure, availability of products and brand communication. Many new large retailers have entered India in the last few years due to increasing interaction of Population at international level, the emergence of largest middle class, the rising affluence of young Indian population along with heightened awareness of global brands and international shopping experiences.

Besides, the Indian rural market is a huge market with a lot of potential in it. The rural market is growing at least 5 times the rate of the urban market. Nearly 70% of the Indian population is living in rural areas. Importance is, thus, given to rural market in the modern times due to saturation attained in the urban market.

Presently, rural consumers prefer to meet their day-to-day needs from village shops but due to availability of better infrastructure and communication they may like to avail improved service of organized marketing efforts and thus, provide the largest market potential.

In developing retailing strategy, the supply chain management is to be given due importance. An advantage can be enjoyed by the companies which can manage supply chain in an efficient and effective way and get a competitive advantage in the market place.

In the end, it can be said that the organized retailing has a future in India. Retailing scene will be different in 2020, the year of vision.

REFERENCES

Amanpreet Singh, Gurgaon: Asia's Mall Capital, bt trends, *Business Today,* Jan4, 2004.

B. Raja Shekhar, Strategies of Supply Chain Management in Global Economy, *Indian Journal of Marketing,* Volume XXXIV, No.4, April 2004, pp 24-26.

Gitanjali Bhatnagar, Retail Revolution, *Indian Journal of Marketing,* Vol. XXXIV, No.11, November 2004, pp 13-17.

K Manjunatha, Rural Marketing – Prospects, *Indian Journal of Marketing,* Vol. XXXIV, No.6, June 2004, pp 24-25.

M. V. Subha, Managing Supply Chain *Indian Journal of Marketing,* Volume XXXIV, Number: 4, April 2004, pp14-15.

Power brands- the 80:20 strategy, *Indian Management,* Dec, 2004, pp 42-44.

Rajnish Tulsi & Prof. Amit Mookerjee, Retail Formats: Patronage Behaviour of Indian rural Consumers, *South Asian Journal of Management, Vol.11, Issue No3, July-Sept. 2004, pp 57-71.*

Raju M Rathod, Challenges and Strengths of Super Market, *Indian Journal of Marketing,* Vol. XXXIV, No.4, April 2004, pp 29-30.

25

LIBERALIZING INTERNATIONAL TRADE IN SERVICES: CHALLENGES IN E-GOVERNANCE AND SERVICE BRANDING

Komal Chopra

INTRODUCTION

Recent Interest in Services Liberalization by Developing Countries: The area of services is rapidly becoming as important in economic terms for developing countries as it is for developed ones. It is by now well accepted that services play a critical role in determining both the quality and speed of the process of economic development, and that a competitive economy cannot exist without an efficient and technologically advanced service sector. Despite this realization, many service sectors remain fairly closed for the majority of developing countries.

Characteristics of Services Transactions: Services are ubiquitous in a modern society; they are multidimensional, and they play a crucial role in economic development. Services encompass many different economic activities. They can be defined as activities that add value either directly to another person or to a good belonging to another person. Services possess three main characteristics that make them very different from goods; they are intangible, though often incorporated in tangible products; they are non-storable; and they involve a simultaneous action between the service provider and the service consumer.

With respect to trade, the simultaneous nature of service transactions impacts upon how international transactions in services are conducted. If a service producer in one country possesses a desired service, then he must somehow interact with service consumers in other countries to provide it. Services have in fact often been characterized as "non-tradable" in the sense that provision of services to foreign markets often necessitates the movement of capital (economic activities set up through foreign direct investment) or labor (personnel to manage such activities or to provide different types of expertise, including basic labor). In the case of services, the few that cross borders do so incorporated into products, as computer programs in diskettes, or air transport through aircraft, or films in videotapes. Or they may be transmitted via the telecommunications networks. Most services, however, are supplied directly by their providers in a foreign market, and for this reason cannot be dissociated from international movement of capital or labor, as well as accompanying knowledge and technology.

Contribution of Services to Economic Development: While in the past the growth of services was perceived as a by-product of development in the primary and secondary sectors and the slow growth of productivity in the service sector was thought to be a drag on long-term economic growth, today this perception of the service sector has changed dramatically. Services have taken center front on the stage of economic development. This is due to the so-called "services revolution" characterized by the rapid expansion of knowledge-based services and the growing tradability of services. Information technology has transformed service industries to the point where the development of services is regarded not as a consequence but as a precondition of economic growth. Knowledge-based industries, including professional and technical services, information technology services, banking and insurance, and education, are the driving forces behind the transformation of the service sector.

Dramatically declining costs of information technology are permitting the development of the service sector to effectively bridge the income gap through "leapfrogging" various stages of economic development. Efficient and competitive service suppliers from developing countries can foster economic convergence with high-income countries. These bold statements are based on the remarkable changes that have taken place in the world economy in the service sector over the past two decades.

Opportunities for Services Exports by Developing Countries: Technological innovation in the process of economic growth places the service sector in a strategic position. To an ever-greater extent, the quality of a country's services represents the measure of its economic and social development. Realization of these facts has heightened the interest of developing countries in looking towards the service sector for its potential contribution to spur more rapid growth and development.

In the area of international trade, services are contributing on a larger scale than ever before to enhance foreign exchange earnings by developing countries. The application of new technologies in the telecommunications and computer-related areas has created major new opportunities for developing countries to provide commercial service exports at long distance, possibly doubling the present value of such exports (now around $180 billion) within a few years. Some developing countries have traditionally shown a revealed comparative advantage in service exports (including Egypt, India, Malaysia, Mexico, Thailand, and Panama, among others). Areas of comparative advantage vary as between construction services (Republic of Korea), personal services (southeast

Asian economies), transport (Singapore), finance (Hong Kong and Panama), and tourism (many smaller developing economies). Exports of computer-related and various forms of data processing activities provided on a long-distance basis by developing countries are growing at remarkable rates (India, various Caribbean countries). Besides long-distance services, there remains much scope for expansion in other areas of traditional service exports by developing countries, particularly tourism, which remains the largest single source of foreign exchange earnings from services for these countries. Certain niches in industrial country markets are also being created by suppliers in areas such as advertising and film production.

The Challenges of Liberalizing Trade in Services: The intensity of regulation present in many service activities contributes to the complexities of liberalization of international service transactions. Again, trade liberalization in the services area does not always equate with deregulation, as a country can deregulate a services activity without inviting foreign competition.

Liberalization of international service transactions poses considerable challenges, which are quite different from those in the goods area. The fact that barriers to trade in services are present in national economies in the form of legislation and administrative practices and not found at the border, make them less transparent than tariffs and quotas, and more difficult to assess their restrictive impact. Moreover, there is not always a clear line between a "measure affecting trade in services" and a "barrier affecting trade in services." What one government may feel is a necessary regulatory measure, applied in a non-discriminatory manner, may in fact constitute a *de facto* trade barrier to a foreign service supplier. It is clear, however, that all regulatory measures which are applied to foreign service providers in a discriminatory manner constitute barriers to trade. Barriers to international service transactions are by definition non-tariff in nature. This is due to the intangible and non-storable nature of service transactions, so that any barrier must be applied to either the service consumer or to the service supplier as they interact across borders.

Measuring such non-tariff barriers in the services area poses formidable challenges, and very few systematic attempts to do so have been undertaken. This is because of the specific problems encountered when trying to quantify aspects of the services sector.

Several developments in international trade in services impact strongly on developing countries: First, the world-wide diffusion of information technologies (IT) has created new export opportunities for developing countries in IT services. While some services, such as international transport and tourism, have been traded internationally without much fanfare for many decades, several recent developments have raised new concerns about how international trade in services impacts on developing countries. A few developing countries, most notably India, have benefited from this progress as their IT-related service exports increased markedly over the last decade. This raises the question of whether, and how, this pattern could be repeated elsewhere.

Second, the renewed focus on poverty reduction in international aid policy, epitomized by the Millennium Development Goals, has drawn attention to the role of those service sectors (e.g., water, electricity, health care, and telecommunications) that are crucial for improving living standards and for increasing the competitiveness of export industries in developing countries. Frequently these services used to be provided (if at all) by loss-making state enterprises at less than satisfactory quality. With support especially from the World Bank and other development banks, many developing countries have embarked on sectoral reforms that have frequently involved foreign investors when privatizing service suppliers and the setting-up of new regulatory bodies. The mixed outcomes of such reforms raise the question of what lessons should be learned from the experience and how policies for service sector liberalization and reductions in import barriers should be designed in the future.

Third, with the conclusion of the Uruguay Round of trade negotiations in April, 1994, the liberalization of service imports became institutionalized in the world trading system. While the Uruguay Round succeeded mostly in establishing a conceptual and institutional framework for service sector negotiations, with little actual liberalization induced by the round itself, analytical work since the late 1990s has demonstrated the large potential benefits of liberalizing market access for foreign service suppliers, especially in business services. This raises the question of how developing countries should position themselves in the ongoing Doha Round talks on services if and when these proceed to the stage of serious negotiations.

These three core questions, while broadly interconnected, relate to analytically separate issues—technological, economic, institutional, and political; service imports vs. exports (each under different modes of supply); multilateral, bilateral and unilateral policies. These diverse analytical issues reflect the fact that services constitute a large, heterogeneous sector and that priority policy concerns are therefore highly subsector- and country-specific.

GOVERNMENT SERVICES AND INTERNATIONAL TRADE

Last decade has witnessed a change in Governmental mindsets, functioning and execution. With the spread of information technologies and world wide web, certain demands have arisen like which touched the vital areas of Governmental functioning such as right to information, transparency in functioning and speedier decisions. Governance has become more citizen centric than ever.

Governments worldwide are faced with the challenge of transformation and the need to reinvent government systems in order to deliver efficient and cost effective services, information and knowledge through information and communication technologies. Development of Information and communication technologies catalyzed and led up to E-governance, which has now become the most talked buzzword the world over.

Before touching the issues, it is quite important to clearly understand the meaning of E governance and E government. For this purpose the following definitions of E governance hold good – "The application of electronic means·in (1) the interaction between government and citizens (G2C) and the government and business(G2B), as well as (2) in internal and external government operations(G2G) to simplify and improve democratic, government and business aspects of governance. (Baackus Michael, 2001)

"E governance is that form of governance which seeks to realize processes and structures by harnessing the potentialities of information and communication technologies (ICTs) at various levels of government and the public sector and beyond, for the purpose of enhancing good governance." (Katherine Reilly, 2002)

E-government on the other hand refers to the facilitation of the delivery of government services, it has a focus on information technology. It can be defined as, "E-government uses computing and telecommunications technologies to make radical changes to the delivery of government services to their citizen customers and the general public(G2C), businesses(G2B), employees(G2E), and other governments(G2G)." (Carolyn Purcell, 2002)

Broadly speaking, e-governance can be defined as the use of information and telecommunication technologies, especially the Internet, to enhance access to and delivery of government services to benefit citizens, businesses and the staff of the public sector. It is the Internet, with its capacity to break the barriers of time and distance and to bring together a wealth of information from a virtually unlimited number of sources, that is creating the possibility of reorganizing and networking government services to make them more user centric, transparent and efficient.

Electronic Governance is the application of Information Technology to the processes of Government functioning in order to bring about Simple, Moral, Accountable, Responsive and Transparent (SMART) Governance. Electronic governance also involves transformation from being a passive information and service provider to active citizen involvement. Evolution of E-Governance is a highly complex process requiring provision of hardware, networking, software and re-engineering of the procedures for better delivery of services.

Traditionally, the interaction between a citizen or business and government agency took place in a government office. With emerging ICT it is possible to locate service centers closer to the clients. Such centers may consist of an unattended kiosk in the government agency, a service kiosk located close to the client, or the use of a personal computer in the home or office. E-Governance is an opportunity to take advantage of the increased productivity and reduced costs that can be achieved using Internet based technology. Even better, E-Governance can enhance the citizen's access to government information and services (both central and local), and can provide new ways to increase citizen participation in the democratic process.

As one can conclude, E-Governance may include very broad range of services for almost all segments of society. The most common areas of E-Governance applications are:

- Electronic commerce and business regulations
- Taxation and revenue
- Law enforcement and courts
- Digital democracy
- Agriculture
- Education
- Health
- Transport

SCOPE OF E-GOVERNANCE

Electronic Service Delivery (G2C): Delivering information and services electronically to citizens and businesses. The objective of the G2C category is to provide one-stop on line access of information and services to individuals. Citizens should be able to find what they need quickly, easily and accessing them in minutes or seconds, instead of days or hours. This involves Governance processes involving significant citizen interface. For example, Utility bill payment, Issue of driving license, Birth/Death registration, Property Tax etc

Government to Business Transactions (G2B): The goals of the G2B category are to reduce burdens on business, provide one-stop access to information and enable digital communication using the language of e-business. This involves interactions between Government & Business. For example, E-Procurement, E-payments, Company Registrations, Trade Licenses/Permits etc.

Internal and External Government Administration (G2G, G2E): Improving efficiency, effectiveness, and transparency of intra-department and inter department interactions within government, and with government employees. The G2G primary goal is to enable state, District Administration and local governments to work together more easily to serve the citizens in a better way using ICT applications. This involves Internal Government processes (intra and inter-departmental). For example, Workflow Automations of internal Administrative functions (Employee Information System, accounting, payroll etc), Project Monitoring, Repository of Parliament Questions & Answers etc.

Foreign Trade (G2X): Increasing exports and tourism, government to government interactions, expatriates, foreign investors.

MOTIVATING FORCES BEHIND E-GOVERNMENT

There are a variety of motivations that may drive a government's decision to embrace e-government as an approach to governmental reform. How governments define, describe, and justify their e-government initiatives can provide some insight into how the role of the citizen and citizenship may be affected. In some cases, government officials may be trying to break with past practices and develop new processes and organizational cultures to bring about a major shift in how governance is carried out. In other cases they may be motivated by an interest in streamlining and enhancing existing functions to achieve better efficiency and enhanced service delivery. Motivation may also come in the form of responding to outside forces, such as the demands of citizens, businesses, and other actors who interact with the government. For example, mature democracies, which generally have well established their legitimacy with internal and external constituencies, may be driven more by an interest in enhancing internal efficiencies and instituting marketization practices. In contrast, transitional democracies with newer governments may perceive a need to improve openness and citizen opportunities to solidify their legitimacy, and thus may emphasize reforms such as transparency and attracting economic development. In most countries e-government initiatives are the result of a blend of motivations, although one or two specific motivations may be particularly emphasized above all others. The exact combination of these motivations reflects both the country's current state of economic and political development, as well as the interests of its political leadership. While the number of motivations is countless, some of the most significant reasons used to justify e-government initiatives can be identified.

Efficiency: One of the chief reforms invoked to advance e-government initiatives is efficiency, which includes a focus on customer service and improved resource management. In both mature and transitional democracies alike, limitations on government budgets have helped drive an interest in using information technology solutions to streamline procedures and trim costs.

However, in the case of less wealthy countries, information technology investments can represent a significant proportion of their resources, creating a greater urgency for positive results. In e-government projects, this anticipated efficiency can take many forms. Some projects seek to reduce errors and improve consistency in outcomes by automating standardized tasks. Other e-government initiatives attempt to reduce costs and layers of organizational processes and bloated bureaucracies by re-engineering and streamlining operating procedures. While these actions can often lead to the elimination of duplicative positions, the reduction of the amount of time spent on repetitive tasks, such as processing

Marketization: Related to efficiency are attempts to infuse market forces into the relationships between governments and their various constituencies (e.g., citizens, businesses, other government agencies, etc.). Marketization is often seen as a means to improve the quality, range, and accessibility of services, while achieving better efficiencies and cost controls. In many cases, marketization reforms include efforts to identify and apply best practices from other areas of the public and private sectors. It is also common for marketization initiatives to refer to citizens as customers or consumers, as a means to emphasize the importance of being citizen-centered rather than government-centered. Some of these efforts are driven by the business community. In many industries, the use of electronic means to carry out various activities, such as procurement, sales, and hiring is commonplace.

New and Improved Services: Very closely related to marketization, enhanced information and service delivery is often cited as a motivating reason for e-government projects. In contrast with marketization, which tends to focus more on transforming the ethos of the bureaucracy, the motivation to provide new and improved services tends to focus more on improving the citizen's experience interacting with the government when seeking out information or trying to obtain various services. In addition to enhanced efficiency, the quality of services may be improved through quicker transactions, improved accountability, and better processes. The evolution of e-government and technology also creates the potential for new services to emerge.

Decentralization: Also related to marketization, another objective of some e-government initiatives is the decentralization of decision-making and service provision to sub national levels of government. This is more likely to be a goal in countries covering a large geographic area with a heterogeneous population where one-size-fits-all solutions may be less useful. It can often be more difficult to effect change in large organizations with entrenched bureaucracies than small agencies with narrower, more clearly defined responsibilities. Decentralization provides the opportunity for small scale projects to be launched with fewer resources as test cases. It also allows entrepreneurial leaders to emerge and seize opportunities that might otherwise go unrecognized. Successful local governments may in turn become the targets of many G2G efforts with other government entities at the local and/or national level due to their relative proximity, geographically and politically, to citizens.

Administrative Control: While not mutually exclusive to decentralization interests, efforts to improve administrative control over the state and its citizens also motivates some e-government initiatives. Conventional wisdom has suggested that the Internet and information technology can serve as important democratizing influences. However, these same technologies can also be used to facilitate online monitoring, track citizen and bureaucrat activities, and collect information for data mining analytical activities. Enhanced administrative control can be used to crack down on corruption and inefficiencies with in government, as well as to identify potential areas of resistance and strengthen a government's monopoly on power. For transitional democracies, such administrative control may be seen as important to facilitating faster economic development and maintaining stability as the country attempts to cope with the 'growing pains' associated with such a transformation.

Citizen Demand: Another motivation is citizen demand, especially by younger citizens and those accustomed to using electronic transactions in other areas of their lives (e.g., banking). Some observers expect the citizen demand for e-government to increase significantly over the next ten years as young people, who are now growing up with mobile phones, personal computers, and the Internet as a routine presence in their lives, become adults. It is possible that this new generation of citizens will be more likely to become participant citizens if the means to do so are similar to the ones they use for personal and professional activities. Citizen demand may also be driven by increased time pressures. As citizens feel they have increased demands placed on their time, they may look for ways to reduce time spent standing in lines and taking care of administrative tasks. One way to do this is to be able to complete routine governmental transactions, such as renewing a license or applying for a permit online.

Increased Citizen Participation: With or without citizen demand, another motivating interest of some e-government advocates is increased citizen participation in government. Increased participation can lead citizens to feel they have a greater stake in the functioning of government, which may help build enthusiasm to propel e-government projects even further. Citizen participation can take many forms, including, but not limited to, higher voter turnout, increased input to rulemaking procedures, or greater interaction with other citizens on important issues. Governments may try to build citizen participation through many means. One way this could occur is by connecting people who live in remote areas of the country so that they can send and receive information more easily. A second way suggested by some observers is through increased participation in government by younger adults. A second way is to specifically target demographic groups that have been traditionally less engaged in politics. In some countries this may be younger adults who are less frequent voters. In other countries, it may be certain ethnic groups whose interests are underrepresented. A third approach is to foster a greater civic culture through the creation of forums that could enhance citizen-to-citizen (C2C) interaction by providing opportunities for people with similar interests, opinions, and concerns, who may be geographically separated, to interact and share information.

Transparency: Generally, and especially in transitional systems, the lack of political transparency has been associated with governmental corruption. Frequently, this takes the form of bureaucrats requiring payments from citizens to perform routine tasks such as permit approvals or license renewals. A lack of transparency can lead to increased costs for completing routine transactions, make democratic accountability nearly impossible, and contribute to increased cynicism about a government on the part of its citizens as well as potential external allies and investors. A government may use e-government initiatives in an effort to eliminate rent-seeking behavior on the part of bureaucrats and increase both political and economic transparency. Such initiatives may be designed to improve accountability, decentralize control, remove bottlenecks in routine transactions, increase the reliability and predictability of government actions, and better ensure equal access to information and services.

Economic Development: Directly related to transparency, a government's interest in economic development can also be a motivator for embarking on and showcasing e-government projects, particularly if the goal is to attract outside investment. To make its country more appealing to potential investors, a government may try to emphasize the quality of its workforce, the condition of its infrastructure, and its ability to provide necessary services. E-government initiatives are one way to demonstrate its commitment to reform, as well as its ability to compete in the information economy. It may also be used to build confidence in its business and regulatory environment, build out its technological infrastructure, and develop its domestic industries.

The E Governance System is supported by five pillars :

- Computers: All hardware and software requirements of governance
- Connectivity : All carrier systems, bandwidth etc.

- Content: The information that is exchanged between the "consumers" of the system
- Consumers: All the human substitute systems that access and use the "content"
- Confidence Building: Those measures that help the citizens develop confidence in the e governance and encourages them to take to the e transformation.

ISSUES IN IMPLEMENTATION

Infrastructural Issues: The infrastructural issues which are important are poor rural telecommunications network, power problems in various states, and network connectivity. Unless these three areas are improved, an effective e governance programme can not be implemented.

Social and Cultural Issues: E-governance implementation leads to information sharing at each small unit level in the masses, high awareness and transparency in governmental functioning. This also needs a strong back end functional support to successfully maintain the e governance initiative; in the absence of which the system will collapse. Due to corruption deep routed in the political and administrative system, majority of the people at the authoritative positions in the respective functional departments may dislike the transparent and smooth working after e governance initiative. Such cultural habits are difficult to fight with which is an essential prerequisite of the e governance. Resistance of staff is also a very likely aspect which needs to be taken care of by taking steps in advance and by spending goodwill among the employees.

On the other hand, people always fear to experiment new things, newer means of functioning. In the initial stages, any e governance project is likely to face criticism and setbacks because of lesser public participation. Further owing to lower literacy rate in majority of the Indian states, the reach of the project remains restricted to the literate people in the society.

Security Issues: Defining a security policy can be a complicated task as each Government must decide beforehand which aspects of protection are most important, thereby compromising between security and ease of use. Various security issues involved are

- Authenticity of the information sent across the web. The use of digital signatures is therefore much more required in case of Government documents.

- Confidentiality of any transaction or information available on the network is a very crucial matter and is therefore of vital importance to the successful e governance implementation.
- Cryptography is an important process to protect the information from unauthorized users and is an inseparable part of network security. Tested encryption software be installed before initiating the e governance.
- Maintaining and assuring Integrity of the information is also an important aspect of digital security, which becomes all the more important in e governance.
- Continuous availability of information 24 hrs a day is important for efficient and effective functioning of the e governance system. This is in fact, a key distinguishing feature of the e governance system.
- Network Security by using multi level barriers be in place for effective protection of the networks. These may use password schemes, biometrics, SMART card authentication and firewalls.

Hardware and Software Issues: Identifying the appropriate hardware platforms and software application packages for cost effective delivery of public services is an important ingredient of the e governance system. This can be achieved by

- Making the knowledge repository widely available through appropriate Demo- Mechanisms
- Offering a Basket of these models to the States, Departments both in the Center and the State, which could be suitably customized as per location and work specific requirements. Towards this end we envisage to have State level models, District level models and Ministry/Department level models;
- This offer is to be supplemented by incubating and initiating efforts in this direction by various organs of the Govt. Amendment in State laws through study and consultation.

Administration Issues: A strong political will and less corruption, encompassing potential changes with regard to physical, technical and human resource infrastructures and honest welfare measures are central to effective administration of e governance. A change in the mindset of people in the government and clear thinking about what needs to be achieved and where to get the expertise and solutions to achieve it in a cost-effective, time-bound manner leads to effective e governance. Setting up a governing body on e-governance for the country might help. The idea should be to further the governance processes toward easier, better citizen-friendly schemes as and where required. According to an observation, hardware and software constitute only 10% of the problem, while 85% of the problem is an organization management problem that is internal to the government.

Delivery of public services like Utilities, Rural and Urban development schemes through EDI, Internet and other IT based technologies would necessitate procedural and legal changes in the decision and delivery making processes as well as institutions, which would mean a complete revamp of the Government decision management involving faster decision mechanisms, less red tapism, changes in organization structures making it more flatter, higher delegation of authority and changes in legal provisions. These measures would lead to

- Organisational and institutional changes effecting both people and methods at all interfaces of the delivery Chain
- For this, acceptance of this Changed Processes would have to be properly understood, accepted, internalised, adopted and improved to enable full advantages of the technology being adopted in the first part of Smart Governance
- De-layering of the decision making levels leading to re-engineering and appropriate sizing of the decision making machinery
- Training and acclimatization of the personnel at all levels more so at the lower rung of Government management organisations.
- Loss of vested interests and assumed power as well as authority both amongst the legislature and the executive

Financial Issues: Apart from the ambitious work plans, the financial issues related to e governance have to be weighed in terms of available resources both in the Plan sector and outside it. It is here that leveraging of ongoing projects can be made more cost and value effective with the use of IT in a modulated fashion without any critical incremental costs.

The Private sector resources have to be also carefully dovetailed with their commercial interests and those of the Government to provide Value Added Services. The Kiosks by themselves can bring in little in terms of better delivery of Services, unless the same are made economically viable and of demonstrated use to the Stakeholders, viz the Public and the Citizenry. Higher cost for high end applications is another attention area.

Redefined Government Structure with IT: In the traditional structure of Government, citizens are interacting with different departments of the Government independently. Information systems are developed by the Departments for monitoring the delivery of services to the citizens. Information flows up and down the administrative hierarchy of the department in the form of periodical returns, MIS and Government orders.

Ultimately, for realizing the full potential of IT and setting in the elements of Good Governance it is essential to have a common Information system across the various Government Departments. Citizens would have access to these information systems without having to bother which department it belongs to. Government is treated as a single entity and one can drill down or across to the requirement seamlessly. It is an integration of various departments and services given by the Government using IT. Standardization for uniformity, Ease of working through avoidance of redundant activities by integration across the departments will enable delivery of Anytime, Anywhere, Anyhow services to the citizens.

GOALS AND SUCCESS STORIES OF E-GOVERNANCE

E-governance is the process of service delivery and information dissemination to citizens using electronic means. By virtue of advantages of electronic medium, e-governance provides the following benefits over the conventional system (along with national and international success stories for achieving these goals):

Better Service Delivery to Citizens: Government service delivery, particularly to the most needy, is an essential part of any poverty alleviation strategy. The following case studies highlight uses of e-government tools in projects focused on improving delivery of services to citizens.

***Land/Property Registration in Andhra Pradesh*:** Land registration offices throughout Andhra Pradesh now operate computerized counters to help citizens to complete registration requirements within an hour instead of several days, as was necessary under the earlier system. The lack of transparency in property valuation under the old system resulted in a flourishing business of brokers and middlemen leading to corruption. Antiquated procedures such as manual copying and indexing of documents, and storage in paper forms in ill-maintained backrooms have all been replaced.

Bhoomi: Online Delivery of Land Titles in Karnataka: The Department of Revenue in Karnataka has computerized 20 million records of land ownership of 6.7 million farmers in the state. Previously, farmers had to seek out the Village Accountant to get a copy of the Record of Rights, Tenancy and Crops (RTC) -- a document needed for many tasks such as obtaining bank loans. There were delays and harassment. Bribes had to be paid. Today, for a fee of Rs.15, a printed copy of the RTC can be obtained online at computerized land record kiosks (Bhoomi centers) in 140 *taluk* offices. The remaining 37 *taluks* are expected to have a Bhoomi center by March 2002. In the next phase, all the *taluk* databases are to be uploaded to a web-enabled central database. RTCs would then be available online at Internet kiosks, which are likely to be set up in rural areas.

Gyandoot: Community-Owned Rural Internet Kiosks: In awarding the Gyandoot project the Stockholm Challenge IT Award 2000 in the Public Service and Democracy category the jury described it as "a unique government-to-citizen Intranet project ... with numerous benefits to the region, including a people-based self-reliant sustainable strategy. 'Gyandoot' is recognised as a breakthrough in e-government, demonstrating a paradigm shift which gives marginalised tribal citizens their first ever chance to access knowledge, with minimum investment." The project also was awarded the CSI-TCS National Award for Best IT Usage for the year 2000.

Improved Services for Business: Many government services and regulations are aimed at businesses (domestic and international), not everyday citizens. In increasingly competitive markets, the quality and efficiency of these interactions has received growing attention.

Philippine Customs Reform: Using an "off-the-shelf" customs application package as the main building block, the Philippines Customs Bureau has developed an on-line system to process clearance of imports, payment of duty, and delivery of release orders for shipments to leave the docks. The new on-line system has lessened the cost of trade for businesses, reduced opportunities for fraud, and helped the Bureau to maximize revenue collection.

Vietnam's Tale of Two Cities: Hanoi and Ho Chi Minh City each launched Web development projects for business service agencies in 2000. The two websites (Hanoi Ministry of Planning and Investment and Ho Chi Minh Department of Planning & Investment) are designed to serve as the first point of contact for potential investors, especially foreign investors. The sites are now interactive, content rich, and have the potential to set standards for related agencies elsewhere in the country. The implementation challenges in these two cities varied, but were mostly of a non-technical nature, including an over-reliance on outside consultants.

Transparency and Anticorruption: "There is increasing evidence that corruption undermines development. It also hampers the effectiveness with which domestic savings and external aid are used in many developing countries, and this in turn threatens to undermine grassroots support for foreign assistance." -- James D. Wolfensohn, President, The World Bank

Central Vigilance Commission Website: A Bold Anticorruption Experiment: In an effort to propagate the idea of zero tolerance for corruption, the Central Vigilance Commission (CVC) in India has begun to share with citizens a large amount of information related to corruption. The CVC website has published the names of officers from the elite administrative and revenue services against whom investigations have been ordered or penalties imposed for corruption. Newsweek magazine carried an article about this effort, calling it E-shame.

***Cristal: A Tool for Transparent Government in Argentina*:** The mission of the Cristal Government initiative, launched by the current administration, is to disseminate online, and in an easily understood format, all information concerning the use of public funds in Argentina. This includes information not only about the amounts of money devoted to different programs, but also how these funds are administered.

Computerized Interstate Check Posts in Gujarat: Through the use of computers and other electronic devices at 10 remote interstate border check posts in Gujarat, India, a team of savvy public officials have reduced corruption and significantly increased the state's tax revenue.

Empowerment Through Information: Information is a critical ingredient for development. The more information that the poor possess, the greater their sense of empowerment. Empowered citizens can more readily hold governments accountable. With greater information the poor also are better able to organize and take actions to improve their quality of life.

Colombia's Government Portal: The government of Colombia made a serious commitment to e-government in 2000-01, mandating that all federal government agencies develop an Internet presence, and creating a unit in the Office of the President to assist and monitor their progress. The Colombian government also developed an Internet legal framework, investment plans, and strong relationships with the private sector in ICT-related projects. The centerpiece of this initiative is the State of Colombia Portal (PEC)

Empowering Dairy Farmers through a Dairy Information & Services Kiosk: In recent years, the milk co-operative movement initiated by India's National Dairy Development Board (NDDB) has led to a substantial increase in milk production in India. The two main reasons for this increase are more efficient collection of milk and higher profits for producers, both of which have been influenced by IT. This case describes the automation of the milk buying process at 2,500 rural milk collection societies. It also describes the extension of the co-op database through the creation of a Dairy Information Services Kiosk (DISK). The Kiosk makes it possible for co-operatives and farmers to manage a database of all milch cattle and access a dairy portal with information about valued services. The case demonstrates the willingness of rural farmers to invest in technology, provided that it can deliver real value.

Efficient Government Purchasing: Governments are the largest purchasers in all economies, and for both moral an political reasons they should buy goods and services in the best way possible. One dollar paid in excess of the best possible price is a dollar less to provide health care, social security or public housing.

Chile's Government Procurement E-System: Recognizing the potential benefits of IT, the Chilean Government established a Communications and Information Technology Unit (UTIC) in 1998. The UTIC was given the mandate of coordinating, promoting, and advising the Chilean Government on the development of IT in the areas of employment, information and communications. One area of reform in which the UTIC was particularly successful was in pushing forward a comprehensive reform of its procurement system. Chile's experience with e-procurement has made business opportunities with the Chilean Government more transparent, reduced firms' transaction costs, increased opportunities for feedback and cooperation between firms and public agencies, and sharply reduced opportunities for corruption.

Philippines Pilot E-Procurement System: In November 2000, the Procurement Service of the Department of Budget and Management (PSDBM), with the assistance of the Policy, Training, and Technical Assistance Facility (PTTAF) of the Canadian International Development Agency, launched the Internet-based Electronic Procurement System (EPS) pilot. The System has generated lower costs for government and increased transparency.

SERVICE MARKETING ISSUES OF E-GOVERNANCE

E-government has changed how citizens and government relate to each other and brought forth new concepts of citizenship both in terms of needs and responsibilities, also a paradigm shift in the work culture of the government from the conventional methods into an integrated internet infrastructure system, a convergence of communications with Information technologies and opened up a new vista of possibilities of providing accessibility to the government services by the citizen, so that they don't have to travel miles away to get various services done at each and every government offices.

The expectations of the citizens and the ever increasing population with attendant problems compel and government to prioritize its activities to the need and demand of the citizen for providing basic amenities, infrastructural development, etc.. whereas on the other hand it is forced to down size the number of employees to limit the expenditure incurred, due to budgetary constraints and at the same time it is supposed to deliver "Good Governance".

'Good Governance' connotes the widest meaning of the three phrases. It encompasses the entire process of public administration, the processes underlying the formulation of public policies, the HRD efforts required for re-skilling the government machinery, prioritization, efficient management of public resources and above all re-designing the various instruments used to realize the concept of a welfare state. **'SMART Government'** is an acronym for Simple, Moral, Accountable, Responsive and Transparent Government. It is the image of an ideal government through the eyes of its constituents. **e-Government** is a subset of the concepts of Good Governance and

SMART Government. It is the very specific task of using the tools offered by Information Technology in various aspects of the process of governance with the objective of achieving efficiency, transparency, accountability and user-friendliness in all the transactions that the citizens and businesses conduct with the Government – that is, providing digital interface in the G2C and G2B interactions.

Public managers worldwide aspiring to improve the quality of government services are increasingly deploying E-government strategies that apply the capabilities of information and communication technologies to redesign government services.

However, as government organizations make subsequent investments to reposition their services around an E-government agenda, executives and managers of public organizations are experiencing great challenges in managing E-government systems successfully. E-government systems consist of complex process innovations and reengineering strategies that rely heavily on the systematic integration of old and new information and communication technology components with critical functions of the service delivery system. E-government systems also involve some level of coordination and communication with almost every functional unit of the organization where working relationships among employees are constrained by new and old business processes, and layers of complex institutional and organizational policies, practices, and norms (Kling, 2000). Consequently the likelihood of a government organization finding success in its E-government strategy depends on how well its managers can leverage its technology, organizational, and human resources.

Apart from the technological and organizational issues, governments need to work on the service marketing issues also wherein they need to position their service appropriately in front of its individual and government customers. In this context the following aspects have to be planned out:

Gaps Model of Service Quality: Keeping this framework in mind, governments need to work on understanding the expected level of service of the consumers. They need to manage their service delivery as per the expected level. Finally they have to keep up to promises that they make to the customers so that all the gaps can be filled.

Understanding Domestic and International Consumer: consumers differ in their buying habits, demographics, socio-cultural orientations, technology adaptation, customer care requirements, service standards expected, service quality desired, their role in service delivery, and many more customer related issues. Any government need to analyze these issues of both national international consumers and then plan accordingly.

Employee's Role: the most important task for the government is to instill the philosophy of customer service into the employees because they are the final face of the service provider. Only when the employees strongly feel about the customer, his requirements, the standard and quality desired by him, he would be ready to accept the change management process to give importance to customer and his needs. For this Service-Profit Chain and Service Triangle Frameworks need to be studied.

Brand Image: more than the above parameters, government needs to work on its image as well. For this it has to strategize its plan of action as to how it will associate itself with superior service delivery, emotional benefits, value, credibility, communicating the promise of quality, differentiation with other governments, and many more issues which go into making a favorable brand image of a government.

Delivery and Monitoring Systems: in today's marketing environment, it is not just enough to deliver as per the promise. The provider of the service has to continuously live up to the rising expectations of the consumers. For this proper delivery and measurement systems should be put in place to keep a track of how the service is being delivered and measured.

CONCLUSION

The prospect of E-government is very promising. As the cases in the study show, government organizations are developing highly innovative E-government applications in efforts to improve governance, and services, and enhance citizen participation.

Users can conveniently examine demographic trends in their communities, review service delivery performance in their neighborhoods, participate in policy decisions in their regions, and address emergency management issues.

Multi-sectoral public-private partnerships (Best, 2002) should be the starting point for e-governance and social change. With this leverage, the Government has to work at several levels to build "trust" with cynical generations of Indian citizens. It has to start viewing its engagement with customers through a "Lifecycle" lens. When and where does the government intervene in the citizens' lives, and how can those transactions be made more meaningful, satisfying, and profitable. The last couple of years have seen e-governance drop roots in India. IT enables the delivery of government services as it caters to a large base of people across different segments and geographical locations. The effective use of IT services in government administration can greatly enhance existing efficiencies, drive down communication costs, and increase transparency in the functioning of various departments. It also gives citizens easy access to tangible benefits, be it through simple applications such as online form filling, bill sourcing and payments, or complex applications like distance education and telemedicine.

Systems such as e-governance evolve through the creation and destruction of successful structural attractors at different stages. It has been described earlier in the paper that top down planning approaches for e-governance have a greater risk involved due to their singular reliance on one point of conceptualization and service delivery. Additionally, the *richness* of interactions and transactions possible through a continuously evolving e-governance system cannot be charted out by a central planning authority.

The underlying *structure* gives rise to *emergent activities.* The structure embodies individuals, primary and tertiary stakeholders and groups, organizations, supply chains and backend logistics, social/political networks, and bureaucratic power centers. This structure, when steered through a set of heuristics, best practices, and continuous engagement, leads to positive feedback loops and morphogenesis (growth).

As government organizations make subsequent investments to reposition their services around an E-government agenda, executives and managers of public organizations are experiencing great challenges in managing E-government systems successfully. This study examines how various human, organizational, and technological factors influence the performance of E-government systems technological factors have important consequences for e-government development, executive leader's commitment to e-government, performance-based incentive systems, and social networks mediate the performance of E-government.

INDIA AS A HUB OF GLOBAL HEALTH CARE THROUGH MEDICAL TOURISM

P. Kannadas and C. Muthuvelayutham

India is the fastest growing economy in the world. Tourism is one of the largest contributors to a country's Gross domestic product. Medical tourism is the fast and more revenue generating than ordinary tourism. The world also prefers recuperation combined holiday vacations. How India is having the competitive edge over the other countries is examined in this paper.

The world health care market is estimated around $3 trillion, India is having a market for Rs1030 billion, which is 5.2% of GDP. At the same time India is having a potential to generate Rs 2320 billion to Rs 3200 billion, which is 6.2% to 8.5% of GDP by the year 2012.

India is having a tradition of curing the diseases by it's pristine medical systems like Ayurveda, Yuani and Homeopathy. In addition to that India is emerging as a hub for cheapest allopathic treatment at world class standard at worlds cheapest price. Now India is earning 900 million dollars through medical tourism. It is having a potential to tap $ 1.1billion to 2.2 billion by the year 2012, which is 7.8% of GDP. The market for medical tourism is growing at 30% a year.

India ranks fourth largest country in attracting medical tourists. The top three countries are Thailand, China and Brazil. Thailand alone is attracting 1 million tourists every year. But India is attracting less than that. Last year alone 1.5 Lakh visited for medical treatment in that 40,000 from Bangladesh to West Bengal.

The standard for heart surgery accuracy in USA is 98.8% but India is having a accuracy rate of 98.6%. But in USA and UK the patient's waiting time is much.

This paper throws the undercurrent activities carried out by the Medical organizations and the role played by both state and central governments in respect of medical tourism. This paper also analysed the economic contributions by the state of Tamil Nadu especially Opthamalic patients visiting to Madurai Aravind eye hospital and sangara nendralaya at Chennai.

Tourism has become so important and competitive that many countries have set up their national tourist organization to attract foreign tourists. The income generated through abundance of tourist flow helps the countries to surge forward economically. The Indian Government, through adequate media coverage and other kinds of publicity, has made moves to welcome tourists with the twin purpose of friendly inter-national bond, besides an eye on the income and jobs that they generate. Initially the Government of India did not consider tourism as an important economic activity. In recent years the trend has changed. There is a substantial realization of the importance of tourism as an economic factor. As a result allocations for publicity and infrastructural developments have been enhanced.

ECONOMIC ASPECTS OF TOURISM IN INDIA

Tourism has provided direct employment for 50 lakh people. Among the immediate beneficiaries are hotel owners, travel agents, taxi drivers, airlines, transporters and tourist guides. In certain parts of India, like Kashmir, tourism is the only flourishing industry. The main economic impact of tourism is in foreign exchange earnings. The second is on the generation of employment. There is also the substantial contribution to regional development. It is now generally accepted that international tourism constitutes one of the most vital of global trade flows. The Indian Tourism Development Corporation (ITDC) working under the Ministry of Tourism and Civil Aviation is a part of the National Tourist organization of India. India is the fifth most favoured destination in the world for tourism. Now it is the boom time for India to achieve significant milestones.

MEDICAL TOURISM

This is a new kind of tourism slowly and steadily moving towards the centre stage in inter-national tourism. In India, in particular, it is now making very significant strides. One of the principal reasons for its unexpected and unprecedented foothold in India is the presence of world-class medical facilities, and the fact that they are provided for a fraction of the amount they cost in foreign and developed countries. Gone are the days when the affluent in India went abroad in search of world class hospitals and medical treatment, demanding prohibitive expenditure. Now the tide is turning inwards. A number of private hospitals in India offer packages designed to attract foreign patients, with airport-to-hospital bed transfer service, internet access and other facilities. Some packages include add-ons, such as a yoga holiday or a trip to the world famous Taj Mahal.

Health Sector in India has improved tremendously in the last two decades. Medical tourism, as a result is a big foreign exchange earner, attracting patients world wide, particularly from South east, Asia, Middle East and Africa. There are multispeciality hospitals across the Indian subcontinent that offer the prospective patients a wide choice. Cardiac care techniques in India are at par with the best in the world. The top hospitals in this sector are Escorts, Delhi, AIMS, Delhi and Apollo Hospitals Chennai. For oncology India has the services of Tata Memorial Hospital Mumbai, Apollo Cancer Hospital, Chennai and Kidwar Memorial Institute, Bangalore Table 26.1).

Table 26.1: Top Ten Hospitals in India

Rank	Hospital Name	Place
1.	All India Institute of Medical Sciences	New Delhi
2.	Apollo Hospitals	Chennai
3.	PG Institute of Medical Education and Research	Chandigarh
4.	Christian Medical College	Vellore
5.	Breach Candy Hospital	Mumbai
6.	National Institute of Mental Health and Neurosciences	Bangalore
7.	Jaslok Hospital	Mumbai
8.	Bombay Hospital	Mumbai
9.	Tata Memorial Hospital	Mumbai
10.	Indraprastha Apollo Hospitals	New Delhi
	Sanjay Gandhi Postgraduate Institute of Medical Sciences	Lucknow
	Escorts Heart Institute and Research Centre	New Delhi

Source: The Week.

Six specialties, namely oncology, cardiology, neurology, orthopedics, gastroenterology and nephrology command the most number of patients. The areas pioneered by AIIMS include multiorgan-transplants. In oncology radical surgical and radiation therapies substantially elevate the cure rate. CMC Vellore attracts poor and rich patients from all over India and abroad. NIMHANS, Bangalore attracts patients not only across the country, but also from foreign countries and the Gulf.

With world class health care professionals nursing care and treatment cost almost one-sixth of that in the developed countries. India is witnessing 30 percent growth in medical tourism per year. According to a Confederation of Indian Industries -Mckinsey study, medical tourism can contribute Rs. 5000–10,000 crore additional revenue for up-market tertiary hospitals by 2012.

India is the most touted health care destination for countries like South-East Asia, Middle East, Africa, Mauritius, Tanzania, Bangladesh and Yemen with 12 percent patient inflow from developing countries.

Indian Government has woken up to realize the potential of medical tourism. The concept of medical tourism is gaining momentum in India with both Indian and foreign insurance companies looking at India as a prospective health care destination, with corporate hospitals that can compete globally.

Realising the potential, hospitals have now started tying up with facilitating agencies like tour operators and have taken to marketing and advertising their services in the form of treatment packages for foreign patients to give a fillip to the health tourism sector.

Experts feel that Indian healthcare institutions should tie-up with multi national insurance companies to offer healthcare services to patients from abroad in order to improve medical tourism. They advocate accreditation of healthcare institutions by a foreign agency, marketing and advertising of health care institutes, the facilities and treatment packages they offer to patients from abroad, as some of the components that need to be given a serious thought, if medical tourism has to really take off in a big way.

A provision for room-sharing facilities and special wards for patients from abroad, proper visa facilities and preferential treatment at immigration are other subjects which need to be addressed. Anupam Verma, director, administration, Hinduja Hospital, has gone on record that "other ways of exploring this sector are through seminar and exhibition, which helps feature the healthcare industry and the medical sector globally". According to Dr. Keval Jain, Consultant Internal Medicine, Sir HN Hospital. "Medical tourism can be improved, if we have a good infrastructure in place to deliver quality healthcare to the foreign tourists. Now, big and large hospitals, in small towns and cities, have a good set-up to offer treatment to foreign patients".

Dr. Atul Marwah, Head, Nuclear Medicine, Bombay hospital has this to state. "Medical tourism can be promoted by marketing the medical expertise and facilities to the American and European countries. Some accreditation programmes need to be devised by the Medical Council of India (MCI) to ensure that General Medical Council, UK could accreditate the healthcare institutions in the country."

COST ADVANTAGE

Many countries are trying to position number one in the world healthcare. But India is having cost advantage than any other countries. India's comparative cost can show its strength (Table 26.2).

Health check-up tests like blood tests, electro cardiogram tests, X-rays, lung tests and abdominal ultrasound costs in UK $4345, in USA $574, in Europe €500 but in India it costs $84 only.

Table 26.2: Co..iparative Cost of Healthcare

Category	USA (Cost in $)	India (Cost in $)
Heart Surgery	30,000	8,000
Bone Marrow Transplant	2,50,000	69,000
Liver Transplant	300,000	69,000
Orthopedic Surgery	20,000	6,000
Cataract Surgery	2,000	1,250
Dental Care		
Filling	300-400	20
Root canal	3,500	200

Source: http//www.ilse2004.qvt.edu.av

PROFESSIONAL EXPERTISE

According to the Dr. Devi Shetty of Narayana Hirudayalaya who performed the heart surgery on Baby Noor Fatima of Pakistan, Indian Doctors would define the surgical procedures in next 10 years. When a surgeon in US retires he would have done 2,500 operations, but an Indian doctor in their 30's would have completed this level.

Sixty percent of the Indian Doctors are having international qualifioations and also some kind of exposure to British and U.S protocols.

As stated above, with cutting-edge technology, instant treatment and quality services in the healthcare industry at reduced prices, combined with an opportunity for traditional rejuvenation therapies, India is fast becoming the medical hub of foreign countries. Today people from other countries are visiting India for their medical treatment in large numbers. India is fast becoming a health tourism hub. One of the reasons for attracting foreign tourism is the low-cost quality treatments that include a wide range of traditional Indian methods covering the whole gamut from Ayurveda, Homeopathy, Naturopathy to Yoga and a host of other rehabilitation and rejuvenation therapies. Medical tourists, mainly from Europe, South Asia and the Middle East have begun to find sanctuary in India. Our country is slowly becoming the healthcare destination of the world.

World class treatment is offered in many hospitals in India by a team of dedicated medical care practitioners who do their best to offer personalized care to the patients suffering from serious medical problems, at various stages of afflictions. The patients find themselves in congenial surroundings. In most hospitals and centres where Ayurvedic and Naturopathy treatments consisting of oil massage and mud smearing are required, every care is taken to make the patients feel at home and are also protected from anxiety stages.

The standard accuracy rate in the USA one of the topmost of the developed countries for heart surgery is 98.8%. It will be of great interest to compare the achievement of a third world country like India in this field. India has managed to maintain 98.6% which compares most favourably with that of the USA. The world average for the post operative infection rate is 1 percent. India is streets ahead having registered 0.3% rate level.

NO WAITING TIME

One thing which has managed to draw, as if by magic, a large number of foreign tourists to India for medical treatment is the wonderfully shortened waiting time for undergoing surgery and other effective medical treatments for killer diseases. It is normal for patients in the foreign countries like the USA and the UK to wait for a minimum period of two months for undergoing critical surgeries. In India such surgeries are generally done in one or two weeks time, at the most. There are many instances where even major surgeries are done at a few days' advance notice, if there is an imperative need for an emergency surgery. The situation might change for the worse and longer queues are in the offing, in the future, if the exodus of foreign medical tourists manages to pickup dynamic momentum. If it happens, the positive aspects completely neutralize the flip side.

The one area where medical tourism in India has to keep pace with the world standard is in the transportation and communication field. The travelling facilities in India, though far better than those in the past, leave much desired, compared to the amenities enjoyed in same of the top class developed countries. We need to have better rail and plane links, to provide an effective and quick network across the length and breadth of our vast country.

WAYS AND MEANS

The government of India has to lead the country from the front in the matter of bringing India to the central stage in medical tourism. Cohesive and well-planned steps are to be taken in tandem with the state governments. These things are easier said than done. It is indeed a Herculean task to make the central and state governments function effectively in harmonious uniformity of design, purpose and goal. At this juncture we are reminded of the words of Swami Vivekananda, who in the last century went and conquered America by his dynamism and eloquent address at the conference of Religions of the World at Chicago. What he said, in general about the need for awakening of man in the field of spiritualism, can be applied to the field of transport and communication in medical tourism in India today. "Awake, Arise and stop not, till the goal is reached." The true goal is not a will o' the wisp. It is very much a concrete reality within our reach. What is needed is pragmatism combined with the real idealistic needs. India can outstrip most of the countries in this industry if tackled with imagination and day-to-day realism. The suggestions offered are to be implemented and tested to meet the present needs.

The Indian Government has been taking a fresh book to know whether there are serious roadblocks to be removed in order to enable this important sector of a pioneering industry to get a steady accelerated growth on the fast track. In keeping with such a goal, the Government of India has taken the important decision of allowing the operation of private airlines. The tie up with strategically placed centres of multi specialty, centres of medical care can definitely boost the medical tourism industry. The new airlines are allowed to operate to any airport in India. A few private companies have started operation of small airlines. It is to be remembered that any tourism development is concerned with a wide range of services, transport, accommodation and the infrastructure Medical tourism is fast becoming a major economic activity and a global phenomenon. What is needed to be stressed here is the social and philanthropic parameters of tourism industry.

There are special reasons why medical tourism in India should claim to be not only exotic but also wonderfully unique. Look at the amazing varieties of holistic medical care that can be provided to foreign patients today in India which is undoubtedly cost effective. India is now the hub of medical healing systems comprising Reiki, Pranic healing, Yoga, Meditation and Music Therapy. A detailed examination of those healing systems and their long term benefits are beyond the scope of this paper covering briefly and graphically the widening horizons of medical tourism envisaged in India of the 21st century. If proper publicity is given there is likelihood of a real flood of patients to India from the far-flung corners of the world for cheap medical care leading to lasting cure of their maladies in the most salubrious and stress-free circumstances, resembling a home away from home.

Indian hospitals can move for accreditations certificates from international agencies like JCAHO (Joint Commission Accreditation of health care Organization). Our corporate hospitals have infrastructure and equipments second to none in the world. Yet, steps can be taken to raise them to a still higher level.

It is suggested that a separate wing in most of the major hospitals that attract medical tourists be introduced and properly streamlined. According to WHO, it is imperative, keeping in mind the likely inflow of vast numbers of foreign medical tourists, that steps are taken for an increase of beds to the tune of 80,000 per annum in the ensuing five years to effectively meet the mind-boggling demand for incessant medical services for foreigners.

For the success of this future venture it is absolutely necessary that the tourism health information and communication departments close their ranks and put up a sustained and dependable joint venture so that there is no sagging of the morale of the aspiring participants and supporters of medical tourism. The concept of 'Tourism Police' is to be given more thrust. A police force endowed with the duty of safeguarding the interests and securing and facilitating the many urgent and essential needs of the tourists could be a good idea. Women tourists will feel a greater service of security and confidence.

There is great need to plug all the loopholes in the legal side of tourism. If the tourists and their families are familiar with their rights and duties and the legal tangles there are immense benefits. The legal aspect in health tourism is to be carefully drafted to avoid disputes.

When a two and half year old Pakistani girl was admitted in the Narayana Hirudhayalaya in Bangalore to undergo an open heart surgery, it created a good will between the two countries. When the parents were ready to pay the bill, the doctors here refused to accept the fee for surgery. Fees for the other Medical tests were paid by the good hearted Indians. It was a good sign of Medical diplomacy by the Indians and Indian Government.

The first and second generation expatriate Indians who are living in different parts of the world estimated to be 20 million strong are the very good potential for the Indian Medical Tourism.

A FOOT IN OPHTHALMOLOGY

The single largest cataract surgery provider in the world is Aravind eye hospital in Madurai. It has given eyesight to 13 million people and performed 1.8 million surgeries in a span of 26 years. A cataract surgery costs US $ 1650 in US hospital, but in Aravind the same quality surgery is US $10. These hospitals manufacturing division Aurolab which prepares the Intraocular lenses (Iols). In America it costs US $100 but it sells here at US $ 4-6 per lens. It offers free service to 70% of the patients but earns 40% of profit. One third of the patients who could afford to pay for the services they received subsidize the rest (2/3) of the patients who could not afford the expenses. It attracts foreign patients from Singapore, Malaysia and Srilanka. It has branches at Tirunelveli, Coimbatore, Theni and Pondicherry. Each day across 5 Aravind eye hospital 4055 out patients per day are checked, 542 surgeries per day are carried out. A cataract surgery takes 10 to 20 minutes. Assembly line operation process is performed here. The founder Dr. V. Govindappa Venkataswamy has started his mission by saying that when Mc Donald's could sell billions of low-cost burgers, he could also sell millions of low-cost sight-restoring operations.

APOLLO HOSPITALS GROUP

The Apollo Hospitals Group, India's first corporate hospital has been recognized as the 'Architect of modern health care' in India. It has done over 7,50,000 surgeries, and over 10,00,000 surgical procedures over the years. It has created a niche in cardiology. Over 2,00,000 angiograms, 16,000 angioplasties and 35,00 mitral balloon valvuloplasties performed. It attracts many foreigners.

SANKARA NETHRALAYA

One of the leading eye hospitals in Chennai runs with a partnership with Apollo hospitals. It has also performed over 35,000 surgeries and accounts for 30,000 surgical procedures annually. Many foreigners to this clinic are attracted thanks to quality and services at reasonable rates.

Rupa Chandra, Professor at the IIM, Bangalore states "The estimate is that the health care market in the Organization of Economic Cooperation and Development countries alone is worth $3 trillion and expected to go up to $4 trillion in 2005." In 2004 just five countries in Asia - Thailand, Malaysia, Jordan, Singapore and India-tackled among themselves about 1.3 million medical travelers and earned over $1 billion in treatment costs alone. Elsewhere around the world, Hong Kong, Lithunia and South Africa are emerging as big medical health care destinations.

Medical tourism has accelerated in the past five years or so. It has developed a massive movement for two critical reasons. The first is the demographies of the developed nations and the problems of healthcare systems. The number of elderly people is expected to double in the next fifteen years. Hence there is a big surge in demand for healthcare.

As the health needs increase exponentially the health care system in the developed countries begin to crack under pressure. The doctors and nurses in the UK and the US are not able to keep pace with the demands of the ageing population. This creates the push factor.

The pull factor, on the other hand, is being created by some developing countries like Thailand and Malaysia. They have good doctors and excellent facilities. India is now attracting a large number of medical tourists because of the presence of adequate facilities for medical care of world class standard. Prathap C Reddy Chairman of Apollo hospital Groups spoke with verve and enthusiasm when he confidently claimed that "The competence and skills of Indian doctors is accepted internationally."

Though the movement has not survived its teething problems, medical care has come under the radar of both the WITO and W.T.O. In the late 1980's and early 1990's most medical travallers coming to India were from the Arab countries, Africa and South-east Asia. But now there is a significant number from the CIS nations.

India does have an edge if it wants to tap the medical traveller market. It churns out over 20,000 doctors in a year. The Apollo Hospitals group has treated about a lakh foreign patients till date. Apollo has tied up with NIIT and Aptech so that attendants of patients0 who come for 2-3 months can take short-term IT courses.

A recent study by Mckinsey & company estimated that India could earn revenues of $1 billion from medical travel. But for that to happen, the government and private hospitals have to make a united effort. Improving the connectivity of Mumbai and Delhi with Hyderabad and Chennai could do much for the foreign patients. Apart from conventional medical treatment retirement homes for the aged could usher in greater opportunity for the widening of the pastures for medical tourism in India.

SUMMING UP

Medical Travel is the most visible face of the increasing global trade in healthcare services. The WTO expects three other modes to become significant. One is 'cross-border delivery of trade'. It covers a wide range from shipment of laboratory samples, consultation via mail channels to the electronic delivery of health services. The record is telemedicine. The third mode covers the setting up of hospitals in a country by a medical group with a base in another country.

According to the CII Mckinsey report the total healthcare market in India could rise from the current Rs. 1030 bn (5.2% of GDP) to Rs 2320 bn-Rs 3280 bn which mean that India could spend 6.2 - 8.5% of its GDP on healthcare by 2012. Medical tourism business could bring $1.1 bn - $ 2.2 bn into the country by 2012. Medical tourism in India is growing by an estimated 30% a year.

Last year as many as 1.5 lakh medical tourists visited the country and it has immense potential to attract more. From Afro-Asian countries alone the contribution by patients who seek treatment abroad comes to $10 billion. If India can tap even a fraction of that market the financial benefits could be quite staggering. The global opportunities in this sphere have to be capitalized by the combined strategic moves of the government and corporate hospitals. The future of Indian economy is directly linked to the gold mine uncovered by the future prospects of medical tourism.

REFERENCES

Apollo Hospitals Pioneering health care", Global CEO, January 2005.

Aseem Anand, "Dictionary of Tourism" K.S. Paperbacks, New Delhi, 110002.

Best Hospitals, The Week, 18 January 2004

Datta, Prosenjit & Krishnan, Gina S. "The health travallers", Business world, 22 December 2003.

http// expresshealthcaremgmt.com

http// globalpolicy.org

http// moneyweek.com

http// us.rediff.com.

http// www.ilsc2004.qvt.edu.av

http// Yale global .yale.edu

Kartham, Anil Kumar and Dutta, Sanjib, "Dr. V of Aravind Eye Hospitals – A 'Level 5' Leader", Case Folio, June 2004.

Rao, N. Janardhan and Zaheer Feroz, Destination India: Medical Tourism, Chartered Financial Analyst, January 2005.

27

INDIAN BANKING: MANAGING TRANSFORMATION THROUGH INFORMATION TECHNOLOGY

R.K. Uppal

Transformation is a dynamic process during which all known tenors undergo metamorphosis. It is a fluid state with uncertain outcome. Due to its fluidity, it is difficult to determine its course. The significant transformation of the banking industry in India is evident from changes that have occurred in the financial markets, institutions and products. While deregulation has opened up new vistas for banks to augment revenues, it has entailed greater competition and consequently greater risks. Cross-border flows and entry of new products, particularly derivative instruments, have affected significantly on the domestic banking sector, forcing banks to adjust the product mix, as also to affect rapid change their processes and operations in order to remain competitive to the globalize environment. All this necessitates a transformation: a transformation in the mindset, a transformation in the business processes and finally, a transformation in knowledge management. Hence, during transformation, all known parameters of the earlier regime continuously change. Managing transformation is, thus, a challenging task. When the required outcome of the transformation is pre-set, as in Indian banking today, managing transformation presents both a great challenge and an opportunity also.

The present paper has national and international status. The findings of the paper may be helpful for the banking industry, particularly; it will be very helpful for our public sector banks. After making a comprehensive discussion regarding the use of various IT delivery channels of various products and services in banks, this discussion will become very useful for those banks, which are managing transformation through IT. They can modify some services, delivery channels as per the requirements of the customers, it will further helpful to improve the CRM in banks, and it will be more useful for those banks, which have still not fully adopted IT in banks, particularly public sector banks.

INTRODUCTION

The changes after Liberalization and Globalization process instated since 1991 significant impact on the financial system particularly on the banking industry. The fast pace of changes have radically and perceptibly transformed the operational environment of the banking sector. The IT revolution is of entirely changing the way banking business is done and has considerably widened the range of products and increased the expected demand of the bank customers.

Indian banking and financial system in the new millennium is facing a series of new challenges. The challenges are manifold and multidimensional under the influence of globalization, coupled with the adoption of new technology and stiff competition arising out of the changing situation. The financial and banking sector reforms introduced in early nineties in Indian economy primarily aimed at viable and efficient banking system in India. Recommendations made by the Narasimham Committee-I (1991) and II (1998) for asset classification, asset-liability management (ALM), income recognition, capital adequacy, disclosure norms, risk management etc. in conformity with the global standards have explained the majority of our banks to quite tough, rather different situations at the initial stage of their complementation and a few of them are still is in incompatible phase. However, alternating doses of re-capitalization for union govt., remarkable transformation has brought in their operations and functionality.

Stiff global competition, rapid technological changes, volatile interest rates, entry of NPSBs, economic and other conditions etc., have created significant pressure on stability and viability of Indian Banks, which were still experiencing reduction in profitability, declining productivity, deterioration in quality of assets, overstaffing, obsolete technology etc. To repose themselves to become cost-effective and market oriented for their survival and growth of new environment changes have created the compulsion on Indian Banks.

In order to meet the global challenges of new economic environment and explore the emerging opportunities, an organization has to reset its structure to make it compatible and adaptable. In the backdrop of transformed phase of banking and financial sector reforms, Indian banks spread across the country with cultural diversity and demographic variations; need to have a fresh look at their organizational structure. Banks are confronted with relentless pressure of global competition. Consequently, restructuring has become necessary to build sustainable competitive advantage for the achievement of global standards.

Restructuring of financial sector is a multidimensional approach consisting of administrative restructuring, capital restructuring, corporate debt restructuring, human resource restructuring etc. Banking restructuring is a total restructuring/re-engineering of banks. It is an orchestrated changes i.e. changes in culture, strategy, vision, management style etc.

Meaning of Bank Transformation

1. The term transformation in Indian Banking Industry relates to intermediately stage when the industry is passing from the earlier social banking era to the newly conceived technology based customer - centric and competitive banking. The activities and banks have grown in multi-directional as well as in multi-dimensional manners.
2. During transformation, all known parameters of the earlier regime continuously change.
3. The current transformation process in the Indian Banking has many aspects. They pertain to:

- Capital Restructuring
- Financial Re-engineering
- Information Technology
- Human Resource Development

IT in banking has been used in four major ways:

- To handle a greatly expanded customers ways
- To reduce substantially to real cost of handing payments
- To liberate the banks from the traditional constraints on time and place and
- To introduce new products and services.

Table 27.1: The Cost Advantage of E-Delivery Channels in Indian Banks

Cost, if transaction is made through Branch	Rs. 50 per Transaction
Cost, if transaction is made through ATM	Rs. 15 per Transaction
Cost, if transaction is made through Internet	Rs. 4 per Transaction

In ICICI Bank, UTI, HDFC Bank, ABN Amro Bank, only 10% of the total transactions take place through the net.

Table 27.2: Impact of Various E–Delivery Channels in Indian Banking Industry (2000-2003)

Name of the Bank	Technology	Customer Base
ICICI Bank	ATMs (125-1750)	2 Million – 5 Million
UTI Bank	ATMs (647 - 1000)	Servicing a base of 1.3 million customers and 90% of total cash withdrawals is through ATMs
ABN Amro Bank	–	92% withdrawals through ATMs. 2.5 lakh customers added through ATMs

Indian PSBs, Corporation Bank, SBI, PNB, OBC, SBP is also using limited ATMs and they are sharing ATMs.

The virtual financial services can largely be categorized as follows:

Automated Teller Machines

- Cash withdrawals
- Fast cash
- Details of most recent balance of account
- Mini-statement
- Statement ordering facility
- Deposit facility
- Payments to third parties

EFTPoS

EFTPoS card used to initiate transaction

- Authorization and transaction capture processes take place electronically.
- Transaction confirmed manually.
- Funds not debited electronically.

Remote Banking Services

- Balance enquiry
- Statement ordering
- Funds transfer (payment) to third parties
- Funds transfer between customers different accounts
- Order traveler's cheques and other financial instruments.

Services Not Available Through Remote Banking

- Cash withdrawal
- Cash/ cherub deposit
- Sale of the more complex types of financial services such as life insurance mortgages and (pensions).

Remote Banking Interface

- Automated voice-response system
- Interactive television
- Internet terminal
- Screen phone
- Personal digital assistant
- Other people provide the information

Smart Cards

Stored value cards

As a replacement for all types of magnetic stripes cards

- ATM cards
- Debit cards
- Charge cards
- Credit cards
- One smart card to carry out all these functions
- One smart card can contain the functionality of several different types of cards issued by different banks while running different types of networks.
- Smart card a truly powerful financial token, giving user access
- STM
- Debit facility
- Charge facilities
- Credit facilities
- Electronic purse facilities at national and international level.

INTERNET BANKING

The latest wave in IT is Internet banking. It is becoming more obvious that the Internet has unleashed a revolution that is affecting every sphere of life. Internet is an interconnection of computer communication networks spanning the entire globe, crossing all geographical boundaries. Touching lifestyles in every sphere the Net has redefined methods of communication, work, study, education interaction, health, trade and commerce. The Net is changing everything. From the way we conduct commerce, to the way we distribute information. Being an interactive two-way medium, the Net, through innumerable websites, enables participation by individual in B2B and B2C commerce, visits to shopping malls, books-stores, entertainment sides, and so on cyberspace.

REVIEW OF LITERATURE

Arora, K. (2003) also highlighted the significance of bank transformation. Technology has a definitive role in facilitating transactions in the banking sector and the impact of technology implementation has resulted in the introduction of new products and services by various banks in India.

Brett (1997) studied the changing in old money structure into E-Money. Now days the banks are providing different cards (Smart Card, Credit & Debit Cards) to their customers.

Bakshi, S. (2003) said that good governance is of interest not only to an individual bank but also to the society in which it operates-the basic objectives being protection of depositors and safeguarding the integrity and soundness of the system.

Clifford (2002) studied the impact of IT on the financial services. The dimensions of banking business are changing in the new economy. In many banks, transformation is managed by IT.

Chachadi, A.H. (2003) given his views that we have to hone our skills in developing an appropriate culture, which is characterized by teamwork commitment and a problem solving approach.

Das, S.C. (2003) said that manpower management is undoubtedly the most important rather the most sensitive and critical areas of management that needs to be handled with utmost care and diligence.

Federick & Phil. (2000) analyzed the E-Loyalty. According to them, the unique economics of e-business make customers loyalty more important than ever.

Garg, I. K. (2003) highlighted the challenges faced by the banks in the present transition mode. He also suggested that continuous change must be adopted as a culture and appropriate institutional arrangements must be made to facilitate it.

Jalan, B. (2003) rightly expressed his view in the Bank Economists' Conference - (2003), a forward-looking approach to our long-term vision must focus on building human resources in a continuous cycle of competency and development.

Mohan, R. (2003) expressed his views regarding the transformation in Indian Banking that if Indian Banks are to compete globally, the time is opportune for them to institute sound and robust risk management practices.

Robert, T. Parry (2000) said that transformation is taking place amid broader changes in banking sector and suggest three principles to cope up with the transformation. He concluded that countries adopting the suggested principles are benefiting from the increasing globalization of financial services; hence other should follow the road map.

Sankarn, S. (2001) concluded that in the era of transformation banks should go for mergers and acquisitions to improve their size, skills and services. He suggested that Indian Banking has to operate with a global mindset even while fulfilling local banking requirements.

The review of literature on various aspects of bank transformation concludes that transformation is taking place and IT is playing vital role in bringing this transformation and it is need of the hour to manage this transformation with IT.

PRODUCTIVITY AND PROFITABILITY AT BANK GROUP LEVEL

Overall productivity (employee, branch & operational) is the highest in foreign banks as this group deserve because it shows that its labour productivity is 4.5 times more than Public Sector Banks, branch productivity is 22 times more than that of PSBs. Whereas operational productivity is 1 to 2 times more than PSBs (Tables 27.3 to 27.8).

It shows that foreign banks are much more efficient as compared to other groups. Foreign banks appear to be more efficient users of input quantities to produce given output as compared to other bank groups. But private sector banks also following these banks with the minor gap in its productivity from the foreign banks productivity as New Private Sector Banks labour productivity in terms of business per employee is 8.43 cr. per employee but foreign banks shows this ratio at 9.42 cr. per employee with the gap of only 1 cr. per employee. Similarly branch productivity of NPSBs in terms of business per branch (158.12 cr. per branch) is 4.5 times less than that of foreign bank's branch productivity (668.77 cr. per employee). In the same way, operational productivity in terms of net profit as percentage of total assets is also 1 to 2 times less of NPSBs as compared to the operational productivity of foreign banks. This group does not show stability in its results, which proves from its C.V. ratio i.e. maximum in almost all the parameters of the productivity. The lower productivity of new private sector banks (G-IV) could be because these banks are in the expansion phase and could have higher amount of fixed assets employed, which have yet to start generating returns.

The public sector and old private sector banks have shown lower productivity as compared to NPSBs & Foreign Banks. Actually, they are flush with deposits but have few lending due to the risk factor. The low productivity and profitability in public sector banks as compared to new private sector and foreign banks is due to:

- Heavy initial cost
- Resistance to change by senior staff/unions
- More interference by govt.
- Inadequate infrastructure
- Less innovative activities and new products/services
- Increasing NPAs due to more priority sector lending with political interference
- Less knowledge of competition i.e. no competitive strategy
- No emphasis on public relations
- Lack of technology (adoption and application)
- Vast branch network
- Management of across border changes- cross-cultural differences and need for continuous realignment due to volatile changes in the international operating environment.

Table 27.3: Productivity of Nationalized Banks (G-I)

Year	Per Employee Productivity			Per Branch Productivity			Financial Productivity As Percentage of Total Assets						
	D/E	C/E	B/E	D/Br	C/Br	B/Br	II	IE	S	NII	NIE	Br	NP
2001	1.08	0.52	1.60	16.70	8.08	24.78	9.09	6.19	2.90	1.14	3.71	2.57	0.33
2002	1.31	0.67	1.97	18.83	9.62	28.46	8.78	6.03	2.75	1.49	3.55	2.06	0.69
2003	1.45	0.76	2.21	20.77	10.85	31.62	8.39	5.39	3.00	1.67	3.69	2.02	0.98
2004	1.68	0.87	2.56	23.80	12.36	36.16	7.43	4.38	3.05	1.86	3.73	1.87	1.18
Average	1.38	0.71	2.09	20.03	10.21	30.26	8.42	5.50	2.93	1.54	3.67	2.13	0.80
S.D.	0.25	0.15	0.40	3.02	1.85	4.83	0.72	0.82	0.13	0.31	0.00	0.30	0.37
C.V.%	18.12	21.13	19.14	15.08	18.12	15.96	8.55	14.91	4.44	20.13	0.00	14.08	46.25

Source: Performance Highlights of Public Sector Banks, 2001-04

Table 27.4: Productivity of Public Sector Banks (G-II)

Year	Per Employee Productivity			Per Branch Productivity			Financial Productivity As Percentage of Total Assets						
	D/E	C/E	B/E	D/Br	C/Br	B/Br	II	IE	S	NII	NIE	Br	NP
2001	1.08	0.52	1.60	23.02	11.09	34.11	8.47	5.68	2.79	1.30	3.54	2.24	0.55
2002	1.24	0.58	1.82	25.83	12.10	37.93	8.62	5.91	2.71	1.34	3.28	1.94	0.77
2003	1.38	0.67	2.05	28.79	13.93	42.72	8.26	5.50	2.76	1.62	3.47	1.85	0.91
2004	1.54	0.79	2.33	31.76	16.18	47.94	7.46	4.62	2.84	1.99	3.80	1.81	1.03
Average	1.31	0.64	1.96	27.35	13.33	40.68	8.20	5.34	2.78	1.56	3.52	1.96	0.82
S.D.	0.20	0.12	0.31	3.77	2.24	5.99	0.52	0.57	0.00	0.32	0.22	0.19	0.21
C.V. %	15.27	18.75	15.82	13.78	16.80	14.72	6.34	10.50	0.00	20.51	6.25	9.69	25.61

Source: Performance Highlights of Old Private Sector Banks, 2001-04

Table 27.5: Productivity of Old Private Sector Banks (G-III)

Year	Per Employee Productivity			Per Branch Productivity			Financial Productivity As Percentage of Total Assets						
	D/E	C/E	B/E	D/Br	C/Br	B/Br	II	IE	S	NII	NIE	Br	NP
2001	1.33	0.69	2.02	17.33	9.00	26.33	9.54	6.97	2.57	1.22	3.07	1.85	0.72
2002	1.49	0.78	2.27	19.04	10.00	29.04	9.35	6.93	2.42	2.35	3.67	1.32	1.09
2003	1.73	0.93	2.66	21.50	11.63	33.13	8.50	6.03	2.47	2.25	3.54	1.29	1.17
2004	2.07	1.10	3.17	24.83	13.17	37.99	7.51	4.95	2.56	2.00	3.40	1.40	1.16
Average	1.66	0.88	2.53	20.67	10.95	31.62	8.73	6.22	2.51	1.96	3.42	1.47	1.04
S.D.	0.32	0.18	0.50	3.26	1.83	5.08	0.93	0.95	0.00	0.51	0.26	0.27	0.21
C.V. %	19.28	20.45	19.76	15.77	16.71	16.07	10.65	15.27	0.00	26.02	7.60	18.37	20.19

Source: Performance Highlights of New Private Sector Banks, 2001-04

Table 27.6: Productivity of New Private Sector Banks (G-IV)

Year	Per Employee Productivity			Per Branch Productivity			Financial Productivity As Percentage of Total Assets						
	D/E	C/E	B/E	D/Br	C/Br	B/Br	II	IE	S	NII	NIE	Br	NP
2001	5.06	2.43	7.49	75.22	36.08	111.30	8.17	6.03	2.14	1.35	2.67	1.32	0.81
2002	4.91	4.16	9.06	90.25	76.48	166.73	4.52	3.33	1.19	1.20	1.91	0.71	0.47
2003	4.64	3.59	8.23	93.34	72.19	165.53	8.13	6.43	1.70	2.57	3.37	0.80	0.90
2004	5.24	3.72	8.95	110.47	78.40	188.87	6.66	4.68	1.98	2.11	3.26	1.15	0.84
Average	4.96	3.48	8.43	92.32	65.79	158.12	6.87	5.12	1.75	1.81	2.00	1.00	0.76
S.D.	0.25	0.74	0.73	14.46	19.97	33.00	1.72	1.41	0.42	0.65	0.67	0.29	0.19
C.V. %	5.04	21.26	8.66	15.66	30.35	20.87	25.04	27.54	24.00	35.91	33.50	29.00	25.00

Source: Performance Highlights of New Private Sector Banks, 2001-04

Table 27.7: Productivity of Foreign Banks (G-V)

Year	Per Employee Productivity			Per Branch Productivity			Financial Productivity As Percentage of Total Assets						
	D/E	C/E	B/E	D/Br	C/Br	B/Br	II	IE	S	NII	NIE	Br	NP
2001	4.60	3.57	8.18	356.96	277.09	634.04	8.28	5.98	2.30	2.38	5.40	3.02	0.94
2002	5.37	4.23	9.60	403.66	318.07	721.73	8.47	5.93	2.54	2.90	5.30	2.40	1.32
2003	5.88	4.43	10.31	383.94	288.99	672.93	7.67	4.33	3.34	2.64	4.42	1.78	1.56
2004	5.44	4.13	9.57	367.54	278.83	646.37	6.59	3.13	3.46	2.95	4.77	1.82	1.50
Average	5.32	4.09	9.42	378.03	290.75	668.77	7.75	4.82	2.97	2.72	4.97	2.26	1.33
S.D.	0.53	0.37	0.89	20.38	18.96	38.86	0.85	1.38	0.58	0.26	0.46	0.58	0.28
C.V. %	9.96	9.05	9.45	5.39	6.52	5.81	10.97	28.63	19.53	9.56	9.26	25.66	21.05

Source: Performance Highlights of Foreign Sector Banks, 2001-04

Table 27.8: Statistical Analysis of Various Parameters of Productivity

Year	Labour Productivity			Branch Productivity			Operational Productivity As Percentage of Total Assets						
	D/E	C/E	B/E	D/Br	C/Br	B/Br	II	IE	S	NII	NIE	Br	NP
G-I													
Average	1.38	0.71	2.09	20.03	10.21	30.26	8.42	5.50	2.93	1.54	3.67	2.13	0.80
S.D.	0.25	0.15	0.40	3.02	1.85	4.83	0.72	0.82	0.13	0.31	0.00	0.30	0.37
C.V.(%)	18.12	21.13	19.14	15.08	18.12	15.96	8.55	14.91	4.44	20.13	0.00	14.08	46.25
G-II													
Average	1.31	0.64	1.96	27.35	13.33	40.68	8.20	5.34	2.78	1.56	3.52	1.96	0.82
S.D.	0.20	0.12	0.31	3.77	2.24	5.99	0.52	0.57	0.00	0.32	0.22	0.19	0.21
C.V.(%)	15.27	18.75	15.82	13.78	16.80	14.72	6.34	10.50	0.00	20.51	6.25	9.69	25.61
G-III													
Average	1.66	0.88	2.53	20.67	10.95	31.62	8.73	6.22	2.51	1.96	3.42	1.47	1.04
S.D.	0.32	0.18	0.50	3.26	1.83	5.08	0.93	0.95	0.00	0.51	0.26	0.27	0.21
C.V.(%)	19.28	20.45	19.76	15.77	16.71	16.07	10.65	15.27	0.00	26.02	7.60	18.37	20.19
G-IV													
Average	4.96	3.48	8.43	92.32	65.79	158.12	6.87	5.12	1.75	1.81	2.00	1.00	0.76
S.D.	0.25	0.74	0.73	14.46	19.97	33.00	1.72	1.41	0.42	0.65	0.67	0.29	0.19
C.V.(%)	5.04	21.26	8.66	15.66	30.35	20.87	25.04	27.54	24.00	35.91	33.50	29.00	25.00
G-V													
Average	5.32	4.09	9.42	378.03	290.75	668.77	7.75	4.82	2.97	2.72	4.97	2.26	1.33
S.D.	0.53	0.37	0.89	20.38	18.96	38.86	0.85	1.38	0.58	0.26	0.46	0.58	0.28
C.V.(%)	9.96	9.05	9.45	5.39	6.52	5.81	10.97	28.63	19.53	9.56	9.26	25.66	21.05
Industry													
Average	1.52	0.82	2.33	24.76	13.25	38.00	8.16	5.43	2.73	1.68	3.62	1.93	0.85
S.D.	0.28	0.18	0.46	4.00	2.60	6.60	0.63	0.70	0.15	0.72	0.14	0.30	0.28
C.V.(%)	18.42	21.95	19.74	16.16	19.62	17.37	7.72	12.89	5.49	42.86	3.87	15.54	32.94

In other words, the main challenges ahead in the new millennium in banking and financial sector contain changing economic and banking environment, global competition, capital structure, transparency in reporting accounts, employee productivity, governance, technology support for enhancing customer services, WTO and PSBs, corporate governance, in global banking regulatory framework, risk management, market discipline, sound human resource management, training and development etc.

POLICY IMPLICATIONS AND RECOMMENDATIONS

Based on the above analysis and observations, I would like to suggest evolving strategy in the days to come to manage bank transformation with IT particularly in PSBs to improve the productivity and profitability of the banks in the following ways:

1. In the liberalized, globalized and highly competitive environment, Indian Banking Industry should manage each and every activity through cost effective IT. PSBs should speed up technology up gradation even in the semi-urban and rural sector branches.
2. More awareness should be created regarding the IT in banks.
3. More training should be given to the staff in PSBs.
4. For improving the share of banks, the low-cost deposited action plans should be prepared for those centers where there is adequate potential for deposit mobilization.
5. For those centers where inadequate potential for business development is available, an strategy should be formulated for considering the merger and relocation of branches within the framework of RBI guidance.
6. A strategic action plan should be initiated for reducing NPAs through IT.
7. In order to involve all members in business development and build team spirit at the branch level, regular staff meeting must be organized at least fortnightly or monthly. In this case, IT can play vital and effective role.
8. To create awareness about the management of NPAS, profitability consciousness, planned business development etc., suitable training programming require to be organized for loss-making branches of e-banks and IT can helpful to create this type of awareness.
9. IBI should stop copying the western banking models and should take special care to understand the local ethos and cultural backdrop. Indian bankers should try to promote innovations (through IT0 and creativity taking into account the local ethos.
10. With increasing competition among the banks, to meet customer expectations, banks should offer a broader range of deposits, investments and credit

products through diverse distributional channels including ungrounded branches, ATMs, telephone and Internet. For this banks should:

- Become more customer-centric, offering a wide range of products through multiple e-delivery channels.
- Pay greater attention to profitability (through IT) including cost reduction and increasing fee-based income.
- Become proficient in managing assets and liabilities according to risk and return.

All these changes require vision, determination and extensive communication across all levels in the organization so that the vision and mission of the banks is communicated and understand down the line.

11. Domestic banks should begin to make them as competitive as possible. They should also increase their productivity and profitability because in the highly competitive and open economy, size is no longer a key indicator in the banking industry.
12. Indian banks should concentrate on asset quality and earnings.
13. In the emerging scenario, with more and more global players operating in India, there has been an urgent need to serve the customers promptly and efficiently through IT.

- Bank should regularly update themselves with economic and trade related developments
- Bank should launch an awareness-building programme for understanding the WTO and various e-delivery channels
- Bank should help their customers in formulating strategies for achieving global competitiveness.
- VRS should continue and should not be one-line affair.

14. Autonomy in HRM areas such as deciding categorization of banks, vacancy placements should be given to banks.
15. An efficient capital market should be developed to channalize private savings into infrastructure financing.
16. Use of IT should be increased to manage transformation substantially in banks and cope with rising volumes and reduce transaction cost and processing.
17. A constructive and serious measure should be initiated for:

- Better and Cheaper access to basic infrastructure requirements such as power, telecommunications i.e. VSAT, leased lines etc.
- Creation of customer awareness and education for technology adoption are imperative.

- The IT Act, 2000 should be implemented in totality to handle legal issues.
- Connecting branches into boutiques catering to the requirements of clients and re-engineering the functions of branch banking using technology and delivery channels.
- Setting up of e-banking group to provide grid principles for risk management of e-banking activities.

There are immense opportunities IBI to overcome these challenges. They can convert these challenges into opportunities with IT. Information Technology will be the important issue in ensuring survival of banks. It is no longer a matter of choice but compulsion. However, at the same time, technology has to be cost effective, customer-driven and implement able. So far, technology has been used only for transaction processing. Time has come to make use of it for decision-making and efficient payment mechanism.

Last but not the least, PSBs have also to appreciate that any technology upgradation programme cannot succeed without pains of restructuring and sacrifices by all the stakeholders for which realization has yet to come.

REFERENCES

Arora, Kalpana (2003), 'Indian Banking: Managing Transformation Through IT', IBA Bulletin, Vol. XXV, No. 3 (March), pp: 134-138.

Avasthi, G.P.M. (2000-01), 'Information Technology in Banking: Challenges for Regulators', Prajnan, Vol. XXIX, No. 4, pp: 3 -17

Bajaj, K.K. (2000), 'E-Commerce Issues in the Emerging Hi -Tech. Banking Environment', The Journal of The Indian Institute of Bankers, (Jan- March)

Bakshi, S. (2003), 'Corporate Governance in Transformation Times', IBA Bulletin, Vol. XXV, No. 3, (March).

Bhasin, T.M. (2001), 'E-Commerce in Indian Banking', IBA Bulletin, Vol. XXIII, Nos. 4 & 5, (April – May).

Chachadi, A.H. (2003), 'HRD as a Strategic Tool in Organizational Transformation in Indian Banks', IBA Bulletin, Vol. XXV, No. 3 (March), pp. 114-120.

Das, S.C. (2003), 'Managing Transformation In Indian Banking Through HRD', IBA Bulletin, Vol. XXV, No. 3, (March)

Ganesh, S. (2001), 'Frauds In A Computerized Environment', IBA Bulletin, Vol. XXIII No. 12 (Dec.), pp: 19-25

Garg, I.K. (2003), 'Indian Banking in Transition: Some Management Challenges', IBA Bulletin, Vol. XXV, No. 3, (March), pp: 121-123

Gupta, R P. (2001), 'Banking In The New Millennium: Strategic Management Issues', IBA Bulletin, Vol. XXIII, No. 3 (March), pp.38-45

Jalan, B. (2003), 'Strengthening Indian Banking and Finance: Progress and Prospectus', IBA Bulletin, Vol. XXV, No. 3 (March)

Kulkarni, R. V. (2000), 'Changing Face of Banking From Brick and Mortar Banking to E- Banking', IBA Bulletin, (Jan.)

Mohan, R. (2003), 'Transforming Indian Banking: In Search of a Better Tomorrow', IBA Bulletin, Vol. XXV, No. 3, (March).

Nair, S.N. (2000), 'E-Commerce and The Emergence of E-Banking', IBA Bulletin, Vol. XXII, No. 10, (Oct.)

Shapiro, C (2000), 'Will E- Commerce Erode Liberty', Harvard Business Review, (May- June)

Shastri, R.V (2001), 'Technology for Banks in India- Challenges', IBA Bulletin, Vol. XXIII, No. 3, (March). pp: 23-45

Trivedi, A. K. (2003), 'Indian Banking: Managing Transformation' IBA Bulletin, Vol. XXV, No. 3, (March)

28

IMPACT AND IMPLICATIONS OF GLOBALIZATION ON MANAGEMENT EDUCATION

Sapna Hooda

Good education aims at the development of balanced personalities who are culturally refined, emotionally stable, ethically sound, intellectual alert, socially efficient, spiritually upright and physically strong. Good education also aims at developing men who can play as well as work; men who can consume as well as create. Santosh Arora on vocational education

This philosophy is the very basis of management education.

India and Indian law underwent a paradigm shift in the last decade. There have been fundamental and favorable changes in the economy, government policies, outlook of business and industry, and in the mindset of the Indians in general. It has emerged as a service oriented economy and is now a front-runner in the emerging knowledge based new economy. The economy has become a high-growth one in the long term. The realm of management education is undergoing metamorphosis. This is not limited to Indian alone but is a global issue. The key success factor under the given situation will lie not only getting it from the west if we can do that management institutes in India each setup role models for other developing countries.

It is becoming imperative to infuse "Indian ,ness" in the curriculum of our management education instead of waiting for the west to make the first move. This could be done by introducing separate courses like political and economic history of India, "business ethics", "The Indian way", "Indian scripture and Vedic management principles, Vedic mathematics and so on. This might also mean the million of contemporary India researches on various subject taught for this the business and management schools together should undertake a joint effort to respond proactively to the changing scenario. They together will have to think globally and also act globally.

IMPACT OF GLOBALIZATION ON MANAGEMENT EDUCATION

Economic reforms initiated by Govt. of India are creating new forces that are revolutionizing the ways of managing the business and other organizations. The emergence of global village with IT revolution has brought fastest ever changes in all walks of life in an unprecedented manner. More and more economic alliances, multinational corporations hi-tech managers, e-business etc. are governing the business scene today. The competition has taken a major leap forward from local to universal demands where value addition is the key to survival of the fittest. The emergences of supra-national corporate ethos and new strategic alliances cutting across the socio-eco culture barriers have become inevitable for any competing economy. The new environment poses exciting opportunities not only in the form of scale and spread of business operation, but also in terms of technology transfer, technocrats and professionals. In the light of all these, fast emerging changes in the environment create vast opportunities for the management education in a global perspective.

GLOBALIZATION OF EDUCATION

Nobel Laureate Joseph Stiglitz defines globalization as "removal to free trade and the closer integration of national economics (Stiglitz, 2002, p. ix). In other words, economic globalization refers to the integration of different economies of the world through trade, investment and migration of people. Broadly Globalization mans integration of economies and societies through cross country flow of information, ideas, technology, goods, services, capital, finance and people."(Rangrajan: 2003 p.729).

Connectivity is the essence of globalization. It is argued that more free trade means more welfare to the people. However, Inequity in the distribution of income among and within the countries is yet to be tackled.

The revolution in information and communication has rendered education portable, flexible, non-linear and student centric globalization in education refers to integrating an international dimension into teaching, learning and services functions of the institution. The concept of quality assurance is based on the western parameters or formulations. The management view of quality implies the totality of features and characteristics of products and services that bear on its ability to satisfy stated or implied needs. (Mohanty and Lakhe: 2002, p.2) In development parlance, quality is all that enhances the quality of life. In Indian tradition quality in education encompasses not only a product and a process, but also a thought as well. Quality education means the transformation of individual and society to higher physical, intellectual, emotional aesthetic, moral and spiritual attainment.

MANAGEMENT EDUCATION FOR VALUE DEVELOPMENT

The essence education is so that the information must lead to knowledge and knowledge must lead to wisdom. The S.B. Chavan committee report presented to the Rajya Sabha on February 26,1999 states," Values are principles which direct actions and activities. If management education is identical to information, libraries are the greatest Sages of the world and encyclopedias are Rishies. The attempt to qualify quantity of education merely with reference to product and process would defeat the very purpose of management education.

The market has acquired the center-stage today. Management Education is considered to the private good rather than the public good. The attempts are made to build and strengthen the relationship between education and economic performance. The university is becoming a profit making enterprise. The withering of the state patronage in the wake of globalization process is compelling the universities to adopt institutional technology strategy in order to translate the mission and methods of the university into business and operational terms (Talgeri, 1999, P.57).

FREE TRADE IN EDUCATION

General agreement of India in services (GATS) has identified education as one of the 12th century; the volume of trade in education has been estimated to be the tune of 50 Billion Dollars, with an annual growth rate of 19 to 12%. The free trade scheme as envisaged under GATS will guarantee that academic institution or other education providers would be free to

- Export and Import degree, diploma programmes
- Award degree, diploma and certificates with minimal restrictions
- Invest in overseas educational institutions
- Employ instructors for their foreign ventures
- Setup educational and training programmes through branches, franchise, distance and online learning technologies without controls.

The objectives of management education in this globalization era are:

- Self-Learning: Preparing students for learning from diverse sources of information on their own.
- Linked Learning: A variety of information about a single topic and the ocean of information useful for day-to-day living requires linked learning.
- Synthesis of knowledge: With information explosion, students are expected to evolve and develop the skills of synthesis of knowledge.
- Team working and Adaptability: Team working is the pre-requisite for survival, and in a boundryless world, only those who will adapt, will survive.
- Uniculture: With the intermingling of diverse cultures, a uniculture society is emerging. Compatibility with such a society will have to be inculcated in the formative years of the students.

- Professionalism: Professionalism shall be the sine quanon of all economic activities and compromises shall have no place in the quality of products or services delivered.

To keep pace global environment management schools will have to develops global business managers will have to develop global business managers professionals entrepreneurs, consultants and academicians who possess an understanding of global business scenarios prevailing imaging and in the offing. Under such circumstances the implications for the management schools may be indicated as:

- Developing tomorrow's business leaders and managers is not a job that today's either the business houses or the management schools can do alone by themselves. The two working together must do it. It would require both systematic learning and development oriented work exposure during studentship.
- Management schools can no longer define its audience as one group comprising merely of students. In fact, these must organize themselves for working effectively with five-district group.

1. The students: Whether on campus or in distance education programmes.
2. The alumni in mid-careers: Whether as a contribution faculty or seeker of knowledge upgrade or advice from his teachers and peers or up to date information / literature on a particular topic.
3. The practicing professionals: Again as a contributor faculty or seeker of knowledge upgrade or advice or information / literature.
4. The top management of established business as students of custom tailored knowledge upgrades, providers of work exposure opportunities to students as well as the critical appraisers of the school's overall performance.
5. The peer management schools: For continuous exchange of students, faculty members, up to date information and literature and also for establishing a collective think tank for evaluating prevailing, emerging and in the offing business scenarios.

CONCLUSION

Management schools in India have come along way since their inception and also have proved their mettle by preparing the trained manpower needed by the country's business as and industries. Globalization has introduced unprecedented changing in every facet of national life, including the businesses and industries and the way are managed. Now the business and management schools together should undertake a joint effort to respond proactively to the changing scenario;

they together will have to think globally and also act globally. It is aptly said: "As with the self so with universe." The connectivity of self with the universe is inherent in the Indian management school of thought. Thus, India has to learn from itself and search a way out from within to truly integrate educational aspects with the global society.

REFERENCES

Ahlawat, Pradip, et al. (2001). Role of Information Technology in Enhancing Academic Productivity, in University New, 39 (42) October 15-21.

Joshi J.P. (2003). Globalization: A need for change in Educational Management System, in: University New, 41 (20), May 19-25, P.1

Nayar, Baldev Raj (2001). Globalization and Nationalism, New Delhi: Sage Publications. P.16.

Rangarajan C. (2-3) 'Globalization and its impact in Kapila, Uma "Indian Economy Since Independence", New Delhi: Academic foundation.

Sharma, S.K. (1997). Globalization of Indian Business Education: To be or not to be. That's the Question, in University New 35 (17), April 28, P.5.

Talgeri, Pramod, (1999). Globalization and farewell to classical University, Higher Education: Challenges and Golden Jubilee year, University of Pune.

Part IV: Management Functions in the Emerging Scenario

29

SUPPLY CHAIN KNOWLEDGE MANAGEMENT: TECHNOLOGY STRATEGY

A. Lakshmi Kanth

ABSTRACT

Fundamental changes have occurred in today's economy. These changes alter the relationships we have with our customers, our suppliers, our business partners, and our colleagues. This paper examines some of the developments underlying these changes, particularly the emergence of Internet and related technologies, for supply chain management. It also describes how these developments have presented companies with unprecedented opportunities to gain lasting competitive advantage. This paper examines the general trends of what we call here the networked economy.

Knowledge of Suppliers business issues, market dynamics, company vision, the competition, Purchasing strategy, and products (or) services themselves, helps purchasing people, establish and maintain credibility. To the extent Purchasing people must compete based on the added value of their knowledge, they must be able to easily access, learn and apply knowledge. Knowledge about Supplier behavior and preferences obtained through finding patterns in purchase or simply codifying the experience of Purchasing people who interact with customers, processes and innovations to improve the efficiency of operations and tools to predict the growth of demand or evolution of demand. With the rapid growth of Purchasing automation and such online technologies as Lotus Notes and Intranets, many corporations have rushed to deploy systems for distributing information and documents of all kinds to their purchasing people. Purchasing guides, training materials, audio and video tapes, sets of overhead transparencies, collateral, proposals, memos, e-mails, and new documents in online databases often cover the same ground in a slightly different ways, and are very difficult to use if one is in a hurry to find needed information.

This paper explores the specific Supply Chain knowledge management activities from the various sectors like Automobile, Cement, Furniture industry, Hotels, Tourism industry, financial services, Information Technology Enabled Services (ITES). For the analysis purpose 75 valid Questionnaires (filled by the Purchasing persons from various sectors) were considered. Results of the study have been analyzed using statistical techniques. Finally we suggest the future directions of research.

1. INTRODUCTION

Today's competitive business environment provides many opportunities for success-unprecedented access to global markets, stronger relationships with trading partners and improved ability to identify and grow key customers. However, organizations wanting to achieve this success must be willing and able to optimize their cultural structure, adopt innovative work processes, strengthen relationships with key trading partners, demonstrate clear worth in the supply chain and capture and leverage best practices within their organization. Organisations must take technology investments that allow for flexibility and rapid deployment, as time is a precious asset and business conditions change regularly. With the evolution of business and the increase in market expectation, it is becoming imperative for the various players in the continuum to work cohesively. This has led various components in the entire chain to have better coordination, communication and collaboration. The degree of complexity varies for different organizations and many of them are also in various stages of implementation.

Knowledge management is first and foremost a management discipline that treats intellectual capital as a managed asset. Many innovative organizations are examining how they can better manage their intellectual capital through the emerging field of knowledge management. Many fortune 500 companies are adopting knowledge management techniques combined with cultural and process changes, with enabling technology to realize the bottom line result. The primary tools applied in the practice of knowledge management are

- Organizational Dynamics
- Process Engineering
- Technology

This three work in harmony to streamline and enhance the capture and flow of organizations information and knowledge and delivers it to the teams, engaged in accomplishing specific tasks.

Davenport and Prusak's definition of knowledge: "knowledge is a fluid mix of framed experience, values, contextual information, expert insight and grounded intuition that provides an environment and frame work for evaluating and incorporating new experiences and information. It originates and is applied in the minds of knower. In organizations, it often becomes embedded not only in documents or repositories but also in organizational routines, processes, practices and norms".

"All of life and business is a game of odds. Just as HR policies increase the odds of employee retention, a good customer service increases the odd towards repeat business. Knowledge management is about increasing the odds towards knowledge being transferred, utilized (and contribution) to innovation."
-E.D (Institute of knowledge management, IBM)

In simple terms knowledge management means management of organizational knowledge for creating business value and generating competitive advantage. Knowledge management enables the creation, communication and application of knowledge of all kinds to achieve business goals. Knowledge management addresses business problems particular to your business-whether it's creating and delivering innovative products or services; managing and enhancing relationships with existing and new customers, partners, and suppliers; or administering and improving work practices and processes. This paper comprises of the following:

1. Introduction
2. Review of literature
3. The 24 Drivers of knowledge Management
4. Supply Chain Knowledge Management
5. Research Design
6. Research Methodology
7. Analysis of Survey
8. Conclusion

2. REVIEW OF LITERATURE

Data quest estimates that companies would spend over $ 4 billion on knowledge management initiatives, to leverage their knowledge resources. Survey response indicated that many executives were involved in some kind of knowledge management initiatives as a part of managing special tasks and projects. Survey result of 31 executives is shown in Table 29.1. It is clear to us that sales and marketing is highly preferred in terms of knowledge management initiatives.

Organizations were interviewed, and interestingly many organizations believed that it is possible leverage business growth through knowledge management (Table 29.2)

Table 29.1: Knowledge Management Initiatives

Various Business processes	12
Sales and Marketing	10
Customer Information	8
Employee Information	7
Product Development	7
Competitive Intelligence	3
Trends Analysis	2
R&D	1

*Multiple responses allowed.

Table 29.2: Knowledge Management as a Business Strategy

Possible to leverage business through KM	81 per cent
Can't Say	13 per cent
Not Possible	6 per cent

Information technology plays an important role in enabling the process of knowledge management across the distributed enterprises. KM is a multidisciplinary field such as, information technology, interpersonal communication, organizational learning, cognitive science, motivation and training and business process analysis. Specific roles are played by various enterprise wide initiatives listed below:

- Intranet
- Document Management System
- Information retrieval engines
- Relational and object databases
- Electronic publishing
- Groupware and workflow system
- Help-Desk system & Corporate yellow pages
- Brainstorming Applications
- Data warehousing, data mining & Knowledge warehouse

3. THE 24 DRIVERS OF KNOWLEDGE MANAGEMENT

Knowledge Centric Drivers

1. The failure of companies to know what they already know.

2. Knowledge velocity and sluggishness.
3. Problem of knowledge walkouts and high dependence on tacit knowledge.
4. The need for systematic unlearning.
5. The need to deal with knowledge-hoarding propensity among employees.
6. The emergent need for smart knowledge distribution.

Technology Drivers

7. The death of technology as a long-term differentiator.
8. Compression of product and process life cycles.
9. The need for perfect link between knowledge, business strategy and information technology.

Organizational Structure Based Drivers

10. Functional convergence.
11. The emergence of project-centric organizational structures.
12. Challenges brought about by de-regulation.
13. The inability of companies to keep pace with competitive changes due to Globalization.
14. Convergence of product and services.

Personnel Drivers

15. Wide spread functional convergence.
16. The need to support effective cross functional collaborations
17. Team mobility and fluidity.
18. The need to deal with complex corporate expectations.

Process Focused Drivers

19. The need to avoid repeated and often expensive mistakes.
20. Need to avoid unnecessary re-invention.
21. The need for accurate predictive anticipation.
22. The emerging need for competitive responsiveness.

Economic Drivers

23. The potential for creating extra ordinary leverage through knowledge; the Attractive economics of increasing returns.
24. The quest for a silver bullet for product and service differentiation.

4. SUPPLY CHAIN KNOWLEDGE MANAGEMENT

With the rapid growth of sales automation and such online technologies as Lotus Notes and intranets, many corporations have rushed to deploy systems for distributing information and documents of all kinds to their Purchasing people. As markets and products change with accelerating pace, purchasing people must assimilate and apply vast amounts of current information about their markets, their competition, and the solutions they can get from their suppliers. The recognition that Purchasing people are knowledge workers, perhaps the most overburdened of all, is gradually dawning on senior purchasing executives in the most forward thinking companies. It is becoming obvious to such executives that knowledgeable purchasing people can offer a significant competitive advantage at every stage of the sales process. Knowledge of supplier's business issues, market dynamics, company vision, the competition, purchasing strategy, and products or services themselves, and helps purchasing people establish and maintain credibility. They can identify the customer's pressing needs and configure optimal solutions, sell the benefits of those solutions, and guard against competitive challenges.

On the other hand, those working today in nearly all functions within business organizations suffer from severe information overload. Purchasing people are perhaps the most overloaded of all. Information of many types, in many different forms and media, pours in on the purchasing person. Dozens or even hundreds of documents are intended to provide purchasing people with the knowledge they need to compete. Yet because the information generally arrives from many different sources, neither its content nor format is consistent. Purchasing guides, training materials, audio and video tapes, sets of overhead transparencies, collateral, proposals, memos, emails and now documents in online databases often cover the same ground in slightly different ways, and are often very difficult to use if one is in a hurry to find needed information. The result is a scarcity of knowledge in an abundance of information.

Without information, no supply chain would be able to function successively or competitively. Supply management organizations would be operating independently and internal departments would be working in silos. There would be little feedback on whether the organization was meeting the needs of its customers. Thus, the informational supply chain is critical to the success of supply management organizations and their suppliers. Within this supply chain, the type of information exchanged and its usage can be a deciding factor in how strategic an organization becomes in the market place. Unless information is accessed or shared and then used by supply managers, there is little chance that any competitive advantage will be realized. Consider the value potential between explicit information and tacit knowledge.

Explicit Supply management information: Data, reports, and procedures retained within an information technology system. This information is readable and communicable. For example, a supply manager inputs the number of orders received each week into an information repository system. This data can be retrieved and explained explicitly to others in the supply management department or organization.

Tacit supply Management knowledge: Deeper experience, expertise, and know-how of the organization. This knowledge is undocumented and exists in the minds of employees. For example, a retiring senior supply management executive demonstrates how to analyze various reports to forecast the next year's inventory. Without sharing this knowledge with the supply management executive demonstrates how to analyze various reports to forecast the next year's inventory. Without sharing this knowledge with the supply management staff, the department may be unprepared to effectively gauge the inventory needs of the organization after the executive retires.

Research has shown that the importance and criticality of the human aspects in supply chain are becoming increasingly apparent. Harrison (1999) studied the human resource approaches used in two supply chain units of an automotive manufacturer. He identified large differences in approach between a world-class and a non-world-class unit. The world class unit concentrated far more on the human factors, in particular, building trust and team work. The CLM (1999) published an extensive review of job descriptions for logistics and supply chain personnel. These include the ability to communicate and negotiate across functional terrain and even companies involved in the supply chain (representing different cultures).Rather, it means leveraging people as one central feature of the agile supply chain. A survey undertaken by price-water house coopers of 400 of the largest European companies(Waller,1998)found that the biggest barrier to change in European supply chain projects was "Culture"(not language or IT systems as one may expect).Culture is a product of the values and beliefs of an organization. Supply chain partners expect supply chain managers to be sensitive to the cultural context in which they are intending to institute change.

A detailed survey by the society of Human resource management (Fitz-Enz, 1997) further emphasized the need for emotional intelligence in achieving the supply chain excellence. They analyzed a series of top companies, selected for profitability, cycle times, volumes and other key performance measures. It was found that the outstanding companies had, amongst others, the following competencies in managing their "human assets":

- Open communication and trust building with all internal and external stakeholders;
- An interest in building relationships inside and outside the organization;
- Collaboration, Support and the sharing of resources;
- Passion for work; and
- An environment where innovation, risk taking and learning are promoted.

The Survey study concluded that in order to develop these capabilities, supply chain managers may need to:

- Show positive emotions, e.g. passion, enthusiasm, sincerity, humility, integrity etc., and learn how to control disruptive emotions
- Be open and genuinely share information – adopt collaborative rather than competitive behaviors
- Be sensitive to others who are different from oneself-learn how to step into the world of others and see things from their point of view
- Learn how to build rapport, actively listen and to read all the non-verbal cues
- Take an interest in non-work matters such as current affairs, the arts, the business in which they work, etc.
- Develop the ability to challenge their horizons, extend their locus of influence
- Become a master at networking and Practice the art of brainstorming to develop alternative and creative ideas and strategies.

5. RESEARCH DESIGN

- Working in conjunction with a select group of industry practitioners to find the status of supply chain knowledge management, it was decided that the research design of the present study would be as follows:
- Search secondary sources of information-Journals, magazines, Newspapers, the Internet, promotional material for educational offerings, company advertisements.
- Analyze the secondary search information obtained.
- Determine the primary research needed to aid practitioners in finding the status of Supply Chain knowledge management practice in Indian organizations. Conduct a primary research among supply chain Knowledge management professionals.

6. RESEARCH METHODOLOGY

This research was clearly exploratory. Information was first obtained from key individuals in various companies. We discussed the role of Supply chain knowledge management using semi-structured questionnaires. The semi-structured questionnaire along with informal discussion was used to gather the relevant data. We have identified the various knowledge management components and observed in the established brands how their knowledge management process is actually working. We surveyed 75 professionals to exactly know how the supply chain knowledge management process is working in the various companies. We further used multiple response questionnaires to find out the key benefits sought from application of knowledge Management.

To increase the face validity each one of the items were defined. We realized that validity and reliability were difficult to measure precisely in qualitative research. Qualitative assessment is largely the product of the interaction of the researcher with the phenomenon. We have tried to do a fair amount of justice to that, through evolving the questionnaire over the entire period of our study.

7. ANALYSIS OF SURVEY

1. Major obstacles of knowledge management implementation are shown in Table 29.3 (Respondents answers in percentages):

Table 29.3: Major Obstacles of Knowledge Management Implementation

Culture Resistance	48 per cent
Lack of incentive	19 per cent
High Cost	10 per cent
Not Required	5 per cent
Others	6 per cent
Inadequate Technology	2 per cent

2. Knowledge Management objectives are shown in Table 29.4 (Respondents answers in percentages):

Table 29.4: Knowledge Management Objectives

Revenue Growth	35 per cent
Cost Cutting	10 per cent
Improved Customer Service	6 per cent
Improved Quality	4 per cent
Improved Business process	45 per cent

3. We have asked the respondents (Purchasing People) in order to know the Supply knowledge management process in their organization. Table 29.5 gives the results (which are calculated in percentages).

Table 29.5: Supply knowledge Management Processes

Particulars	Unsatisfactory	Moderately Satisfied	Satisfied	Good	Excellent
Current Information	7.4	3.7	1.8	33.3	40.8
Information about Competition	11.1	11.1	11.1	18.5	48.2
Regarding Company Vision	3.7		7.5	22.2	66.6
Purchasing strategy	7.4	3.7	29.6	33.3	26
Current Pricing	3.7	7.4	18.5	25.9	44.5
World wide Purchasing calendar	14.8	7.4	14.8	25.9	37.1
Mergers & Acquisitions within the sector	14.8	7.4	14.8	25.9 t	37.1
Purchasing Guides	3.7		11.1	33.3	51.9
Training Materials			14.8	33.3	51.9
Audio & Video tapes	18.5	11.1	18.5	33.3	18.6
Sets of overhead transparencies	22.2		14.8	11.1	51.8
Collateral	7.4	7.4	3.7	7.4	74.1
Proposals	14.8	11.1	3.7	25.9	44.5
Memos	14.8	3.7	3.7	11.1	66.7
Purchasing Libraries	29.6	7.4	11.1	14.8	37.1
Brochures	7.4		7.4	18.5	66.7
Presentation Sets	18.5	3.7	7.4	14.8	55.6
Demonstrations	14.8	7.4	7.4	11.1	59.3

4. In order to know the Supply Chain manager's capability of using the information technology we have asked the questions pertaining to that (whether they uses it or not) Results are given in Table 29.6.

Table 29.6: Use of Information Technology by Supply Chain Manager

Per cent

Particulars	Yes	No
E-Mail	96.2	3.8
Database Program	81.5	18.5
Online Documentation	81.5	18.5
Hypertext multimedia authority Tools	29.6	70.4
Expert Systems	51.8	48.2
Lotus Notes Groupware	48.2	51.8
HTML based Java Appn.	18.5	81.5
Internet & Intranet Technologies	96.2	3.8

5. Key Benefits derived by the organization after integrating the supply chain are shown in Table 29.7.

Table 29.7: Key Benefits of Integrating Supply Chain

Per cent

Key Benefit	Yes
Online Purchase Information. For e.g., POs, Delivery Schedules, Delivery Orders, Goods Tracking, Invoice Details	84
Instant Notification of any changes in the Purchase Information via e-Mails	95
2D/3D product visualization	99
Integration with Vendor's Information System via Data Download/Upload	88
Effective Inventory Control	99
Dramatic Reduction in Transactions Costs	92
Reduction in Administration Costs due to Phone/Fax/Mails/Personal Visits	89
Increase in operating efficiency	88
Increase in supplier competitiveness by providing online supplier Ratings	92
Increase in Customer Base	95

Contd...

Major reduction in the cycle time for Ordering to Delivery	84
Real-time Analysis of Market Trends	90
Online Vehicle Tracking	96
Consignment Tracking by Customers	93
Improved EIS Drilldown approaches about Billings, Transactions	98
Informed Decision Making	99
Fleet Management	92
Warehouse Management	98
Reduced Administrative Costs	91

6. Key benefits derived by using the supply chain knowledge management software are shown in Table 29.8.

Table 29.8: Key Benefits of Supply Chain Knowledge Management Software (Per cent)

Key Benefits	Yes
Reconciles and Optimizes the conflicting goals of different divisions or departments	94
Increases efficiencies by standardizing business processes	96
On-line/Real time information throughout all the functional areas of an organization	98
Data Standardization and accuracy across the enterprise	99
The Analysis and Reporting that can be used for long term planning	100
Reduces enterprise expenses	94
Early Risk Resolution, Early error and gap detection	92
Increases adaptability to changing work conditions	87
Reduces inventories, personnel, total logistic costs, manufacturing costs, outside warehousing, procurement costs	92
Managers needs right information at right time so that they can predict trends, budgets and keep top management informed well in advance	98
Top management needs system so that they can dig out information on their own without any dependency on managers or employees	91
Increases customer satisfaction	98
Increases Production capacity	95

7. Managerial Problems which can be encountered during the Knowledge Management implementation phase are shown in Table 29.9.

Table 29.9: Problems Encountered during Knowledge Management Implementation (Per cent)

Managerial Problems	Yes
Project Cost overruns	90
Conflicts with business strategy	87
Employees resistance to change	74
Conflicts with consultants	82
Internal conflicts	87
Conflicts with vendors	76
Project Delays	90

8. CONCLUSION

Today, the integrated supply chain has emerged as an increasingly dominant model. The future may be a learning supply chain that adds collective knowledge management and learning capabilities that would allow a dynamic responsive supply chain that simultaneously assures fairness of returns through transparency and full interdependence. The real conclusion of the analysis may that full set of benefits ascribed to any integrated supply chain was never really within the capabilities of most forms of the integrated supply chain. In particular any of the benefits demanding knowledge sharing, faster response to changing markets, shorter product realization cycles, and lower product development costs, would be much less likely to arise from channel masters or chain webs. Only knowledge sharing and learning throughout the supply chain would create value.

REFERENCES

CLM, (1999), the growth and development of the logistics personnel, CLM, OAK Brook, IL.

Devrics, e. J., and H.G. Brijder, "Knowledge management in hybrid supply channels: A case study". Int. J. Tech. Management, 5-8(2000): 569-87

Fitz-Enj, J., (1997), the truth about best practices, Human Resource Management, 36, 1, pp.97-104.

Lazzarani, S.G., F.R. Chaddad, and M.L. Cook. "Integrating supply chain and network analysis: The study of Net chains".-Chain and Network science 1(2001):7-22

Lee, C.C., and J. Yang. "Knowledge Value chain". -J. Manage. Develop. 9(2000).

Mason-Jones, R., and D.R. Towill. -"Total supply chain compression and the agile supply chain", Int.J.Prod.Econ.62 (1999)

Von Hippel, E. The sources of Innovation. New York: Oxford University Press, 1988.

Waller, A., (1998), Supply chain management: Barriers to change, Cranfield School of Management Logistics Workshop Series, October.

Williamson, O.E. Markets and Hierarchies: Analysis and antitrust implications. New York: The Free press, 1975.

30

MANAGERIAL ROLE IN INTERNATIONAL MARKETING STRATEGIES

S.K. Bhatt, Arunabh Mishra and Julius Mogaka Gekonde

INTRODUCTION

Each and every country in the world be it developed or under developed are always having the main goal of increasing its nature of production with the main target of fulfilling the exact wants and needs of its people with comparative objective of raising the standard of living of its people over the same

Various sectors of production as well as service sector like factories, commercial sectors and even offices are exactly aiming in producing a variety of goods and services in order to satisfy the host of human needs and wants.

However Abraham Maslow has given various human needs as: physiological or biological needs, social needs, self fulfillment needs, self actualization needs, and many more.

In addition to the above it's good for us to understand the meaning of the term "good" actually these are tangible things desired by people and of which human is willing to in cure the cost or pay price. The above so said goods include consumer goods like convenience goods, shopping goods and specialty goods, industrial goods like raw material, fabricating materials, components part, installation, accessories and many more others.

On the other side service are those intangible activities which are offered for sale in connection with sales of goods of which comparatively includes personal and house hold services, business services, advertisement and hotels as well as tours courts.

However, the term "Market" is Alatin award marcatus which means merchandise trade or business is conducted.

"Markets" are people with money to spend and desire to spend it – canon and witched.

"Market include both place and region in which buyers and sellers are in free competition with one another"

Apart from the above other legalistic economic and even factual or descriptive definition has been given over the same.

(The main objective of marketing is; to develop an intelligent appreciation of modern marketing practices and influences the marketing situation in the international level, developing broader framework for thinking about the nature of marketing in the international facet,) to provide sound guiding polices in relation to marketing procedure and also to ensure complete implementations, to provide sound intensity on one's feeling and participation to allow the creation of an open minded with hopeful to researchers, to show the other sources of information for marketing and many more.

We have to know that a market may be defined by the nature of demand and it's the demand which exactly creates the supply of the goods. Equally it has to be clear that it's the consumer demand that comparatively influence the nature of the supply. However it's the marketing opportunities that equally represent customer needs and desire.

MARKETING MIX

The consumer environment, competition, marketing institutions, and even the nature of the legal system and the main uncontrollable elements which the marketers has to take into consideration while holding an in depth analysis of both external and internal uncontrollable elements.

+ (Actually it's comparatively very much clear that marketing mix can exactly differ from one geographical region to the other, due to the following factors:

- Economic Factors
- Social Factors
- Cultural Factors
- Political Factors and even
- The commercial environmental factors)

It's clear that according to our findings, the international marketing efforts,) and even the environmental parameters become so very much important which can comparatively be treated as marketing mix of any geographical region or country.

Tallor made marketing mix for each country or geographical region to fulfill its uncontrollable marketing g environment forecasting such as consumer environment, competition, marketing institution and even the legal system of each geographical region.

We have to take into consideration that each of the internal elements of the exactly marketing mix is a controllable factor in nature. Equally it has to be noted that in each of the element must also in turn be actually be fully tuned with exactly everyone of the external uncontrollable environmental forces like

- cultural forces

- social forces and even
- legal forces

It has comparatively to be noted that international marketing also follow the same principles like that of domestic marketing. It is quite good for us to know that marketing principles and universally common to any geographical region.
One has to know that in any geographical market there must be four blending ingredients of marketing mix like:

- Product
- Price
- Promotion
- Distribution

A good marketer must have good product, good and fair price and also sound promotion as well as good nature of distribution for the reputed global marketing. He/she has to know that global marketing mix must always be based on exactly and up to date reliable as well as adequate information of the above said uncontrollable forces of marketing.

The marketer has to know that each and every country is having various marketing environment as social cultural political and even the legal. Comparatively it has to be so very clearer that the international marketer is bound to hold on the reorganization that every marketing environment defer from place to place as well as nation to nation than that of the same country state.

MARKETING DECISION AND INTERNATIONAL ENVIRONMENT

A marketer has to be very much acknowledged that the marketing decision making with the main objective of capitalizing the global marketing opportunities is exactly similar in nature of the decision making process of home or domestic markets. We have also been informed that the four main marketing elements like Product, Price, Promotion and even the Distribution are equally related to the international marketing. In addition to the above one has equally to take into consideration that there are international marketing segments which are equally based on demographic social and even the cultural factors that may equally attracts the consumer buying systems.

Comparatively the main composition of the international marketing environment that has to be taken into consideration is:

- Cultural Factors
- Economic Factors
- Commercial Factors
- Legal Factors and
- Political factors.

We have to know that all the above forces exactly represent a given informational inputs which shape the exactly nature of the global marketing mix which might be suitable for a specific marketing of global geographical area.

MARKETING SEGMENTATION ON GLOBAL SCALE

When we talk of marketing segmentation we actually mean the modern marketing strategy in nature. The international marketer has to divide the global market into the various division or submarkets or segments whichever the sense.

The international marketer has to ensure that each sub-market as mentioned above has similar responses to the exact marketing inputs. We have to know that such market segmentation help to sub division instead of spreading the marketing effort over the same.

However, the following are the main ways of sub-dividing the global marketing;

Social economic variables like

- Age
- Sex
- Family size
- Income
- Occupation
- Family life cycle
- Race
- Religion
- Social class and many more

Behavioral patterns like

- Usage rate
- Buying motives

INTERNATIONAL MARKETING DECISIONS

According to our findings, some firms they just enter into the base of the international or global marketing without taking the following in to the consideration:

a) Marketing decision
b) Global marketing selection decision
c) Global market entry decisions
d) Global marketing mix which includes:

- Product mix decision
- Distribution decision

- International pricing decision and
- Promotional decisions

GLOBAL MARKETING

Global marketing essentially deals with the nature of the trade patterns like:

- Import patterns
- Export patterns

In addition to the above, the global marketers has also to take into consideration the trade polices and trade practices of various geographical countries since they are the main determinant of the buyer-seller behavior in the global markets.

Also the nature of the trade polices and even the trade practices are not the same in various geographical countries because of some restriction, these makes the call for a well trained human resources in the sector of global marketing.

We have also acknowledged that global business transaction have to be sound planned and objectives oriented in nature.

MAIN REGULATION FOR GLOBAL MARKETING

The developing countries like Kenya, India, and many more others have to be very much keen with there nature of global trade so that to maintain their balanced points of marketing.

The global market regulation like exchange control and even import export regulation must be possible position.

The following are the main regulation devices:

a) Trade barrier like:
- Levels
- Custom duties

b) Non Tariff Barriers like
- Quantity restrictions
- Foreign Exchange Restrictions
- Consumer Formalities
- Preferential Arrangements
- Technical Regulations
- Administrative Regulations
- And many more

c) Trade Arrangements
d) Joint Commissions
e) Trade blocks

However the global marketers is always faced with various problems like distance transport, Language, Customs, Traditions, National laws, Currencies, Weights, Marketing methods, Risks and uncertainty, Custom formalities, Exchange formalities, Exchange Controls, Payment of dues, Shipping and Insurance and many more. The only way out to the above is to be well equipped on how to be in control of the same.

The nature of the import substitutions has to be equally limited with the main objectives of concerning foreign exchange. Also its nature should be modified so that to promote the export promotions.)

The export trade, in India is equally governed by the satisfactory control like, control of export-import, control over foreign exchange and quality control. The main stages for export in India are as:

- Quanta ion and order
- Shipping and credit Enquiring
- Custom and exchange formalities
- Preparation for Exports
- Placing the goods on board
- Securing of mates receipt
- Effecting marine insurance
- Securing Bills of lodging
- Securing other Shipping documents
- Securing Payments
- Obtaining various export incentives

In addition to the above, the import producers that the marketer has to take in to the account are:

- Placing of an indent
- Terms of payment
- Customs formalities
- Clearing Arrangements

GLOBAL EXPORT PROMOTION

The global marketer must take in to consideration that sound export promotion is the main determinant of his/her progress. Hence the global marketer must equally larger the creation of the sound incentive so that main increases the nature of his/her exports in the global markets.

However the main factors that main increases and even so diversities the global marketers export are:

- The nature of the price of the goods to be comparatively exported must be competitive.
- The nature of the quality goods to be exported must also be comparable with rival geographical market.
- Science the Global price level must be high the domestic market become the only solution.
- The Global Marketer must conduct sound Global market research.
- The nature of the business must be equally higher.
- Sound planned diversification of the Global market is also very much important.

EXPORT PROMOTION MEASURES IN INDIA

The following are the main export promotions measures in India:

- Sound cash compensatory assistance
- The Indian Global marketer gets exemption from customs duty.
- Sound supply of the raw materials.
- There is an exemption of excise facilities to the main global marketer.
- Marketing development alliances are the other main export promotions.
- Bilateral trade agreements.
- Export marketer training.

The main problems facing the export promotions are the ever an increasing in the internal price level which are comparatively influenced by the nature of inflation which raise the comparative cost of production poor and low business. Morality is the other obstacles and the efficiency of the main Global exporters.

The Export-Import bank was created in 1981 as the stationary corporation. It was migrated with the lead back with the authorized capital of 200 crore. In order to finance the global export-import and at the same time to conduct the global marketing promotion of the export and import of the goods the export-import bank was launched over the same.

REFERENCES

Carnot, Principles of Economics.
Chapman Economics
Clark and Clark, Principles of Marketing (1945).
Drucker P.F., The Practice of Management (1954).
Duddy and Reizan marketing – An Institutional Approach. (1953).
Francis Geoffrey K, Modern Marketing Management (1978).
Kotler P., Marketing Management Analysis: Planning and Control.
Kulkarni K.R., Agricultural Marketing in India (1956).

Lorenzo A., Market Reports (1948).
Maslow Abraham Motivation and Personality (1954).
Onkvist Shaw, International Marketing Analysis and Strategies
Pyle G.F., Principles of Marketing (1936).
S.A. Sherlekar, Modern Business Organization and Management.

31

DYNAMICS OF RURAL MARKETING

Meera Kulkarni and Vaidehi Pandurengan

ABSTRACT

A thorough understanding of the rural markets has become an important aspect of marketing in the Indian marketing environment today. This attraction towards the rural markets is primarily due to the colossal size of the varied demands of the 700 million rural people. In fact, the rural markets are expanding in India in such a rapid pace that they have overtaken the growth of urban markets. This rate of growth of the rural market segment is however not the only factor that has driven marketing managers to go rural. The other compelling factor is the fact that the urban markets are becoming increasingly complex, competitive and saturated.

Rural market comprises of 40 per cent of middle class and 60 per cent of its disposable income. C.K. Prahalad points out, "If we study single study shampoo market, we find that 67 per cent of the market is among the poor and 50 per cent of the volume". Going by National Council for Applied Economic Research, India, the millennium belongs to Class III & IV rural - urban towns.

Despite of the great opportunity that the rural market holds tackling the dynamics of it is a challenge for the marketers. It is therefore important for the marketers to understand the rural consumer so that he can plan his strategies in such a manner that they produce the desired results. To achieve this the main concerns are - providing access to credit or ways to enhance income; creating innovative product, packaging & logistics; shaping aspirations through communication & education.

NGO's have been able to reach with their "products" into deep interiors of this difficult and unfathomable market- right from creating awareness to acceptance of their socially useful products. Thus for the corporate to be profitable despite of its dynamics it has lot to learn from NGO's.

In this paper through case study method an attempt is made to understand how NGO's can help in providing early detection of potential problems, attitudinal shifts, creative ways to overcome barriers, which could help in handling rural dynamics. And also an attempt is made to understand the profitability model corporate use, so that they too can plough back more into rural system.

Though marketers have understood the mighty power of "Bottom of the pyramid" a successful structure is yet to emerge combining the strengths inherent in this market with the NGO experience.

The synergy between NGO and corporate is probably where lies the Win - Win situation for all!!

INTRODUCTION

A thorough understanding of the rural markets has become an important aspect of marketing in the Indian marketing environment today. This attraction towards the rural markets is primarily due to the colossal size of the varied demands of the 700 million rural people. In fact, the rural markets are expanding in India in such a rapid pace that they have overtaken the growth of urban markets. This rate of growth of the rural market segment is however not the only factor that has driven marketing managers to go rural. The other compelling factor is the fact that the urban markets are becoming increasingly complex, competitive and saturated.

Further, the vast untapped potential of the rural markets is growing at a rapid pace. The policies of the government largely favour rural development programmes. This is clearly highlighted by the fact that the outlay for rural development has risen from Rs. 14,000 crore in the 7th plan to Rs 30000 corers in the 8th plan period. These figures also prove that the rural market is emerging stronger with a gradual increase in disposable income of the rural folk. In addition, better procurement prices fixed for the various crops and better yields due to many research programmes have also contributed to the strengthening of the rural markets. Thus, with the rural markets bulging in both size and volume, marketing manager will be missing a great potential opportunity if he does not go rural (Table 31.1).

DYNAMICS OF RURAL MARKET

The buying behavior demonstrated by the rural Indian differs tremendously when compared to the typical urban Indian.

- The values, aspirations and needs of the rural people vastly differ from that of the urban population. Basic cultural values have not yet faded in rural India. Buying decisions are still made by the eldest male member in the rural family whereas even children influence buying decisions in urban areas. Further, buying decisions are highly influenced by social customs, traditions and beliefs in the rural markets. Many rural purchases require collective social sanction, unheard off in urban areas.

Table 31.1: How is Rural Money Spent?

Expenditure	Percentage
Groceries	34
Agricultural inputs	14
Medicines & health care	9.5
Apparel & footwear	8.1
Fuel	6.4
Vehicles	5.2
Personal care	5.2
Interest payment	3.9
Savings	3.1
Household maintenance	2.5
Hard liquor & tobacco	2.3
Entertainment & music	1.7
Jewellery	1.7
Consumer durable	1.6
Home textiles	0.5
Home Appliance	0.3

Source: KSA Technopak.

- Another contrasting feature is the precision in the assessment of purchasing power of the consumers. In urban markets, income levels are generally used to measure purchasing power and markets are segmented accordingly. However, this measure is not adequate for defining the purchasing power in rural areas because of the single fact that rural incomes are grossly underestimated. Farmers and rural artisans are paid in cash as well as in kind. However, while reporting their incomes, they report only cash earnings, which then affects the calculation of their purchasing power. This is the reason why marketers are often surprised to find that people who, according to their surveys and estimates do not have the purchasing power to do so sometimes consume their products.
- One of the characteristics of rural consumer is the variability in income size and patterns. Somebody gets daily wages while someone else earns weekly

salaries. Yet another might be paid on a monthly basis. Given this scenario, it is often said that if a rural consumer buys daily, he has 365 opportunities in a year to switch brands. Developing brand loyalty is a real challenge in a market like this

- The most important element in rural communications is that you have to integrate 3 things as you communicate: communication (the exposure to a message), trial or demonstration (convincing) and final sale. There has to be a concept of touch and feel within the communication itself that you have provide as you create communication for rural consumer. Wall paintings, van advertising were the mode of advertising in past but today's world there is hardly any van advertising. There are about 47,000 haats in our country. In Maharashtra there are 4000 haats and there are 5 types of haats in broad terms. So one can create channels. It's a battle of the ability to notice, create, use and build on that.
- India is a very large country with, different socio cultural aspects, income levels, educational levels, poor CNS penetration, long distances etc. The rural retailer does not stock huge quantities so that you may supply him only once in a month. And you can't block your money too. In such a scenario, how do you develop your logistics model? How do you solve this distribution problem?
- Rural credit is virtually non-existent. 80 per cent of urban durable sales depend on hire purchase. This concept of hire purchase still hasn't entered rural India. As a result, what is happening is the second-hand sets, which, are exchanged in the urban market, are sold in rural areas.

COMPLEXITIES OF INDIAN RURAL MARKET

- When price is the issue, in India we have seen that every time the telephony rates fall the market grows in the circumference to include the next lower income layer. The Indian mobile market is expected to double every year. The volume offset the price disadvantage.
- When product is to be considered we that in India Gillette found its surprise that man preferred the old double-edged blade to twin blade as three out of every four Indian shaves without running water, which only former can accommodate. The R&D at Gillette used this opportunity to introduce Vector plus-a razor with a knob that when pressed separates the blades making it easy to improve hair (overcoming the problem of flowing water to clean the shaving system).
- In case of creating finance facility it is imperative to develop good distribution network and an effective credit delivery mechanism so that larger

penetration of the market is possible at lower cost of operation. Technology can come to aid here. As in case of ICICI bank, that is developing ATM for around Rs 30000(as against 60000 today).

12.5 per cent of world's population lives in rural and semi urban area, in India and 700 million of Indian population live in rural areas. The opportunity in terms of volume is colossal. "If we study single study shampoo market, we find that 67 per cent of the market is among the poor and 50 per cent of the volume" Dr. C.K. Prahalad.

Despite of the great opportunity that the rural market holds tackling the dynamics of it is a challenge for the marketers. It is therefore important for the marketers to understand the rural consumer so that he can plan his strategies in such a manner that they produce the desired results. To achieve this the main concerns are – providing access to credit or ways to enhance income; creating innovative product, packaging & logistics; shaping aspirations through communication & education. Thus for the corporate to be profitable despite of its dynamics it has to learn from NGO's.

In this paper effort has been made to understand how a corporate could use NGO's experience to tackle complex and dynamic rural market. The effort is to be profitable despite of its dynamics.

Dynamics of rural market cannot be understood by being on the sideline through primary or secondary data. One has to get totally involved in the rural life, get them involved in the process of development and create a overall environment of confidence and trust.

The experience of the NGO can be taken as an example to see how their initiative and commitment has been acceptable at village level, while corporate experience has been studied for the witnessing translation of profitability.

Although NGO's activity in rural development has primarily been in the areas of economic field i.e. development of agriculture & rural industries etc. but it has also helped in establishment required special infrastructure, services in the area of health & nutrition, education & literacy, family planning, basic civic amenities etc. The basic aim is to improve the quality of life in the natural way. The focus of attention is the rural poor. This has been so done that this benefit is translated to them in a way that it is sustainable despite their presence or absence. They have been able to bring forth participation of the people, which is central to their empowerment. Inculcation of participatory attitude in the minds of the rural people is done through education, extension work & demonstration work and projects. From initial indifference or reluctance they are capable of moving their target group towards realizing their potential in such a sensitive way that they do not appear threatening or overbearing. Further, the entire system is kept so transparent that the presence of any disguised covert intentions in their agenda is absolutely absent. Thus high level of trust is created all throughout -their upliftment is the key to the effort. The main objective of this method is to make the rural target audience realize his potential strength, develop his own capacity for growth and use his abilities for his benefit and to the benefit of his family & community at large.

Corporate if are able to adopt the method of total involvement in rural life will be able to handle the dynamics if rural marketing. Thus the Hypothesis formed is

The success in rural marketing depends very much on the ability of the organization to win the trust through peoples participation.

Case study method has been applied to understand the effect of integrated rural development. Integrated rural Development is aimed at total development of area and people, by bringing about the necessary institutional and attitudinal changes and delivering a package of services through extension methods to encompass not only the economic field but also establishment of required special infrastructure and services in the area of health, nutrition, education, family planning, basic civic amenities etc. The basic aim of it is to improve the quality of life. This participatory development of the rural people can be taken as an example and experience to bring about greater leverage to make rural marketing more profitable.

Two cases have been closely studied – the NGO experience of BAIF & the corporate experience of ITC, to check them for similarities & differences and draw out important learning's from them.

CHONDHA EXPERIENCE OF BAIF

It was March, 1946 - the dawn of Indian Independence. The brief sojourn of the Father of the Nation - Mahatma Gandhi to Urulikanchan, a backward village near Pune, marked the turning point in community development. Promotion of community health through nature cure became a reality with the establishment of a Nature Cure Center, managed by his trusted disciple Manibhai Desai.

Unemployment, underemployment and erosion of natural resources being the root causes of poverty, Manibhai promoted income generation activities as the main plank of development. Cultivation of high yielding varieties of food crops, vegetables and fruits was his first successful venture but his successful experiments for improving non-descript cattle through cross breeding had greater potential to generate gainful self-employment for most of the poor farmers.

The encouraging response from the rural community motivated Manibhai to establish the Bharatiya Agro Industries Foundation (BAIF) at Urulikanchan near

Pune in 1967 and later renamed as BAIF Development Research Foundation, to replicate his novel programme in rural development. Presently, the organization is professionally managed by a team of multidisciplinary experts, under the guidance of the Board of Trustees.

In Navsari district of South Gujarat, at Chondha village a weekly bazaar is held on Sunday during the period of December to June. This village which earlier saw migration of its local inhabitants after harvesting of paddy, today witnesses the village inhabitants as members of different people's organizations –milk cooperative, watershed committee, Ayojan Samiti, Chonda bazaar Samiti etc.

In 1987,it was after carefully watching the successful implementation of the 'Wadi' programme in Valsad district by BAIF, did the people of Chonda opt for it. It was through this programme that they first experienced success through an organized effort in controlling the damage caused from stray cattle damaging their fields. These supervisors & wadi workers selected from the village were highly motivated & selfless villagers are chosen as supervisors who got no honorarium for their work. This committee was known as **Dhor Bhandi Panch.** The villagers then enthusiastically joined the cattle development scheme introduced by the Government- 75 crossbreed cows were purchased through this scheme. In 1989, a Milk Cooperative was formed with active cooperation of wadi holders. Conflicts were resolved at village level meetings with mediation from village leaders. The cooperative is being effectively managed & about 500 liters of milk is supplied to it.

The BAIF staff was regularly giving technical inputs on health & sanitation. Slowly, awareness level increased among the people. An **Ayojan Samiti** was formed having representative membership (rotating) in order to take collective decision & action regarding wadi programme, improved agricultural practice, water resource development & health intervention. Women started participating. This exposure reinforced the principles of community management – emphasizing on representativeness, communication, conflict resolution, planning & collective decision making.

In 1992, under the guidance of BAIF, **Manav Vikas Mandir**, a trust formed by five villages, was established. Mahua oil extraction unit and purchase of 4 acre plot for high school (Funded by profit of the former) is to its credit. This was an exercise of congregation of people from different villages to achieve symbiotic goals. It gave an opportunity to develop skills- communication, decision making, negotiating. Over a ten-year period this village is a witness to many changes – increased income level, pucca houses, children getting higher education. More importantly increased self-esteem, confidence, change in mindset, a feeling of togetherness has generated. This resulted in increased keenness to take up initiatives that benefit the larger community.

Over a period of time the **Bazaar Samiti** was a result of this learning. Though from 1995, the villagers wanted to start a weekly bazaar to sell their agricultural produce, it was only in 1997 that they could see it crystallizing. It all started with collecting of funds for construction of temple in the village, which in itself worked as a support drawing majority of villagers supporting this initiative. Bazar samiti was formed selecting one representative member from each helmet. It is an informal body selected by the villagers on whom they trust as their leader. The village annual fair is decided by them they promote the activity, find interested party, design layout of the fair, drinking water and other facilities. They collect cess from traders, which are based upon the size of the stall. Unlike most of the cases where this amount is kept with panchayat, in the case of Chondha it is bazaar samiti, which keeps and maintains the collection-, which would contribute in the building of village temple later on.

It was decided that bazaar would be held on Sunday- to draw larger crowd and to avoid disturbing the school adjacent to the ground. The first hurdle was to get the traders to participate. The traders were already engaged in holding a Sunday bazaar in two villages 35 Kms from Choda and were ready to participate on any other day than Sunday, which was totally not agreeable by the members of Samithi. Undeterred by the response 21 December 1997(Sunday), the first weekly bazaar was held with local shopkeepers & vegetable vendors stalls to sell their goods.

Gradually sales picked up. The initially hesitant and reluctant traders soon started approaching the Bazaar Smithi to seek permission to trade on Sunday Bazaar. In 1999 some traders preferred trading in Unai a pilgrimage center. This led to lowered participation in Bazaar. The samithi members took this opportunity to encourage local villagers to take up trading. The members educated the villagers on opportunity for earning additional income and also advised on products that had good demand.

Now there are about 50 traders (men and women) dealing in vegetables, grocery, poultry, garments etc. Goods to the tune of Rs30000 –Rs40000 are traded every Sunday. Peaks sales are witnessed during Holi festival, when 150 traders participate and 10000 people visit the stall. About 50 per cent traders are resident of Chondha and 90 per cent of these are wadi holders.

Soon members of Mola Amba village, 7 Kms away, took guidance from Chondha Bazaar Samithi and set up a weekly Bazaar on Tuesdays. The villagers of Hanvetmal also set up a weekly bazaar on Sunday- but this has not affected the interest and attendance of Chondha bazaar.

Bazaar was place were everything was available for villager's requirements-they did not have to leave the village for procurement of the necessities. To add more visitors a suggestion was made to have health camps, cattle faire etc. Success of this model sees it replicated in other areas too[1].

This is an example of a NGO working very closely with the rural villages bringing overall development. BAIF helped the people in becoming self-sufficient by making them realize the opportunities of rising income, which in turn helped in developing self-confidence the people. The improvement was not only in terms of income but also in terms of improving the quality of life by regularly giving information about health & sanitation. Finally BAIF also managed to forma trade center through bazaar Samithi that helped the economy of villages to roll on.

BAIF's effort has now made the village economically and socially developed to accept higher standards of living because of rise in income and developed logistics through. Bazaar Samithi. This the groundwork required by the corporate to start and develop the market for the product.

CORPORATE EXPERIENCE THROUGH ITC

With a product created in the rural market, ITC was able to successfully move it forward by creating a forward chain. They did this simply by strengthening the backroom power of information.

The success of **ITC's e-choupal** is key to this. The e-choupal aimed at using Internet to source relevant information at the village level & share it with the farmers. The resultant networking was found to be cost effective, reliable and assured the farmer of good price for their produce connecting this underserved metamarket 2001 has served ITC rich dividend.

ITC had been facing certain problems. It did not have desirable control over the supply chain of agricultural produce. It resulted in erratic procurement volumes costs, no control on the quality of the produce, problems of physical distribution (transportation, warehousing, handling) and dealing with middleman power games. Further they could not eliminate all the intermediaries from this process as some crucial functions were being performed by them specially logistics management.

The farmer on the other hand seemed to have resigned to his fate of drudgery. Trapped in the vicious cycle of low investment, low productivity, low margins, weak market orientation, low risk taking ability and low value addition the Indian farmer appeared to be destined for being globally uncompetitive. The aim of

ITC's distribution initiative was to integrate ITC's association with rural suppliers as well as develop new markets for their own & third party goods.

The initiative, in phased manner, served four markets the;

- Bulk crop market –soybean, wheat etc;
- Aqua products- shrimps;
- Plantation products – coffee;
- Value added products for export- fruit pulp, basmati rice etc.

At ITC, they figured out that their solution lay with "information edge", which could be translated by rampant usage of the Internet. Working towards this direction, they first set networking the villages to give Internet connectivity through the e-choupal, which was equipped with a PC. So for the Soya farmers of Madhya Pradesh ITC invested 1-3 lakh and launched its e-choupal project. They created a website-**www.soyachoupal.com.**

The management of this operation was very simple. The e-choupal was headed by a **Sanchalak**(convener) who had three fold function- coordinate group of villages & perform documentation work, supplies farm inputs from ITC & partner companies to farmers (prices & related information) and working for a good relationship between farmers & ITC. They were given a commission of 0.5 per cent for each ton of Soya procured by them for ITC. To ITC this also provided backward flow of information – feedback & innovative ideas. For the existing commission agents at the mandis their role was remodeled. They were called **Samyojaks** (coordinators) and had to do the following function – provide spot quotes after examining produce & transporting this produce to ITC collection center. They were paid 1 per cent commission for each ton of Soyabean sold to ITC (they made profits through volume of trade). Both these members were trained for using the PC & internet.

Many problems were faced but ITC overcame them. They used technology to overcome – speed of connectivity bandwidth, basic telephone connectivity. Familiarizing the farmer to use the PC and facilities from the Internet. They had to even lobby with some state governments to waver the Agricultural Produce Marketing Committee Act, which made it mandatory to buy certain commodities (soybean, coffee & wheat) only through Government designated mandis. By end of 2002, 976 e-choupals were spread in 7000 villages trading soyabean worth 1.6 billion.

For coffee farmers of Karnataka, in December 2000, ITC set up75 kiosks in 125villages. There was lesser scope for disinter mediation as the growers were sophisticated and the existing value chain is strong & efficient. They created a website- www.aquachoupal.com. In Andhra Pradesh in Feb 2001.It covers the shrimp farmers in 300 villages through 55 kiosks. Since high costs, high risks and high perishability is involved here, already well to do & very demanding (bargaining for price) farmers exist.

In November 2001, ITC started the e-choupal program for wheat growers of Uttar Pradesh covering 1500 villages through 180 kiosks.

From 2002, ITC also started trading in products of other companies through its kiosks – Nagarjuna fertilizer, Monsanto etc. The sanchalaks took orders from the farmers & delivered goods at a commission of 5 per cent to them and 10 per cent to ITC. The sanchalaks also started selling life insurance policies of LIC & others.

ITC's e.choupal is a example of a corporate which has empowered through completely taking over all links in supply chain management and made it profitable for themselves. This concept has been economically beneficial and sustainable to all those companies that tried in to tap the rural market in this adventure. The way this momentum is gathering strength ITC plans to target international export worth $ 400 million in 2005.

MANAGERIAL IMPLICATIONS

Marketers of today try to extend marketing plans that they use in urban areas to the rural markets and face, on many occasions failure. The recent data of the Business World 27 Dec 2004 states that the ranking of all the companies which are mainly targeting rural markets is going down (Table 31.2).

Table 31.2: Ranking of Companies Targeting Rural Markets

Corporate	Rank 2004	Rank 1999
HLL	5	1
Nestle India	28	12
Nirma	54	46
Dabur India	60	37
Gillette	65	41
Britannica	78	30
P& G Hygiene & health care	81	33

Do they need to adopt a strategy that appeals individually to the rural audience and formulate separate annual plans and sales targets for the rural segment? Managerial implication of the cases studied above will help us understand how rural dynamics could be handled through people's participation.

If we take the example of BAIF and ITC both have worked closely with the villagers though BAIF has done it very intensely. The origin or benefit occurred from the product has benefited the geographical area of work i.e. the community there. This close interaction has helped them get a deeper understanding of the rural customs beliefs traditions which could in turn help them in buying decision.

Working closely with the rural people has helped in creation of wealth through peoples participation and thus improve the standard of living, which helps in the assessment of the purchasing power and variability in income patterns. This helps in collecting Interpretive research data through Ethnography.

To create the right channel of communication to establish brand loyalty, because it is a battle of ability to notice, create use and build on that. Though in consumer market, pace has many a times created the edge, for the rural markets loyalty building is an essential ingredient. For this the time frame is much longer than what traditionally is allowed by selling or marketing activity. The NGO has been accepted because they keep their presence and focus for longer period of time. High level of trust is a result of this. Their dedication to the 'product' success is measured on a larger time frame.

It can be argued here that in case of profit generating organizations, where performance review is done on smaller time frames, this appears far fetched. But the author thinks that this is an empathetic learning- to invest in rural markets the psyche of the rural poor should be given a deeper understanding. Since they are not early adopters they still need more time for product acceptance. They spend only 1.6 per cent of their income on consumer durable i.e. they can forgo it easily. To translate this into purchase they cannot to be pushed and hurried (by short lived promotions). Rewards will come with time. So patience here is the key to this success replicating in consumer market.

In India experience of e-choupal is a pointer to improvement of productivity due to efficiency in supply chain. ICICI and HLL are currently working on a partnership web experiment with farmers of Hoshangabad district of Madhya Pradesh, which has witnessed an increase in productivity by 70 per cent. Hindustan Lever Limited has initiate "Project Shakti" It covers 5000 villages in Andhra Pradesh, Karnataka, Madhya Pradesh and Gujarat. By 2010, Hll plans to reach 1 lakh villages and 100 million rural consumers.

Being associated with NGO ensures customer loyalty. The association of corporate with one NGO gives it an edge and also makes it difficult for other companies to enter the market.

Develop right logistics model to solve the distribution problem to cater to the needs of people in far flung rural area,

Chonda Bazaar Samithi case we see that wider participation leads to success of an intervention. This was a place were everything was available for villagers requirements they did not have to leave the village for procurement of the necessities.

Success of this model saw it replicated in other areas too. Market like this is a perfect solution to solve distribution and logistic problem because it centers the selling process.

Village market is an opportunity to use NLP (Neuroliguistic Program) techniques to sell the product.

Today 80 per cent of urban durable sales depend on hire purchase. This concept of hire purchase still hasn't entered rural India. This is because there is a high capital requirement unmet rural areas. It is important to note that unless an opportunity to increase the standard of living and simple banking system is provided to the entire community, it will not lead to acceptance consumer durables.

ICICI is India's largest private sector bank. Following the success story of ITC's e-choupal, ICICI bank has decided to set up e-kiosks in the rural markets of Maharashtra, Gujarat, Rajasthan, Andhra Pradesh & Tamil Nadu. This is going to enable farmers to access agricultural information, mandi prices, health& education related information and financial services at the village level. To support this effort ICICI has collaborated with agri-input providers(Agri Universities), procurement firms, Veterinary hospitals & telecommunication providers to support this kiosk network.

The farmer can use this e-kiosk facility in three ways: with a problem related to crop/ cattle, they can access and refer to a data base for a solution; capture image using a webcam & sending it to an expert for advice; chat with a professional for advice and best practices. ICICI also plans to provide other financial products to rural customers – insurance products on life, rainfall, accidents & health and general insurance; investment services (stock, bonds & mutual funds); gold purchase; credit products (micro loans, agricultural loans & personal loans); transaction & bill payment services[3].

NGOs understanding of the community and identification of needy, is unbiased. This will get corporate good and reliable work force that could represent successfully (in terms of reach and profitability). The roles of Sanchalak and Samyojaks with e-choupal are a pointer here. HLL under project Shakti has patterned with several NGO's in Andhra Pradesh to promote SHGs (self help groups) supported by micro credit. Besides being greater reach to HLL products, they are generating incomes and developing entrepreneurial skills. HLL is committing itself to huge training inputs and there are also now efforts to make some of these SHGs sourcing point of product sold in rural market.

In both the cases we see certain similarities and dissimilarities they're of power of patience to be appreciated in case of BAIF. From Chodha case we wee that wider participation leads to success of an intervention. Selfless and motivated individual, timely communication, collective decision-making etc. is what has led to the success of this project. The intervention has lead to overall development of the village. The communication by the NGO is kept simple, establishes relatedness in their circumstances and very local.

This gives it the flavor of being genuine, understandable and so gets accepted. Corporate have to learn to fit into rural psyche in this regard. This is a great learning for the FMCG category. To stay in this market they have to invest in terms of time and commitment.

The knowledge that has flown out of this is to be taken seriously in translating it pragmatically. To bring about change in mindset C.K. Prahalad questions following areas of blocks- the poor is not the target; bottom of the market is not important for long-term interests and that intellectual excitement lies in the developed markets. As suggested here, NGO's will have to move from ideological rhetoric to strategic role. Corporate will have to respect the importance of local knowledge and wisdom that are coded in traditional, cultural and community practices of which the NGO have good understanding. There is certain divergence in their views on natural capital. It is imperative for the survival of both to understand and recognize community as a stakeholder. Corporate responsibility will be to partner with local communities/NGO initiatives prevent ecological, environmental and health catastrophe. Thus engagement and not exclusion is the way forward. The author argues that unless this synergy is sought or more emphatically drawn out, the rural market will remain isolated and untapped much to the chagrin of all concerned.

REFERENCES

Gupta Inderjit, ITC's Rural Symphony, Business world, January-20-03.
ITC e-Choupal, Business World, Feb-4-02.
Sarma Das Suman, ITC May Ferry LIC to Rural India.
www.BAIF.org
www.digitaldividend.org
www.hll.com

ALIGNING INFORMATION TECHNOLOGY TO GLOBAL BUSINESS STRATEGY

Jaspal Singh, Baldev Singh and Manohar Singh

INTRODUCTION

Information technology infrastructure investments are an extremely important part of global business and constitute a major portion of IT investments in many organizations. IT infrastructure investments include investments in connectivity, systems integration, and data storage that may be used by multiple applications. Prior research has recognized the importance of a flexible IT infrastructure as a source of competitive advantage. The continuously growing importance of information technology (IT) requires organizations to integrate IT decisions with their common planning and decision-making processes at all organizational levels. Aligning IT with global business strategy focuses on the two-way link between business strategy and IT strategy. Its purpose is to help organization to allocate resources more effectively by improving the IT investment decision process, and to increase the value from IT through practices that help to find opportunities to use IT capabilities to influence business strategy, as well as support or execute current business strategy. In our global village, information technology IT is no longer a cost of doing business. Relegated to the position of administrative support function since its inception, IT has awoken and taken its place at the business table. For leading-edge firms today, information technology is nothing less than a competitive weapon.

It is clear that even though information technology (IT) has evolved from its traditional orientation of administrative support toward a more strategic role within an organization, there is still a glaring lack of fundamental frameworks within which to understand the potential of I/T for tomorrow's organizations. In this paper, we are conceptualizing and directing the emerging area of alignin IT to global business strategy. This approach concentrate on fundamental domains of strategic choice: business strategy, information technology strategy, organizational infrastructure and processes, and information technology infrastructure and processes.

IMPACT OF IT

The role and impact of information technology on today's organizations has significantly changed over the last decade. Across a wide spectrum of markets and countries, IT is transcending its traditional "back office" role and is evolving toward a "strategic" role with the potential not only to support chosen business strategies, but also to shape new business strategies. Yet, there is increasing concern that the anticipated value of the investment in IT is not being achieved. How do we reconcile the dramatic increase in the role of IT in organizations and markets with the evidence of minimal productivity gains at an aggregate level of the economy?

This paper is of the view that the inability to realize value from IT investments is, in part, due to the lack of alignment between the business and

IT strategies of organizations. This paper views strategy as involving both formulation (decisions pertaining to competitive, product-market choices) and implementation (choice that pertain to the structure and capabilities of the firm to execute its product-market choices). Our concept of strategic alignment is based on two fundamental assumptions: One, economic performance is directly related to the ability of management to create a strategic fit between the position of an organization in the competitive product-market arena and the design of an appropriate administrative structure to support its execution. This assumption is consistent with the generally accepted axiom that strategic choices in the external and internal domains should be consistent. Two, It is to contend that this strategic fit is inherently dynamic. The choices made by one business enterprise, or firm (if fundamentally strategic), will over time evoke imitative actions, which necessitate subsequent responses. Thus, strategic alignment is not an event but a process of continuous adaption and change.

In this context, a critical lever for attaining this dynamic capability is not a specific set of sophisticated technological functionality but the organizational capabilities to leverage technology to differentiate its operations from competitors. In other words, no single IT application--however sophisticated and state of the art it may be--could deliver a sustained competitive advantage. Rather, advantage is obtained through the capability of an organization to exploit IT functionality on a continuous basis. This requires a fundamental change in managerial thinking about the role of IT in organizational transformation, as well as an understanding of the critical components of IT and its role in supporting and shaping business strategy decisions.As we know, views are different on the changing role of IT within organizations, managers are still confronted with basic concepts like:

IMPLICATIONS OF IT

Implications of IT in different business operations today and tomorrow i.e. Alternative perspectives for leveraging information technology capabilities for business operations, Locus of IT competence "inside" or "outside" the operation, Role of senior management for leveraging IT capabilities, Role of IT outsourcing, Appropriate criteria for assessing IT-based benefits, We attempt to answer these and related. Let us consider how organizations are leveraging IT capabilities to shape and support their business strategies.

We have real life examples with us where IT becmoes essential to the welfare even survival of many organizations. Air line reservation system through information technology is nothing less than a competitive weapon by all airlines. Consider another example of banking industry. In banking sector, all the baks trying to provide their best services to the customers so that they compete to other banks or say for their survival, it is must. Accepting telephone bills, ATM facility, online banking, mobile banking etc nothing less than alligning IT with business strategy. Whether these strategies are applicable in local businesses, they will equally impact on global business strategy.

With the use of electronic filing of individual income taxes, many tax-return preparers have created new electronic linkages with retail financial instutions that enable interested tax-payers, for a fee, to receive refunds at the time of electronically filing their return. Electronic connection between the filers and the Internal Revenue Service, combined with superior capability to check for errors, has become an important competency in this fast-changing marketplace.

Integrated information systems are in use by multinational companies to redesign key business processes that affect their ability to manage the movement of products through their global distribution channels. Due to this, these firms achieve significant improvements in operating costs and, more importantly, increased ability to respond quickly to local market conditions and requirements.

These some examples highlight different facets of aligning IT to global business strategy.

ALIGINING IT TO STRATEGY

Our concept of strategic alignment is based on two building blocks: strategic fit and functional integration. The former recognizes the need for any strategy to address both external and internal domains. The external domain is the business arena in which the firm competes and is concerned with decisions such as product-market offering and the distinctive strategy attributes that differentiate the firm from its competitors, as well as the range of "make-versus-buy" decisions, including partnerships and alliances. In contrast, the internal domain is concerned with choices pertaining to the logic of the administrative structure (functional or divisional or matrix organization) and the specific rationale for the design and redesign of critical business processes (product delivery, product development, customer service, total quality), as well as the acquisition and development of the human resource skills necessary for achieving the required organizational competencies.

Within the business domain, the fit between external positioning and internal arrangement has been argued to be critical for maximizing economic performance. The fit between external positioning and internal arrangement is equally relevant within the IT domain. More specifically, Further IT strategy should be articulated in terms of an external domain--how the firm is positioned in the IT marketplace--and an internal domain--how how the IS (information systems) infrastructure should be configured and managed. However, it is suggested that managers are more often comfortable with their capability to understand positioning choices in the business marketplace (where their products are sold) than with their understanding of how to be strategically positioned in the IT marketplace (where they obtain critical technological functionality that supports and shapes their business strategies). This is partly due to the fact that strategy--as a management concept--has historically been applied to the output market rather than input markets and that IS strategy has often been viewed as a functional, internal response to the business strategy.

POSITION OF IT IN THE ORGANIZATION

The position of the organization in the IT marketplace involves three sets of choices:

Scope of Information Technology: Those specific information technologies (for example, electronic imaging, local-and wide-area networks, expert systems, and robotics) that support current business strategy initiatives or could shape new business strategy initiatives for the firm. This is analogous to business scope, which deals with choices pertaining to product-market offerings in the output market.

Systemic Competencies: Various attributes of IT strategy (for example, system reliability, cost-performance levels, interconnectivity, flexibility) that could contribute positively to the creation of new business strategies or better support of existing business strategy. This is analogous to the concept of business distinctive competencies, which deal with those attributes of strategy (pricing, quality, value-added service, superior distribution comparative advantage to a firm over its competitors.

IT Enablement: selection and use of mechanisms (for example, joint ventures with vendors, strategic alliances, joint research and development for new IT capabilities) for obtaining the required IT competencies. This is analogous to business governance, which involves make-versus-buy choices in business strategy. Such choices cover a complex array of interfirm relationships such as strategic alliances, joint ventures, marketing exchange, and technology licensing.

In a similar way, the internal information system domain must address at least three components, namely:

Information System Architecture: choices that define the port-folio of applications, the configuration of hardware, software, and communication, and the data architecture that collectively define the technical infrastructure. This is analogous to the choices within the internal business strategy arena to articulate the administrative structure of the firm dealing with roles, responsibilities, and authority structures.

Information System Processes: choices that define the work processes central to the operations of the I/S infrastructure such as systems development, maintenance, and monitoring and control systems. This is analogous to the need for designing the business processes that support and shape the ability of the firm to execute business strategies.

Information System Skills: choices pertaining to the acquisition, training, and development of the knowledge and capabilities of the individuals required to effectively manage and operate the IS infrastructure within the organization. This is analogous to the skills required within the business domain to execute a given strategy.

As IT emerged as a critical enabler of business transformation with capabilities to deliver firm-level advantages, it is imperative that firms also pay attention to the three external components of IT strategy. Hence, we this paper of the view that IT strategy should be elevated from its traditional internal focus to address external issues of how well the firm is positioned in the fast-changing IT market-place.

INTEGRATING BUSINESS AND IT DOMAINS

The need to integrate the IT strategy and the business strategy has long been advocated by both researchers and practitioners. This dimension specifically considers how choices made in the IT domain impact (enhance or threaten) those made in the business domain and vice versa. However, much of current research has focused only on issues of integrating the internal IS strategies (IS infrastructure and processes) with internal organizational requirements as a response to business strategies.

Strategic integration, is the link between business strategy and IT strategy reflecting the external components. More specifically, it deals with the capability of IT functionality to both shape and support business strategy. This capability is particularly important as IT has emerged as an important source of strategic advantage to firms. These second type, termed operational integration, deals with the corresponding internal domains, namely, the link between organizational infrastructure and processes and IS infrastructure and processes. This type highlights the criticality of ensuring internal coherence between the organizational requirements and expectations and the delivery capability within the IS function.

ALIGNMENT PERSPECTIVES

Business Strategy as the Driver: The first two cross-domain relationships given here arise when business strategy serves as the driving force. This perspective is anchored on the notion that a business strategy has been articulated and is the driver of both organizational design choices and the design of I/S infrastructure.It is important to identify the specific role of management to make this perspective succeed. Specifically, we contend that top management should play the role of the strategy formulator to articulate the logic and choices pertaining to business strategy, whereas the role of the IS manager should be that of the strategy implementor, one who efficiently and effectively designs and implements the required IS infrastructure and processes that support the chosen business strategy. The performance criteria for assessing the IS function within this perspective are based on financial parameters reflecting a cost center focus.

Technology Transformation: This perspective involves the assessment of implementing the chosen business strategy through appropriate IT strategy and the articulation of the required IS infrastructure and processes. In contrast to the strategy execution logic, this perspective is not constrained by the current organization design, but instead seeks to identify the best possible IT competencies through appropriate positioning in the IS.

CONCLUSION

The globalization of economy has opened up vast avenues of growth for the business organizations. Hence one universally superior mode to formulate and implement strategy is required. The dominant alignment perspectives that use the strategies as the driver are equally useful and powerful in thinking about the role of IT in organizational transformation. It is in fabour of organizations that their managers do not consider IT as a panacea and consequently focus only on those two perspectives with IT strategy as the starting point that are namely, competitive potential and service level. It is not arguable that business strategy should always be the starting point and adopt only the other two perspectives on strategic alignment. The potential for IT impact is so varied and complex that the executive must consider these perspectives and be prepared to make adaptations continuously.

REFERENCES

A. C. Hax and N. S. Majluf, The Strategy Concept and Process: A Pragmatic Approach, Prentice-Hall, Inc., Englewood Cliffs, NJ (1991).

E. R. McLean and J. V. Soden, Strategic Planning for MIS, John Wiley & Sons, Inc., New York (1977).

J. C. Henderson, J. F. Rockart, and J. G. Sifonis, "Integrating Management Support Systems into Strategic Information Systems Planning," Journal of Management Information Systems 4, No. 1, 5-23 (1987).

J. N. Luftman, P. R. Lewis, and S. H. Oldach, "Transforming the Enterprise: The Alignment of Business and Information Technology Strategies," IBM Systems Journal 32, No. 1, 17-39 (1993, this issue).

John C. Henderson, N. Venkatraman, "Strategic alignment: leveraging information technology for transforming organizations ,"IBM Systems Journal, March, 1993

M. Broadbent and P. Weill, "Improving Business and Information Strategy Alignment: Learning from the Banking Industry," IBM Systems Journal 32, No. 1, 162-179 (1993, this issue).

M.M. Parker and R. J. Benson, with H. E. Trainor, Information Economics: Linking Business Performance to Information Technology, Prentice-Hall, Inc., Englewood Cliffs, NJ (1988).

N. Venkatraman and J. C. Camillus, "Exploring the concept of 'Fit' in Strategic Management," Academy of Management Review 9, 513-525 (1984).

N. Venkatraman, "Information Technology-Induced Business Reconfiguration: The New Strategic Management Challenge," The Corporation of the 1990s, M. S. Scott Morton, Editor, Oxford University Press, Oxford (1991).

W. H. Davidson, "Beyond Re-engineering: The Three Phases of Business Transformation," IBM Systems Journal 32, No. 1 65-79 (1993).

W. R. King, "Strategic Planning for Management Information Systems," MIS Quarterly 2, No. 1, 27-37 (1978).

33

CONSUMPTION BEHAVIOR OF YOUNG CONSUMERS IN PAKISTAN

M. Mahmood Shah Khan

ABSTRACT

The study reports the empirical research for consumption behavior of Pakistan consumers. Study develops a scale includes thirty items of buying decision and categories them into three houses of preferences: 1) Product Preferences, 2) Pattern Preferences, and 3) Decision Preferences. The study takes the convenient random sampling of 254 respondents of FMCG (fast moving consumer goods) in Lahore and analyzes the data using various statistical tools. The study investigates the relationship of individual's profiles like income of the family head, age, gender with purchase preferences or their influence on buying decision-making process.

Finally study reports the research findings under three houses of preferences identified by respondents towards their consumption behavior and purchase pattern.

The results indicated that the young buyers always buying preferences to multinational quality products, like to shop with friends from the specific products shops and most of the time, their buying decisions are based on the their own personal experience.

INTRODUCTION

The debate over globalization, its effects and occurring changes in cultural and social values produce big considerations for the companies especially working in foreign countries. Developing scenario of free market in a global village is reshaping the consumption habits and purchasing style of every region. Such kind of dynamic nature of the market creates need for the companies to understand the values, attitudes, cultural specifications and changing buying pattern and consumption behavior of consumers of the host country. People consume resources to survive and make their lives simpler. Consumers' efforts to use the resources more efficiently have evolved the consumption behavior over the time. A continues change in consumption pattern has created the new product development priorities of producers accordingly.

Today markets are not as were a century before, when consumption was based on necessities and spending on luxuries was considered wasteful. The revolution of consumption in these days is pursuaded by the developemnt of new technologies which has had resulted in the form of mass production. Facing the tough competion, the producers started influencing the consumption behavior, convincing people to buy things, by altering basic institutions and even generating a new ideology of pleasure. *(Allyn and Bacon, 1999).* This change in coming age will continue and consumption pattern will be transformed into new shapes. The extent of the changes needed in consumption patterns is illustrated by the problem of climate change.

By 2050, the world's population could have grown to about 10 billion. "Worlds' consumption has expanded at an unprecedented pace over the 20th century, with private and public consumption expenditures reaching $24 trillion in 1998, twice the level of 1975 and six times that of 1950. In 1900 real consumption expenditure was barely $1.5 trillion."*(UNDP, 1998).* The trend of emerging boundaries is destroying the traditional distinctions among countries. A global consumer class is emerging, sharing common lifestyles despite being separated by great distances. The companies producing FMCG should stop wasting their time looking for the "hippest" or "coolest" gimmicks and instead concentrate on understanding what consumers are thinking (Joeri Van den Bergh 2000). The markets is observing changes in attitudes and thoughts, changes in prosperity and standards of living, changes in commercial techniques and promotional skills, sometimes changes even in the law itself. In order to enahnce progress and proseprity in the country, we need to enhance the consumption rate. The single most important measure of economic growth is, after all, the gross national product (GNP). It is a measure of the success of a consumer society, obviously, to consume.Our consumption of goods obviously is a function of our culture. With the change in culture consumtpion habits are influenced and dramaticly changed.

This scenario in Pakistan is developed by good economic indicators and market conditions like: consumer fianancing, increasing FDI, trade agreements with neighbor countries, boom in capitial market and strong reserves. The economic stituation of Pakistan riase the need of such investigation, which provides emparical evedince for consumers' preferences comparatively youngsters towards their priorities and product choice. Youngsters are usually prospective buyers of consumer goods and extensively targeted by the producers of FMCG in Pakistan.

CONSUMERISM IN PAKISTAN

Pakistan has a very strategic location in the world especially in South Asia. The country, having more than 150 millions people, largely concentrated in the 18-35 years age bracket along with a propensity to consume of nearly 76 per cent, is the biggest *buy argument* for the consumer sector in Pakistan. A population growth rate of 2 per cent coupled with a nearly 0.3 per cent annual rise in the degree of urbanization are likely to be strong drivers of the Pakistani economy.

The sheer size of Pakistan's growing population, its high degree of urbanization and its high propensity to consume clearly defines the market size of the consumer and allied companies. With real growth in the Pakistani economy expected to continue accelerating over the next few years, the market for consumer products is also expected to continue expanding at a rapid rate and thus offers a great deal of attraction to potential investors.

With the stock market currently in a consolidation phase and with the possibility of a rapid rise in the index looking relatively unlikely, investors, in our opinion, are likely to be looking for a sector that offers three main qualities: (a) sustained growth, (b) a defensive position relative to the market and (c) dividends. We can easily expect that the consumer and allied sector fit these requirements perfectly. That is why; many new companies from China, India and from the different parts of the world are entering into the Pakistan market and making their investments. Pakistan recently has successfully experienced the process of deregulation, attracted new investments and entered into free trade agreements with many countries of the region. Consumer financing is at boom and banks are giving persuasion to the micro credit schemes in the market. In the nutshell, this whole scenario obviously demands an empirical investigation of consumptions behavior and preferences towards product choices and buying patterns of the consumers particularly from the young ones lay between 18 to 30 age-bracket.

LITERATURE REVIEW

Consumption behavior and change in buying pattern has been widely discussed in literature. Now the consumption behavior is characterized by rapid and persistent changes in the consumer environment such as changing lifestyles, the changing role of women, increasing per capita income, advancement in communication resources and coming generation. Producers need to consider ways of anticipating such changes in order to use them to the competitive advantage of a company. *Martin G Letscher (1990)* urged to make this change in the social environment as a source to create opportunities for a company. *Ekerdt David J (2004)* discussed the cultural construction of the assisted living consumer. They indicated the complexity of consumption pattern with cognitive impairments, family demands, payment sources, and the very novelty of the assisted living philosophy. *Joeri Van den Bergh (2000) claimed that* in order to understand how mainstream teenagers will be thinking in the future, we have to listen to the underground cultures now. Their thoughts and visions will "bubble up" in the mainstream of youth behavior. They said "*Street Trends* is a fine first introduction into the minds of our youngest generation".

Michael F. Smith (1999) in his study contrasted out shopping, shopping behavior, intentions, retail satisfaction and its antecedents between city shoppers and suburban shoppers. He found that, "urban retailers must attempt to attract suburban and urban shoppers in an attempt to overcome the potentially negative effects of urban resident out shopping to the suburbs". *Packard Vance (1960)* pointed out the serious social, economic and environmental consequences of an unchecked expansion in consumption. He urged the need to make consumption patterns sustainable. *Juliet Schor (1998)* reported an estimate that by 1996, the emerging middle class of China, India, Venezuela, Brazil, Argentina, South Korea, Taiwan, Indonesia, Malaysia and Thailand amounted to roughly 750 million, almost as many of the 880 million consumers in the industrialized countries. *Tacoma (1996)* said that already the richest fifth of Chileans and Malaysians enjoy higher incomes than the average German or Japanese. Polly Ghazi and *Judy Jones (1997)* Reported that East Asians are now "leaders of post-modern consumerism", renowned for their extravagance in luxury goods and prompting the establishment of a National Campaign against Excessive Consumption in Korea recently.

Despite the recent shock to living standards in Asia, there is no reason to believe that the upward surge in consumption will not continue in emerging economies over the long-term. Meanwhile, the poorest fifth of the world's population continues to be left out of the global consumption, with the average African household consuming 20 per cent less than it did 20 years ago. *Eco-Efficiency report (1998)* supported this as saying "In China alone, the spread of car ownership will attain the current levels in the UK by 2020. That means 400 million more cars.

STUDY SAMPLE AND DATA COLLECTION

The study selects FMCG (fast moving consumer goods) as a representative of consumer goods in Pakistan. FMCG is one of the fastest growing segments and effectively covers more than 85 per cent of the country's consumption. The FMCG includes various categories of products/brands as food, apparel, stationary and house hold goods consumed frequently and used on daily basis. The consumers of FMCG are frequent buyers hold extensive buying experience and make regularly changes in his consumption behavior and buying pattern.

The study collected the required data through a valid and reliable questionnaire, which consists of ***thirty*** variables. Three houses were developed included house of product preference, which contained eleven items, house of pattern preference, which contained seven items and house of decision preferences, which contained *twelve* items of study interest. Each house is discussed separately along with included items.

This questionnaire covers *thirty* items in total. In answering the questions, respondents were assured of the confidentiality of their responses and their names were not disclosed. Lastly, five-point Likert type questionnaire was designed scaling factors ranging 1 stands for "strongly disagree" to 5 for "strongly agree".

The questionnaire were personally administrated and were collected there of. This exercise was conducted in front of the different departmental stores; consumer's goods retail outlets and different academic institutions in the selected areas of Lahore.

Customers were selected based on the required criteria: frequent users of goods and well-experienced customers of FMCG products. Therefore, 270 randomly completed questionnaires out of 300 were easily achieved. Sixteen carelessly filled questionnaires were rejected to further and strength the quality of data. Finally the 254 questionnaires were taken for analysis purposes.

RESULTS AND DISCUSSION

The paper tried to explore the young customers' preferences and priorities towards a brand. The study conducts research through three dimensional research instruments, consisted of product preferences, pattern preferences and decision preferences. The study collects the data through a questionnaire with ***30*** items with convenience sample of 254 respondents randomly (Table 33.1). For the analysis purpose, One-Sample statistics were applied. All items contained significant variance ($P < 0.05$) with Standard deviation of more than one. In order to measure the internal consistency and reliability of scale Alpha coefficient is computed.

The scale got total reliability score 0.74, which is reasonable in the case of thirty items. In behavioral and attitudinal studies Alpha score more then 0.70 is considered satisfactory (Nunnally, 1978). For the preferences measurement total scores are taken and divided by hundred for analysis. Finally table of frequency distribution is made for respondents profile and results are analyzed through percentage scores.

Table 33.1: Respondent's Profile

Profile N= 254	Frequency	Percentage
Gender:		
• Female	67	26
• Male	187	74
Age:		
• Less then 20	129	50
• 20 to 30	94	37
• 30 to 40	27	10
• 40 to 50	4	2
Income:		
• Less than 10,000	21	8
• 10,000 to 20,000	79	31
• 20,000 to 30,000	98	39
• 30,000 to 50,000	56	22
Profession:		
• Private Job	50	20
• Govt. Job	40	16
• Own business	135	53
• Unemployed	29	11

Table 33.1 outlines the respondents' personal characteristics. Respondents profile is collected through four aspects: gender, age, and income of family and profession of family head. The data shows that 26.0 percent of the respondents are female and 74.0 percent are male. This may give a limitation to study findings, as females in Pakistan culture are not very much comfortable with such kind of research participation. In the area of age, data shows that 50 percent respondents are less than twenty years old and 37 percent are within the age group of 20 to 30. The customers of consumers goods are usually adult or in young age. These findings may provide the future concerns to the FMCG producers as data is mostly related to youngsters. In the area of income only 8 percent respondents are of less than ten thousand per month income. Thirty percent people are of ten to twenty and 40 percent respondents are of twenty to thirty thousand per month income. The 60 percent respondent's falls in the income bracket of around twenty thousand, which indicate the middle class segment, which is frequently buyer of FMCG.

Almost 20.0 per cent of the respondents work with private sector while 53.0 percent holds their own businesses. Only 16 percent respondents belong to government jobs and 11 per cent are unemployed. The respondents ratio of people having their own business indicated the strong relationship with FMCG customers as industrialist usually are considered as lavish consumers and spend more than general society.

Table 33.2 shows the house of product preferences, indicating the customer's priorities towards product features. This house includes eleven items of the scale outlining the product features. Group A in house of product preference shows that customer gives high priority towards brand. Pakistan consumers, especially, the urban people are convinced by the strong brand name. Second thing which attracts their mind is stylish feature of product than the seek uniqueness in a product. The data indicates that customer gives least value to the imported things as compared to brand, style and uniqueness. Group B shows that customer put highest emphasis on quality, in other words customers of the urban society in Pakistan are quality conscious. They seek quantity after the quality and then considered packaging. Price feature of product is least important as compared to quality, quantity and packaging. Group C outlines the customer trend in consumption towards the brands of multinationals. Customer holds high level of trust on multinational products and gives lower priority to national level brands and least important to local manufactured items.

Table 33.2: House of Product Preferences

Preferences Group A	Scores (%)	Preferences Group B	Scores (%)	Preferences Group C	Scores (%
• Branded	9.88	• Quality	10.47	• Multinational	9.66
• Stylish	9.82	• Quantity	10.16	• National product	8.69
• Unique	9.29	• Packaging	8.62	• Local product	7.71
• Imported	8.98	• Price	8.43		

Table 33.3 has the house of pattern preferences. This house consists of seven items, indicating the customers buying pattern or preferences while going to shopping. The data in Group A show that customer prefers to shop in specialized departmental stores, started developing in Pakistan. The shops have their specialty in their brands can more successfully attract and win the customers attention. Secondly people go to big Bazaar as AnarKali and Liberty market in

Lahore. General departmental stores stand third in importance hierarchy. Results show that customers of Pakistan do not give much consideration to the traveling for shopping or prefer the nearest shop

Group B provides the insight of Pakistan consumers as they go for shopping. They prefer to go with friends and feel much comfortable. Their second priority is to go with family. These results may be the out come of married respondents, as they usually need to make purchases with family. Consumers in Pakistan are not very much willing to do shopping alone.

Table 33.3: House of Pattern Preferences

Preferences Group A	Scores (%)	Preferences Group B	Scores (%)
• Special shops for specific goods	9.96	• With friends	10.07
• Big markets (Bazaar)	8.91	• With family	8.49
• Departmental stores	8.37	• Alone	6.52
• Nearest shops	8.55		

Table 33.4 describes the preference that influences a customer decision about a brand/product. The house of decision preferences contains thirteen items indicating the external intangibles or tangibles aspects related to purchase decision. The study investigates the importance of these external variable and their influences on customers purchase decision. Group A of house of decision preferences shows that customer's first priority while selecting a brand is the latest design. After the latest design, customers seek product match or contrast then considered the fashion. Results show if during a fashion season new design come, customer will move towards the latest design and ignore the fashion. Customer will try to create uniqueness as concluded in Table 33.4. Discounts and schemes are less important when compared to new design, contrast and fashion.

Group B supports the results in Table 33.4 as friends have most dominant influence on purchase decision. These results may be affected by the respondent's rate of their age as 50 per cent are youngsters and fall under 20 of age bracket. Therefore parents on their product choice make second big influence. In case of married people or family spouse have influences on purchase decision.

Table 33.4: House of Decision Preferences

Preferences Group A	Scores (%)	Preferences Group B	Scores (%)	Preferences Group C	Scores (%)
• Latest design	10.3	• Friends	9.16	• After my own experience	9.15
• Matching (Contrast)	10.01	• Parent	8.86	• Frequent advertisement	8.64
• Fashion	9.49	• Spouse	7.01	• Seller's Reputation	7.95
• Discounts and sale offers	9.42			• Recommendations by friends	7.44
• Schemes /prizes/ coupons	7.42				

Group C outlines the decision preferences as customers are inspired by trust via external aspects. The data show that customers mostly prefer to experience the product and then get trust about it. They give first priority towards self-experience while trusting a brand. Frequent advertisement also helps to gain the customer trust and influence on purchase decision. Market reputation of the seller stands third and word of mouth got least importance in influencing the purchase decision. In the case of FMCG product are fast moving and their consumption is very frequent in human life. Therefore, in case of FMCG word of mouth do not play very strong role. For the purchase of a sweet or pair of shoes, customer is not willing to consult his or her various friends. In purchasing decision, the information lies in the subconscious of consumers have strong influence on a buying decision, which is poured by producer with frequent advertisement of their brand.

CONCLUSION

Consumption habits and purchasing style of every region is reshaped by free market in a global village. Such kind of dynamic nature of the market stresses the companies to understand the values, attitudes, cultural specifications and changing buying pattern and consumption behavior of consumers of the host country.

The study collects the required data through a specifically designed questionnaire, which consisted of thirty items. Three houses were developed includes house of product preference, which contains eleven items, house of pattern preference, which contains seven items and house decision preferences which contains twelve items of study interest. Each house is discussed separately along with included items

Table 33.1 provides the overview of respondents taken into analysis. 26.0 percent of the respondents are female and 74.0 percent are male. In the area of age, 50 percent respondents are less then twenty years old and 37 percent are within the age group of 20 to 30. Table 33.2 provides the results of House of Product Preferences, concludes that the respondents are convinced by the strong brand name. Second thing which attracts their mind is stylish feature of product then they seek uniqueness in a product. Group B shows that customers of the urban society in Pakistan are quality conscious. They seek quantity after the quality and then considered packaging. Price feature of product is least important as compared to quality, quantity and packaging. Group C outlines the customer trend in consumption towards the brands of multinationals. Customer holds high level of trust on multinational products and gives lower priority to national level brands and least important to local manufactured items

Table 33.3 indicates customer preferences to specialized stores, started developing in Pakistan. The shops have their specialty in their brands can more successfully attract and win the customers attention. Secondly people prefer big Bazaar as Anarkali and liberty market in Lahore. General departmental stores stand third in importance hierarchy. Results show that customers of Pakistan do not give much consideration to the traveling for shopping.

Group B provide the insight of Pakistan consumers as they go for shopping. They feel much comfortable to shop with friends. Their second priority is to go with family. These results may be the out come of married respondents, as the spouse directly influences their buying decisions. Consumers in Pakistan are not very much willing to make shopping alone.

Table 33.4 provides the customer behavior about external aspects associated with purchase decision. Discounts and schemes are least important things when compared with new design, contrast and fashion. They give first priority towards self-experience while trusting a brand. Frequent advertisement also helps to gain the customer trust and influence on purchase decision.

Appendix Table 1

One-Sample Statistics					
	N	Mean	Std.d	T-values	Sig. (2-tailed)
UNIQ	254	2.6	1.4	28.6	0
IMPRT	254	2.8	1.3	34.5	0
BRAND	254	2.9	1.2	38.7	0
SRYTLSH	254	2.9	1.3	35.9	0
QUALTY	254	3.0	1.2	41.9	0
QUANTITY	254	3.1	1.0	50.5	0
PAKGING	254	3.3	1.0	50.4	0
PRICE	254	3.3	1.1	47.1	0
LOCAL	254	3.3	1.5	36.0	0
NATIONAL	254	3.4	1.2	43.7	0
MULTNAT	254	3.4	1.1	49.5	0
BIGMKT	254	3.4	1.1	50.4	0
DEPRTMNT	254	3.4	0.9	57.7	0
SPECSHOP	254	3.5	1.3	43.9	0
NEARSHOP	254	3.5	1.2	45.9	0
ALONE	254	3.5	1.1	50.2	0
FRIENDS	254	3.6	1.1	50.2	0
FAMILY	254	3.6	1.1	50.1	0
FASHION	254	3.7	1.2	46.8	0
LATSTDSG	254	3.7	1.1	52.7	0
MATCH	254	3.7	1.1	52.2	0
DISCOUNT	254	3.8	1.2	50.9	0
SCEMES	254	3.9	1.1	54.5	0
SPOUSE	254	3.9	1.1	57.8	0
PARENT	254	3.9	1.1	58.1	0
FRIEND	254	3.9	1.0	62.0	0
RECFRND	254	4.0	1.0	61.5	0
ADVERTS	254	4.0	1.1	59.8	0
TRSTSELL	254	4.1	1.1	62.3	0
XPERIENC	254	4.4	1.0	71.3	0

Appendix Table 2

RELIABILITY ANALYSIS - SCALE (ALPHA)				
Reliability Coefficients				
N of Cases = 254.0			N of Items = 31	
Alpha = .7400				

Appendix Table 3: Study Scale

Aspects	
1.	I prefer to choose the goods if they are Unique
2.	I prefer to choose the goods if they are Imported
3.	I prefer to choose the goods if they are Branded (By company name)
4.	I prefer to choose the goods if they are Stylish
5.	I always prefer to purchase from Big markets (like Anarkali Bazaar)
6.	I always prefer to purchase from Departmental stores
7.	I always prefer to purchase from Special shops (shops for specific goods)
8.	I prefer to choose the goods if they are Nearest shops
9.	I prefer to purchase the goods of Local producers
10.	I prefer to purchase the goods of National producers
11.	I prefer to purchase the goods of Multinational producers
12.	For shopping, I always prefer to go Alone
13.	For shopping, I always prefer to go With friends
14.	For shopping, I always prefer to go With family
15.	While purchasing, I prefer to consider Fashion
16.	While purchasing, I prefer to consider Latest design
17.	While purchasing, I prefer to consider Matching (contrast)
18.	While purchasing, I prefer to consider Discounts and sale offers
19.	While purchasing, I prefer to consider Schemes /prizes/ coupons
20.	While purchasing, my priorities are towards Branded/ Packed
21.	While purchasing, my priorities are towards Quantity
22.	While purchasing, my priorities are towards Packaging
23.	While purchasing, my priorities are towards Price
24.	My purchase decisions are influenced by Spouse (wife or husband)
25.	My purchase decisions are influenced by Parents
26.	My purchase decisions are influenced by Friends
27.	My trust on products, is based on Recommendations of friends
28.	My trust on products, is based on Frequent advertisement
29.	My trust on products, is based on Market reputation of seller
30.	My trust on products, is based on My own experience

REFERENCES

Allyn and Bacon, 1999,, "*Global Problems and the Culture*", of Richard Robbins Capitalism", , p. 210

Ekerdt, David J, 2004, "*Consumption and Meanings of Age*" , Journals of Gerontology Series B: Psychological Sciences & Social Sciences; Mar, 2004, Vol. 59B Issue 2.

Joeri Van den Bergh, 200, "*Book Review*", Journal of Consumer Marketing Volume 17, Number: 2, 2000, pp. 172-185

Juliet Schor, 1998, "*The Overspent American*", Basic Books, New York, 1998

Martin G Letscher, 1990, "*Fad or Trend?, How to Distinguish them and Capitalize on them*" Journal of Services Marketing 1990 Volume: 4 Number: 3

Michael F. Smith, 1999, "*Urban versus suburban consumers: a contrast in holiday shopping purchase intentions and out shopping behavior* ", journal of consumer marketing, Volume 16, Number: 1, 1999 pp. 58-73

Nunnally, J.C., 1978, Psychometric Theory, McGraw-Hill Book Company, New York.

Organization for Economic Cooperation and Development, "*Eco-Efficiency*", OECD, Paris, 1998

Packard Vance, 1960, "*The Waste Makers*", Penguin, Harmondsworth, 1960

Polly Ghazi and Judy Jones, 1997, "*Downshifting*", Coronet, London, 1997

Rio de Janeiro, 1992, UNCED, Agenda 21, UN, 1992

Tacoma, 1996, "Yearning for Balance", Merck Family Fund Tacoma, 1996

VENTURE CAPITALISTS: AN INDIAN PERSPECTIVE

Neeti Agrawal

ABSTRACT

Over the years industrial financing has become an area of exotic financial instruments, high technology and innovations. Indian economy has already witnessed emergence of several financial institutions and growing capital markets, which have undergone a drastic change. The most notable change is the arrival of venture capital institutions to cater to the needs of industrial ventures involving high-risks on account of technology development and up gradation.

In India the venture capital existed in informal form in the 19th century but the formal process of introducing venture capital to the Indian financial sector started with recommendation of R.S. Bhatt committee in 1973 to form a venture corpus of Rs. 100 crore. Then the seventh five-year plan in 1985 emphasized the need for developing a venture funding system in India. The actual process started in 1988 with government coming up with certain guidelines and setting up of a venture fund. Since then the amendments have been made, still the industry is not growing fast.

Since this avenue has not been as popular as the other financing alternatives, much academic research has not been done on the topic in India. The present work aims at providing an insight to the venture capital industry in India, with special reference to the problems faced by venture capitalists Efforts have been made to analyze the Indian scene with a different perspective.

INTRODUCTION

Venture capital as the new phenomenon appeared in the world of business after the Second World War. Similar to the banking industry, the venture capital industry serves as a link between investors and investee firms. However, the participation of venture capitalists is far more extensive and individual. VCs play the role of a resource manager. Venture capital is the equity finance in relatively new companies and is termed as a risky capital

Venture capital industry in India is a fourteen-year-old industry, yet it is a neglected one even though India has had a network of development financial institutions for more than four decades, in addition to a reasonably well-developed banking industry. The institutions like ICICI, IDBI etc. have been providing financial support to a variety of projects, including new industrial projects, during this period. Entrepreneurs with no proven track record but with a professional or managerial background have often obtained assistance from these institutions. The stock market conditions do support the new companies and businesses by subscribing to their public issue but the volatile market conditions pose some problems.

Indian transition of VC industry goes back more than 150 years when many of the managing agency houses acted as VCs providing both finance and management skill to risky projects. It was due to the managing money system through which Tata Iron and Steels and Empress Mills were able to raise equity capital from the investing public. The Tatas were the pioneers in starting the managing agency house, named Investment Corporation of India in 1937 which acted as VC and promoted hi-tech entrepreneurs such as CEAT tyres, Associated Bearings, National Rayon etc. (Gordon & Natrajan, 1997). Managing agency system was abolished later and the public sector term lending institutions took the baton with meeting a part of venture capital requirement through seed capital and risk capital for hi-tech industries, which were not able to meet promoter's contribution. All these institutions only supported sound technology, while technology development remained largely confined to government labs and academic institutions.

Concept of venture funding entered India nearly after 25 years of its existence elsewhere. The IDBI has been managing venture capital fund scheme established by the Union Government in 1986. The ICICI in association with the UTI has set up a venture finance company named TDICI, which commenced its operations in 1988. Canara Bank launched its funds in 1989. Private sector has large number of players. Credit capital venture fund (I) ltd., supported by Asian Development Bank (ADB) and Bank of India. ANZ Grindlays Indian Investment fund is another fund supported by NRIs (Avadhani, 1991).

The need for specialized venture capital institutions has been felt for quite some time even though the development banks in India play an important role in financing new entrepreneurs and form an integral part of the financial system. The need is because of the following factors:

- Requirement of due diligence.
- Financing highly risky investments.

- Willingness to support new technologies and innovative projects.
- Monitoring of the financed projects.

Apart from these factors it is necessary to have these institutions to invest in the equity of small companies to any significant extent.

Venture capital is money provided by professionals who invest alongside management in young, rapidly growing companies that have the potential to develop into significant economic contributors. Professionally managed venture capital firms generally are private partnerships or closely held corporations funded by private and public pension funds, endowment funds, foundations, corporations, wealthy individuals, foreign investors, and the venture capitalists themselves.

INDIAN IT INDUSTRY

The information and communication technology (ICT) revolution opens up the new prospects for mankind. The third millennium witnesses a new role that developing countries and nations with transitional economies may play in the world economy landscape. India's unique experience in IT is definitely worth studying. Within a short period of time, it has managed to build a powerful ICT industry with a dramatically growing software export sector (www.auriga.com, 2001). Government incentives and liberal policies relating to IT companies have resulted an impressive boost in the IT industry revenues. In 1991-2000, the Indian IT industry has recorded an average annual revenue growth of about 50 per cent.

Venture capital financing is different from the conventional mode of financing and the difference lies in terms of uses, securities and requirements. Every mode of financing has its respective advantages and disadvantages. Most people define **'Venture Capital'** as the money for start-ups and good ideas. Private investors or 'angels' are the principal source of capital for most start-ups and good ideas. Many venture capital companies however define venture capital as money for expansion of an existing business. Clients who rely on the fund managers to make appropriate investment generally fund large venture capital companies (Preparing for venture capital, Jeffrey M. Stoller; http:/ www. venture capital.com). It can also be defined as an equity/equity related investment in a growth-oriented small/medium business to enable the investors to accomplish corporate objectives, in return for minority shareholding in the business or the irrevocable right to acquire it. Over the years the concept has shifted from technology oriented manufacturing organizations to being very close to 'private equity class' for unlisted new companies in all sectors of the economy irrespective of the nature of their projects (Khan, 1998).

PROCESS OF VENTURE CAPITAL INVESTMENT

Contrary to popular perception, venture capital plays only a minor role in funding basic innovation. Venture money is not long-term money. The idea is to invest in a company's balance sheet and infrastructure until it reaches a sufficient size and credibility so that it can be sold to a corporation or so that the institutional public-equity markets can step in and provide liquidity. In short the venture capitalist buys a stake in an entrepreneurs idea, nurtures it for a short period and then exits with the help of an investment broker. Venture capital niche exists because of the structure and rules of capital markets (Zider, 1998). Normally the investment is in the risky project with expected higher returns. Basically such kinds of funds are invested in industries, which are unable to get funds through conventional sources. This type of funding may be by way of investment in the equity of the new enterprise or a combination of debt and equity, though equity is the most preferred route. Most of the ventures financed through this route are especially in the industries like InfoTech, electronic, biotech and communications or in short can be said to be ICE industries.

Normally the investment process includes the following steps: (Avadhani, 1998)

1. Establishment of contact between the entrepreneurs and the venture capitalists;
2. Preliminary evaluation;
3. Detailed approval;
4. Sensitivity analysis;
5. Financing the new venture portfolio;
6. Monitoring the project and post investment support.

MECHANISM OF VENTURE CAPITAL FINANCING

VCF is no longer about seed financing a small amount of capital extended to an investor to prove a concept or start-up financing funds given for product development and marketing provided the company has been in business for a short while. Instead it's all about extending finance to firms that have already managed to reach a certain level of operations (Dhawan, 1997). The venture capital industry in present times covers the broad spectrum of investment interest from product concept to product development, commercial stage improvement as well as meeting the second stage requirement of funds for expansion. These are the steps during which the risks of enterprise are high due to technological innovations and uncertainty in the market conditions (Mishra, 1996). There is a paradigm shift in venture capital industry. Table 34.1 summarizes this shift.

Table 34.1: Stages of Venture Capital Financing

Stages	Name	Stages of Project
I	Seed	Conceptualization/planning
II	Start-up	Operational/production
III	I round/Expansion	Expansion in production/marketing
IV	II round/ Mezannine	Last stage before public offering
V	III round/Buy-out	Acquisition of a product line business
VI	IV round/Turnaround	Reestablishment of business

Source: Dhawan, 2000, loc.cit.

RESULTS AND DISCUSSION

We could be on the threshold of a glorious revolution powered on by ideology and the individuals pursuing their own dreams. Change is the buzzword in the 21st century. This changing market scenario brings in the concept of different alternatives in different sectors. Past fourteen years (since liberalization), financing sector saw a great change in India. Here comes in the concept of different funding alternatives for start-ups as well as developing and established companies. Many new players have entered to change the structure of the economy. The new entrepreneurs do have new ideas, technological skills but lack proper management and funds. This is where venture capitalists/angels come in and help the new ideas to take a real shape.

A primary investigation was carried out to find out the problems of venture capitalists as well as venture capital backed companies. A survey was conducted for select companies. 45 venture-funding companies were chosen. Out of the 45 companies only ten replied, that too without the financial data. Efforts have been made to maintain the accuracy while interpreting the results but the process was difficult as the data was insufficient. The percentage calculation was done to reach the conclusion.

A survey says that eight of the richest men in India are first generation entrepreneurs (Outlook, Oct. 16, 2000). A study of global entrepreneurship done in 2001 shows that India is among the top three in largest number of entrepreneurs. The other two are U.S. and Brazil. India was ranked ninth amongst 29 countries relating to entrepreneurial activity, as measured by the percentage population involved in the start-up process or in a business less than four years. It also shows that less than 1 per cent adult population invested in start-up business, which was amongst the lowest in the countries surveyed.

RESULTS: VENTURE CAPITALISTS

The primary survey indicates that the investment in early stage was more (approx. 53 per cent) as compared to later stage and acquisition stage. The mentality of the Indian investor does not support this view. The main reason for this is the availability of foreign/private venture capital funds.

- The respondents feel that board of directors with a stake of approximately 73 per cent dominates the participation area of the firm. This shows that the board of directors plays a decisive role in the management process.
- Approximately 66 per cent investors preferred young entrepreneurs with new ideas and technical skills and the secondary data does support the view that venture capital financing is normally for the new entrants.
- Venture capital assistance was provided more (approx. 58 per cent) for the new product development than for the product modification or research and development.
- The equity mode of financing remained high.
- The availability of funds for new entrants was more, therefore the investors favoured the venture capital assistance for new product development and the general size of the assistance was quite high.
- The survey also revealed that approximately 80 per cent finance was for the information and technology sector and that too in the early stage.
- The problems due to government regulations were found to be more (approx. 73 per cent) than at the individual or entrepreneurial level.
- Since maximum investment is by foreign or private funds, the most popular exit route opted is Initial Public Offering or going public.

PROBLEMS OF VENTURE CAPITALISTS

The venture capitalists face lot of problems while investing in a company whether new/ established. Some of the problems, which could be deciphered through the survey, are as follows:

- Most of the VCs felt that they did not get supporting loans or funding at the time of crisis or temporary illiquidity.
- The VCs feel that though the proposals with new ideas are available in large number but the quality proposals are only few.
- The VCs face difficulty in reselling the investments at a time when the money invested is not received on time.
- The strict guidelines do not allow VCs to invest in any other field except

greenfields/small units.

- It is difficult to raise equity from the market, as the risk associated is quite high.
- Banks or other financial institutions are not eager to provide overdraft facilities to VCs because of high-risk nature of the investment activities.
- The VCs face difficulty due to multiple legislation i.e. they have to register with SEBI as well as RBI and to avail tax benefits, have to register with Central Board of Direct Taxes (CBDT). Many VCs feel that getting registered with one regulatory authority in itself is quite cumbersome, hence registering with three regulating bodies, poses more problems.
- One of the major problems is Disinvestment process. In a country like India, where capital markets are quite volatile, it is very difficult to exit through primary or secondary market. The failure of OTCE in India has led to further problems.
- Since venture fund is a long-term illiquid investment, funds are locked up for a longer period.

SUGGESTIONS

Since the eligibility criterion by Venture Capital Companies (VCC) is based on government guidelines, the choice of quality proposals is restricted. India is self-sufficient to have indigenous technology; hence the government can relax certain conditions, which will help the industry to grow. VCCs/VCFs feel that there is lack of awareness at the small and medium level firms about the advantages of venture capital. What the VCs feel about the venture capital industry is summarized below:

- Majority of VCs feel that their income should be tax-exempted fully in view of high risk involved in financing a new venture.
- Some feel that the income of VCCs/VCFs should be tax deductible from other incomes for five years after financing a particular unit.
- Almost all the VCs surveyed agreed that the venture capital industry should be treated at par with the mutual fund industry.
- VCs felt that the self-regulatory (like IVCA) body should regulate the financing process rather than the legislative enactment.
- VCFs must be allowed to use a wide range of financing instruments apart from the equity.

Venture capital has been given due importance in Budget 200-01 and SEBI has been made the nodal agency for its entry and monitoring. But the controversy regarding the tax structure still persists. Contrary to the K.B. Chandrashekhar

Committee's report on venture capital, such capital has been treated like any other equity capital and not been given the special "pass through" status it deserves (Sengupta, March 12, 2000). The Chandrashekhar Committee report says that VC funding is dominated by foreign funds, which account for 80 per cent of the business (Tripathi, 2000). This shows that even after so many years the Indian funds could not bring themselves at par with the foreign funds.

To Sum up the analytical study, it can be said that venture capital is basically equity finance in relatively new companies. The venture capital funding requires lot of patience as it has a substantial degree of active involvement with the promoters of the business. This type of funding is expected to provide superior returns essentially through capital gains at the time of exit. The basic objective of the venture capitalist therefore, is to achieve capital gains of his/her equity at the time of exit, and the loan finance will only be supplementary to this main objective.

Finally it can be stated that the venture capital though being a risky mode of financing is a better alternative as it gives higher returns. If the venture capital industry has to survive in these changing times, the venture capitalists must:

- Have a clear focus in their business with clear, prioritized objectives;
- Focus on specific industry niches;
- Manage portfolios ruthlessly.

Venture capital is quite well developed in the developed countries but it still has to get its due importance in India. Venture capital industry feels that there is a need for separate laws for developing venture capital in India.

REFERENCES

Avadhani, V.A. (1998. 'Venture capital funds' in Investment and securities markets in India. Last edition. Himalaya publishing house. P. 183.

Dhawan, R. (November22-December 06, 1997). 'Financing Venture Capital 2000'. Business Today.06, 139-147.

Gordan, E. & Natarajan, K. (1997). 'Venture Capital' in Emerging Scenario of Financial Services. Second Edition. Himalaya Publishing House, Mumbai.

Khan, M.Y. (1998). 'Venture Capital Financing' in Financial Services. First reprint. Tata Mcgraw-Hill Publishing Company Limited, New Delhi.

Mishra, K. Asim. (1996). 'Venture Capital Financing In India'. Shipra Publications, New Delhi.

Tripathi, Roop. Rishi. (April 15-30, 2000). 'IDEAS'. Advertising & Marketing. 12, 2, Pgs. 30.

Zider. Bob. (November- December, 1998). 'How venture capital works'. Howard Business Review. Pgs. 131-139. (October 16, 2000).

WEB ENABLED SUPPLY CHAIN MANAGEMENT

Prashant M More

ABSTRACT

Co-operative behaviour forms the basis of today's successful business. To achieve a high degree of co-operation it is necessary for key supply chain partners to share information. Equally or more importantly is the willingness to share strategic information so that firm can jointly plan the best ways and means to satisfy requirements. The purpose of the paper is (a) to bring forward the need of web based transactions and (b) to enable the supply chain partners to share information through web based transaction system.

With the help of case study in automobile company, recommendations regarding the information gap which are to be filled in procurement transaction are given and it outlines the problem areas in the supplier end of supply chain. Further the paper suggests the web based system (solution) which can be deployed for better information sharing between supply chain partners.

Lastly paper gives input for building up of web based transaction system that would make the real time data available and fetch the benefits of the deployment to supply chain people who deal with continuous changes in market demands, production plans and production setups.

AUTOMOTIVE SCM–SUPPLIER'S COLLABORATION

According to Roger Blackwell, a business Professor at Ohio State University, "*Supply Chain Management is all about having the right product in the right place, at the right price, at the right time, and in right condition.*"

Before moving to what services can be provided on web in reference to supply chain it is necessary to have a look at the motive behind formation of the supply chain which is derived from two paradigms.

First, the fundamental belief is that co-operative behavior will reduce the risk and greatly improve the efficiency of overall logistical process. To achieve a high degree of co-operation, it is necessary for key supply chain participants to share information. Such information sharing should not be limited to transaction data.

Equally or more important is a willingness to share strategic information so that firms can jointly plan the best ways and means to satisfy requirements. This co-operative paradigm is based on the belief that information collaboration is essential to allow participating firms to do the right things faster and more efficiently.

The second paradigm is elimination of waste and duplicate efforts. At the root of this paradigm is the fundamental belief that substantial amounts of inventory deployed in a tradition channel constitute a risky commitment. Sharing information and jointly planning can eliminate or reduce risk associated with much of these inventory speculations. In fact, if information is shared and used properly, much of the inventory positioned between end of a production line and the customer checkout can be eliminated from the channel. (ref: p102/"Logistical Management" by Donald .J. Bowersox & David .J.Closs/1986/McGraw-Hill)

In short to better balance supply with demand and optimize the efficiency of your supply chain, you need to collaborate more closely with your suppliers and customers - today's competitive environment demands it. We will consider a scenario in automobile company where SCM has been implemented through ERP product.

The paper outlines a problem area in the supplier end and suggests the improvement. The business process of Procurement is also studied with the objective of improving it with the help of internet technology.

An Auto company has a ERP setup, which has been/can be supported by SCM implementation. However even with this implementation, auto company have had limited success in the Supplier's Integration. We feel that the Web technology would be in a position to bridge this gap with discernable advantages.

CASE STUDY OF AUTOMOBILE COMPANY

The Current Business Process of Procurement is as follows:

The demand is fed into the ERP application and the MRP run is performed. The BOM (Bill of Materials) is exploded and the output that is generated is the procurement details for the next 7 days. The details of the items required is then distributed to the corresponding "Buyers". "Buyers" are executives who "father" a set of items from the sourcing, to quality analysis, to costing, to procurement until the item is fitted into the vehicle. Thus a specific buyer monitors the entire life cycle of a specific item in auto company. This buyer is in constant communication with the vendors or "Supplier".

The buyer segregates the item requisitions into procurement lots for the suppliers. Thus he allocates the quantity for each supplier to provide. He then charts out the individual "Delivery schedules" and posts them on the web site.

The suppliers log into this web site and access the various transactions.

The supplier then sends back the Invoice and the Goods Delivery Note. auto company would send back the RIR (Receiving and Inspection Report) and also the payment status details.

ISSUES FOR A MORE SUCCESSFUL SUPPLY CHAIN

1. Though the "Data Pipe" is available, the quality of the data and making sure it's the right data for the decisions that need to happen through establishing information systems capable of sharing real-time, accurate and relevant information is not in place. This data helps maintain records but does not help taking decisions.
2. Getting small businesses on to this technology is difficult and thus it is felt that, ideally, only the 1st tier(A –class) of suppliers will be able to make use of this facility.
3. The "Third Party Logistics" though present are not a part of these transactions through the web site.
4. The suppliers are sourcing the data. If it could be pushed into their system then they would be more enthusiastic about the usage and dissemination of data.
5. The data flows are related only to individual suppliers and Auto Company. Auto company could also look at exposing the data between suppliers and the also the "Third Party Logistics" company.

Thus auto company require a solution that would seamlessly integrate the suppliers and its SCM applications, that would help take decisions and that would spread the benefit of seamlessly accessing data by disseminating this data to all concerned. After all the suppliers in the Supply Chain are considered as an integral part of the organization and active collaboration with them would lead to lesser costs and better profits.

IMPROVED SCM THROUGH COLLABORATION

Organizations are not happy just sourcing data from their trading partners; they also want to use this data to collaborate. Collaboration brings about a amalgamation of common goals and thus the movement towards the achievement of these then becomes relatively easier. The data exposed by the application layers between auto company and its trading partners would only benefit transactional abilities they do not benefit collaborative systems.

Collaboration in the Planning, Forecasting and Replenishment of requisitioned items for production in B2B exchanges and collaboration in the Transport Management are the new age paradigms that are being executed in

Business Processes. auto companies has already taken a step in this by implementing "Third Party Logistics" in the upstream processes of the SCM efforts.

Simply put it means that data and access to the data should be available seamlessly across the extended SCM partners. This would help collaboration in Supply Chain execution. The e-business rules are forcing the partners to shorten planning cycles and they need to re-plan and re-allocate and also expedite execution. Thus it requires processes of building orders forecasts / Delivery schedules into Shipment forecasts / Advance Shipment Notes and insuring their accurate fulfillment in a shorter planning window.

The universal objective is to minimize the inventory in the value chain. With most of the loose ends tied up at the Supplier's end and at the auto company end, the link between them could be strengthened to provide further efficiency to the SCM system. Stock availability and the transportation of this stock have mostly been reactionary. Discrepancies or amendments to the Delivery Schedules also result in erroneous shipments. Finding a solution for these issues would result in definite cost savings.

BENEFITS OF DEPLOYMENT

The benefits of services on web being deployed in ABC auto company would be the following:

Adaptability: Services on web is clearly for integration rather than raw development. Development will be minimal since the components already available are to be used. Thus offering shorter delivery cycles for the technology to be implemented and accepted.

Speedy Integration: Enhanced distribution of information and integration, Web services lets the value chain discover the value within and about the organization without complex and time consuming bilateral development.

Interoperability: The seamless integration would be a very beneficial to network the supplier base. This will also help in getting the small businesses on board and thus move the IAI exercise beyond the "I" tier ("A" Class) of suppliers.

Cost Centric: The development and deployment time would be considerably less and with the web site effort to be compared with, we will be able to prove that Web services deployment would be less costly.

Standards: Open standards would be introduced across the supplier network and thus would be ideal and strong basis for future scalability.

Reusability: The services developed will be complete in them selves and could be utilized by the users across the organization.

The necessary Modules needed for these transactions would be made available to the companies on net by paying service charges to the service provider.

SOLUTION TO BE DEPLOYED

We have identified the "Material Delivery Schedule Note" and the "Stock Check" functionalities as the area for deployment of Web Services for auto company

The following criteria may be considered for the success of the pilot project:

1. A web component, which seamlessly pushes the Delivery Schedule to the suppliers and the TPL (Third Party Logistics) without issues of interoperability.
2. All the "Buyers" will be able to access this web and would be available on the Corporate Intranet /Extranet.
3. A web services component that will be able to extract the current stock figures for a specific item from a specific supplier.
4. This component would be available on the Corporate Intranet for "Buyers" to be able to check the stock and then proactively formulate the Delivery Schedule for the suppliers. This will prevent un-necessary delays due to non-conformity of stocks from the suppliers.
5. This component would be available on the Internet for the other Suppliers and also the TPL to be able to check the stock and then formulate the sourcing and delivery processes.
6. Both these components are independent and could be used by any authorized user across the organization.

REFERENCES

B.S.G.K Shastry, R.S.Rajan, A.K.Vij and Rakesh Chaudhary" Value Chain Integration in Project Life Cycle – A Case Study", World Conference on supply chain management (1998).

Donald .J. Bowersox & David .J. Closs" Logistical Management" McGraw-Hill 1986, p102.

Shobha Seturam" IT –Enabled Supply Chain", Proceedings of World Conference on supply chain management (1998).

SUPPLY CHAIN PERFORMANCE THROUGH SCOR MODEL

Prashant More and Rupa S. Bindu

ABSTRACT

In the competitive and dynamic market place, the role of management has turned to be difficult task. SCM forms as important aspect of business and management.

The paper suggest the use of SCOR Model as an effective tool for measuring and evaluating the performance of supply chains which helps to justify the Technical and Financial feasibility of implementing SCM. The basic structure of SCOR is illustrated which revolves around five distinct management processes in the context of different types of production systems. Further it moves down to elaborate the performance metrics at different levels of the model.

Since the launch of SCOR model in 1996,it has been adopted as the cross-Industry Standard in Supply Chain Management by many well known companies worldwide, which has achieved substantial improvements in delivery performance, forecast accuracy and reduction in Supply Chain costs. In this way SCOR model allows an organisation to analyse its supply chain performance and link the results to the Financial Performance.

SCOR IS process reference model designed for effective communication among supply chain partners. It can be adopted as Industry standard - a standard language that helps management to focus on supply chain issues .SCOR is used to describe .measure and evaluate supply chain configuration. If implemented SCOR will definitely prove to be cutting edge tool in improving the present day performance of many existing Supply chains in the Industry. Therefore the implementation of SCOR Model in Indian scenario is recommended.

WHAT IS SCOR?

Supply Chain Management is a systems approach to map the entire flow of information material and, services from raw material suppliers, through factories and warehouses to the end customers. Supply Chain Operations Reference Model

(SCOR) is a leading frame work that enables organisations to describe their simple and complex supply chain network easily using a common set of definitions and processes which allows effective communication among supply chain partners. SCOR is a Process Reference Model that provides a language for communicating among supply chain partners.

Process reference models integrate the well-known concepts of Business process re-engineering, Benchmarking, and process measurement into a cross-functional framework.

A Process Reference Model Contains:

- Standard descriptions of management processes.
- A framework of relationships among the standard processes.
- Standard metrics to measure process performance.
- Management practices that produce best-in-class performance Standard alignment to features and functionality.

BPR: Is the critical analysis and radical design of existing business process to achieve breakthrough improvements in performance measures.

Benchmarking: Is the process of Quantifying the operational performance of similar companies and establishing internal targets based on Best-in-Class results.

Best Practices: The process of characterising the management practices and software solutions that result in Best-in-Class performance.

SCOR Span

"From your supplier's supplier to your customer's customer"

- All customer interactions, from order entry through paid invoice
- All product (physical material and service) transactions, from your supplier's supplier to your customer's customer, including equipment, supplies, spare parts, bulk product, software, etc.
- All market interactions, from the understanding of aggregate demand to the fulfillment of each order.

DEMAND/SUPPLY PLANNING AND MANAGEMENT

Balance resources with requirements and establish/communicate plans for the whole supply chain are decided. Under this process the company should access supply resources, aggregate and prioritize demand requirements ,plan inventories, distribution requirements, production, material and rough cut capacity of all products and all channels. Make/buy decisions are evaluated under this heading. Decision related to long term capacity and resource planning, product phase in /phase out are undertaken in this phase.

Business management rules ,supply chain performance ,data collection are also planned.

Sourcing for stocked, make to order, Engineer to order products

Under this process sourcing infrastructure is managed. Various activities like selection of supply sources, vendor contracts, vendor certification and feedback ,sourcing quality monitoring, scheduled delivery, receipts verification and transfer of products, payment of authorized suppliers, assessment of supplier performance, business management rules, managing the capital assets, supplier network, import/export requirements are undertaken.

Make-to-Stock, Make-to-Order, and Engineer-to-Order products

This process is concerned with production, Execution and managing "Make" infrastructure.

Under production execution activities like scheduling, manufacturing, testing ,packaging, holding and releasing of product are under taken. It also includes the finalisation of Engineering for engineer to order products. Under managing "make" infrastructure, engineering changes, facilities and equipment management, production status and production quality, shop scheduling and short term capacity are planned. Establishing Manage rules, performance, data, in-process products (WIP), equipment and facilities, transportation, production network, and regulatory compliance for production are also included in this domain.

Ordering, Warehousing, Transportation, Installation and Management for Stocked, Make-to-Order, and Engineer-to-Order Products

Under order management activities like maintaining and entering orders, generating quotations, configuring product are undertaken. Further create and maintain customer database, maintain product and price database, managing receivables and credit management also fall under this domain. Management of delivery business rules, performance, information and finished product inventories, capital assets, product life cycles and import/export requirement are also included in this function.

Return of Raw Materials (to Supplier) and Receipt of Returns of Finished Goods (from Customer), including Defective Products, MRO Products, and Excess Products

All return defective product steps include authorizing return; scheduling product return; receiving, verifying, and disposition of defective product; and return replacement or credit. Return MRO product steps include authorizing and scheduling return, determining product condition, transferring product, verifying product condition, disposition, and request return authorization. Return excess product steps include identifying excess inventory, scheduling shipment, receiving returns, approving request authorization, receiving excess product return in Source, verifying excess, and recover and disposition of excess product. Manage Return business rules, performance, data collection, return inventory, capital assets, transportation, network configuration, and regulatory requirements and compliance are a part of Return process.

LEVELS OF SCOR MODEL

At the core of SCOR model is the pyramid of four levels that represents the path the company takes on the road to supply chain improvement.

Level 1: Process Types

It provides the definitions of Plan, Source, Make, Deliver process types and this is a point where the company establishes its Supply chain competitive objective. It is the top most level which forms the basis of competitive performance and accordingly targets are set.

Level 2: Process Categories

It is the configuration level. It defines 30 core process categories and codes that are possible components of a supply chain. Organizations can configure their ideal or actual operations using these processes. *Example*: S1Source from stock, M2-Make to order. Supply chain configuration can be mapped easily using these codes.

Level 3: Process Elements

It provides the information required for successfully planning and setting goals for supply chain improvements. This includes process decomposition , defining process elements ,setting target bench marks ,defining best practices and system software capabilities to enable best practices.

Level 4: Decompose Each Process Element

Level 4 focuses on implementation, i.e. putting specific supply-chain improvements into action. These are not defined within industry standard model as implementation can be unique to each company.

SCOR METRICS

SCOR Model contains a set of metrics in three hierarchical levels.

SCOR Level 1 Metrics: level 1 is the top most level giving the process types at level 1 there are 13 metrics that are displayed in the SCOR card.

Level 1 metrics measure performance in delivery reliability. supply chain flexibility, supply chain responsiveness, supply chain costs and assets. The SCOR Card provides a process measurement tool kit to set targets and track operational performance. Lower level objectives can be derived from the targets at level 1 in the SCOR card.

SCOR Level 2 Metrics: LEVEL2 is the configuration level giving process categories and their standard codes.

SCOR Level 3 Metrics: :Level 3 is the process element level having element definitions, Performance attributes and accompanying metrics are as shown below.

Since the launch of SCOR model in 1996,it has been adopted as the cross-Industry Standard in Supply Chain Management by many well known companies worldwide ,which has achieved substantial improvements in delivery performance, forecast accuracy and reduction in Supply Chain costs[3].In this way SCOR model allows an organisation to analyse its supply chain performance and link the results to the Financial Performance.

SCOR IS process reference model designed for effective communication among supply chain partners. It can be adopted as Industry standard - a standard language that helps management to focus on supply chain issues. SCOR is used to describe .measure and evaluate supply chain configuration. If implemented SCOR will definitely prove to be cutting edge tool in improving the present day performance of many existing Supply chains in the Industry.

For effective implementation of SCM & ERP in Indian Industries it becomes essential to have a system to measure the performance of SCM and justify the Technical and financial feasibility. But in most of the Indian industries as well as some industries in developing countries the SCM and ERP has proved ineffective only because they don't have a structured means to measure the Performance of SCM and link it to the financial returns. Use of SCOR Model would be an appropriate means to enhance and justify the SCM Implementation.

REFERENCES

Balaram Avittahur, Janat shah, "Evaluation of Supply Chain Management Strategies", Proc. Of World Conference on Supply chain Management(1998).

Davis, "Effective Supply chain Management, "Sloan Management Review, vol.34, No.4, 1993, pp 35-46.

John Paul, "Micro Supply Management in Manufacturing and Management", Proc. of International conference on Manufacturing and Management (2004)

Rajesh Silswal & K.Suryanarayan, "Assessing Manufacturing Excellence: A Practice – Performance Gap Model", Proc. Of World conference on Supply Chain Management (1998)

Vasant M. Cavale and Renu L. Rajni, "Benchmarking Global Supply Chains", Proc of World Conference on supply chain management (1998).

37

BUILDING INFORMATION MANAGEMENT

Rachit Garg and Manohar Singh

ABSTRACT

The objective of the paper is to identify the trends in initiating computer-based information systems and to ascertain the experience and perception of chief information officers in India about computerization in their organizations. For the organizations that have not been able to initiate such projects, the objective is to identify inhibiting factors. The findings suggest that CBIS projects will be undertaken by the organizations as a routine process to .enhance their performance. The behavioral factor and the project related factor were the two most important factors affecting success/failure in Computerization projects in India. The results of the analyses show that there are significant relationships among the following variables: Implementation of Computerization Projects: 1. The human factor and user training have a significant positive correlation with the severity in .implementation problems. 2. The degree of complexity in projects compared to the original estimates has a significant negative correlation with the performance of the projects. 3. The performance of the projects has a positive correlation with the satisfaction level.

INTRODUCTION

The worldwide spread of IT is well documented, with diffusion from developed to developing countries and the newly industrialized economies in Asia. Most businesses in the industrial world could not compete, and many could not even survive without computers and software. Now IT is an integral part of the products and services delivered to customers. Today, many multinational corporations and governments are increasingly using IT for international business and commerce. While advanced countries have made use of this technology for years, IT has also started to make inroads into lesser-developed countries. Thus, the level of IT adoption is different from country to country, as are each country's key management information systems or Computer Based IS issues are different. Businesses are generally regulated by a government policy in India. However, in

India, the government aggressively promotes the increased use of IT in business and industry.

Computer related technology or any other technology is essentially neutral: whether IT's application succeeds or fails depends entirely on the decisions that are made on how it shall be used. Also, the impact of IT in less developed countries depends on its adaptation to the local environment. Effective implementation of IT depends on the organization's vision of change, either by deliberate design or as an emergent phenomenon.

Use of Computer: People interact with the IS through a human interface. Culture impacts attitudes towards the use of computers. This impact is enunciated by various theories and the role of individuals' beliefs about their ability to competently use computers. In this paper we have used these four parameters for the measurement of culture:

Individualism versus Collectivism: The extent to which the individual expects personal freedom versus the acceptance of the responsibility to family, tribal or national groups. More individualism will result in more innovation.

Power Distance: The degree of tolerance and inequality in wealth and power indicated by the extent to which centralization and autocratic power are permitted. Higher innovation capacity is more available in societies having less power structure or little difference in power status within organizations.

Risk Avoidance: The extent to which a society avoids risks and creates security by emphasizing technology and buildings, laws and rules, and religion. A high-risk avoidance environment is not conducive to entrepreneurship and hence dampens innovations.

Masculinity versus Femininity: The extent to which the society differentiates roles between the sexes and places emphasis on masculine values of performance and visible achievements. Masculinity refers to assertive, competitive, and firm, whereas femininity culture refers to soft, yielding, dependent, intuitive etc. Radical innovation thrives in more masculine societies.

Levels of IS Growth: Depending upon the level of IS growth, the IT strategy is formulated by the organizations. A proper IT strategy corresponding to a matching stage of IS growth leads to a successful implementation of IS applications in the organizations. According to one indication the organizations should go through six stages of IT growth – initiation, expansion, control, integration, data administration, and maturity. The level of IT adoption and the sophistication of the corresponding management issues increases from one stage to the next, i.e. from underdeveloped to developing to newly industrialized to advanced nations. The important issues in India are currently operational and control oriented. Further, it is not necessary that CBIS development in lesser-developed countries, like India, must parallel the "bottom- up" evolutionary cycle experienced in the developed countries. It is conceivable that developing nations, with proper planning and advances in technology, can leapfrog into advanced strategic uses of IT.

Factors for Success of CBIS: The determinant of successful IS implementation can be grouped into categories as: These categories are frequently interrelated. Some determinants can be classified into two or more categories. IS implementation is often considered as the introduction of change. Reengineering implementation is also viewed as a large-scale organizational change. Therefore, it is reasonable to assume that reengineering implementation can benefit from an understanding of some of the problems faced in general IS implementation. In today's environment, users/customers are faced with similar products, too many options, and lack of time. The customer's natural reaction is to look for the cheapest, the most familiar, or the best quality product. The growth in end-user computing, availability of knowledge workers, trend towards usage of packaged software, and availability of quality-packaged solution, leads to elimination of most of the factors related to quality. Increased competition leads to a receptive environment for adoption of technology.

METHODOLOGY

The study has been defined as an exploratory and descriptive "survey" approach in order to achieve more generalizability and additional richness. The study is divided into three phases: ***Exploratory Study***: In the first phase, an obvious step in an exploratory study, in which interviews can be conducted. The data gathered from a literature search and interviews will be analyzed, and a revised version of the problem list and a questionnaire will be developed. ***Survey and Data Analyses***: In the second phase, a questionnaire survey will be used to answer the research questions. The data found here are quantitative in nature. The data will be used to test the hypotheses using correlation and multiple regressions. ***Computation of Discriminant Functions:*** To determine if statistical differences exist between the average score of manufacturing and service sectors within Indian organizations, discriminant analysis using stepwise variable selection method will be carried out.

LIMITATIONS

It must be stressed that any interpretation of the findings must be made in light of the selected set of variables, issues, and categories. Availability of literature in the area of information technology in context to developing countries is found to be scarce and limited. Any research that uses data gathered for inferential statistics assumes that the data should be collected randomly from the population. Further, the questionnaire survey involved people from various departments such as information systems, general administrative offices, accounting/finance, production, etc. In India there is a limited number of organizations with experience of IT applications for more than five years.

REFERENCES

Boehm, B.W. Software risk management. IEEE Computer Society Press.
Champy, James. Reengineering management: Harper Collins.
Hayes, F. Managing user expectation. Computerworld, 31(4), pp.8-9
Kalakota, e-Business: Roadmap for success, Addison-Wesley
Morris. Reengineering your business. McGraw-Hill.

ENTRY STRATEGIES OF AUTOMOBILE MANUFACTURERS: THE CASE OF INDIAN AUTOMOBILE INDUSTRY

Rajiv Kumar Garg

ABSTRACT

In anticipation of rapid growth, the passenger car market in India is crowded with many multinational companies trying to establish themselves. Most companies have joint- ventures with Indian partners and have entered the market in the last few years. The number of new entrants over a narrow time window of five years is unprecedented. Demand forecasts vary and analysts expect anywhere between 2 and 3.5 million cars to be sold in the next five years. Equity holding for the international partner is usually over 50 per cent and they retain significant managerial control. Most of them have introduced cars in the $15,000 to $35,000 price range, which is viewed as a luxury segment in India. Automobile companies have also chosen to establish exclusive dealerships. Initially, companies have chosen to import completely knocked down (CKD) kits and assemble them in India. However, this strategy is not effective in the long run since such imports attract 50 per cent duty. The major implications are that a shake out is likely and that companies would need to have alternate plans, including introduction of cars in other market segments, lower prices, and exports from India if they cannot establish themselves in the domestic market. The supplier industry is not sufficient and needs to develop simultaneously on all fronts including rapid capacity expansion, acquisition of technology, improvement in manufacturing practices, quality and productivity, adoption of lean manufacturing, and developing product design capabilities to meet the needs of assemblers. Therefore, a critical requirement for rapid growth of the industry is adequate assembler involvement in the suppler industry.

INTRODUCTION

New automobile policy of Government of India, announced in June 1993, attracted a large number of multinational automobile companies to India. These include General Motors and Ford, Japanese, European and Korean companies.

Chrysler is also planning to enter the country with a suitable Indian partner. In addition, there are three existing Indian companies: Hindustan Motors, Premier Automobiles and Telco, and one Indo-Japanese venture, Maruti Udyog Limited already in the passenger car market. Maruti is by far the biggest player with about 70 per cent of the market share. As on today, a total of 20 Automobile companies have either begun operations in India or plan to start soon. The number of new entrants and the level of investment within a very narrow time window of two to three years is unprecedented and seems unique to India. Compared to three major models available in the Indian market until recently, customers can now choose from a wide variety of products.

Some of the entry barriers faced by automobile companies in India are relatively high levels of import duties, a nascent ancillary industry, and product modifications required for relatively poor road conditions. On the other hand, a rapidly growing middle class, rising per capita income, and high levels of latent unsatisfied demand with customers starved of world class options promise enormous opportunities. For instance, from current sales of around 300,000 passenger cars in 1996-97, sales are expected to rise to anywhere between 850,000 to 2 million vehicles by the year 2005. Automobile companies have announced plans to install capacity of around 1 million vehicles by the year 2006. The number of cars sold over the next four years is going to be anywhere between 3 and 5 million vehicles. It is not certain how exactly demand will grow and on what factors it will depend, and whether there is room for so many players. The supplier industry also faces enormous challenges to keep pace with rapid growth. Manufacturing practices will have to change considerably to come closer to lean production. It is also possible that some companies will increasingly use India as a base for exporting vehicles to other countries. These issues will become clear as the future unfolds. At this stage, we describe and analyze the entry strategies of multinational companies in the Indian automobile industry.

ENTRY STRATEGY

Entry strategy for international markets is a comprehensive plan, which sets forth the objectives, goals, resources, and policies that will guide a company's international business operations over a future period long enough to achieve sustainable growth in world markets (Root, 1994). The time horizon we have used for entry strategy research is 1 to 3 years. For a company, each product in foreign market has a different entry strategy. The corporate international entry strategy is a combination of the different entry strategies of its various products in various foreign markets. There are various elements of entry strategy. In this paper, we have considered the following elements:

- Choice of product
- Choice of target market
- Choice of an entry mode to penetrate the target country
- Timing of entry
- Magnitude of investment and area of competitive emphasis
- Marketing plan to penetrate the target market
- Control system to monitor performance in the target market

RESEARCH FINDINGS

The Indian automobile industry is still in its evolutionary stage. There is no widely accepted method of segmenting the Indian market as yet. The segmentation provided in this paper is based on an understanding of the current state of the industry. These segments are quite different from the segments known in the US, European or Japanese markets. The following four segments that have been identified:

- Off-road vehicles, e.g. Maruti Gypsy, Mahindra Armada, Tata Sumo.
- Economy segment, comprising cars priced at less than $13,000 e.g., Ambassador, Premier, Maruti 800.
- Luxury segment, comprising cars within the $13,500 to $33,000 price bracket, e.g., Zen, 118NE, Contessa, Esteem, Sierra, Peugeot, Astra, Cielo, Ford Escort, Volkswagen, Mitsubishi Lancer.
- Super luxury segment, comprising cars priced higher than $33,000 e.g., Mercedes-Benz, BMW and Audi.

This segmentation is largely based on price and reflects the fact that an automobile is currently priced at about 18 to 24 months salary for individuals in the target segments. This is in contrast to western markets where prices are less than 6 months salary. However, middle class incomes are rising rapidly. A model sold in the West is likely to cost more in India for some time to come because of import duties. With progressive reduction in duties and increasing indigenization, prices are likely to come down in the future. The adverse price to income ratio will therefore come down, and is likely to further spur demand. Some automobile companies are also planning to use India as a manufacturing base to supply cars to other countries. This has the added advantage of eliminating duty payments for exported cars.

Appendix 'A' gives the entry strategies of thirteen new entrants to the Indian automobile market, in terms of the different measures of entry strategy identified. A close look at the entry strategies of the multinational companies in the Indian automobile industry points to some distinct patterns. Except for Audi, which is targeting a premium market niche, and Hyundai, the rest of the companies have set up joint ventures with Indian partners. Audi has announced plans for franchising automobiles. Recently, Hyundai has announced plans to enter the country with a wholly owned subsidiary. For most of the new joint ventures, management control lies with the MNCs. For example, though General Motors India is a 50:50 joint venture of GM and Hindustan Motors, ten International Service Personnel from Opel form the entire top management team of General Motors India. Similarly, Ford in Mahindra Ford, Mercedes in Mercedes Benz India Limited, Honda in Honda Siel, and Volkswagen in Eicher Volkswagen exercise significant management control. All these companies have expatriate managers in top positions.

Incremental internationalization is the mode recommended by management scholars (Ansoff and McDonnell, 1990) and observed in a number of studies by researchers from Western countries (Johanson and Vahlne, 1977; and Welch and Luostarinen, 1988). Initial involvement in a foreign market is conceived as a gradual and sequential process by most of the studies. This gradual pattern is thought to be the consequence of greater uncertainty, higher costs of gathering information, and the lack of experiential knowledge in international marketing activities. Several distinct stages are identified along the internationalization process for a firm in a foreign country, including pre-export stage, experimental involvement, active involvement, and committed involvement. However, the multinational firms cited here have directly gone in for active involvement. This could be due to high import duties for cars, inadequate existing capacity, and expectations of rapid demand growth. Most automobile companies have preferred joint ventures even though the government is not restricting foreign companies from setting up wholly owned subsidiaries. Joint ventures provide international companies with partners who understand local markets, government regulations and the supplier industry better, and also reduce initial risks.

An interesting feature of car sales is the use of 'bookings', i.e., getting customers to deposit $500 to $1000 for a car that will be supplied a few months from the date of booking. This method of trying to tie up customers is possible because of the large amount of unsatisfied pent up demand, severe capacity shortages, and the initial glamour for foreign cars. These bookings are so successful currently that a company's entire capacity is booked within a month. Some credit card companies are encouraging its cardholders to book cars by offering to cover them if they choose to default and not buy the car at a later date. The total number of bookings made across all companies is much more than the most optimistic demand estimates.

This suggests that many bookings are speculative and there could be an active secondary market for these bookings as production takes off and deliveries begin. Another factor fuelling advance bookings is the practice of many business houses supplying cars to their executives as perks.

IMPLICATIONS

There are about 20 automobile companies jostling for a market whose size by the most optimistic estimate is around 2 million vehicles per year by the year 2008. Clearly, sufficient room for so many players is not there. This means companies will need to have clear strategies on what they will do if they are not able to establish a viable market presence. One alternative is to use India as a manufacturing base to supply cars to other countries in South East Asia, Middle East and perhaps the Eastern block countries.

The other major implication is that automobile companies need to pay attention to the development of the supplier industry. Rapid growth in assemblers' capacity is possible only if suppliers are able to keep pace with them. The strategy used by Suzuki in 1980 of facilitating joint ventures between its major suppliers in Japan and some Indian companies is a good one. However, the supplier industry needs to grow, acquire new technology, improve manufacturing practices, quality and productivity, and restructure itself into first, second and third tier companies. There is also a lot of pressure on suppliers from assemblers to acquire product design capabilities.

Automobile companies may also need to rethink their strategy of introducing models successful in developed economies into India. High quality roads allowing driving at high speeds of over 50-80 miles per hour over long stretches are still less. These models are still perceived as high priced luxury cars by the middle class. For car sales to really take off, tailored products at lower prices may be an alternative. Automobile companies are also not paying enough attention to vehicles other than passenger cars. There is likely to be a lot of opportunities in products like jeeps, light commercial vehicles, buses and trucks. These markets are growing fast and there is relatively little competition.

This research throws up some interesting areas for future work. One area is comparison of strategies adopted by automobile companies in India and in other emerging markets, and also in Western and emerging markets. Another area of research is the comparison of strategies of companies from various countries, like US, Europe, Japan, and Korea in India. With the passage of time, research can try to establish linkages between entry strategy and performance. One of the most interesting questions will be to research the response of automobile companies to the shake out which many industry analysts expect.

Appendix A
Table 1: US Companies

	General Motors	Ford
Name of company	General Motors India Limited	Mahindra Ford India Limited
Market Segment	Luxury segment	Luxury segment
Partner	Hindustan Motors	Mahindra and Mahindra Limited
Timing of entry	March 1996	Phase 1: May 1996, Phase II: September 1998
Investment	US $117 million	Phase 1: $50 million, Phase II: $800 million
Distribution	Totally new dealership network	Not announced
Plant Location	Halol, Gujarat	Phase 1: Nasik, Phase II: Mardas
Level of indigenization	Current 65 per cent	Not announced

Table 2: European Companies

	BMW	MERCEDES BENZ	AUDI
Name of company	BMW India Limited	Mercedes Benz India Limited	Audi AG
Market Segment	Super-luxury segment	Super-luxury segment	Super-luxury segment
Partner	Hero Motors	TELCO	Ashiya Motors Mumbai
Timing of entry	1998	October 1995	March 1996
Price	US $ 66,667 to 83,333	$ 66,670	$63,333 $100,000
Plant Location	Greater Noida (UP)	Pune	Not applicable
Level of Indigenization	Not announced	5 per cent	Fully imported Car

Table 3: Other European Companies

	Fiat	Volkswagen	Peugeot	Rover
Name of Company	Premier Automobiles Limited	Volkswagen Eicher Limited	PAL Peugeot Limited	Sipani Automobiles Limited
Segment	Economy	Luxury .	Luxury	Luxury
Entry mode	Phase I: technical tie up, Phase II: Joint venture	Joint venture	Joint venture	Joint venture
Partner	Premier Automobiles	Eicher	Premier Automobiles	Sipani Automobiles
Time of entry	Ph I: Feb 1996, Ph II: 1998	1998	1995	1994
Price	$5,000 to $12,000	$18,000 to $22,000	$13,000- $ 16,000	$25,000- $34,000
Distribution	Newly appointed dealers	Not announced	32 dealers with a target of 100	Not known
Plant location	Kurla, Mumbai	Faridabad	Kalyan, Mumbai	Bangalore
Level of indigenization	15 per cent	Not known	25 per cent with a target of 79 per cent	9 per cent

Table 4: Southeast Asian Companies

	Honda	Mitsubishi	Hyundai
Name of company	Honda Siel cars India Pvt. Ltd.	Hindustan Motors Ltd.	Hyundai Motors
Segment	Luxury	Luxury	Luxury
Entry mode	Joint Venture	Joint venture	Wholly owned subsidiary
Partner	SIEL	Hindustan Motors	Not applicable
Time of entry	1997	1997	1997
Price	$ 16,000 to $ 20,000	$ 13,500 to $ 16,000	$ 7,000 to $ 10,000
Distribution	Not announced	Not announced	Not announced
Plant location	Greater Noida	Madras	Madras
Level of Indigenization	55 per cent	52 per cent	Not announced

REFERENCES

Amsden, Alice H.; and Kang, Jong-Yeol. "Learning to be lean in an emerging economy: The Case of South Korea," IMVP Sponsors Meeting, Toronto, Canada, June 1995.

Anderson, Erin; and Coughlan, Anne T. "International Market Entry and Expansion via Independent or Integrated Channels of Distribution," Journal of Marketing, Vol. 51, Jan 1987, pp. 71-82.

Frazier, Gary L.; Gill, James D.; and Kale, Sudhir H. "Dealer Dependence Levels and Reciprocal Actions in a Channel of Distribution in a Developing Country," Journal of Marketing, Vol.53, Jan 1989, pp. 50-69.

Fujimoto, Takahiro ; Nishiguchi, Toshihiro ; and Sei, Shoichiro. "Managing Japanese Direct Investments in Europe: The Case of the Automobile and Auto Parts Industries," IMVP Research Briefing Meeting, June 1994.

Johanson, J.; and Vahlne, Jan-Erik. "The Internationalization Process of the Firm - A Model of Knowledge Development and Increasing Foreign Market Commitments," Journal of International Business Studies, Spring/Summer 1977, pp. 23-32.

O'Brien, Peter ; and Karmokolias, Yannis. "Radical Reform in the Automotive Industry," International Finance Corporation Discussion Paper No. 21, The World Bank, Washington D.C., 1994, 46 pp.

Root, Franklin R. *Entry Strategies for International Markets*, New York: Lexington Books, 1994.

Welch, Lawrence S.; and Luostarinen, Reijo. "Internationalization: Evolution of a Concept," Journal of General Management, Vol. 14, No.2, Winter 1988, pp. 35-55.

Womack, James P. ; Jones, Daniel T. ; and Roos, Daniel. *The Machine That Changed The World*, New York : Rawson Associates, 1990, 323 pp.

39

BRANDING: CHALLENGES FOR GLOBAL COMPETITIVENESS

Ruchi Shah

"The lion is the king of the jungle," Grandma was explaining to her grand kiddos. "It never eats animals which are dead or killed by others. It can even kill an elephant. All animals are afraid of lion". The grandchildren looked completely unconvinced "But granny, the other day I saw a lion chased away by hyenas on National Geographic and also watched, on Discovery, a lion waiting for an old elephant to die to eat it and a baby elephant chased it away", they exclaimed. Similar to grandma many established brands find the consumers in "Knowledge Economy" tough to handle.

ARE WE GLOBALLY COMPETITIVE?

As the distances are crunching with the integration of economies we are heading towards a more global competitive state and again existence and presence would be strictly guided by Darwin's theory- 'Survival for the Fittest'. Networked Readiness Index of the Global Competitiveness report 2004-05 reveals that India ranks 55 in the year 2004 rating, one up from its ranks as fifty-sixth most competitive nation in 2003. This is below China at forty-six (44 in 2003), and it is also below countries as Australia, Canada, South Africa, Mexico and quite a few East European countries.

Sun Tzu says about 'The Art of War' – "All warfare is based on deception. Hence, when able to attack, we must seem unable, when using our forces, we must seem inactive, when we are near, we must make the enemy believe we are far away. When far away we must make him believe we are near Hold out baits to entice the enemy. Feign disorder and crush", and this is almost synonymous to what Al Ries and Jack Trout have put in their book, 'Marketing Warfare'- "the true nature of marketing is not serving the customer, it is outwitting, outflanking and outfighting your competitors."

Contrary to popular opinion a brand is not just a look. Rather it is a trustmark, a legal protection, a warrant and a promise. The answer to Why branding is indispensable is predominantly because it alleviates the probability of perceived risk associated with the product and lets the customer confide in its legitimacy. Though the positioning mantra reminds us that the purpose of marketing is to build a brand in the mind of prospect still Rob Frankel remarked that truly successful brands are perceived by the target audience as the only solution to a particular need. This insight by Frankel highlights two critical components of an effective brand-'awareness and relevance'.

MARKET TRENDS: WHAT IS UP?

The emergence of hyper-competition has transferred power to customers and retailers. One way to retain customers is to develop a holistic relationship with them through brand relationship management, and the main branding challenge from global perspective is to *evangelize its customers from 'brand loyals to brand enthusiasts'*, for every marketing maverick knows that his company needs satisfied customers which is necessary condition for customer loyalty but not a sufficient one. Breathing for a brand in knowledge economy has become a bit tough and a byte uneasy. Brand driven companies like Hindustan Levers and Colgate are struggling to defend their market share and the result is still weak topline growth. The domestic slogging is causing customers to downtrade putting pressure on higher-value branded products. Though Hindustan Lever has in fact announced a power brand strategy in order to avoid spending time and money on weak regional brands and focus instead on winners in its entire portfolio.

Fragmentation is pervasive not only in markets but in media too, which is accruing to the heap of problems for building and sustaining brands. Ten years back, most advertisers could flaunt in a national market via Doordarshan. Now with numerous media vehicle and media types, innumerable players are passionately contributing to cost escalation for the companies. With clients demanding greater value for money and brand losing steam in a tough market, even ad agencies like Rediffusion DY & R, Leo Burnett, FCB Ulka et al are trying to be more than mere creative shops and they are busy innovating and delivering new tools for old brands by bringing in their global branding philosophies like- Brand Asset Valuator (BAV), Brand Belief System (BBS), Chess Team respectively.

DESCRYING GLOBAL-INDIAN CUSTOMERS

At another level there is no question that there is a paradigm shift in the customer-buying pattern in this current economy. They are becoming more sophisticated ipso facto their rising expectations. According to Jean- Francois Nebel of consulting firm Accenture, customers are showing interest in innovative products and customized services. With global brands flirting and enticing their senses, their heightened awareness oscillates amidst the spate of choices available, the tremendous sense of freedom to access the options. As an outcome they are becoming unpredictable and clandestine in their flavours, fragrances, tastes, needs and preferences, demand more value from the brands, and contemplate at the probability of perceived value before they decide to pay a premium price.

Knowledge economy has bestowed his customers with loads of information, myriad choices, greater accessibility, expanded zone of freedom, added convenience and thus honed and grilled them to be more smart and intellectual. Isn't this a vivid indicator for the companies to invest in their brands with more meaning in a holistic sense, and definitely only those brands will thrive which will be able to create most compelling, adorable and consistent experience for their customers, which is only possible if efforts from every chunk of the organization are aligned and synchronized. The depth across the length and breadth of the relationship between the brand and the customer is the foundation of bond betwixt the two, the intensity of which would determine the brand belief for ongoing success and sustained competitive advantage despite of the presence of disruptive forces in the marketplace.

DIAGNOSING BRAND HEALTH

Managers need a strategy to capitalize on the potential of their brands by examining the brand report card, which will highlight the areas which need to be strengthened and concurrently a piece of wisdom where brands need not to be extended beyond their natural limits (despite of the marketing folklore and companies reluctant to stop experimenting this).

Coca-cola started life in 1886 as a soda foundation beverage- a typical local or store brand, and one could witness its prolific spread. Bottling was not an initial priority. In fact two attorneys bought the bottling rights for most of the US for a handsome $1. Nokia was originally a brand of paper and cardboard. It predates coke, tracing its origin back to 1865. Today, it is the world's eighth most valuable brand worth $24 billion. Nokia has been named Manufacturer of the Year at a prestigious mobile phone industry awards ceremony and was presented with the coveted title at the Mobile News Awards held in London on March 17, 2005. So this voyage from a small beginning to a big cheese is an experiencing and experimenting venture.

SKIRMISHING GLOBAL CHALLENGES

Brands confront and combat innumerable challenges in order to live and earn a living. Several strategies could be drafted taking into consideration the following aspects-

Are You Inside the Choice Set? The goal of branding is to get your intuition included in the choice set. Your most important audiences must recognize you as the solution to a need they have. Hence for a brand to be within the consideration set two key components are-'Awareness and Relevance'.

Awareness implies that among 3,000 or so other messages the customer receives in a day, did your audience members notice yours? Did the message figured the ground, did it stood out from the background clutter, did the audience know how and when to respond? Second the relevance constituent, which comes into action after the message is noticed. Did members of your audience begin to sense how the message and you might begin to fill the 'need gap', is the message germane and pertinent to them? Did it have its roots on previous messages? Did it lay groundwork for the future message- did it create a relationship? The branding truism thus is-'the most precious resource of all is someone's attention'.

From Interruption Marketing to Permission Marketing: Movement from one set of circumstances called interruption marketing to another named permission marketing is perhaps one of the most important outcomes of a branding strategy. By interruption marketing you carve and creep your way into the minds of your target audience. The audience is hit with spate of messages after messages. More messages. More ads. More direct mails. However with permission marketing you have done a research, segmented the audience, filtered and refined the offer and used messaging to meticulously weave a network of relationship over time. You have become a partner.

With interruption marketing you are rebuffed, scorned or ignored. With permission marketing you are invited.

Personal Involvement with Brands: Branding is about building and eventually owing a position. Over time you might move from no position to the position you want to hold or from a position you do to a position you want. This sounds easy but it isn't. On one hand brands are difficult to map and establish in this global village but once positioned, a brand and its perceptions that surround, it can be extremely difficult and expensive to disrupt the aura.

Philip Kotler and Karen Fox note that people often develop a high level of personal involvement with their favourite brands and this is backed up by handful of 'laws' among which two in particular are relevant for this conversation-

- The cost to carry out the decision involves major personal and economic sacrifices.
- There's considerable group pressure to make a particular choice or to act in a particular way, and the consumer is strongly motivated to meet the expectations of these peer and reference groups.

The more intense is the halo of positive assumptions, vibes and experiences that builds trust and confidence the higher is the degree of psychological fastening with the brands. The more personal stories and anecdotes that are associated with your brand, the more alive your brand becomes. After all brands are like people- they have a personality, they reflect opinions, have their individual distinct appearances, possess non-similar intonations and tones and bear experiences.

It was year 1895 when King Camp stood before his shaving mirror and just then a thought struck him. His cut-throat razor was performing its job well as usual, but so little of the entire blade was actually used in the process and he wondered about a new type of blade, one practically all edge which minimizes the chances of injuries and cuts to almost negligible and then he pondered to make it all disposable too. So if he could manufacture a blade that was sleek, slim, flat, efficient, disposable and economic then it would definitely induce a market pull. Did I forget to mention that King Camp's surname was Gillette? A good story wrapping a brand, intrinsic to its identity, is an effective way to generate consumer understanding and loyalty.

Building a Brand by Living its Values: Very true said Nirmalaya Kumar, professor of marketing at the fifth Retail Summit organized by KSA Technopack in Mumbai-"values are what is important to companies like Disney and Starbucks. The latter follows a no-ads policy. The challenge lies in capturing the value of the brand and these companies live by the maxim-'Don't advertise the brand-live it".

Marketing brands is increasingly becoming complex for it faces challenges like value- driven consumers who look to buy the cheapest products without compromising quality, hence a dire and rigorous search for a distinctive image in the face of commercial products and retail power is indispensable. Evolution too is necessary for the companies, like P&G has continuously evolved over the years. The evolution is achieved by a lot of initiatives. These include eliminating marginal brands, reducing SKU, controlled new product introductions et al.

Branding Beyond Brandnames: Brand has to build around a philosophy than on certain product attributes and yes its not an easy game, for the society will severely test the philosophy that the corporate brand stood for, and B Muthuraman, MD Tata Steel holds similar consideration. He affirms that one of the key question which determines the long term sustenance of a corporate brand is whether the corporation is meeting societal objectives and whether it has returned some wealth to society in one form or another. Hence powerful brands are sensed through touch, taste, smell, sight and sound. It encompasses everything that affects the emotional tie between the brand and your customers. Its much more beyond controlling colours, fonts, design and the language of your press releases. Hence to create long lasting brands, companies have to build the right kind of experiences around them and these experiences must be consistent across all points of contact, via which moments of truth emanate.

New Munitions for Old Brands: What is happening to brands is happening to ad agencies too, realizing that their services are in the danger of being commoditized, too.

Leo Burnett CEO, Arvind Sharma says: "Brand Belief is to the twenty-first century what 'positioning' was to the twentieth. You might position yourself to be whatever you are, but if you build a healthy relationship with the consumer by living up to a promise, over a period of time, he/she starts believing to you, whatever your positioning. In that sense, your positioning becomes redundant". Challenging some long held beliefs is its Brand Belief System (BBS). The agency believes that the key elements of marketing success are "brand believers" and "brand bonds". The stronger the belief the stronger the bond. On similar veins Ogilvy and Mather uses two tools –Brand Scan and Brand Audit- to deliver more value. After all Customer choice is a sine qua non for business.

Understanding Customer Pain Points: All done to lure customer, but in vain. Again the company is confronted with the same old problems-declining market share, plummeting sales, customer migration and as a result shrinking profits. Where then do companies falter? The answer-corporate lose sight of the basics when it comes to customer management. "We often see some of the worst value creation practices happening from time to time. Most of the initiatives like sending greeting cards and mails to customer only add the frills. They seldom address the pain points", says Rama Bijapurkar of Strategic Marketing Consultancy. No one tries to look at what can be done to improve the service and prevent this from happening next time.

Hence while framing a global branding strategy following five key ideas are to be considered and integrated –

- Your brand is sum of experiences that your customers have whenever they are exposed to moments of truth interfacing your product and this gives your brand depth and endurance.
- You have to control your brand if experiences are planned and conform to your vision. At this level branding is strategic not tactical
- Your brand is consistent if these experiences all convey and say the same thing to your audience and this will generate brand conformity across all venues experiencing great synergy
- Your brand is working if these experience create the desired impression in the minds, hearts and books of your target audience, and this impression is one of

relevance

- Your brand is successful if the perceptions you have created make people act in a right way, which means that do people follow through? Do they demand? do they commit?

BRANDING PERSPECTIVES IN KNOWLEDGE ECONOMY

The LPG era has dovetailed every zone of this living planet to some extent, the result of which is buyer's market replaced by sellers', whereby several brands are vying there chunk out of the coveted pie. The IT boom has made the information availability very easy hence it becomes imperative for the seller to gain knowledge about the customer's needs, socio-economic background and dynamics of decision making to survive.

Enablers of Knowledge Economy: Cable TV and Internet among many other factors have intensified the advent of knowledge economy, for it has played a vital role as a dissemination medium, in a country like India by transcending across all geographical and socio-economic boundaries and creeped inside customers' living rooms. The Cable TV offered unprecedented choice of channel types, from entertainment, news, music, history and inventions to animal planet and this was the impetus behind large-scale customer awareness.

Internet too altogether opened a new chapter in quest for more knowledge. With a click of mouse customer could attain and drench himself into the knowledge ocean. And this unleashed their global aspirations. The interface of developing countries with the developed ones made them realize that future is no ahead of them it has already happened somewhere and the difference lies in the extent of penetration, and pace of acceptance. This ignited the aspirations of customers to consider and recognize brands of international repute, having a stamp of global familiarity or else the realistic chances of survival are almost negligible. The enlightened customer is reluctant to accept any model, which was not successful in world market. Now the task of the brand is to look straight into the eyes of its customers and sense his latent covert needs with a deeper understanding of the changing dynamics.

No doubt the awareness phenomenon was initiated by the brands themselves but once set in, the Herculean task lies in keep going the chain reaction and though the process has started with premium products it would percolate down towards mass products. Contrary to the fact that earlier the chief wage earner in the family always had his way in the matter of household purchases but the scenario has taken a rotation where other members in the family too, backed up by the market information, have access to the choice inventory. Indian youth is considered to be hit and affected by the western winds and like a rebellion questions the basics of Indian culture. And it's the clash against the cultural backdrop that India boasted. Still Coke had understood this "global-aspirations-with-Indian-undertones phenomenon" and was able to tap the potential audience. Understanding the complex psyche of consumer is perhaps the elixir for survival. Branding global or domestic is akin to performing matrimony of your brand with your customer for germinating a lifetime relationship.

Hence the consumer need to know and must be made aware about the following information search parameters-

Physical attributes (e.g. how well does the product perform, how competitive is its price, what functional and emotional benefits it delivers etc.) may require some adaptation to local market conditions and culture: A US laundry detergent (which does not contain perborate) may not satisfy a European housewife, used to washing her laundry at near-boiling temperatures; similarly green monochrome computer monitors may not satisfy the German hacker, who prefers an amber screen.

Style (i.e., how the physical-attributes message is delivered) is even more rooted in culture. Germans, whose ad culture grew from magazines, want hard facts. Latin cultures are inclined to imagery and may resist hard sell. Asians are sensitive to symbolism, Britons to humor, etc. There is some truth to these generalities, even though the rules are often successfully broken.

Character communication is the key element of branding and the backbone of a global branding strategy. It requires an absolute consistency of purpose which one can only achieve by having, at the onset of the communication planning, a very clear idea of the set of values to be linked to the brand. A McDonald's commercial from the US, Germany, Brazil or Japan is readily recognized as a McDonald's commercial, even though it may have been produced locally, and by a different ad agency. It will consistently convey some or all of the values (service, friendliness, understanding of family life etc.), which are attached to the company.

FRAMING GLOBAL BRANDING STRATEGY

Competition is a complex series of moves and countermoves on a global landscape. But what's the best opening move?

"Competing with multinationals can be considered a big game of chess, with each engagement with a competitor broken into an opening, a middle game, and an endgame. In this excerpt, the authors set out best moves for an effective opening. "

Competition among multinationals these days is likely to be a three-dimensional game of global chess: the moves an organization makes in one market are designed to achieve goals in another market in ways that aren't immediately apparent to rivals. We call this approach "competing under strategic interdependence," or CSI. And where this strategic interdependence exists, the complexity of the competitive situation can quickly overwhelm ordinary analysis. As strategists have learned from game theory, the results of any move a player makes stem in large part from the choices his opponent makes. Often those results are nonlinear—that is, out of proportion to the events that provoke them. Furthermore, they might happen far away from the apparent sphere of competition, like the proverbial butterfly that flaps its wings in New York and causes a tsunami in Japan. Most business strategists are terrible at anticipating the consequences of interdependent choices, and they're even worse at using interdependency to their advantage.

With the following mapping tools and techniques, one can have an insight of the whole chessboard—that is, you can anticipate how the moves you make in one market can influence competitive interactions not only in that market but in others far situated prospective and potential markets.

THE OPENING

To uncover—and ultimately exploit—the interdependencies between you and your competitors, you need a clear understanding of your own product categories and the geographic arenas you operate in. So the first step in the CSI process is to set up a table that reflects all your assets and all the territories you compete in. For an example of this, let's consider Unilever, a European consumer-goods manufacturer. The company's well-known brands include Knorr soups, Dove soap, and Snuggle fabric softener.

Unilever competes in three principal product categories—foods, personal care, and fabric care—and in three major global geographic arenas—Europe, the Americas, and the Asia-Pacific-Africa region. In most of those categories and in all of those territories, Unilever's principal rival is U.S.-based Procter & Gamble, makers of Folgers coffee, Pampers diapers, and Tide laundry detergent. Unilever company competes in nine different product and geographic arenas.

Unilever's executives could then drill down further and draw up CSI tables for each product group, for specific types of products within those groups, and for different geographic arenas. For instance, if the company's personal-care group were thinking through its global positioning prospects, a manager in that unit might look at the competition more narrowly, by product type. The personal-care group is responsible for products in the following categories: oral care, grooming, infant hygiene, feminine hygiene, and senior hygiene. So if we continue analyzing Unilever's business opportunities in the same three geographic regions (for simplicity's sake), we see that the personal-care group competes in fifteen different arenas.

Once you've created your tables, the second step in the CSI process is to take a rigorous look at where you stand relative to your main competitor in each arena. The best way to do that is to analyze three important factors: your competitor's potential *reactiveness* to increased pressure in that arena; the arena's *attractiveness* to you; and the *relative clout* each of you brings to the table.

Reactiveness measures how much incentive your competitor has to counter your move. It is based on several subfactors, including your competitor's market share in a particular business arena (the larger the share, the greater the arena's importance to your competitor) and the arena's profitability (the more profitable the arena, the more incentive your rival has to defend it). The final subfactor, your competitor's emotional attachment to the arena, is more difficult to ascertain, but it can be as critical a consideration as share and profitability. Essentially, you should be looking for any non-economic factor that would make your competitor more likely to want to protect the arena—for instance, national or corporate pride, the historical significance of the arena, and any significant sunk costs.

The ultimate purpose of this mapping technique is to help managers plan competitive campaigns in multiple markets, but it is useful for other reasons. Attractiveness, in this scheme, is the mirror image of reactiveness. It's the measure of how important the arena is to you and is based on the same subfactors as reactiveness: How much market share do you have in the arena? How profitable is it? How emotionally attached to it are you?

Relative clout, the third factor, measures who's in a better position to launch, or defend against, a strategic move in the arena. Clout can be determined by looking at the relative sales of a company and its competitor, then adjusting for other factors such as each party's distribution dominance or technology advantages. (Clout measures the ability to fight back, while reactiveness measures the propensity to fight back.)

There's a site that offers the methodology and formulas for measuring reactiveness, attractiveness, and relative clout based on publicly available information—things like a company's individual product sales, a product division's performance compared with that of the rest of the organization, the company's sales in a particular region of the country or the world, and so on. The end result will be numerical ratings for reactiveness, attractiveness, and clout—numbers you can use in the third step of the CSI process, mapping the competitive terrain on a bubble chart. To do this, first plot your competitor's reactiveness along the horizontal axis. Reactiveness increases from left to right, so bubbles further to the right indicate arenas that are more important to that competitor, also known as the defender. Then plot the arena's attractiveness to you along the vertical axis. The higher the bubble, the more attractive the arena is to you. The size of a bubble indicates the defender's market clout—the bigger the bubble, the stronger the competitor. The chart may end up looking something like this:

The bubble chart is useful because it quickly conveys a great deal of information about two competitors' relative positions. For instance, bubble **b** in the upper left appears to be the most appealing arena for the instigator, the company that wants to make an opening move. The size and position of the bubble indicate that this arena is highly attractive to the instigator and that any strategic ploy it launches in this arena would prompt relatively little reaction from the defender. Conversely, the least appealing arena for the instigator is represented by bubble **e**, because it reflects low attractiveness to the instigator and the highest reactiveness score on the chart for the competitor—a promise of much pain for little gain.

Choices get more difficult when comparing bubbles like **d** and **e.** Bubble **d** suggests that this arena would prompt less of a reaction by the defender than bubble **e** would, but the defender has more clout in this product or geographic arena. The instigator would have to make a judgment call about which arena, **d** or **e,** it would best be able to defend from a competitor's retaliation.

The ultimate purpose of this mapping technique is to help managers plan competitive campaigns in multiple markets, but it is useful for other reasons. First, it allows a company to look at its world through its competitor's eyes. Second, the mapping technique can be employed at several levels of granularity to expose competitive opportunities and weaknesses that might not otherwise be evident.

Companies can build charts that focus on smaller geographic areas, such as states or even cities, if the data are available. Even in highly concentrated industries such as consumer soft drinks, where Coca-Cola and Pepsi control 76 percent of the U.S. market, competitive battles are planned down to the level of individual supermarkets in individual cities; the price of a twelve-pack in a suburb of Oakland on Superbowl Sunday is of genuine importance to the outcome of the competitive battle. For companies with less global reach than Unilever, P&G, Coca-Cola, and Pepsi, charting will likely start at a national or regional level.

It's also possible to plot several competitors in each arena to fully understand the dimensions of the competitive landscape. The vertical axis would continue to measure only the instigator's attractiveness scores. The reactiveness scores would then be used to place different competitors along the horizontal axis of the chart, using different colors to identify each competitor. Bubble size would indicate each competitor's clout relative to the instigator—not relative to the other competitors.

CONCLUSION

Think of P&G or Johnson & Johnson (even a new value proposition), do you feel the stimulus of high quality? Isn't it that the tag "made in America" adds strong connotations of quality even if the product is not mad but only assembled in US? Take the case of Levi's or Ray Ban, doesn't it arouse strong aspirational connotations, because of the associations the brand carries and this will let the brand not only command a premium over its competitors but defend itself at the time of adversity too. Such is the spell bound aura of branding.

What brand managers are supposed to do? They must first spot the scotoma-, which is essentially a blind spot, and—as a brand owner—having a blind spot can be fatal to your brand. When the owner focuses too intently on working in his business (as the technical expert) instead of on his business the blind spot develops. Competitive myopia occurs when companies do not monitor their competitors systematically. Competitor information needs constant updating. At least one person should be dedicated to competitor intelligence. Look at probabilities to assess what the competition's next moves will be. The crux is that the brand has to visualize beyond the espying premises and has to dig deep into the minds of its customers in order to volatize the blind spot.

The onset of media of knowledge dissemination has changed typecasts and established practices for the Indian customers. There is a sweeping change in the value orientations, roles and inter-family (or inter-organisation) dynamics. This has brought about some fundamental changes in the way the customers look at and prefer brands. The biggest challenge for the brands is to understand the new market environment and decide the strategies to succeed. The process of change is still not over and only those brands that think of future and act in present are likely to be successful.

Global marketers need to first write a thorough and sustainable Brand Strategy which lists the character traits intended for the brand. Then they should set up an organization which can tactfully direct, teach and evaluate the brand's communication to ensure consistency while at the same time preserving the autonomy (and thereby the quality) of local management.

Let your customers fall in love with your brand and let this legend of romance and courtship culminate in a pious matrimony, betwixt the two, taking away the *share of heart* before *share of mind.*

GLOBALISATION AND BUSINESS MANAGEMENT WITH SPECIAL REFERENCE TO BANGLADESH

Anwar Hossain

INTRODUCTION

Management is the most important factor for economic development of any country. In today's global economy the dynamic role of management can hardly be exaggerated. Harnessing the natural resources, producing crops, exploiting the queries, running business enterprises, and providing the basic amenities of life and above all utilizing the human resources all depend on effective use of knowledge on management. In fact management touches every facet of our life. In this contemporary world rapid progress has been taking place in all spheres of our life due to the splendid synergistic combination of science, technology and management.

GLOBALIZATION

We all understand that globalization is a process of interaction among people, business houses and governments of different countries mainly driven by international trade, investment and augmented by information technology. If we view the recent trend of globalization we see an amazing change that is taking place. Volume of world trade grew by 25 times since 1950. Foreign investment in a single year is now close to 1 trillion dollar. The regional blocks and number of free trade associations like, EEU, NAFTA, ASEAN, BIMSTEC and SAARC is more than 200. In fact the pace at which globalization is taking place in today's world it has really become unstoppable.

At present the world is witnessing a rapid change in all fields of human civilization. The world we knew is shrinking fast paving the way for globalization. In the backdrop of powerful trade and business interests political boundaries are tumbling, geographical obstacles are being leveled down and cultural barriers are being won in a highly competitive world of today. Economic integration among regional blocks is emerging one after another; political boundaries are transcended by such collaboration and cooperation among nations, governments, business houses and social and cultural organizations. Media is playing a powerful role in this process of economic and cultural integration. The open sky invasion of the satellite channel and the cable network has brought the world much closer than before. The overall global trade is increasing phenomenally every year and after. In business the process of going global is largely marked by increasing volume of export and import and greater number of licensing, franchising, strategic alliances, joint venture and setting up of foreign subsidiaries by business houses. Thomas Friedman while describing the trend of globalization summed it up in one sentence that globalization is "farther, faster, cheaper, and deeper."

MANAGEMENT IMPLICATIONS OF GLOBALIZATION

Such changes of galvanic proportion stated above demand a dynamic role of management. Management is dynamic when it is proactive not reactive. A set of managers who smells changes ahead, projects its path and trajectory and stands right there to face it with preparedness of an impending disaster is the one to survive. Those who fail to do so are destined to exit from the corporate world. For today's managers change has emerged as the only constant and the rests are variables. In the backdrop of this crazy time and crazy world as Tom Peter suggested the life cycle of many products has been reduced many fold into weeks from years. Naturally this change driven growth leaves no complacency for management to bask on the sun of their newfound success as some competitor is waiting round the corner to displace their product and or their business.

Mangers of today must always be on guard and ready to adopt change. Sometimes the changes are taking place from within sometimes the organizations are being swept away by changes from around and environment. Fortune smiles on the companies, which can anticipate the wind of change and place their organization and product in line with that. Those who fail to do that become a memory of the past and soon pass into oblivion.

Like the flight of capital labour is also flying although at a slower pace. At present about 80.9 million workers are out in the foreign land. Chinese workers are working in 160 countries of the world so are Indians, Pakistani's and Bangladeshi's

In this age of cutting edge skill, competition is the name of the game and management must be dynamic and ready to face the changes squarely. This ability to adjust to the changing environment makes or breaks a company. Changes might creep in silently or it may come abruptly swamping the organization like an avalanche and in both cases management must not remain unprepared. How little preparedness for catastrophe we have has been laid bare by the recent tsunami that struck the tourist industry by surprise. It will take years for the tourism industry to recoup the losses it suffered.

Management needs to be proactive in anticipating changes that may come from the standpoint of customers, competitors or from the changes in the technology or environment. In today's world drastic change is taking place due to globalization and rapid development of technology. The global economy now witnesses flight of capital from place to place, country to country in search of new market, cheap labour and wholesome profit. The strong resurgence of Asian economy and the galloping pace of economic development of China, India, Vietnam and host of other countries in the region has raised the hopes of millions for a better standard of living and alleviation of poverty. There is no denying the fact that the engine of growth in these nations had been the private sector and giant corporate house, which now expanded their businesses to many other countries.

Multinational and transnational companies now dominate the global economy, the popular mode of joint venture and strategic alliance; licensing and franchising all are indications of global networking.

Our subcontinent is a perfect testimony to the fact that government policies affect the process of globalization. To attract global capital or foreign investment countries in our subcontinent have laid down attractive concessions and investment packages. The government of Bangladesh has set up Export Processing Zones (EPZ) with most liberal incentives and policies for investment and has obtained a remarkable success. China and India have also opened up there economy for the foreign investment with phenomenal success.

ROLE OF WTO AND GLOBAL PARTNERSHIP

WTO, which was created by Uruguay Round negotiations to replace GATT in 1995, is a body to deal with rules of trade between the nations. Since inception it has been an object of controversy with respect to its dominance by the rich nations. Critics point out to the fact that its obsession to free market economy and its role to work as catalyst to economic integration will benefit the rich nations rather than the poor nations. As a platform of 147 nations WTO is the only global organization that deals with rules of trade among nations. In view of that it can play a major role in building global partnership if the inequalities are addressed properly and the interests of the developing countries are not bartered away in the name of free market competition.

POST MFA PERIOD

From the 1st of January this year the multi fiber agreement has come into effect removing the quota system of RMG products in USA. For Bangladeshi RMG companies this is a big challenge. They no longer enjoy the quota and have to compete with China and India for the same products in a free market. Although this change was announced much ahead it will depend on the dynamism of Bangladeshi managers whether they can really survive this challenge. Early statistics show the downward trend in export order to US market of Bangladeshi RMG products whereas the Chinese RMG export has risen steeply in the same market. Needless to say that not all changes will come in phases and with prior warning.

BUILDING GLOBAL PARTNERSHIP IN BUSINESS

Obviously business puts top priority on building global partnership in order to expand their market. Multinational companies are going for huge investment wherever they see profitability. The phenomenal improvement in telecommunication and information technology has made the world financial market to grow, expand and intensify at a pace unheard of before. The ease and speed of transaction of money in the international market has made the international trade deal easier and smoother. The highly aggressive international banks have truly become global by putting their branches in the streets of far - flung cities.

The financial network along with the infrastructure development in telecommunications through submarine cable and satellite connection have revolutionized the system and immensely increased the scope for building global partnership. Under the new set up the list of possibilities is endless. Global tnership in the information technology is a reality now where unique features comparative advantage exist along with decreasing labour cost.

The horizon of telecommunication is also an open field where much can be done to accelerate the pace of development of the developing countries where the tele-density is one of the lowest in the world. The case of Bangladesh can be cited as an example where joint venture between Telenor, a Norwegian tele-company, Marubeni, a Japanese company and Grameen Bank of Bangladesh have set up Grameen Phone a cell phone company which already attained a total client of 2.5 million raising the tele-density of the country to a substantial level and empowered the impoverished village women.

Similarly in context of pharmaceutical industry, biotechnology and genetic engineering building global partnership can work wonder provided the partnership are forged with more egalitarian relationship rather than purely commercial motive of profiteering. In 1982 Bangladesh undertook a pragmatic drug policy, which set the foundation for the growth of its indigenous pharmaceutical industries shunning the earlier dependence on multinational companies for medicine. The result is that the pharmaceutical industry of

Bangladesh has rapidly developed producing ninety percent of its domestic demand for medicine and also having surplus for export.

In the case of Agro-based industry I think we should look from the standpoint of the developing countries where the stakes are really high since the economy of these countries are highly dependent on agriculture. If I am allowed to take the case of Bangladesh once again where agriculture even now contributes 24% to the Gross Domestic Production (GDP) but engages 65% of our labour force, consequently agro based industries are going to touch upon the lives of millions. One should be little cautious however, before making such observation in view of the fact that the 2004 world indicator published by world bank while reviewing the world economy stated that by and large developing countries are gradually shaking off their dependence on agriculture sector and switching over to manufacturing and service sector as the engine of growth. Agro-based industries offer a big promise for quick and expansive expansion in manufacturing concern.

Agro-based industries offer a great prospect to the countries like India, Bangladesh, China and Vietnam having a large mass of population. Marginal and subsistence farmers can obtain relatively higher prices for their commodities when agri-business thrives. However, the same conclusion cannot be drawn in terms of labourers of agro-based industries. Although flourishing agro-business industries may provide job opportunities it may not completely free them from exploitation. (Matiur Rahman & Raymond Wiest, contest and trends of globalization in Bangladesh: A critical agenda, UPL, 2003)

An interesting feature of agro-based industries in Bangladesh is that its products are exported globally. Since the ethnic Bengalis living abroad are the primary customers of the Bangladeshi agro-based products agro-based industries have great export potential. PRAAN a leading agro-based industry in Bangladesh exports its products to fifty different countries. I am sure same situation prevails with the agro-based industries in India.

One of the major beneficiaries of increased globalization has been the entertainment industry. It has really thrived over the years in view of the open access through the sky and the direct link through the Internet. Millions of viewers can now watch their favorite channels and listen to the music they like. The industry as such has changed a lot. Joint collaboration in this sector is also driven by the needs of the people, their taste and their cultural ramifications along with the new technology that has emerged.

Typically there are strong resistances to change. This is quite expected. Many organizations just follow the dictum, "if it is working don't fix it." But one should also remember "what is working today may not work tomorrow." Global economy is changing so should the management to adapt to the change. One should also remember that as there are strong proponents of globalization there are strong opponents of it as well. Those who oppose globalization blame the rich nations and the giant multinationals for their hardcore commercialism, brutal exploitation of natural resources and consequent environmental degradation. They insist that through the process of globalization the rich becomes richer and the poor poorer. However, the latest world development indicators show that while in 2002 the world economy grew by 1.9 percent lower- middle-income economies saw the fastest growth.

CONCLUSION

In fact time has come to accept the change and mold it for better rather than resist it and be crushed under the avalanche of globalization. Our purpose of life will be better served and our wisdom will be better utilized if we build the bridge of friendship and cooperation, mutual trust and adhere to the age old golden rule of "win and win' rather than win and lose in a world where we all are mutually interdependent.

However, all that said and done let me share with you the voice of the teeming millions who are not represented here today but for all practical purpose who are our backbone and who deserve a much better deal than they receive and conclude with the following observation. Globalization is welcome if it is for people not for business alone, if it is for reasonable profit not for exploitation, if it is for peace and not for aggression if it is for improving the quality of our life and not for environmental, moral and spiritual degradation.

PERCEPTIONS ABOUT GENDER DISCRIMINATION AGAINST WOMEN AT WORKPLACE

Kashif-Ur-Rehman, Nasir Ahmed, Muhammad Shahbaz Shabbir and Muhammad Iqbal Saif

This paper explores the perceptions and existence of gender discrimination at work place. A sample of 96 male and female in age group of 19 to 51 years of age from 17 organizations was taken. The questionnaire data analyzed conformed that women do experience discrimination at work place.

INTRODUCTION

Discrimination involves classifying people into different groups (the criteria for differentiation, e.g. gender, race, or class) and according to the members of each class distinct and typically unequal treatments, rights and obligations.

Discrimination generally refers to treating one group of people differently- in a negative way- from another on such grounds as their race (racism), sex (sexism), religion (religious discrimination), ethnic background, disability, sexual orientation, preference, or behavior, or political views. Generally, the aggrieved group is considered by the discriminator as inferior to others.

Discrimination has been a controversial issue in the workplace environment from many decades (Ingkapattanakul & Kleiner, 2001). Discrimination might take place in terms of recruitment, hiring, firing, promotion, employment benefit, working conditions, and treatment with the employees.

Gender – the division of society into male and female – is in many ways the most important discriminator because it cuts across and supplements all the other criteria. Mostly women feel the consequences of gender inequality. Men are simply carved out when biased ness is discussed. "But wait," you will say, "men are not invisible. They are everywhere!" Quite true. Men are ubiquitous in universities, in organizations, and in the public sphere in general. Most people would not dispute that men constitute the overwhelming majority of corporate executives and CEOs, attorneys and law professors, members of collegiate boards of trustees, and state, local, and national legislators (Kimmel, 1998).

Discussions in everyday life are almost exclusively on men in their public activities. Men are discussed as political leaders, military heroes, scientists, writers, artists, and the like. By contrast, when women are discussed at all, the class almost always includes a discussion of femininity, about how the women's experiences as women influenced their experiences in their public activities. It is in this sense that men themselves are invisible as men.

Thus gender is everywhere, and yet masculinity is oddly invisible. It is now understood that gender is one of the central organizing principles around which social life revolves, and one of the basic building blocks of an individual's identity (Lips, 1988). In past generations, social scientists listed class and race as their major categories that defined and delimited social life (Nicholson, 1986). But today, gender has joined race and class in the basic understanding of the foundations of an individual's identity. Gender remains one of the basic criteria for allocation and distribution of rewards in society. It is one of the chief lenses through which we explain economics, social, or political inequality and discrimination. It is a major mode of explanation of everything from sexual behavior to

Voting preferences, and one of the fundamental ways in which to measure social responses.

The problem of gender inequality in the workplace is globally recognized. However, the need for research on this topic in a country like Pakistan is firstly it is a male dominating society and secondly, research on this topic in this geographical area is rare as because it is regarded a sensitive issue.

Consequently, the purpose of the study is to explore the perceptions of men and women regarding this concept. Not only to see how they perceive gender inequality but more importantly to check whether they even accept the presence of the phenomenon at workplace. Furthermore what practices make up gender discrimination in the workplace.

REVIEW OF LITERATURE

Gender discrimination is still a pervasive issue in today's work place for women (Lowry, 1998; Wozencraft, 1999). Gender discrimination has received much attention in economics, sociology, and psychology literatures (Truman & Baroudi, 1994). Economic research often attempts to explain discriminatory practices, i.e. wage and job-level inequalities, by looking at employees in terms of human capital and addressing differences in capital formation as reasons for such inequalities (Darity & Mason, 1998). From a sociological perspective, Bielby and Baron (1986) have questioned the nondiscriminatory structural explanation that women are disproportionately employed in lower paying occupations or smaller, lower wage paying firms. The psychological perspective focuses on cognitive, perceptual, and behavioral biases that can lead to gender discrimination concerning pay, promotions, or job responsibilities (Wright, Ferris, Hiller, & Kroll, 1995). This includes analyses of the impact of biasing factors such as stereotyping based on gender roles (Konrad & Cannings, 1997) or statistical discrimination (Lyness & Judiesch, 1999)and or Perceptions previously held about working women

To examine the impact of gender discrimination of working women, it is important first to consider the attitudes generally held regarding women. Unlike attitudes regarding other stigmatized groups, attitudes regarding women have been found to be surprisingly positive (Eagly & Mladinic, 1989). But this positive bias in favor of women may not extend to women in nontraditional roles. Attitudes toward women in leadership positions are often quite negative (Eagly, Makhijani, & Klonsky, 1992; Glick & Fiske, 1996). Recent theoretical work on the social psychology of Sexism suggests that certain forms of modern Sexism exclude women from high-status roles (e.g. leaders, employers), as well as protect and revere women in traditional roles (e.g. mothering, nurturing), without the antipathy often associated with prejudice. Thus, individuals may simultaneously hold positive attitudes about women, yet negative attitudes about women who take on nontraditional, high-status roles.

The divergence of practice and impression of gender distinctions reveal that gender inequality is still persistent in organizational practices while a dominant perception of equality occurs at the same time (Benschop & Doorewaard, 1998). Organizations that usually claim to encourage equal employment make periodical reports on the wide gaps between males and females working in the same organization. These reports show differences in compensation, as well as low representation in many departments, and greater difficulty for women in balancing family and work responsibilities (Wright and Perrone, 1977). These reports are, however, created by male decision makers, thus they just "feel" that women cannot bear the burden of home and work simultaneously.

A total of hundred individuals (50 men and 50 women) volunteered to participate in the study. In the final analysis, 96 of those questionnaires were returned. This response rate (96%) is consistent with similar surveys of professionals (Wunder & Wynn, 1988;McNevin, Leichner, Harper, & McCrimmon, 1985). The participants were recruited from public and private organizations in Islamabad. Seventeen Public and Private organizations were randomly selected from Islamabad.

Perception of gender inequality scenarios was assessed with a two-part questionnaire. In the first part we asked regarding existence of gender discrimination. Demographic question regarding gender was also asked in this part. In order to prevent participants from trying to give gender-conscious response, they were not asked their name (Steinpreis, Ritzke and Anders, 1999).

Participants encountered a question with 9 different scenarios (Rosell and Hartman, 2001). The scenarios portrayed discrimination from the workplace due to individuals' perceptions. Participants were asked to rate their views about current gender discrimination issues in their respective work places, for example, "Women are not as qualified as men in organizations". The participants then answered on a five-point scale from strongly agree to strongly disagree to the scenario if she or he had felt something similar to the scenario or not.

Participants rated their level of agreement with nine items (Rosell & Hartman, 2001) designed by us to assess attitudes regarding the existence of gender discrimination in the organizations on a 5-point Likert-type scale ranging from(1 to 5), 1 = strongly agree, 2 = agree, 3 = neither, 4 = disagree and 5 = strongly disagree.

The nine items were basically one-line statements to be assessed. These statements contained the common view that the society held about working women. Each participant had to show his or her level of agreement to each of the statements. The nine statements were for men and women to see the divergence in their perceptions and views they held about each item.

Again following Keller(2001) an Independent sample t-test (p=0.05, two-tailed) was used to see group difference in terms of discrimination they had experienced in the workplace due to different scenarios presented to them. Levine's Results were checked on 95% Confidence.

The analysis was done to see how men and women agree or differ on a certain view. Thus for each statement, the perceptions of men and women were measured separately. This was done to see the strength of agreement of men and women individually on a common statement.

The participants filled out the questionnaires in their own organizational setting. One type of questionnaire was distributed to the males and the females so that the responses could be compared against common questions asked. Participants were also allowed to ask any questions during that time.

As employees at all levels were studied, we had to make sure that each participant clearly understood the contents of the questionnaire. That did not seem to be a problem for the middle and upper level employees. However, the lower level employees did seem to have some difficulty in understanding what was required. Thus, we had to personally stand by each respondent to explain what was written and in many cases we even to translate the questions in Urdu (Native language) for better comprehension.

After they completed the questionnaire, the participants also received a debriefing statement, which stated what the research study was about and were thanked for their participation.

Fifty-seven (59.4%) of the respondents out of ninety-six believed that gender discrimination existed in their respective workplaces. This was irrespective of what type or form the discrimination existed in. It conformed the fact that gender discrimination was felt in their organizational setup or not. The results are displayed in Table 41.1.

Table 41.1: Frequency Distribution Showing the Existence of Gender Discrimination at the Work Place

Gender Discrimination	Frequency	Percent
Yes	57	59.4
No	39	40.6
Total	96	100.0

Table 41.2 shows the mean and standard deviation for each scenario for men and women separately. Table 41.3 demonstrates the t-test for the Equality of Means along with its significant value.

Table 41.2: Independent t-test Showing the Degree of Variance among Male and Female Perceptions on Different Scenarios

Variable	Gender	N	Mean	Std. Deviation
1	Male	48	4.2500	.8873
	Female	48	3.8958	1.1344
2	Male	48	2.8125	1.0449
	Female	48	1.8750	1.0442
3	Male	48	3.0625	1.1923
	Female	48	3.1458	1.2202
4	Male	48	2.8125	1.0848
	Female	48	2.0625	.9765
5	Male	48	3.4792	1.1667
	Female	48	3.2500	1.3448
6	Male	48	3.3542	.8377
	Female	48	2.2083	1.0907
7	Male	48	3.3333	1.2772

Contd...

	Female	48	4.1250	1.1553
8	Male	48	4.6250	.5310
	Female	48	4.6667	.7810
9	Male	48	3.2292	1.0364
	Female	48	2.1250	1.2312

Legend
1. Women's role in society is of a homemaker.
2. Working women are not good mothers.
3. Men do not like working women.
4. Women are not as qualified as men in organizations.
5. Women are only hired to make the working environment more colorful.
6. Women are too emotional and weak to take work pressure.
7. Men do not treat women equally as they "feel" they are the dominant section of the society.
8. Children are the responsibility of both the parents.
9. Women cannot take care of home and work simultaneously.

Table 41.3: Summary Result of Independent Sample T-Test

Variables	T	Df	Sig. (2-tailed)
1	1.704	94	.092
2	4.397	94	.000*
3	-.338	94	.736
4	3.560	94	.001*
5	.892	94	.375
6	5.772	94	.000*
7	-3.434	94	.001*
8	-.306	94	.761
9	4.753	94	.000*

* P < .05 Significant

Legend
1. Women's role in society is of a homemaker.
2. Working women are not good mothers.
3. Men do not like working women.
4. Women are not as qualified as men in organizations.
5. Women are only hired to make the working environment more colorful.
6. Women are too emotional and weak to take work pressure.

7. Men do not treat women equally as they "feel" they are the dominant section of the society.
8. Children are the responsibility of both the parents.
9. Women cannot take care of home and work simultaneously.

The means of male and female responses on different gender discrimination factors give us a feel that both groups have different attitude to some of the gender discrimination factors, specially in case of variable 2, 4, 6, and 9. Females are more agreed with the statements than males. However males are agree more with statement number 7 as compared to females.

The results conform that women experienced discrimination in the workplace due to their gender. Out of nine variables under study significant difference at 5% level was found in five variables that include Workingwomen are not good mothers, Women are not as qualified as men in organizations, Women are too emotional and weak to take work pressure, Men don't treat women equally as they "feel" they are dominant in society and Women not can take care of home and work simultaneously.

These findings supports Freeman (1990) and contribute to current knowledge within this area of research. Freeman argued that women's scarcity in top executive positions was not due to personal shortcomings but rather to obstacles and to other persistent discrimination.

Further it was observed that each of the factors did to some extent contribute to the presence of gender biases in the workplace against women. Further research may also show a general discrimination against women in other situations.

CONCLUSION

Inequality seemed to be a highly diversified issue. It rested deeply on attitudes and where these were perceived as disadvantageous to one gender; they were necessarily regarded as discrimination and in turn adversely affected the weaker gender. Obtaining information about attitudes is problematic as they are difficult to concretize and observe. It may be a question of disparaging or unintentional ignoring of a person in a work community. Thus, one thing remained true that people recognized the existence of this phenomenon and even if not the existence, the mere hazards it can cause.

There are implications not only for researchers but also for employed women, employed men, their families, and the employers. Research to see whether the employers had faced gender inequalities could be of importance when looking at discrimination in the workplace due to the gender of the individual. Employers may be more appreciative of someone's agony if they had been victim of this act.

The word "discrimination" has always been perceived to be against *women* and men are simply carved out as being victims. Thus, another implication may be to look at the issue from a different angle. Future researchers may try to probe into this issue so as to balance both sides of the Phenomenon. This would act as a counterbalance and the difference between discriminations against both sexes would be a true measure to see which one is the more deprived and suppressed.

Finally, a detail questionnaire may be more beneficial for such a research. The current research questionnaire had only nine short scenarios and a few close ended questions. A longer questionnaire, including the marital status, the incomc, etc., may bc better able to get results that are more precise. Such a questionnaire would also provide more accurate results if the respondents could include their own opinions rather than forced choice answers.

REFERENCES

Benschop, Y., Doorewaard, H. (1998) Covered by Equality: The Gender Subtext of Organizations Organization Studies.

Bielby, W., Baron, J. (1986). Men and women at work: Sex segregation and statistical discrimination. American Journal of Sociology, 91, 759-799.

Darity, W., Mason, P. (1998). Evidence on discrimination in employment: Codes of color, codes of gender. Journal of Economic Perspectives, 12(2), 63-90.

Eagly, A. H., Mladinic, A. (1989). Gender stereotypes and attitudes toward women and men. Personality and Social Psychology Bulletin, 15, 543-558.

Eagly, A. H., Makhijani, M. G., Klonsky, B. G. (1992). Gender and the evaluation of leaders: A meta-analysis. Psychological Bulletin, 111, 3-22.

Freeman, S. J. (1990). Managing Lives: Corporate Women and Social Change. Amherst, MA: University of Massachusetts Press.

Glick, P., & Fiske, S. T. (1996). The ambivalent sexism inventory: Differentiating hostile and benevolent sexism. Journal of Personality and Social Psychology, 70, 491-512.

Ingkapattanakul, W, Kleiner, B.H. (2001). New developments concerning discrimination in government. Equal Opportunities International. Patrington: Vol. 20, Iss. 3.

Kimmel, M. Integrating Men Into The Curriculum. Cited: 4 Duke J. Gender L. & Pol'y 181– 184

Konrad, A., & Cannings, K. (1997). The effects of gender role congruence and statistical discrimination on managerial advancement. Human Relations, 50, 1305-1328.

Lips, H.A.(1988).Sex And Gender: An Introduction xi (1988).

Lowry, T. (1998, September 3). Another Wall Street firm faces sex harassment charges. USA Today, Section B, p. 1.

Lyness, K., Judiesch, M. (1999). Are women more likely to be hired or promoted into management positions? Journal of Vocational Behavior, 54, 158-173.

McNevin, S.H., Leichner, P., Harper, D., McCrimmon, E. (1985). Sex role ideology among health care professionals. Psychiatric Journal of the University of Ottawa..

Nicholson, L.J. (1986). Gender And History: The Limits Of Socila Theory In The Age Of The Family 36 (1986) (describing how gender differences were considered relatively superficial in comparison to racial differences).

Rosell, M.C., Hartman, S.L (2001).Self-Presentation of Beliefs about Gender Discrimination and Feminism. Sex Roles: A Journal of Research, June, 2001.

Steinpreis, R.E., Ritzke, D, Anders, K.A. (1999). The Impact of Gender on the Review of the Curricula Vitae of Job Applicants and Tenure Candidates: A National Empirical Study. Sex Roles: A Journal of Research, Oct, 1999.

Truman, G., Baroudi, J. (1994). Gender differences in the information systems managerial ranks: An assessment of potential discriminatory practices. MIS Quarterly, 18, 129-140.

Wozencraft, A. (1999). About 900 women will join suit against Merrill Lynch. New York Times, Section C, p. 6.

Wright EO, Perrone L. (1977). Marxist class categories and income inequality. Am. Sociol. Rev. 42:32-55

Wright, P., Ferris, S., Hiller, J., Kroll, M. (1995). Competitiveness through management of diversity: Effects on stock price valuation. Academy of Management Journal, 38, 272-287.

Wunder, G. C., Wynn, G. W. (1988). The effects of address personalization on mailed questionnaires response rate, time, and quality. Journal of the Market Research Society, 30, 95-101.

STRESS MANAGEMENT IN THE BANKING SECTOR

Sandhir Sharma, Pawan Taneja and R.K. Gupta

INTRODUCTION

Banking in India has its origin as early as the Vedic period. It is believed that the transition from money lending to banking must have occurred even before Manu, the great Hindu Jurist, who had devoted a section of his work to deposits and advances and laid down rules relating to rates of interest. During the Mogul period, the indigenous bankers played a very important role in lending money and financing foreign trade and commerce. During the days of the East India Company, it was the turn of the agency houses to carry on the banking business. The General Bank of India was the first Joint Stock Bank to be established in the year 1786. The Reserve Bank which is the Central Bank was created in 1935 by passing Reserve Bank of India Act 1934. In the wake of the Swadeshi Movement, a number of banks with Indian management were established in the country namely, Punjab National Bank Ltd, Bank of India Ltd, Canara Bank Ltd, Indian Bank Ltd, the Bank of Baroda Ltd, the Central Bank of India Ltd. On July 19, 1969, 14 major banks of the country were nationalized and in 15th April 1980 six more commercial private sector banks were also taken over by the government.

By the end of eighties, Indian financial sector had registered tremendous growth in volume and variety. But the country's financial system was saddled with an inefficient and financially unsound banking sector. Some of the reasons for this include high reserve requirements, administrated interest rates, poor supervision, and political interference, inefficient recruitment process, lethargic work force. Last but most important factor, poor performance of Indian banking sector was deprived spirit of competition and absence of any strong competitor due to closed economy which leads to inefficient and incompetent staffing. After 1991 financial sector reforms the doors of Indian economy opened up for the foreign banks and private sector which put forward a synergic impact on the performance and quality of service of Indian public sector bank.

Now this sector has become the inseparable part of Indian economy by the way of creating more employment opportunities. Most of the persons are trying to get job in the banking sector, as in this sector growth is very quick and employees get appreciation for their good work from their bank in the form monetary incentive, promotion in the post or in the form other incentives other then money. So now as in banking sector the concept of human resource is increasing, more and more of the persons are coming to the this sector.

On the other side of this picture, we found the entire banking sector into the phase of transition not only in regard to the financial products and services but also in context of complex and dynamic working environment such as; long working hours, customer interaction, high sales targets, high usage of information technology, multi operations, work overload, role conflicts, growth prospects etc. This resulted into the emergence of stress among the workforce employed in the private banking sector. Actually the banks which promoted the need of change in the banking structure and called PIONEERS were started feeling more stressed as compare to other banks.

STRESS: A BLUEPRINT

But With the growing recognition of the ' Human Relations Approach' in the management of banking organizations, the discomforts and dishonor associated with work are apparently missing today but the intangible vulnerability and hazards in the shape of stress, strain and anxiety are still ingrained in it. This intrinsic and hidden susceptibility, which is more precarious and has been taking the tool on working people, is fallout of the worker and work environment misfit.

"Around 40 percent of the sampled executives say that they frequently lie awake at night or wake up thinking about work problems, while another 33 percent report that they often feel incapable of relaxing at home because of stress", this was the crux of the survey conducted by *Wall Street Journal in 1982,* which so ingeniously conveys that how latently, and relentlessly job stress takes the toll on working people.

Stress had probably been associated even with the life of prehistoric man and is there to stay in every socio- economic setting. The stress level was on the continuous rise because of the increasing competition and attempts at trying to keep pace with the advancement in one's field together with constant threat of falling short of one's own and those of others expectations. The term stress had been borrowed from physical sciences where it was used to mean force, pressure or strain applied on an organism, which resists these forces and struggles to maintain its original position or in other word it can said as Physiological and psychological responses to excessive and usually unpleasant stimulation and to threatening events in the environment.

It was Hans Selye who introduced the concept of stress in life sciences more than five decades ago. Selye observed the reactions of his animal subjects to variety of stimuli (GAS) model, to explain the stress phenomenon; Alarm

Reaction Stage, Resistance Stage, and Exhaustion Stage.

Ever since Selye's pioneering work on stress, researchers of various academic fields to meet their specific requirements have used the term variously. Even the psychologists and behaviouralists have been using the term differently. One group of researchers, viewed stress as a stimulus phenomenon and regarded it, as an external force operating on an individual, who was perceived as a threat, the other group believed that stress should be conceived as an organism's response to internal and external processes that go beyond the limits of physical, psycho-physiological and integrative capacities. There is, however, still another group of analysts who feels that stress is the outcome of the transaction between the stimulus and the response. Most of the behavioral scientists belong to the third category and believe that stress is a situation created by thc interaction between the stimulus or the external force upon the individual and the deviation or the changes made by the individuals in response to that external force.

Stress, therefore, is a dynamic condition in which an individual is confronted with an opportunity, constraint or demand related to what the individual desires and for which the outcome is perceived to be both uncertain and important.

Causes of Job Stress: There were few behavioral scientists that have properly defined the causes of stress in the workplace. According to them stress is a situation which caused by

Feeling of helplessness: Managers often understand problems and have reasonable solutions, but feel powerless to act because of organizational constraints. Feeling helpless and unable to influence a situation can be particularly stressful.

Poor management: the lack of adequate planning and directions along with chronic indecisiveness causes a complaint that the top management cannot or will not talk about certain areas of discord in the organization.

Work overload and work under load: Work overload results if there is too much work to perform in the time available (quantitative), or work that is too difficult for the employee to perform (qualitative).

Where as work under load results from work that is too simple or insufficiently challenging for one's abilities. Both conditions are positively correlated with stress.

Lack of authority and blurred organizational relationships: Another common cause of stress is the inequality between authority and responsibility. Some executives complain that they are given exceptionally high targets to achieve without proper authority to achieve them and if they are unable to do it, they are penalized for no fault of theirs.

Promotion and recognition concerns: This cause of stress centers around the uncertainty regarding future advancement and frustration due to the lack of praise by top management. More over, being by passed for a promotion without being informed about the cause causes inferiority complex and lack of faith in one's ability and leads to tension.

Basic business problem: certain unavoidable accompaniments of job like paper work, budget, deadlines and need to be in touch with latest information causes a great deal of a stress. The following things cause tension:

- Never been able to concentrate on problem for too long.
- Being told to deal with incompetent subordinates or those that refuse to take any initiative.
- Constant telephone interruptions.
- Too many meetings and unnecessary discussions.
- Having to supervise too many unrelated tasks or a variety of tasks at the same time.

Organization Politics: company politics plays a major role in the appearance of stress in an employee's job. It comes in the form of nepotism, favoritism and coteries. More over if in an organization what matters is " whom you know" and not "what you know or do", the employees of that organization who are honest and believe in interest of the organization as hard working employees stop working, are demoralized and stop putting their heart and soul in work.

Harassment: This can come in the form of subordinate manipulation, sexual harassment of females and mental harassment. The subordinates might be asked to tend to the personal work of the superiors, be yes-man to the boss and if he refuses, he might either be asked or might have to bear a constant barrage of taunts and put-downs of his superior. All this leads to stress not only in their organizational level but also in their personal life.

Organizational Structure: Too complicated an organization structure, too much bureaucracy, redtapism, and long chain of communication, indirect methods of passing feedback are all tailor-made for causing stress. The greater the distance of top management form the operative level, the grater the chances of miscommunications leading to misunderstanding and stress.

Personal Relations with Other Members of Organization: If the employee relations are full of friction and mental bocks the whole work atmosphere will suffer. Animosity, quarrels, resentment, bitterness, and misunderstandings spoil the work culture. Any inability to solve the friction causes tension and stress. Peer relations and superior- subordinate relations are the main source of such a friction. Grapevine plays its role and an inability to control the grapevine and other formal channels of communication causes stress in the organization members.

Organizational Change: Organizational change is stressful. Those who view change as exciting and a challenge are less vulnerable than those who resist change or view it as a threat. Diversity within the workforce as well as generational gaps can be stressful.

Role Ambiguity and Role Conflict: Role ambiguity results when job responsibilities are unstructured or poorly defined in the form of performance criteria, work method and scheduling. Role conflict results when there is a disparity between job demands and the employee's personal standards.

Other Stressors: Other then above causes of stress there are few stressors, which were defined in two parts:

Type 1 Stressors: organizational change events.

- Major or frequent changes in instructions or policies or procedures.
- Major reorganization (at least department- wide)
- Sudden significant change in the nature of one's work.
- Sudden significant increase in the activity level or pace of your work.
- New boss or supervisor.
- Required to work more hours per week than normal, due to crises/deadlines.
- Gave major briefing or formal presentation.
- Decrease in status, either actual or in relation to peers.

Type 2 Stressors: stressful daily work conditions.

- I have too much to do and little time to do it.
- Other's demands for my time at work are in conflict with each other.
- I spend my time 'fighting fires' rather than working to a plan.
- Decisions or change, which affect me, are made 'above', without my knowledge or involvement.
- I must attend meetings to get my job done.
- There is conflict between my unit and others it must work with.
- Management expects me to interrupt my work for new priorities.
- I lack confidence in management.

Hence, stress involves an interaction between the person and the environment; it begins with the environmental demand or opportunity for a person to behave and ends with the person's response to that opportunity or demand. These demands and influences combine and continuously pressurize an individual until stress develops.

Effects of Job Stress: If we are talking about the causes of job stress workplace then how can we forget to mention the effects of job stress, which are:

Mass Psychogenic Illness: Mass psychogenic illness is a stress-related disorder manifested in a variety of physical symptoms and popularly called "assembly-line hysteria". It typically afflicts more women than men, strikes suddenly and spreads swiftly Dizziness, nausea, trouble breathing. Social isolation, work-related stress, and poor working conditions may be factors of this.

Burnout: Burnout is a condition of job stress that results from overwork Emotional exhaustion, Depersonalization, Reduced sense of accomplishment, Burnout victims tend to become rigid about their work, following rules and procedures compulsively. It is characterized by exhaustion, apathy, depression, irritation, and boredom; work quality deteriorates but not necessarily quantity.

Burnout victims may feel insecure and have unfulfilling personal lives, and lack self-esteem and personal recognition off the job.

Workaholism: Workaholic is an employee who is addicted to work stemming from anxiety and insecurity, or because of a genuine liking for the job. Workaholics can stress others. Healthy workaholics are work enthusiasts. Unhealthy workaholics are highly involved but derive little satisfaction from their work. Compulsive addiction to work can lead to negative situations (too controlling, rigid thinking, and hard on colleagues and subordinates).

However stress is essentially a psychological and internal phenomenon and its level is subservient to many factors like perception of the individual vis-à-vis his capacity to deal with the situation and the importance of the possible outcome thereof etc. The common connotation which the term 'stress has acquired is a negative one; something, which should be avoided, because stress never effects every body in the same way. Nonetheless, the researchers had, of late, started feeling that a moderate amount of stress is not only essential but also desirable for effectiveness and improvement.

They felt that it is natural and healthy to maintain optimal level of stress and believe that success, achievement and high productivity call for optimum amount of stress. A reasonable level stress is positively related to job satisfaction and involvement for poor performance and physical and psycho-physiological disorders. Similarly, too little stress (hypo stress) is as undesirable as too high stress. Thus, somewhere between these two extremes is the moderate level of stress where performance is optimal. In other words those with high job satisfaction suffer few harmful effects of stress and those with high levels of job dissatisfaction show considerable stress-related effects.

Tackling Job Stress: People differ in their ability to cope with stress producing situations. What seems to differentiate the more successful form the less successful is the awareness of the stress potential in situation, sensitivity to an individual's own reactions and a capacity for alternate responses. So we can say that best strategy of coping with stress is self-management.

Physical Job Environment: A number of stressors, influencing mental and semantic well-being are located in physical job- environment. Dependent upon the situation, we may think of reducing debilitating noise levels, reducing the possibilities of inhaling toxic substance or gasses, air conditioning to level off the effect of extreme heat or cold, improving levels of illumination and reducing reflections from for instance, keyboards; introducing better ergonomically designed office equipments etc.

Organizational Structure: One can think of altering the organization's formal structure, for instance, by making it less bureaucratic, by flattening the organization in order to shorten the chain of information, or by integrating a production department and a technical services department in order to facilitate daily maintenance.

Work Structuring: It is possible to restructure jobs in such a way that they are optimally in accordance with the other process. To reduce workload one may check whether tasks and competencies are optimally delegated to lower levels of management. One can also think of job enlargement, job enrichment for those jobs lacking sufficient stimulation.

Information: information needs to be channeled and apportioned very carefully. It is important that all employees get the right information at the right time to do proper jobs, and it is important that no one 'drowns' in it.

Clarity: Every employee should have clarity, not only regarding his or her tasks and competencies, regarding what others expect to be done, how they think of the work and what the career possibilities are, but also regarding general company policies and the company's results. Such clarity enables one to place one's own job in a broader perspective.

Support from Superiors and Colleagues: support form superiors and colleagues soften the serious effects of stressors. Support may thus act as some kind of buffer. Management and the middle managers should discuss situations, which are ambiguous for the latter. Even without the direct possibility of solving problems the fact that problems are recognized as such may reduce the uncertainty.

Participation: the opportunity to exert more influence on decisions affecting the person himself or his work may lead to more clarity, less conflicts and better relations with others. In participation, middle management should be used more frequently to assist in the organization's policy making.

Training: Training may enlarge the individual's ability to handle stress successfully. Assertiveness training could be particularly valuable, but any training to prepare some one for a new job or novel situations in the job can play an important role.

Job Rotation: it is the almost always used as a tool for management development. However, one could also think of using it as means of letting people work in stressful situations or job for a shorter time, and letting them recreate in easier jobs in between.

Relaxation Techniques: Relaxation techniques are quite popular these days. And they are good method for physical recreation, if their usually mystical ideological elements are taken out. Physical recreation or better relaxation, is important, because stress is accompanied by raised muscle- tension, which raise heart frequency and blood pressure by, in fact, pinching off the arteries.

Stress Chain Reaction: One of the problem faced in organizations when one scan the organization for signs of stress is that it is not always easy to distinguish between cause and effect. Ones skill as an observer of stress in the organization will be helped if one take into account the 'stress chain reaction'—the process by which stress in one part of the social system puts pressure on the other parts. When one tries to look for stress manifested in organization, he must take into account the facts that some pieces in information base will be missing. As a manger one always access the organization system, and stress symptoms exhibited outside the organization may not come to the persons mind. So it is clear that stress brought to work from outside can be difficult to diagnose. So in order to check the sign of stress in office or organization manger must understand the stress chain reaction.

So in the end, we can say that Stress is known to have two dimensions. It can be an individual's best friend or his worst enemy. In case it assumes the role of the latter, it tears one down in a number of subtle ways and hits at physical, mental and behavioral faculties. Challenge related stress leads to fulfillment and achievement of the target. Whereas hindrance related stress leads to frustration and low satisfaction. This is true under the modern belief according to which illness is considered as physiologically and chemically founded and socially and culturally conditioned. This social and cultural contribution to illness is to a great extent, stress causation. All above description gives us the view that it is very difficult for the employee to work without stress in present scenario, but stress is not only costly for the employee but it is costly to employers and correlates positively with health care claims and costs. It causes a loss of work, money, resources for the employer and specially in banking sector, where the competitions so tough in banks that with one minute of carelessness one bank earns profit in crores than other bank.

REVIEW OF LITERATURE

Farber (1983): Research suggested that work-related stress should be conceptualized and studied as a multifaceted problem involving personal characteristics of the individual, situational factors, and the organizational and cultural context in which such stress occurs. He had identified number of personal characteristics associated with an individual's being particularly vulnerable to high levels of stress, which were being too idealistic, setting unrealistic goals for self and clients, over-identifying with others, high need for self-affirmation, and high work orientation.

Pareek (1983): According to him effective coping strategies were 'approach' strategies; to confront the problem of stress as a challenge and to enhance the capability of dealing with it and the ineffective and unpleasant strategies are avoidance or escape strategies. According to his study social support moderates the negative effects of stress on personal wellbeing. He further suggested that organizational stress could best be managed by creating a person-work environment fit.

Mason (1984): In his study he tired to found out stress problem with the executive while they are at job. According to his study we were all born with a primitive survival mechanism called the "Flight/Fight Response." This ancient survival response has been inherited from billions of years of evolution. 5,000 years ago, if a man was confronted by a threat, he could either run away or stand his ground and physically fight against his attacker. His body would automatically prepare for the action required to survive. His heart beat would increase, his blood pressure would go up, his breathing would become more rapid, muscles would tense to prepare for the fight or to flee, his hands would get cool and clammy, digestion and libido would be reduced, and the primitive brain would take over reducing his ability to think clearly, instead making him more reactive to his fear or anger. These "hard-wired" responses that are triggered when we are threatened. The threats today are usually not as life threatening as 5,000 years ago but our sub-conscious perceptions believed that an upset client or a poor contract negotiation are as serious as a life and death confrontation. We only have one way to respond to the stress of change. Even if the change was a positive experience our body responds in part, if not all, the "Flight/Fight Response."

Agrawal (1985): According to him if the individual is linked with the job characteristics, then it will yield the result of low absenteeism and turnover and high work satisfaction. According to him investigating the impact of yoga and meditation on stress experience has been yet another field of fascination. There should be proper therapy to manage the stress.

Neale, et. Al. (1986): They had done a study with the help of extensive mail and telephone survey on the occupational stress of the non- managerial employees. According to their study corporate and labor definitions of the occupational stress were widely divergent. Stress according to their corporate respondents was primarily a question of maladaptive personal lifestyle and poor 'person- environment fitts'. Alternatively, labor representatives portrayed stress as the product of organizational condition that promoted loss of control, workload, or under load.

Repetti (1987): His research suggested that a supportive social environment at work might be associated with higher self-esteem in employees and the reporting of fewer anxious and depressive symptoms. In particular, a supportive supervisor may buffer or compensate for negative work conditions. According to him employees in a stressful work situation were less likely to report negative mental health indicators (depression, anxiety) if they perceived themselves to have a supportive supervisor."

Karasek (1990): He said that job stress occurs because the `demands' of employment exceed the `controls' of the individual needed to interact with those demands. He had given a `Demand-Control Job Strain Model', which had highlighted two key workplace conditions, that increase hypertension: high psychological demands combined with little control in meeting those demands. People with high job demands describe themselves as "working very fast", "working very hard" and not having "enough time to get the job done". And employees with little workplace controls describe themselves as lacking the ability and/or authority to make decisions or impact their job.

Theorell (1990): According to his study researchers had linked job strain with higher rates of heart disease and other physical ailments and had explored the psychological effects of working long hours or being disenchanted with a job. According to him one specific physical problem associated with job strain is hypertension. Hypertension was considered as the world's number one disease, with an estimated 500 million people worldwide currently afflicted. In the United States, 50 million people were having high blood pressure and estimates are that another 50 million are on their way to acquiring the condition. Ironically, in 95% of hypertensive cases the cause was unknown (American Heart Association). While estimates of proportion to heart disease, possibly due to job stresses are great. He had calculated that nearly a quarter of all heart disease could be prevented if we reduced the levels of job strain.

(Shah 1994): His study revealed that role stagnation, inadequate role authority, role erosion is the main source of stress for employees. The banking employees find their carrier development opportunities bleak along with inadequate authority to carry out their responsibilities efficiently. According to his study most of the employees in the banks feel stress of high level. His study suggested that the major reason for the stress was the increasing workload. But mechanization and computerization can reduce the strain of employees caused due to workload.

Williams (1997): He demonstrated that certain psychosocial factors known to predict increased risk of cardiovascular disease were higher among women who reported higher levels of job stress. In his study, he measured the job stress and psychosocial risk factors (i.e. depression and anxiety) from 152 female employees. The results showed that perceptions of low `control' in women were correlated with increased levels of anxiety, anger and depression, reduced levels of social support and a preponderance of negative feelings, compared with positive feelings in working with colleagues and supervisors. Using a canonical correlation, Williams found that 70% of the women were depressed; 70% were anxious; and 83% reported low decision capabilities.

Haldia (1998): He talked about banking sector, that banking is one major industry which is in danger of being" virtually" blown to bits by technology. When banks had a monopoly on certain financial activities there wasn't much pressure to perform and branches proliferated. Now, technology permits almost anybody to become a bank for most purpose. So there is always a stress on the employees to coordinate with the technological changes, to survive in this sector.

Schnall (1998): He had studied 200 men for three years and found that those with the most job stress had significantly higher blood pressure than those with the least. Employees with highly demanding jobs that allow little latitude for making decisions have 3 to 5 times higher blood pressure and are at greater risk of heart disease than workers who do not experience such job stress. Ironically, the study also found that men who were initially in high-stress jobs but moved to low-strain positions saw their blood pressure readings fall over time. In fact, their follow-up blood pressure readings were nearly the same as those who had never been employed in high-stress jobs.

Moniz (1999): According to Moniz the major sources of stress were family, relationships, inflexible work environment, chemical and nutrition's (Caffeine, Bursts of sugar from sweets or chocolate, too much salt), lack job security, role ambiguity, conflicting demands, excessive job requirements, Fatigue and Overwork, Stress due to Change, Internally Generated Stress, Survival Stress. According to him family is a system, which is created by sub system. When one system is in problem then it will affect other system because each system is related to each other.

NIOSH (1999): On the basis of experience and research, NIOSH favored the view that working conditions play a primary role in causing job stress. However, the role of Individual factors is not ignored. According to the NIOSH view, exposure to stressful working conditions (called job stressors) can have a direct influence on worker safety and health. But the factors like Balance between work and family or personal life, support network of friends and coworkers, relaxed and positive outlook, individual and other situational factors can intervene to strengthen or weaken this influence.

LinXie (1999): According to his study in china the profound changes of the Chinese society and state-owned enterprises had created an exceptionally stressful environment for Chinese employees. His study explored the relationship between stressors, stress, and employee psychological and somatic reactions. With blood samples and other health data collected from the subjects. According to his study exposure to chronic stress might affect the physical health and immune system. Most of the cases of immune's diseases in china were related to working age group and it had been seen that most of the diseases were due to job stress.

Manktelow (2000) his study suggested that in order to ease out job stress employee has to use few ways. He first has to identify the short-term stresses, he has to do job analysis in order to manage work overload, must do performance planning to reduce performance stress, use physical relaxation techniques like deep breathing, PMR and the 'Relaxation Response', use the technique of Thought Awareness, Rational Thinking and Positive Thinking.

Puri (2000): According to him there was a paradigm shift in banking. Today the customer will not lap up whatever a bank offers. The bank has to make services available as demanded by the customer and that too tailor-made. So, to maintain its competitive edge the bank has to keep all possible channels of delivery open and to make the employees always on their tows.

Kivimaki, etal (2001) They examined the association between work stresses, according to the job strain model and the effort-reward imbalance model, and the risk of death from cardiovascular disease. According to their study high job strain and effort-reward imbalance seemed to increase the risk of cardiovascular mortality. The evidence from industrial employees suggested that attention should be paid to the prevention of work stress. Mean length of follow up of their study was 25.6 years. After adjustment for age and sex, employees with high job strain, a combination of high demands at work and low job control, had a 2.2-fold (95% confidence interval 1.2 to 4.2) cardiovascular mortality risk compared with their colleagues with low job strain. The corresponding risk ratio for employees with effort-reward imbalance (**low salary, lack of social approval, and few career opportunities relative to efforts required at work**) was 2.4 (1.3 to 4.4). These ratios remained significant after additional adjustment for occupational group and biological and behavioral risks at baseline.

Northwestern (2001) According to their study, Problems at work are more strongly associated with health Complaints than are any other life stressor—more so than even financial problems or family problems. Three-fourths of employees believed the worker have more on-the-job stress than a generation ago. One-fourth of employees viewed their jobs as the numbei one stressor in their lives.

Builder (2002): According to Career Builder's online survey of more than 1,300 U.S. work-related stress had increased from 52 percent in February to an all-time high of 61 percent in May. The gains in job satisfaction and job security had come at the cost of increased stress for many workers. According to the survey, workers reporting job satisfaction was at 66 percent, up from 61 percent in February. The gain in job satisfaction reverses a downward trend that began in August 2001 -- but it was still below levels from January 2001, when 69 percent of workers reported satisfaction with their jobs. Workers' feelings of job security are also up. In May, 70 percent of Career Builder survey respondents felt they had job security, up from 60 percent in August. The unemployment rate was 4.9 percent in August and 6 percent in April.

Armour (2003): According to him the rise in stress — driven by mounting unemployment, leaner workplaces and a jobless recovery — could pose a bottom-line threat to companies as workers suffer more mental and physical health problems related to job pressure. According to him Chicago-based employee assistance provider ComPsych experienced a 23% increase in crisis- and stress-counseling requests from client companies in the first quarter of 2003 compared with the first quarter of 2002. Nearly 30% were because of worker anxiety and terminations. Nearly 35% of workers say they've seen an increase in anxiety and stress-related physical ailments in their workplace in the last year, according to a May survey by The Marlin Co., a North Haven, Conn.-based workplace communications firm. Twenty-seven percent report a rise in emotional problems such as insomnia and depression.

Bryant (2003): In her study she said that there is no shortage of Stress. Pressure. Anxiety. Tension in today's fast-paced, technologically advanced workplace. Her study showed that stress-related disorders were fast becoming the most prevalent reason for worker disability according to the National Institute for Occupational Safety and Health. Job stress and related problems cost American companies an estimated $200 billion or more annually through absenteeism, turnover, accidents, etc. The World Health Organization called job stress a "worldwide epidemic." According to her we couldn't eliminate the stressors of modern work life -- and it's a good thing we can't. We need a certain degree of stress in our lives to spur us to action, challenge our perception of what we are capable of, and help us reach new levels of performance. The trick is learning how to manage the stress versus being overwhelmed by it.

Bunker, Colquhoun (2003): An Expert Working Group of the National Heart Foundation of Australia undertook a review of systematic reviews of the evidence relating to major psychosocial risk factors to assess whether there were independent associations between any of the factors and the development and progression of coronary heart disease (CHD), or the occurrence of acute cardiac events. The expert group concluded that (i) there was strong and consistent evidence of an independent causal association between depression, social isolation and lack of quality social support and the causes and prognosis of CHD; and (ii) there was strong or consistent evidence for a causal association between chronic life events, work-related stressors (job control, demands and strain), Type A behavior patterns, hostility, anxiety disorders or panic disorders and CHD.

Delano (2003): According to Bill Delano the founder of Job Stress Help, an Internet service that provides confidential, individualized advice via email to those experiencing job stressing in order to remove job stress on should develop few habits in him or her. According to his study one should the take breathing breaks, which allow the man to breathe deeply and relax the mind. Than he said that one must have defined that which was the thing making him or her stressful? He must do exercise which helps to release endorphins, which relieves stress. One must be recognized the difference between the things one can control and the things you cannot. Make a list of these two categories and try to stop thinking about those things, which were or are not in your control. He said that try to share the work or load. According to his study Job stress builds when our minds are constantly focused on work. Strive for balance in your life. Make time for family, friends, hobbies and, most importantly, fun.

Mellor (2003): According to his study Job stress was taking a big bite out of the profits of Canadian companies, Workplace stress costs Canadian companies about $16 billion per year in profits. According to him dealing with job stress is not just about looking after companies people, it also made a bottom-line business sense. The costs of employee stress include absenteeism, low productivity, high turnover; disability claims, accidents and drug plan costs. He as per his study said that a company could boost profits by 14% a year just by dealing with workplace stress. Where as management style or the "culture of an organization" was the biggest factor in employee stress according to him. He said that employees who have little control over their environment or what happens to them at work are likely to feel the most stress. His study said that getting rid of the stress in an organization must start at top.

Tangri (2003): According to him researches in Canada on work-life conflict showed that 22 per cent of workers who reported having supportive managers experience high stress at work, as compared with 78 per cent of workers who reported having non-supportive managers. Based on research studies, Mr. Tangri had developed a formula to help companies determine what stress is costing their organization. It involved calculating 19 per cent of absenteeism costs, 40 per cent of employee turnover costs, 55 per cent of Employee Assistance Program costs, 30 per cent of short- and long-term disability costs, 10 per cent of drug plan costs and the total costs of workplace accidents and workers compensation claims due to stress." Making these calculations will provide with a conservative estimate," he said.

OBJECTIVES OF THE STUDY

- To assess the nature, degree and sources of job stress in banking industry.
- To study the techniques being used by the banks to ease out the stress.

RESEARCH METHODOLOGY

The study was descriptive in nature. The data was collected through primary source by using unbiased, structured and undisguised questionnaire. All employees of private banks were considered as the Universe and sample unit for the research included any individual who was the employee either of a Private Sector Bank. Target population of the research included all the employees of HDFC, ICICI, IDBI bank at its Ludhiana branch and the method used for selecting sample was stratified sampling technique; the population was stratified as managers and executives. Managers include sales managers, relationship managers, branch managers and regional heads. Executive includes marketing executives, financial consultant, and direct sales team (DST).

The size of the sample was restricted to 100 employees comprised of 4 managers (sales manger, branch manager, relationship manager, regional manager) and 20 marketing executives from IDBI bank, 8 managers (sales manger, branch manager, relationship manager, regional manager) & 30 marketing executives from ICICI bank and 8 managers (sales manger, branch manager, relationship manager, regional manager) & 30 marketing executives were taken from HDFC Bank.

More number of managers and executives were taken form both HDFC & ICICI bank because these banks were having two-two more branches in Ludhiana city as compare to IDBI. So 4-4 managers were taken under the study from both branches and 15 –15 executives had been taken from these branches.

RESULTS OF THE STUDY

A. About the Respondents (Table 42.1): Majority of respondents under the study were working with the banks for more than 3 years.

Table 42.1: Work Experience of Respondents in Banks

Years	No. of Respondents	%age of Respondents
Less then 1 yr	27	27
From1 to less than 2yrs	18	18
From 2 to less than 3yrs	26	26
More than 3 yrs	29	29
Total	100	100

B. Reason for Joining the Bank (Table 42.2): The study revealed that earning handsome income was the first reason to join banking sector by majority of respondents followed by other reasons such as good career growth, brand image and better facilities

Table 42.2 Reasons for Joining Particular Bank

Reasons	No. of Responses	%age of Responses
Brand image	40	23
Good carrier Prospective	45	26
High income	53	32
Better facilities	33	19

C. Number of Respondents Feeling Stressed: 93% of the respondents under study were found under heavy stress.

D. Nature of Stress Faced by Bank Employees (Table 42.3): The study concluded that majority of the respondents i.e. 52% were found suffering from mental and physical stress. 27% of the respondents complained about moral stress (when the targets are not achieved) and environmental stress (hectic working conditions and noise). Rest of the respondents blamed social stress and self induced stress (stress which arises due to our own imagination and constant but negative thinking) as critical factors of their worries and pressure during job.

Table 42.3 Nature of Stress Faced by Respondents

Nature of Stress	No. of Responses	Percentage
Moral Stress	40	14
Mental Stress	75	27
Physical Stress	70	25
Environmental Stress	37	13
Social Stress	33	11
Self- Induced Stress	27	10
Total	282	100

E. Degree of the Stress Faced by Respondents (Table 42.4): The study found that Mental and Physical stress were causing high degree of stress as compare to moral, environmental, social and self induced stress.

Table 42.4: Degree of Stress Faced by Respondents (No. of Respondents = 93)

Nature Of Stress	Frequency of Stress	Mean Score	Degree
Moral stress	99	1.06	Medium
Mental stress	191	2.05	High
Physical stress	187	2.01	High
Environmental stress	64	0.69	Low
Social stress	48	0.52	Low
Self- induced stress	40	0.43	Low

F. Difficulties Faced by Employees Due to Stress (Table 42.5): Majority of respondents complained about the problem of physical disorder, deteriorating in work quality, depression, lack of confidence and reduction in the sense of accomplishment due to the stress conditions in the organisation. The study revealed that organizational conflicts, emotional exhaustion were the other results of the stress

G. Causes of Stress (Table 42.6): Inadequate working conditions, Time Schedule, Role Overloading, low salary and Role Stagnation were identified the most prominent reasons for stress in any banking organisation followed by other reasons such as Role ambiguity, Inadequacy of the resources, role conflicts, market saturation, lack of supervisory support and competition.

Table 42.5: Difficulties Faced Due to Stress

Difficulties	No. of Responses	Percentage
Physical disorder	70	19
Work quality deteriorates	54	15
Work quantity deteriorates	50	14
Reduced sense of accomplishment	41	11
Emotional exhaustion	25	7
Conflicts with colleagues	40	10
Depression	49	13
Lack of confidence	39	11
Other	0	0
Total	368	100

Table 42.6: Important Causes of Stress

Dimensions	Frequency	Total Respondents	Mean Score	Importance	Rank
Role stagnation	355	93	3.82	Important	5
Role ambiguity	335	93	3.61	Important	6
Role conflicts	290	93	3.12	Important	8
Role overload	375	93	4.03	Very important	3
Lack of group cohesiveness	256	93	2.75	Indifferent	13
Personal/ resource Inadequacy	297	93	3.19	Important	7
Constraint of change	269	93	2.89	Indifferent	11
Inadequacy role Authority	277	93	2.98	Indifferent	9
Inadequate working Condition	377	93	4.05	Very important	1
Low salary	365	93	3.93	Important	4
Competition	259	93	2.78	Indifferent	12
Market saturation	273	93	2.94	Indifferent	10
Time schedule	376	93	4.04	Very important	2

G. Techniques Used by Banks to Remove the Stress (Table 42.7): As per the study, weekly parties and informal get together has been found the most popular technique used by banks to ease out the stress among employees followed by other techniques such as payment of incentives, review of performance on quarterly basis, monthly trips, appreciation letters and employee assistance programs.

Table 42.7: Techniques Used by Banks to Ease Out Stress

Techniques	No. of Responses	Percentage
Weekly Parties or get together	75	22
Monthly trips	56	15
Employee assistance programs	20	5
Heavy incentives then salary	76	20
Behavior modification program	20	5
Quarterly review of performance and training	82	20
Appreciation letters for excellent performance	51	13
Total	380	100

H. Effectiveness of Stress Busting Techniques in Order to Remove Stress (Table 42.8): The study found that monthly trips, parties and quarterly review of performance, incentives highly effective & popular techniques followed by banks to ease out the stress.

CONCLUSION

The study found majority of the respondents under stress due to Inadequate working conditions, longer time Schedule, role overloading, low salary, role Stagnation, Role ambiguity, Inadequacy of the resources, role conflicts, market saturation, lack of supervisory support and competition. If we look at these reasons, we find it the way, presently; most of the organizations are working in competitive environment. Business world has become mercurial and in such a turbulent environment we find most of the organizations suffering from inadequate working conditions, longer time schedules, Role overloading, low salary and Role stagnation, Role ambiguity, Inadequacy of the resources, role conflicts, market saturation, lack of supervisory support and competition resulting into high degree of stress over the employees. Majority of the organizations have come up with the new techniques of easing out the stress among employees such as quick incentives, family get together, promotions, trips, indoor sports room etc. to relieve their employees from this distress.

Table 42.8: Effectiveness of Stress Busting Techniques

Techniques	Frequency	Total Respondents	Mean Score	Effectiveness	Rank
Parties	235	100	2.35	Highly effective	1
Monthly trips	225	100	2.25	Highly effective	3
EAP	153	100	1.53	Effective	6
Heavy incentives	233	100	2.33	Highly effective	2
Behavior modification Program	153	100	1.53	Effective	6·
Quarterly review of Performance	212	100	2.12	Highly effective	4
Appreciation letters for excellent performance in month	171	100	1.71	Effective	5

REFERENCES

Arroba, T. and James, K. Pressure at Work- A Survival Guide. 1st ed. New Delhi: Mc-Graw-Hill Publications, (1987).

Agarwal, M. A Study of Stresses Among University Students. Ph. D. thesis, University of Allahabad, Allahabad, (1985).

Builder, C. "Survey: Job stress on rise" Journal of American City Business, (2002).

Colquhoun, D. M. Stress and coronary heart disease: psychosocial risk factors.

Giga, S. I. And Hoel, H. Violence and stress at work in financial services. Karasek, R. "Health risk with increased job control among white-collar workers", Journal of Organizational Behavior, (1990), 171-185.

Kaur, G. Stress and You. 1st ed. Delhi: New Century Publications, (2003).

Pareek, U. "Organizational Role Stress". In. L.D. Goodstein and J. N. Pfeiffer (Eds.), The 1983 Manual for facilitators, Trainers and Consultants. San Diego, California: University Associates, (1983).

Palmer, S. and Dryden, W. "Stress management: approaches and interventions". British Journal of Guidance and Counseling, 1994, 5-12.

Sangmi, and Din, U. M., "Emerging Dimensions of Business", 1st ed. Delhi: New Century Publications, (2003).